Athens

timeout.com/athens

Published by Time Out Guides Ltd, a wholly owned subsidiary of Time Out Group Ltd.
Time Out and the Time Out logo are trademarks of Time Out Group Ltd.

© Time Out Group Ltd 2007
Previous editions 2004, 2005.

10 9 8 7 6 5 4 3 2 1

This edition first published in Great Britain in 2007 by Ebury Publishing
A Random House Group Company
20 Vauxhall Bridge Road, London SW1V 2SA

Random House Australia Pty Limited 20 Alfred Street, Milsons Point, Sydney, New South Wales 2061, Australia
Random House New Zealand Limited 18 Poland Road, Glenfield, Auckland 10, New Zealand
Random House South Africa (Pty) Limited Isle of Houghton, Corner Boundary
Road & Carse O'Gowrie, Houghton 2198, South Africa

Random House UK Limited Reg. No. 954009

For further distribution details, see www.timeout.com

ISBN 10: 1-84670-032-9
ISBN 13: 978184670 0323

A CIP catalogue record for this book is available from the British Library

Printed and bound by Firmengruppe APPL, aprinta druck, Wemding, Germany

The Random House Group Limited makes every effort to ensure that the papers used in our books are made from trees
that have been legally sourced from well-managed and credibly certified forests. Our paper procurement policy can be
found on www.rbooks.co.uk/environment.

Time Out Guides Limited
Universal House
251 Tottenham Court Road
London W1T 7AB
Tel + 44 (0)20 7813 3000
Fax + 44 (0)20 7813 6001
Email guides@timeout.com
www.timeout.com

Editorial

Editor John Shandy Watson
Deputy Editor Ros Sales
Consultant Editor Diane Shugart
Listings Editors Andrea Gilbert, Laura McDowell
Proofreader Simon Cropper
Indexer Jonathan Cox

Managing Director Peter Fiennes
Financial Director Gareth Garner
Editorial Director Ruth Jarvis
Deputy Series Editor Dominic Earle
Editorial Manager Holly Pick
Assistant Management Accountant Ija Krasnikova

Design

Art Director Scott Moore
Art Editor Pinelope Kourmouzoglou
Senior Designer Henry Elphick
Graphic Designer Gemma Doyle
Junior Graphic Designer Kei Ishimaru
Digital Imaging Simon Foster
Ad Make-up Jodi Sher

Picture Desk

Picture Editor Jael Marschner
Deputy Picture Editor Tracey Kerrigan
Picture Researcher Helen McFarland
Picture Desk Assistant Troy Bailey

Advertising

Sales Director Mark Phillips
International Advertising Manager Kasimir Berger
International Sales Consultant Ross Canadé
International Sales Executive Charlie Sokol
Advertising Sales (Athens) Natassa Vassilakis
Advertising Assistant Kate Staddon

Marketing

Group Marketing Director John Luck
Marketing Manager Yvonne Poon
Sales and Marketing Director North America Lisa Levinson

Production

Group Production Director Mark Lamond
Production Manager Brendan McKeown
Production Coordinator Caroline Bradford
Production Controller Susan Whittaker

Time Out Group

Chairman Tony Elliott
Financial Director Richard Waterlow
Group General Manager/Director Nichola Coulthard
Time Out Magazine Ltd MD Richard Waterlow
Time Out Communications Ltd MD David Pepper
Time Out International MD Cathy Runciman
Group Art Director John Oakey
Group IT Director Simon Chappell

Contributors

Introduction John Shandy Watson. **History** Nick Wyke. **Athens Today** Diane Shugart. **Architecture** Martin Olofsson. **Greek Myth & Legend** Amanda Castleman. **Where to Stay** Despina Zefkili (*Design central* John Shandy Watson). **The Acropolis & Around** Cordelia Madden. **The Historic Centre** Niki Kitsantonis. **Kolonaki & Around** Andrea Gilbert. **North of the Acropolis** Joanna Kakissis. **Greater Athens** Nikos Pitsiladis. **Piraeus** Niki Kitsantonis. **Beaches** Laura McDowell. **Restaurants** Diane Kochilas (*Greek wines* Cordelia Madden). **Cafés** Joanna Kakissis. **Shops & Services** Cordelia Madden. **Festivals & Events** Joanna Kakissis. **Children** Stella Sevastopoulou. **Film** Leonidas Liambeys. **Galleries** Andrea Gilbert. **Gay & Lesbian** Leo Kalovyrnas. **Music** Martin Olofsson. **Nightlife** Laura McDowell. **Sport & Fitness** John Hadoulis, Will Vassilopoulos (*A fighting chance for football* John Hadoulis). **Theatre & Dance** Nikos Pitsiladis. **Attica & the Mainland** Diana Farr Louis. **North-east Peloponnese** Diana Farr Louis. **Island Escapes** Niki Kitsantonis. **Directory** Andrea Gilbert.

Maps john@jsgraphics.co.uk, except page 256, used by kind permission of Attiko Metro SA.

Photography All photography by Karl Blackwell, except: page 12 akg-images/Erich Lessing; page 15 Mary Evans Picture Library; page 16 Victoria & Albert Museum/The Bridgeman Art Library; page 19 Archaeological Receipts Fund; page 20 Bettmann/Corbis; page 23 Roger Viollet Collection/Getty Images; pages 24, 164 AFP/Getty Images; pages 35, 100 Maxime Gyselinck; page 80 Reuters/Yannis Behrakis (Greece); page 163 Thanos Iliopoulos; page 171 © Warner Bros. Pictures 2007; page 180 Stefanos.
The following images were provided by the featured establishments/artists: pages 47, 168, 199, 211.

The Editor would like to thank Manos Hatzimalonas and Makis Peppas at the Greek National Tourist Organisation (UK), Kostas Konstantinidis at Olympic Airlines, Jo Brown at ZFL PRCo, the management and staff at Athens Art Hotel, Baby Grand Hotel, King George Palace and Ochre & Brown, Elinda Labropoulou, Rachel Howard, Debbie Ellis and all contributors to previous editions of *Time Out Athens*, whose work forms the basis for parts of this book.

Contents

Introduction   6

In Context   11

History   12
Athens Today   26
Architecture   30
Greek Myth & Legend   35

Where to Stay   39

Where to Stay   40

Sightseeing   59

Introduction   60
The Acropolis & Around   62
The Historic Centre   77
Kolonaki & Around   86
North of the Acropolis   91
Greater Athens   96
Piraeus   100
 Map: Piraeus   101
Beaches   103
 Map: Beaches   105

Eat, Drink, Shop   107

Restaurants   108
Cafés   133
Shops & Services   140

Arts & Entertainment   161

Festivals & Events   162
Children   166
Film   168
Galleries   172
Gay & Lesbian   175
Music   179
Nightlife   187
Sport & Fitness   194
Theatre & Dance   199

Trips Out of Town   203

 Map: Trips Out of Town   204
Attica & the Mainland   205
North-east Peloponnese   213
Island Escapes   219

Directory   223

Getting Around   224
Resources A-Z   228
Vocabulary   237
Further Reference   238
Index   239
Advertisers' Index   244

Maps   245

Athens Overview   246
Street Maps   248
Greater Athens   253
Street Index   254
Athens Metro   256

Introduction

If you haven't been to Athens for a few years, you'll be surprised by how much the city has changed. And if it's your first visit to the Greek capital, you may wonder what all of the gripes were about, and why many visitors only dropped in for a day or two to quickly see the archaeological sites and then dash off to the countryside or the islands.

For both locals and tourists, the city has become a much more pleasant place in which to linger. You can easily spend days mooching about the sights, dawdling over a frappé at one of the café tables that seem to spill across pavements all over the city and, having set your internal clock to Athens time, heading out for a late dinner at one of the many restaurants that are taking Greek cuisine to new heights or one of the tavernas that inspired them. There's a vibrancy to the nightlife that you'll most likely find infectious – at some point you'll find yourself in a trendy bar in hip and happening Psyrri or an arty event in even more cutting-edge Gazi.

Much of this change of spirit can be attributed to the 2004 Olympics, which kick-started numerous projects throughout the city, from a general scrubbing up of streets and squares, and an astonishing number of hotel refurbishments to the construction of sports facilities and vast improvements to the region's transportation network. The creation of swathes of new pedestrianised areas now makes strolling the sights a pleasure.

Even more impressive is that the Olympic gold rush wasn't the end of the changes. Athenians, always so cynical about whether anything will ever get off the ground in their city, are having to think again, to avoid being surprised when a project comes in on time, on budget and looking rather good. But for every Benaki Museum annexe or new station added to the metro network there's a New Acropolis Museum. And though the giant structure's shell is now finally constructed, its opening has been put back yet again, until the beginning of 2008 (at the earliest).

Still, Athens continues to capitalise on its assets. When the Parthenon first catches your eye – as you emerge from a metro station or look along a concrete-blocked street – the effect is magical, especially when it's lit up at night. It is one of the most recognised (and most copied) structures on earth; French poet Lamartine called it 'the world's most perfect poem in stone'. Beneath the Acropolis is the Ancient Agora, where democracy was born in the fifth century BC and Socrates taught young Athenians to question everything.

But this city is no ancient world theme park. It lives and works in a busy patchwork of styles and periods: around the Ancient Agora; in tiny old neighbourhoods like the villagey Anafiotika at the foot of the Acropolis; in the neo-classical buildings that staked Greece's claim to modernity and nation-statehood in the early years of independence; in icon-filled Orthodox churches; and in the generic-Mediterranean concrete buildings that are homes and offices for most Athenians. Wherever you are, there's a certain energy about Athens today. It's also a much more pleasant place – one where you'll want to spend more than just a couple of days.

ABOUT TIME OUT CITY GUIDES

This is the third edition of *Time Out Athens*, one of an expanding series of Time Out guides produced by the people behind the successful listings magazines in London, New York and Chicago. Our guides are all written by resident experts who have striven to provide you with all the most up-to-date information you'll need to explore the city or read up on its background, whether you're a local or a first-time visitor.

THE LIE OF THE LAND

Athens is a city of distinct neighbourhoods, and we have used these to structure our sightseeing chapters: these broader area designations are a simplification of Athens' sprawling geography and most are not official names you'll see on signposts. We hope they'll help you to understand the city's layout and to find its most interesting sights. For further orientation information, *see p60*; a map showing the divisions is on page 246. For consistency, the same areas are used to divide other chapters, such as Restaurants.

The back of this book contains street maps of central Athens on pages 248 to 252, along with a full street index. Pinpointed on the maps are the locations of each hotel (❶), restaurant (❶) and café (❶) featured in the guide. For all addresses throughout the book, we've given a

map reference, along with details of the nearest metro stop or bus route. In addition, you'll find an overview of the central neighbourhoods and the suburbs of the greater Athens area, as well as a transport map. The maps start on page 245.

ESSENTIAL INFORMATION

For all the practical information you might need for visiting the area – including visa and customs information, details of local transport, a listing of emergency numbers, information on local weather and a selection of useful websites – turn to the Directory at the back of this guide. It begins on page 223.

THE LOWDOWN ON THE LISTINGS

We've tried to make this book as easy to use as possible. Addresses, phone numbers, transport information, opening times and admission prices are all included in the listings. However, businesses can change their arrangements at any time. Before you go out of your way, we'd strongly advise you to phone ahead to check opening times and other particulars. While every effort and care has been made to ensure the accuracy of the information contained in this guide, the publishers cannot accept responsibility for any errors it may contain.

PRICES AND PAYMENT

We have noted where venues such as shops, hotels, restaurants and theatres accept the following credit cards: American Express

(AmEx), Diners Club (DC), MasterCard (MC) and Visa (V). Many will also accept other cards and/or travellers' cheques.

The prices we've listed in this guide should be treated as guidelines, not gospel. If prices vary wildly from those we've quoted, ask whether there's a good reason. If not, go elsewhere. Then please let us know. We aim to give the best and most up-to-date advice, so we want to know if you've been badly treated or overcharged.

TELEPHONE NUMBERS

The country code for Greece is 30. Almost all Athens numbers start with 210, which needs to be dialled both from outside and inside the city. Where no alternative exists, we have given (and stipulated) a mobile telephone number. These start with '6'. For more details, *see p235*.

TRANSLITERATIONS

There is no standard system for the transliteration of Greek characters. We have chosen a method that reflects pronunciation as closely as possible. However, we have frequently broken our own rules where there seemed good reason to do so: for proper names with a well-established spelling; or when people or businesses had their own preferred version, for example. We have chosen, however, not to duplicate the spellings given on street signs, since these are inconsistent and unrecognisable in speech. It's better to follow a map.

LET US KNOW WHAT YOU THINK

We hope you enjoy *Time Out Athens*, and we'd like to know what you think of it. We welcome tips for places that you consider we should include in future editions and take note of your criticism of our choices. You can email us at guides@timeout.com.

Advertisers

There is an online version of this book, along with guides to over 100 international cities, at **www.timeout.com**.

Time Out
Travel Guides
Worldwide

All our guides are written by a team of local experts with a unique and stylish insider perspective. We offer essential tips, trusted advice and honest reviews for everything you need to know in the city.

Over 50 destinations available at all good bookshops and at timeout.com/shop

Time Out Guides

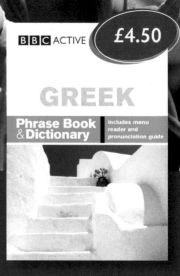

In Context

History   12
Athens Today   26
Architecture   30
Greek Myth & Legend   35

Features

Three wise guys   15
Traces of Byzantium   19
All change   20
Key events   25
If you build it, they will come   28
Neo-classical Athens   31
Designs on tomorrow   34
Gods almighty   38

The Mall Athens. *See p140.*

Alexander the Great. *See p17.*

History

It all started here.

From the cradle of Western civilisation to a ransacked outpost of the Byzantine and Ottoman empires, Athens has seen some dramatic highs and lows over the years.

Graves and wells of neolithic settlers dating back three millennia before Christ have been found on the slopes of the Acropolis. But the city's founding myth rose out of a heroic showdown between the male god of the sea, Poseidon, and the female goddess of wisdom, Athena. Both were laying claim to Attica, the region in which the city is located. According to legend, when Poseidon struck the rock of the Acropolis with his trident, a horse leaped out of rushing water. Athena replied by striking a nearby rock with her spear, and an olive tree appeared. The gods of Olympus declared Athena the victor and she became protectress of the town, giving the city its name and, with the olive tree, an important symbol of peace and prosperity.

EARLY DAYS, DARK DAYS

By 1400 BC the Acropolis had been fortified as a Mycenaean citadel. The Mycenaeans lived in independent communities clustered around palaces ruled by kings and dominated by a centralised religion and bureaucracy. Their kingdoms were a breeding ground for myths, and yielded the sources of the sack of Troy (which took place some time between 1230 and 1180 BC) and the destruction of Thebes that would inspire Homer when writing *The Iliad* four centuries later.

Under Dorian assault and amid internal strife, most of the Mycenaean culture in Greece collapsed in 1200 BC. Somehow, though, the invasion bypassed Athens. But Athens couldn't avoid the shadow that veiled Greece during the period 1050 to 750 BC, the Greek Dark Age. The bitter infighting of the Mycenaeans had caused widespread poverty; the population plummeted and many people migrated to the Aegean Islands and the coast of Asia Minor.

BIRTH OF A CITY STATE

The collapse of Mycenaean civilisation left a political vacuum in Greece. Around 800 BC, Athens began incorporating the outlying villages into its city state (polis), and within 50 years ruled the whole of Attica. By this time, other Greek cities had also organised themselves into independent city states, the most powerful being Chalcis, Corinth and Eretria. The main goal of the city state was to avoid strong central political power and to share authority among its citizens. Power, however, was still largely concentrated in the hands of the wealthy and privileged.

A cultural and economic revival accompanied the emergence of the city states across Greece, and inspired new styles of warfare, art and politics. Greek colonies were established as far away as the Black Sea, present-day Syria, North Africa and the western Mediterranean.

Athens enjoyed a period of peace and remained the leading artistic centre in Greece until about 730 BC, when it was superseded by Corinth, culturally and politically. The introduction of coinage and the spread of alphabetical writing came to Athens second-hand via Corinth. It would take until the late Archaic Age (700-500 BC) for Athens to gain any real political clout.

FROM TYRANNY TO DEMOCRACY

The Archaic Age is so called because of its plodding pace of change in comparison to the hyper-progressive Classical Age that succeeded it. It was, nevertheless, a seminal period, with startling innovations in architecture and art, not to mention the poetry of Homer.

In Athens, city government developed into an annually appointed executive of nine archontes (chief magistrates). After serving his term, an archon became a life member of the Council (called the Areopagus, because it met on the hill of Ares). An aristocratic group known as the Eupatridai ('sons of good fathers') had an exclusive right to these posts. The governing class was responsible for war, religion and law. Its hierarchy depended on wealth, gained either from commerce or agriculture.

'Draco's code dealt with minor crimes, such as the pilfering of cabbage, by capital punishment.'

The replacement of monarchy by an oligarchy of nobles had left the common people with few rights. The resulting social tensions prompted a move towards tyranny, where despotically inclined individuals temporarily seized power in the city states. Continued unrest and the constant threat to the aristocracy's supremacy led to the archon Draco's strictly defined law code in 621 BC. It was a harsh code (hence 'Draconian') that sidestepped pressing issues and dealt with minor crimes, such as the pilfering of cabbage, by capital punishment.

Relief came in the guise of Solon, a poet who became archon in 594 BC. His revised code alleviated the system of land tenure and debt for the peasants and implemented trial by jury. He reorganised the state by breaking the exclusive power of the aristocracy and established four classes of Athenian society based on agricultural wealth. A new council was set up, the Boule of 400 Representatives, a sort of popular assembly that sat alongside the Areopagus. Among Solon's other initiatives, he encouraged the development of lucrative olive and wine production in Attica, reformed the law courts and coinage, and invited foreign businessmen to the city.

Solon may have paved the way to Athenian democracy ideologically, but in practice many of his reforms failed. As controversy grew around the rule of the archontes, the opportunistic military leader Pisistratos seized power in 560 BC. Although he was expelled twice, Athens flourished under his rule.

Arguably the most benign of Athens' many tyrants, Pisistratos assembled a hefty navy and extended the city's boundaries on land. He improved the water supply and commissioned the Temple of Olympian Zeus and the rebuilding of the Old Temple of Athena on the Acropolis. Keen on culture, he sponsored historians, poets, sculptors and orators and revitalised the Festival of the Great Dionysia, which rivalled those at Olympia and Delphi.

Pisistratos died in 527 BC. He was succeeded by his son Hippias, who, though a patron of poets, became increasingly tyrannical after surviving an assassination attempt in 514 BC in which his brother Hipparchos was killed.

By 510 BC, following a consultation with the Delphic Oracle, Cleisthenes, son of Pisistratos' rival Megacles, had rallied the support of the Spartans, the premier power of the time, and managed to drive Hippias out of Athens.

Cleisthenes took over Athens, allied himself with the ordinary people (demos) and brought Solon's reforms back. He created ten new tribes based on place of residence to avoid the old political ties of kinship that had existed. Each tribe was composed of demoi (village units) with their own political apparatus. The Assembly (an attempt to make the different factions and regions of Athens into one people) became the focus of political decision-making.

Cleisthenes introduced the political safety valve of ostracism, whereby citizens could agree to remove a troublemaker for ten years. This was democracy of sorts. All adult male citizens could speak and vote for, or against, motions put before the Assembly, but women, slaves and those not born of Athenian parents were excluded from the political process.

BELLIGERENT ATHENS

Athens had to get a series of Persian wars out of the way before it could fully blossom as the cosmopolitan centre of its 'empire'. Twenty years after his expulsion, the exiled Hippias tried to settle old scores with the help of a Persian army headed by Darius, only to be trounced at the Battle of Marathon. In 490 BC, Darius amassed an army at least 30,000 strong on the plains of Marathon. Famously, a messenger ran the roughly 42 kilometres (26 miles) from the battle site to Athens to announce the news, and his efforts are immortalised in modern marathon races.

Darius expected an early surrender, but instead the vastly outnumbered Athenian hoplites made an impromptu charge and with their superior armour, astonishingly, drove the Persians away. In the war's sequel, ten years later, a fearsome army returned under the command of Darius's son, Xerxes I. By the time the invaders reached Athens, the vastly outnumbered citizens had been evacuated and the Persians burned an empty city. Then, at the Battle of Salamis, the Athenian general Themistocles ingeniously defeated the Persian navy by luring its ships into a narrow channel, where the heavier Greek vessels proceeded to ram and sink them. The string of victories sent the Greeks' confidence sky-high.

'Athens and Sparta would soon be at each other's throats.'

But for Athens and Sparta, the spoils of war were short-lived, for they would soon be at each other's throats. Both sides began collecting allies – Athens sided with the city states in northern Greece, the Aegean Islands and the west coast of Asia Minor, while Sparta formed the Peloponnesian League with its neighbours, Olympia and Corinth. Athens' Delian League of city states, so called because its treasury was originally located on the sacred island of Delos, moved to Athens in 454 BC. Gradually its members became more dependent on their head city, and the Athenian Empire was formed.

Pericles (495-429 BC), a politician from a distinguished local family, is the protagonist of Athens' Golden Age. He used tributes coaxed from members of the Delian League and materials brought back from expeditions to territories in Phoenicia and the Black Sea region to transform the city.

Eventually Pericles overstretched the empire by advising war on too many fronts at once, while at the same time stirring up resistance among allies by making harsh demands on them for protection against the Persians. In 446 BC Athens and Sparta agreed to a 30-year peace treaty. But the mutual mistrust continued.

GOLDEN AGE

With the unflappable Pericles at the helm, peace – coupled with unprecedented power and income – heralded Athens' heyday as the intellectual and cultural centre of Greece and beyond. In just a handful of decades, from approximately 470 to 430 BC, many of the city's iconic buildings were constructed. The Acropolis (see p64), left ravaged by the Persians, took shape again. The fusion of Ionic and Doric order columns in the Parthenon and the sheer beauty of the Erechtheum proclaimed the city's imperial pre-eminence.

The rooftop pediments of other majestic buildings, including the Temple of Hephaestus (or Theseion; see p76), the Propylaia and the Temple of Poseidon at Sounion (see p207), strove ever upwards. Such buildings would prove to be the blueprint for the architecture of elegance and power down through the ages.

The progressive climate of the period allowed the arts full creative freedom. Drama entered its own golden age, with the innovative political satire of Aristophanes and classical tragedies of Aeschylus, Sophocles and Euripides (see p202 A dramatic start); Pindar penned lyric poetry, while Socrates, and later Plato and Aristotle, laid the basis of Western philosophy (see p15 Three wise guys). The glories of the Golden Age were recorded by the historians Herodotus and Thucydides. The latter employed a scientific approach that, for the first time, attempted to clear the historical landscape of dim myths and divine actions.

Sculptors abandoned the rigid formal styles of the Archaic Period for more naturalistic poses. During the fifth century, even the much-prized Attic red-figure pottery reached its artistic zenith, with detailed everyday scenes and mythological stories fired on black vases and wine vessels.

Pericles was at the vanguard of this progress. He never ranked higher than a general, but his sound intelligence and charisma as an orator allowed him to dominate the political scene and oversee the city's extraordinary boom.

Although Pericles also had praise for an individual's freedom, his ardent imperial streak still favoured the subjugation of former allies. In terms of political and legal rights, Athenian citizenship was deemed superior to that of other cities within the empire. Out of a population of 200,000 at its peak, only 50,000 males were full citizens. In the mid century, at Pericles' request, citizenship was restricted to those born of two Athenian parents; this protectionism arguably

Three wise guys

In the fifth and fourth centuries BC, a trio of super-brains hit the city of Athens. Proffering radical ideas on just about everything, from theology to politics, these philosophers made an impression that endures today.

No Adonis, the short, stub-nosed **Socrates** (470-399 BC) preferred the immediate impact of an argument in the Agora to putting pen to papyrus. The Socratic method of solving a philosophical problem – often one concerning moral concepts like goodness or justice – by asking questions became a basis for Western philosophy. A spiritual man, he believed that true moral wisdom lies in the self and that a person's soul is directly responsible for his or her happiness. Because Socrates claimed to know nothing, the Delphic Oracle called him 'the wisest man in Greece'. In 399 BC a jury of democrats found him guilty of impiety and of corrupting the young. He was condemned to death. Rather than take voluntary exile, he swallowed hemlock after explaining to his friends the immortality of the soul and his fearlessness in the face of death.

Born to a well-off Athenian family, **Plato** (427-347 BC; *pictured*) was an instinctive authoritarian who admired the Spartans' ruthless discipline and loathed the limp-wristed democrats who had condemned his mentor Socrates to death. He believed we all possess immortal souls and, ergo, that learning is just recollection from the soul's previous existence. To escape a dim ever-repeating existence we must train our minds to seek a better, 'more real' world. A staple on university reading lists today, Plato's *Republic* is a model for a society blissfully in tune with itself, where commoners and soldiers are governed by wise philosopher-chiefs.

Born in Macedonia, **Aristotle** (384-322 BC) enrolled at Plato's Academy at the age of 17, and studied there for 20 years. After a spell as tutor to the young Alexander the Great, in Asia Minor, he returned to Athens to set up his own university, the Lyceum. He believed that everything has a final cause or potential function, from simple objects to complex human beings; therefore there must be one divine first cause or 'prime mover'. He wrote over 400 works covering just about everything from crustaceans to the constitution. His observations of the anatomy of marine life laid the blueprint for zoology, and his study of logic using syllogisms (deductive arguments) was unsurpassed until the 20th century.

backfired, as the conquered upper classes were unable to become part of the Athens project.

Pericles' achievements were multifarious. He proposed the building of the Long Walls around Athens' southern perimeter (linking the city to the port at Piraeus), commissioned the Parthenon, introduced the theorica, a state allowance to encourage poorer citizens to attend the theatre, and was a friend and sponsor to many of the leading philosophers and artists of the day, in particular Anaxagoras, Sophocles and Phidias. But with Pericles' demise and the onset of war, the Golden Age lost its sheen.

BACK TO THE FRONT

The Peloponnesian War ran from 431 to 404 BC, triggered when Athens placed Corfu,

a colony of Corinth, under its power. Thanks to Thucydides, detailed accounts of the war still exist. He attributed the 'real' cause of the conflict to Sparta's fear of Athens' expanding imperialism. On paper, Athens had the superior navy; Sparta, the sharper infantry. Pericles' strategy, therefore, was to make sudden navy raids and then retreat behind Athens' defensive walls when Spartan soldiers attacked. The plan might have worked, had an epidemic in 430 BC not killed thousands of Athenians packed inside the city, including Pericles himself.

Athens held on for ten more years despite the devastation of its countryside and the loss of income from its silver mines and olive groves. After victories for both sides, including the prestigious capture of 120 Spartan soldiers, the

Raphael's painting of **St Paul** preaching at Athens. *See p18.*

fragile Peace of Nicias, named after the chief Athenian negotiator, was agreed in 421 BC.

But a succession of generals turned their backs on Sparta's offers of peace and took increasing risks. In 413 BC, an overstretched invasion force led by Alcibiades, an ambitious student of Socrates, suffered a catastrophic defeat at Syracuse in Sicily. The damage was massive: more than 40,000 Athenian troops and as many as 200 ships were lost in Sicily.

Before leaving for war, it was alleged that Alcibiades had taken part in a spree that desecrated the Herms, sculpted heads of the god Hermes that protected doorways throughout the city. Recalled from Sicily for trial, he fled to Sparta rather than face the Assembly, and was condemned to death in absentia. After upsetting the Spartans by seducing the wife of one of their kings, Alcibiades sought refuge in Persia. He was itching to return to Athens, though, and, with the promise of Persian support, made contact with some Athenian oligarchs who were looking to take advantage of the ferment in the city. In 411 BC a moderate oligarchy failed and democracy was restored. Alcibiades switched sides to the democrats and led a four-year campaign, regaining Athenian control in the Aegean. He rode back into Athens a hero and that year led the religious procession to Eleusis. Pursued by multiple enemies, Alcibiades was eventually blamed by the fair-weather Athenians for a naval defeat at Notium and he retreated to the safety of a castle.

The situation deteriorated in Athens when, in 406 BC, a 5,000-strong crew drowned and the people accused the generals of not having done enough to rescue the sailors. The generals were tried en masse at the Assembly, but Socrates, who happened to be chairman, refused to conduct the case as it contravened an Athenian citizen's right to an individual hearing. Such was the rancour among the people that they condemned the generals anyway. Six, including the son of Pericles, were summarily executed. As Aristotle later noted, ancient democracy was ever susceptible to mob rule.

By 404 BC, the population of Athens had grown, but food lines were still cut off. The city had no choice but to surrender, and its walls were supposedly dismantled to the sound of flute music while the freedom of Greece was proclaimed. The war ended Athenian hegemony and shut down the Delian League. Sparta installed a brutal puppet regime in Athens called the Thirty Tyrants. This lasted only a year before Athenian rebels restored democracy.

MACEDONIA RISING

Although the fourth century BC began with the unjust death of Socrates, the baton in the quest for absolute truth was passed on to Plato and Aristotle (*see p15* **Three wise guys**), who became regular fixtures debating in the Ancient Agora (*see p75*). The Monument of Lysicrates (*see p71*) was built, and the polished speeches of Demosthenes, delivered at the people's

Assembly, became another highlight of city life in this period. Fourth-century BC Greece was marked by complex power struggles between new alliances, even more wars and a shift from city states towards monarchy.

During the first third of the century, Sparta and Thebes became embroiled in a feud that ultimately weakened both sides. Athens, fearful of the growing power of Thebes, her north-western neighbour, switched allegiance and formed a coalition with Sparta. In 378 BC Athens revived her maritime ambitions and formed the Second Athenian Confederacy, composed of the cities and islands of the Aegean and Ionian seas. However, it lacked the backbone of the Delian League, having neither the resources nor the determination to impose its will, and soon overreached itself.

Ready to capitalise on the power vacuum among the squabbling Greek states was new player Macedonia. Its rise as a superpower was inspired by its king, Philip II, and his son Alexander the Great (*photo p12*).

Athens, which had allies on the north-western border, had always been happy to see Macedonia weak. A step ahead of his fellow Athenians, Demosthenes realised that Philip's expansionist policies represented a real threat. In a series of well-varnished speeches known as the Philippics, he warned the Athenians how their indifference contrasted with Philip's energy and decisiveness. His powerful oratory, though, went unheeded.

'On the news of Alexander's death, the people of Athens danced in the streets.'

The Macedonians made their move in 338 BC in a battle at Chaironeia, in central Greece. Fighting side by side in a phalanx formation and armed with 4.3-metre (14-foot) spears, Philip's light-footed army became a lethal porcupine that could skewer enemies before they got too close. After the victory, Philip sent Alexander to Athens on a diplomatic mission to placate the Greeks by returning the ashes of the Athenian dead who had fallen in the battle. He made no punitive demands and asked only that Athens should ally itself with Macedonia.

Alexander didn't linger in Athens. Instead he marched east to create the Persian Empire by conquering territory from present-day Turkey to as far as Afghanistan, while still only in his twenties. Apparently he loved Homer so much that he slept with a copy of *The Iliad* under his pillow. On news that his brilliant life had been cut short by an illness in 323 BC, the people of Athens reputedly danced in the streets.

In the squabbles among generals following Alexander's death, Athens tried to seize back its independence, but was effortlessly defeated. Surrender meant the end of its proud tradition of naval power and the abolition of democracy.

FROM CITY STATE TO EMPIRE
In 307 BC Demetrios 'the Besieger' (so called for his assault on the island of Rhodes) freed Athens and re-established democracy. This marked the beginning of the Hellenistic Age, which is characterised by a shift in perception from an insular city-state mentality to a view of the individual as part of an expansive empire. Adherents of Diogenes – particularly the Cynics, but also the Epicureans and Stoics – considered the achievement of self-sufficiency a means of protecting man from a random world at large. These new philosophical patterns were reflected in the arts. Portraits expressed not only the public role of the sitter, but also his or her inner thoughts and feelings. Sculpture was less serene than in the classical period; it began to embody the sensual and a sense of life's drama. Much impressive construction took place throughout the wider empire, but in Athens, notably, the Tower of the Winds (*see p74*) and the Stoa of Attalos (*see p76*) were built, the latter's neo-classical style echoing the glories of the past.

In 267 BC, Athens and Sparta, with support from the Egyptian king Ptolemy II, attempted one last time to undermine the Macedonian hegemony. Demetrios' son Antigonos, however, proved too strong; when he counter-attacked not even the Spartans could save the day. Athens endured a Macedonian garrison until 229 BC, but, although the city lost any further political claims to lead Greece, it remained an intellectual and cultural centre.

ROMAN OCCUPATION
In the second century BC, Rome, the region's growing superpower, began to wrest power from Macedonia in Greece. But it was not until 86 BC that the Roman general Sulla occupied Athens. One of his first acts, as a punishment for Athens support of Mithridates' rebellion in Asia Minor, was to knock down its walls and siphon off art treasures to decorate Rome.

Under the Pax Romana (the imperial peace inaugurated by Augustus in AD 31), Athens benefited from Roman patronage as the intellectual capital of the Graeco-Roman world. In AD 66-67, Nero toured Greece and won all that he turned his hand to, from athletic to musical challenges – only a brave opponent would defeat a psychopathic emperor. Tourists and the sons of Roman nobility, such as Cicero and Horace, flocked to see Athens' ancient sites and to study at its renowned university. As a token of the esteem with which Rome held all things Greek, emperors began to honour leading Greeks by electing them for the Roman senate, and inaugurated a panhellenic festival.

Around this time, modifications were made to the Acropolis with the construction of an elegant circular temple dedicated to Rome and Augustus, eastwards of the Parthenon; and the Emperor Claudius built a grandiose stairway leading to the Propylaia, which provided a formal, symmetrical approach to the sacred hill.

But of all the Roman Emperors, it was the passionate philhellene Hadrian (117-138) who made the biggest impact on the city and its heritage. Not only did he introduce the Greeks to Roman laws and give them the rights of Roman citizenship, but he also repaired earlier fire damage to the Parthenon and built the Library to the east of the Ancient Agora. In addition, he solved the crucial problem of the city's water supply by building a great reservoir on the slopes of Lycabettus Hill, which collected water brought there by channels from Mount Parnes. His impressive architectural contributions included the completion in 131-32 of the Temple of Olympian Zeus (*see p83*) and the erection of a huge gateway leading to the peribolos (precinct) of the temple, the Arch of Hadrian (*see p83*).

Equally evident today is the Odeon of Herodes Atticus (Herodeion; *see p66*), a Roman imperial theatre built into a natural slope of the Acropolis in the middle of the second century by the eponymous rich man and tutor to Marcus Aurelius. The auditorium could seat 50,000, and still hosts productions of the great Greek dramas today (*see p199*).

During the reign of Valerian (253-60), the walls of Athens were rebuilt – but not well enough to repel the Germanic Heruli tribe, who stormed the city in 267 and left it in rubble. The remaining Athenians moved to a small area to the north of the Acropolis, where they fortified new walls built of marble salvaged from the ruined buildings.

THE COMING OF CHRISTIANITY

According to the Roman writer Petronius, in the early first century AD one could find more gods than citizens in Athens. In 52 AD, St Paul preached the gospels on the Areopagus (*see p66*; *photo p16*). As the apostle shared his news with the Epicurean and Stoic philosophers on walks through the temples, he was shocked to discover a city full of idols (though he was impressed by its beauty). The Athenians relished hearing about a religion whose god 'does not inhabit temples'. It appealed to them on a moral and intellectual plane, but they mocked the concept of resurrection. A handful,

however, did convert to Christianity, long before Constantine made it Greece's official faith in 323, when he moved his capital from Rome to the Greek city of Byzantium, renaming it Constantinople.

During the fourth and fifth centuries, Athens experienced a brief regeneration, with its neo-Platonic philosophical school attracting important students (such as Julian the Apostate, Basil and Gregory) from all over the known world, only to fall into oblivion after Emperor Justinian closed them down in 529. By then, Athens, tormented by waves of Slavic barbarians, plague and earthquakes, had long since faded under the shadow of Constantinople. For the next seven centuries, Athens passed through another dark age, demoted to the rank of a bit-player in the Byzantine empire and minor centre of religious learning and devotion.

INSTABILITY, THEN OTTOMAN RULE

From the 13th century, a host of outsiders took advantage of Athens' run-down state. First came the French. After the creation of the Latin Empire of Constantinople in 1204, the city passed to Othon de la Roche, a French noble who became megaskyr, or great lord of Athens and Thebes. He was succeeded by his nephew, Guy I; Athens prospered under Frankish rule.

Then, in 1311, the duchy was captured by a band of Catalan explorers who, a year later, offered the ducal title to King Frederick II of Sicily, a member of the house of Aragón. The Aragón clan carried the title, but Athens was in fact governed by the Catalan Grand Company, an unreliable mercenary force.

As the French feudal culture faded, Athens sank into insignificance and poverty, notably after 1377, when the succession was contested in civil war. Peter IV of Aragón took over in 1381, but ruled from Barcelona. On his initiative, the duchy was settled by Albanians.

'The fall of the Acropolis marked the beginning of nearly four centuries of Ottoman rule.'

Athens again shone briefly after its conquest in 1388 by Nerio Acciaioli, lord of Corinth and member of a family that was 'plebeian in Florence, potent in Naples and sovereign in Greece,' according to the historian Edward Gibbon. Nerio helped to establish many of his compatriots as merchants in Athens.

The next 50-odd years witnessed a tug-of-war for the city between the Republic of Venice and the Ottoman Turks. The Venetians held Athens

Traces of Byzantium

From the sixth to the 13th centuries, Athens was immersed in a dark age. Plato's Academy was closed in 529 by Emperor Justinian, and the former cradle of civilisation became a provincial satellite of the Byzantine Empire, whose thriving capital had shifted to Constantinople.

Justinian removed many columns from ruined temples to use in the building of the Hagia Sophia in Constantinople. He is also said to have re-used the Ionic columns of the ancient temple of Apollo when he founded the fortress-monastery of Daphne, 11 kilometres (7 miles) north-west of central Athens, on the old Sacred Way to Eleusis. Only one of those columns remains in the portico; a certain Lord Elgin shipped the others to London.

The diminished city was typically medieval, with narrow streets following the route of the wider Roman ones and houses built around courtyards. Athens' magnificent ruins served as a reminder of past glories. Athens was repeatedly ransacked; all that remains from this period are the foundations of some of the ancient temples that had been converted for early Christian worship, and a handful of churches from the 11th and 12th centuries built on the Byzantine cross-in-square plan. In fact, Athens has the highest concentration of Byzantine churches in the whole of Greece.

Byzantine architecture formed a bridge between the classical and medieval periods, and between the East and the West. Typically, architects subscribed to the ancient practice of building on the foundations of previous churches or temples. The use of broad, high domes and elaborate decoration can be seen in a cluster of churches in central Athens, including the **Kapnikarea** (*see p79*), and the churches of the **Saints Theodore** (*see p78*), **St Catherine** (*see p71*) and the **Holy Trinity** (*see p71*). The renovated **Byzantine Museum** (*see p82*), where archaeologists have discovered the site of the Lyceum, has an excellent collection of religious art, icons, mosaics and rare manuscripts.

In the early 11th century, an unknown patron, possibly Emperor Basil II (aka 'the Bulgar-Slayer'), cleared the ruins of the **Daphne Monastery** (*see p206*) and built a new cross-in-square church of the octagonal type, with a vast dome, and embellished it with splendid mosaics (*pictured*) representing the Christian cosmos. Although more than three-quarters of these have been lost, the monastery, which was designated a Unesco World Heritage Site in 1990 and damaged by the earthquake in 1999, is being restored and should be open to visitors again soon.

from 1394 to 1402, but in 1456 the fall of the Acropolis to the Turks marked the beginning of nearly four centuries of Ottoman rule.

Athens once again declined. The remaining Greeks lived a semi-rural existence. They paid a tax to the Turks, but Jesuit and Capuchin monasteries still thrived. The Erechtheum was used as a harem, and the Parthenon, which had already been converted into a Christian church with a campanile, was refashioned into a Turkish mosque, complete with minaret.

A French naval officer visiting in 1537 wrote: 'Athens, once worthily called the flower of the world, has now, under heavy servitude, sunk to being the poorest and most miserable of cities.'

When Venetian troops besieged the Acropolis in 1687, the Parthenon, which had been used by the Turks as a gunpowder store, was heavily bombarded, resulting in an explosion; until then the sacred hill had been virtually intact. The Parthenon took a further hit in 1801, when the British ambassador to Constantinople,

All change

By the time three million visitors descended on Athens for the 2004 Olympics, the city had had plenty of time to prepare for their arrival. But an extraordinary influx of 400,000 refugees in 1923 left it shell-shocked for years afterwards.

Following World War I, the army of the emergent state of Turkey had begun an offensive against the one million Greeks still living in the area then known as Asia Minor. The Turks torched all the Greek sections of the city of Smyrna, where hundreds of thousands of Greek Christians had taken refuge. Up to 300,000 were reported killed. The Allies refused to send aid, having earlier condemned the Greek decision to reinstate its monarchy. Tension and fear between Greek Christians and Turkish Muslims ran high in Greece and Turkey.

In 1923, the Treaty of Lausanne was signed, restoring territory to the Turks and incorporating the plan of a Norwegian diplomat called Fridtjof Nansen to combat the problem of cultural tensions. There was to be a giant exchange of populations, based on religious identity. The Orthodox Christians, largely ethnic Greeks from parts of Turkey such as Anatolia, were to return to Greece, while Muslims living in Greece would move back to Turkey. As a result, 380,000 Turkish Muslims had to emigrate from Greece, while 1.1 million Greek Orthodox Christians moved back over the Turkish border. The resulting chaos was such that the League of Nations established a Commission for Refugees, with Nansen as its first secretary.

Over a million people poured into Greece, destitute and desperate. In Athens, refugees camped out on the beaches, in the ancient palace, opera house and Parthenon. Winter brought an outbreak of pneumonia, and many refugees brought smallpox and typhus with them. Tent cities were set up around Athens and the harbour of Piraeus, which quickly grew into long-term shanty towns. The population of Piraeus more than doubled, as new settlements with poignant neo-Turkish names such as Nea Kokkinia and Nea Smyrni sprang up.

A combination of post-war poverty and the 'catastrophe' of the influx affected politics. As coup followed counter-coup, the immigrants were slowly absorbed into an unstable Athenian society, but the country was unable to support its new population. Overcrowding, unemployment and famine became the norm, until the instigation of martial rule in 1936 restored some order to the capital. Cultural shifts occurred as the Byzantine side of these new Greeks emerged. In the refugee areas of the city, clubs modelled on the 'cafés aman' of Asia Minor began to appear, and the folk music of the two cultures began to meld.

Despite the desperate conditions, tensions between old and new Athenians were minimal. There was less diversity after the population exchange than there was before: the immigrants were all Orthodox Christians, the majority of Muslims had left and Greece became a country that was unified and even insular.

Lord Elgin, detached much of the frieze around the temple and shipped it to London.

Gibbon described the Athenians as 'walking with supine indifference among the glorious ruins of antiquity.' Foreign visitors were more enthusiastic: the 1762 publication of *Antiquities of Athens* by the Society of Dilettanti prompted many travellers to visit the city as part of the Grand Tour, and proved highly influential on Western neo-classical architecture.

GERMAN AND BRITISH ATHENS

In the late 18th century, the Greek nationalist movement gained momentum with the founding of a number of secret societies financed by exiled merchants. They were spurred on by philhellenic Western European intellectuals such as Goethe and Byron, who did a first-rate PR job for the Greek cause. During the War of Independence, Athens changed hands several times between the Turks and Greek liberators, with the Acropolis, as ever, the seat of power.

'When plans for the new nation were drawn up, Athens only held about 4,000 people.'

By 1827, when the Turks recaptured the hill (which they were to hold for the next six years), Athens had been all but evacuated. Even in 1833, when plans for the new nation had been drawn up by the 'Great Powers' of Western Europe, Athens only held about 4,000 people, housed below the north slope of the Acropolis.

Modern Athens began to take shape in 1834, when it took over from Nafplio as the capital of a newly independent Greece. If Ioannis Kapodistrias, the mastermind of the War of Independence, had not been assassinated in 1831, the chances are that the capital would have remained in Nafplio. As it was, the reasoning of the mediating powers was for the most part symbolic. They imposed a hereditary monarchy on Greece: at the age of 17, the Bavarian Otto I became the first king of the Hellenes (1832-62).

Installed in the only two-storey house in the city, the teenage monarch set about rebuilding much of Athens along neo-classical lines, using German and French architects. The idea was to re-create the glories of the ancient city: broad streets were laid out in grid patterns, incorporating showpiece squares such as Syntagma, and lined with grand public buildings like the Royal Palace, the University, the Academy (built in marble from Mount Pentelicon) and the Observatory. (*See also p31* **Neo-classical Athens**.)

In keeping with the spirit of the new nation, German archaeologists, most notably Heinrich Schliemann, began stripping away the Frankish and Turkish embellishments on the Acropolis and Parthenon, and at other key sites. Clearly impressed by these treasures on a visit in 1848, the English author Edward Lear wrote: 'Poor old scrubby Rome sinks into nothing by the side of such beautiful magnificence.'

By most accounts, 19th-century Athens was a mild-mannered city of elegant, tree-lined avenues. Its dwellings, built for the nascent professional classes, were similar in style to those of Victorian London. Most of these Ottonian-style houses have long since been replaced by concrete, though some of the best surviving examples are on Leof Vas Sofias.

In 1843, the explosive combination of Otto's autocratic rule and cronyism, the continued interference of foreign powers, and declining economic conditions, led to a bloodless revolution in Athens. The people joined forces with political and military leaders to insist on the restoration of the constitution.

In the 1850s, the population still numbered only 20,000, and economic progress was slow. There were no railway routes into the city, roads were poor and the export of currants provided the only source of national income. It was out of a climate of despondency that the governing creed of the century, the 'Great Idea' (Megali Idhea), developed. The thesis advocated a new Greek Empire by the gradual enlargement of Greece's territory at the expense of the declining Ottoman Empire; but for the rest of the century, it was to create tension between liberal and conservative forces. One expression of rebellion against tradition was an enthusiasm for use in literature of the demotic (popular) language over catharevousa (a simplified form of ancient Greek), a debate that led to riots in Athens in 1901.

Between 1854 and 1857, the occupation of Piraeus harbour by the French and British armies increased discontent among Athenians and eventually led to the expulsion of King Otto in 1862. This had been facilitated by a new generation of graduates from Athens University, which had been re-opened in 1837. However, much to the chagrin of Greek intellectuals (and due to British influence in the Ionian Islands), George I was enthroned in 1863. He ruled until 1913 and proved a more capable leader than Otto (even if during the first 17 years of his reign there were nine elections and 31 governments).

Athens arguably deserved its fin-de-siècle tag as the 'Paris of the eastern Mediterranean'. The opening of the Corinth Canal, begun in AD 62 and completed in 1893, made Piraeus one of the world's great ports. The merchant navy expanded, and a shipping boom sparked a growth in manufacturing and banking.

Athens had a chance to show off its achievements to the world in 1896, when it hosted the first modern Olympic Games. But such progress was precarious. A year later, when a dispute broke out over the control of Crete, the Turks were poised within a few days' march of Athens. Once more the city was saved from the Turkish army by the Western powers.

POPULATION BOOM

The leader of the uprising to liberate Crete in 1905, Eleftherios Venizelos, was summoned to Athens following a coup d'état in 1909. Appointed prime minister in 1910, he was an advocate of liberal democracy who doubled Greek territory during the Balkan Wars (1912-13) and sided with the Allies in World War I.

In March 1913, after King George was assassinated by a madman, his son Constantine became king. Constantine, who was married to the sister of the German Kaiser, didn't want to get involved in World War I and this caused tension with Venizelos. For the first three years of the war Greece remained neutral and the city was occupied by British and French troops.

Greece's catastrophic post-war invasion of Smyrna resulted in the 1923 Treaty of Lausanne, which implemented a controlled form of ethnic cleansing and signalled the end of the Great Idea. In an exchange of religious minorities, 400,000 Turks left Greece, and 1.5 million Christian refugees, mainly Greeks, arrived from Asia Minor (see p20 **All change**).

FASCIST THREAT, COMMUNIST REVOLT

Although a republic was established between 1924 and 1935, its existence was threatened by repeated military coups. When Venizelos was exiled in 1935, King George II was restored to the throne by a rigged plebiscite. He installed General Ioannis Metaxas as prime minister, who ruled as a fascist-style dictator whose secret police dealt ruthlessly with leftist opponents. Metaxas is best known for his curt reply of '*ohi*' (no) to Mussolini's request in 1940 to allow Italian soldiers to cross Greece. Apparently his actual words were '*C'est la guerre*', but the proud Greeks prefer to remember the more emphatic, apocryphal riposte. The day of the rebuttal, 28 October, is now celebrated as a national holiday.

In April 1941, Hitler's armies advanced suddenly into Greece. Athen's inhabitants suffered extreme hardships during the three-year German occupation in World War II, especially during the winter of 1941-42, when hundreds died daily from starvation.

During the war, the luxurious Hotel Grande Bretagne (see p45) in Syntagma Square housed, successively, the Greek, German and British headquarters. Churchill, who was in Athens to show his support for the Greek government against the communists, escaped a bomb placed in the hotel's basement in December 1944 by staying aboard *HMS Ajax* in Piraeus harbour.

In December 1944 an open communist revolution broke out in the Thissio area after a demonstration had been fired on by police in Syntagma Square. Traces of action from the Battle of Athens that ensued can still be seen on some buildings in the city. For a brief time, the government held only the Parliament building, neighbouring embassies and a part of Syntagma Square, and the palace garden was used as a common grave. British troops eventually restored order, and at a conference called by Winston Churchill on Christmas Day, an armistice was arranged; under its terms Archbishop Damaskinos became regent.

'More Greeks were killed in the civil war than during World War II.'

The civil troubles of 1944-49 between pro- and anti-communist factions seriously retarded the city's recovery. Athens was virtually severed from the rest of Greece by roadblocks. More Greeks were killed in the civil war than during World War II. In response to the distress and disorder, over a million Greeks set sail for a more peaceful and prosperous existence in Canada, Australia and America. Many of those who stayed behind headed for Athens in search of work.

After its wars, Greece was isolated as the only non-communist state in the Balkans. Communism was declared illegal, and the government introduced its infamous Certificate of Political Reliability (that gave proof that the holder was not a Red), which remained valid until 1962, and without which Greeks couldn't vote or easily find a job.

In the 1950s and '60s, the metropolis began to take on the sprawling shape that characterises it today. Land clearance for suburban building caused run-off and flooding, requiring the modernisation of the sewer system. The Mornos River was dammed, and a 160-kilometres (100-mile) pipeline was built to supplement Athens' inadequate water supply.

Ideological conflict and political instability led to the seizure of power by a military Junta in 1967. Andreas Papandreou, who would later be prime minister, called it 'the first successful CIA military putsch on the European continent.'

German planes in formation above the Acropolis during World War II.

During this time, persecution and censorship ruled. Greece's favourite actress, Melina Mercouri, was disenfranchised while out of the country, rembetika clubs were shut down, and productions of the classical tragedies were forbidden. During this dictatorship of the Colonels (1967-74), many of the Turkish houses of Plaka and other neo-classical buildings were destroyed.

On 17 November 1973, student demonstrations against the Junta at Athens Polytechnic were brutally ended when tanks moved in, killing dozens. The occasion provided the name for Greece's lethal November 17 urban guerrilla terrorist group, which has killed 23 targets, including British Brigadier Stephen Saunders, shot dead at point-blank range in Athens' traffic in June 2000.

MODERN ATHENS

The Junta was finally felled in July 1974, after it had precipitated the Turkish invasion of northern Cyprus following a disastrous plan to assassinate President Makarios. Konstantine Karamanlis, a leading politician in voluntary exile, returned to streets full of jubilant crowds. As the new prime minister, Karamanlis noted: 'We invented democracy. We were into it before it was cool.' A ban on communist parties was lifted, and later that year the Greeks voted by two thirds for the abolition of the monarchy.

The new republic now looked to Western Europe, with the goal of joining the European Economic Community. On 1 January 1981,

thanks to the manoeuverings of Karamanlis, Greece became the tenth member of the EEC. Later that year, Andreas Papandreou's Panhellenic Socialist Movement (PASOK) formed Greece's first socialist government, appealing to the electorate with the simple slogan '*Allaghí*' (change). Melina Mercouri was appointed minister of culture, and wasted no time launching a campaign to return the Elgin Marbles to Greece. In 1985 Athens became Europe's first Capital of Culture. The 1990s were characterised by austere cuts by the government to attain some sort of economic stability, and reactive strikes.

ATHENS THE MEGACITY

Since World War II, Athens has drawn more than three million people from the countryside, and now contains more than 40 per cent of the country's population. In such a megalopolis, the Greek saying that Athens is merely 'the largest village in Greece' is now seriously challenged.

A series of governments had neglected the city's expansion problems, and by the early '90s Athens was saddled with a deserved reputation as one of the most traffic-polluted cities in Europe. In 1994, as a response to the worsening *nefos* (smog) that was affecting ancient buildings and monuments, traffic restrictions were introduced in central Athens.

The failed bid for the 1996 Olympic Games inspired some improvements to the city – primarily a shiny new metro system and a gleaming modern international airport. But

Opening ceremony of the 2004 Olympics.

it was the awarding of the 2004 Games a year later that galvanised planners into action. Plans were disturbed when an earthquake measuring 5.9 on the Richter scale shook the city on 7 September 1999. It was the most powerful to hit the region in almost two centuries, killing 120 people and leaving 70,000 homeless.

Following the death of Papandreou in 1996, the Blairite Costas Simitis steered Greece to the European Monetary Union in January 2001, when the euro replaced the drachma. A year later, the city elected its first female mayor, Dora Bakoyianni, who narrowly escaped an assassination attempt soon after her election.

In March 2004, Costas Karamanlis followed in the footsteps of his uncle (former prime minister Konstantine Karamanlis) by leading the conservative New Democracy Party to victory, narrowly defeating another big family name in Greek politics, the incumbent leader of the Socialist party, George Papandreous. Karamanlis is credited with transforming his party's dated, conservative outlook with more attractive and pro-European policies.

Later that year, on 13 August, the Olympic torch was lit in Athens at a spectacular opening ceremony. Despite worries about potential terrorist attacks, a huge security and volunteer operation ensured that the 28th Olympiad ran

smoothly. 'The Olympics came home and we've shown the world the great things Greeks can do,' said Gianna Angelopoulos, president of the Games organising committee.

There are mixed feelings among Athenians about the legacy of the Games. The city's transport infrastructure is radically improved, with 120 kilometres (75 miles) of new roads, nearly eight kilometres (five miles) of new metro lines, a 24-kilometre (15-mile) tram network, an ultra-modern traffic management centre and one of the best airports in the world. This in turn has helped to tackle the notorious smog that shrouded the city in the post-war years. But critics point out that sustainable development targets were not achieved, and not all of the 65,000 promised permanent jobs have materialised.

Politically, Karamanlis has attempted to put Greece on a more stable economic footing, introducing measures to tackle unemployment and bring inflation under control. He has been hampered in his efforts by strikes, including by rubbish collectors, which had a real impact on tourism in Athens in the summer of 2005.

In addition, a festering bond scandal that ran through 2007 has dented the credibility of Karamanlis's New Democracy Party. 'Return the money,' has become the mantra of the opposition party, PASOK, referring to the alleged removal of money from pension funds. However, the next election, due to be held in 2008, is expected to be a close-run affair. This is partly because, according to some polls, PASOK is seen by voters as even more undesirable.

With Greece's neighbour, Bulgaria, and other east European countries now part of the EU, the government has been pushing to give Greece an edge in the region. A €210-million broadband rollout programme for provincial Greece is part of this drive.

Greece's long and troubled relationship with Turkey appears to have reached a period of relative stability. Although many disputes are unresolved, the Greek government supports Turkey's bid to join the EU on the basis that it would bring increased regional stability.

In the summer of 2007, a heatwave pushed temperatures to 46°C (115°F) and prompted the government to activate its Xenocrates emergency plan, which requires state buildings to provide air-conditioned spaces to the public. Hundreds of forest fires spread across central Greece, there were at least a dozen heat-related deaths and power blackouts occurred in Athens as the demand for electricity, needed to power air-conditioners, overloaded the grid. A portent of the future? Could it be that global warming will assert itself as the crucial issue for Athens – and Greece – as the 21st century progresses.

Key events

3200 BC Bronze Age in Cyclades and Crete.
c3000 BC Neolithic settlements on
the Acropolis hill.
1450 BC Mycenaeans in Knossos.
c1400 BC The Acropolis is fortified.
1230-1180 BC Destruction of Troy.
1200 BC Collapse of Mycenean culture.
800 BC Athens expands by incorporating
its surrounding villages into its city-state.
776 BC The first Olympic Games take place.
750-700 BC Homer writes *The Iliad*
and *The Odyssey*.
750-500 BC The Archaic Age.
594 BC Solon becomes archon of Athens.
496 BC Birth of dramatist Sophocles.
490 BC The Athenians defeat the Persians
(led by Darius) at the Battle of Marathon.
480 BC The Persians burn Athens.
470-430 BC Pericles' programme of civic
improvement focuses on the Acropolis.
454 BC The Delian League moves to Athens,
signalling the start of the Athenian Empire.
431-404 BC Peloponnesian War between
Athens and Sparta.
427 BC Birth of philosopher Plato.
399 BC Socrates is sentenced to death.
387 BC Plato sets up his Academy.
338 BC After winning the battle of
Chaironeia, the Persians, led by Philip II,
gain control over Athens.
336 BC Philip II's son Alexander
(the Great) inherits control of Athens.
323 BC Death of Alexander the Great.
322 BC Death of Aristotle and Demosthenes.
330-215 BC Euclid and Archimedes develop
their mathematical theorems.
267 BC Athens fails to rise
against Macedonia.
148 BC Romans conquer Macedonia.
86 BC Roman general Sulla occupies Athens.
AD 31 The Pax Romana is inaugurated
by Emperor Augustus.
52 St Paul preaches the gospels to Athenians.
66-67 Emperor Nero tours Greece.
124-31 Emperor Hadrian begins architectural
reconstruction in Athens.
232 Constantine moves the capital of
the Roman Empire to Constantinople.
380 Emperor Thedosius declares Christianity
the official religion of the Empire.
529 Emperor Justinian closes down
the philosophical schools in Athens.
600-1300 Athens goes into decline. Its
temples are converted to Christian churches.

1054 The Christian church is divided
into Roman and Greek orthodoxies.
1300-1456 A series of invaders (Franks,
Catalans, Venetians, Turks) occupy Athens.
1456 The Turks occupy the Acropolis.
They rule Athens for the next four centuries.
1687 In an attempt to recapture Athens,
the Venetians bombard the Parthenon.
1801 Lord Elgin removes part of the frieze
around the Parthenon and ships it to London.
1821 Start of the Greek War of Independence.
1828 Creation of the first free Greek state.
Its president is Ioannis Kapodistrias.
1831 Kapodistrias is assassinated.
1832 The Great Powers of Western Europe
impose Bavarian King Otto as ruler.
1834 Athens becomes the capital of Greece.
1893 Opening of the Corinth Canal.
1896 The first modern-day Olympic Games
take place in Athens.
1910 Eleftherios Venizelos is appointed
Prime Minister.
1912-13 The Balkan Wars double
the territory belonging to Greece.
1913 King George is assassinated.
1917 Greece sides with the Allies in
World War I.
1923 Treaty of Lausanne authorises a
population exchange in Asia Minor. Greece
gains in excess of one million refugees.
1935 Venizelos is exiled; power is given
to general Ioannis Metaxas.
1941-42 German occupation.
1944 An assassination attempt against
Winston Churchill fails. The communist
revolution starts.
1944-49 Civil war tears Greece apart.
A mass exodus begins.
1967 The Junta seizes power.
1973 Student demonstrations against
the ruling colonels end in a blood bath.
1974 The Junta collapses.
1981 Greece's first socialist government
is elected. The country joins the EEC.
1985 Athens becomes Europe's first
Capital of Culture.
1994 Traffic restrictions are introduced
in Athens in an attempt to reduce pollution.
1997 Athens is awarded the 2004 Olympics.
1999 An severe earthquake hits Athens.
2001 The drachma is replaced by the euro.
2004 Athens hosts the XXVIII Olympiad.
2007 Heatwave-sparked forest fires burn
in the countryside around Athens.

Athens Today

A city that's constantly reinventing itself.

Viewed from the plane, as it circles the Attica basin for the landing at Eleftherios Venizelos Airport, Athens looks like an enormous pool of spilled concrete that has seeped down to the sea. Patches of colour are rare in this swill of grey, which seems ready to swallow the few islands of green that mark the city's main parks, including the National Gardens, Pedion Areos and Lycabettus Hill.

However, at ground level, the Greek capital is transformed as mulberry and olive trees soften its harsh edges. Café tables and chairs cram the pavements, creating the illusion in districts like Kolonaki or Thissio that you're in the midst of some vast living room rather than the streets of a bustling city. The ugliness witnessed from the air disappears and an alluring capital with a unique vibe begins to take shape. At ground level, the extraordinary Greek light loses its harshness and envelopes monuments, old and new.

The secret of the city's charm is its capacity to surprise even its most world-weary residents. A wander around Athens might reveal a flash

of the Parthenon between the congested streets of the commercial centre, or the reflection of a neo-classical column or pediment in the glass façade of an office building, seeming to appear out of nowhere. Athens today is a city that veers between the sublime and the surreal.

CHANGE IS GOOD

The Greek capital's latest transformation began with the 2004 Olympics. The city's justifiably jaded residents had feared that the pre-Games spruce-up would be the beginning and the end of regeneration, but it has proved to be an ongoing process. For one thing, some projects slated for completion in time for the Olympics – most notably the New Acropolis Museum (*see p28* **If you build it, they will come**) – are still works in progress. Meanwhile, scaffolding is still coming down from various buildings to reveal gorgeous façades that enhance the city's appearance. New projects are also being planned, including a massive arts complex on the site of the old racetrack at the southern end of Syngrou (*see p34* **Designs on tomorrow**), and gentrification schemes are being linked to

Athens Metro.

the construction of new home stadiums for the city's two Super League football franchises, Panathinaikos and AEK Athens.

One less tangible legacy of the Olympics is that it has helped Athens' denizens see the capital with fresh eyes. Slowly, they have begun to reclaim public spaces such as the Zappeion, the National Gardens, Syntagma Square and the pedestrian walk skirting the base of the Acropolis, where on holidays you'll see families indulging in the Greek village habit of the *volta*, or stroll.

'Playgrounds, walkways and cafés have sprung up in the voids between the beachside clubs.'

City planners continue to expand the reach of bus lanes and metro lines into the suburbs, altering how Athenians move around the city. Even the tram, initially reviled for its sluggish pace between Syntagma and the coast, has brought change to the coastal areas, where playgrounds, walkways and cafés have sprung up in the voids between the beachside clubs. The city is still congested with cars, and parking is as acute a problem as garbage removal, but car parks and recycling bins are now becoming common sights, forcing the city's inhabitants to grudgingly abandon their old habits of leaving vehicles and trash willy-nilly on the pavements.

If Athens seems tidier these days, it's also because the unsightly signage that was pulled down for the Olympics hasn't been allowed to creep back up. There's also been a change in scale: global retail and food chains have pushed out smaller businesses, injecting an aesthetic uniformity into high streets, and local stores and cafés have imitated the look. New shopping malls on the city's periphery, meanwhile, are tugging its centre of gravity outward – an impact that's only now beginning to be felt. The effects of these changes are already noticeable, not just in the city's physical structure but in its residents' lifestyles. Longer, uninterrupted (globalised) trading hours are altering social habits, with the afternoon nap the first victim, though Athenians still find time to linger at cafés, eat dinner late and stay out later still.

NOT QUITE GOING TO PLAN
Reality bites the first-time visitor to Athens. Even with regeneration, what strikes you first is its lack of 'old world' elegance, save for a sprinkling of neo-classical buildings (*see p31* **Neo-classical Athens**) amid the sea of glass, chrome and concrete. This is the Athenian paradox: an ancient city that is also very new, with almost nothing to bridge the historical gap between the city of Pericles and the capital founded by idealist philhellenes in the early 19th century, following Greece's liberation from the Ottoman Empire.

Athens is set in a basin, cupped by three ranges – mounts Hymettos, Pendeli and Egaleo – that spills into the sea in the south. Once a

If you build it, they will come

Even seen up close, the small block of marble seems hardly remarkable – except, that is, for a tiny inscription identifying it as a fragment from the Parthenon's frieze. But this was enough to put a broad smile on the face of Greece's culture minister, George Voulgarakis, as he showed off the eight-by-eleven-centimetre (3.2 by 4.3 inches) carving of a man's heel in September 2006, when the piece was officially presented to Greece by the University of Heidelberg. It was, as Voulgarakis said, a 'momentous' occasion – although university officials, not wishing to set a precedent for other disputed art works in European museums, said the Acropolis was a special case.

The fragment was the first piece of the **Parthenon** (*see p30 and p64*) to be returned to Greece – a symbolic gesture that Greeks hope will be imitated by others, notably the British Museum. For it is there that the Elgin (ahem, Parthenon) Marbles have been on display since the mid-1930s, having been removed from the Acropolis and taken to London in the 19th century by Lord Elgin, the British ambassador to the Ottoman Empire.

The **New Acropolis Museum** (*see p74*), whose opening has yet again been pushed back (from the summer of 2007 to early in 2008), is the climax of an international drive for the marbles' return, which was spurred in the '80s by the late actress and then culture minister Melina Mercouri and her husband

filmmaker Jules Dassin. Pride of place in the sleek new building, designed by Swiss architect Bernard Tschumi, has been given to the gallery intended to house the 17 marble sculptures – roughly half of the 160-metre (525-foot) frieze – in the possession of the British Museum. Located on the top floor, the gallery has been designed so that its glass walls and roof direct visitors' gaze to the Parthenon, at almost eye level, a few hundred meters away. But with the British Museum showing no signs of softening on the issue of the marbles' return, the room that is meant to be the heart of the new museum may stand empty for the forseeable future.

There are other pieces of the Parthenon – all larger than the fragment handed over by the University of Heidelberg – in other European museums and public collections, including the Louvre and the Vatican. And while Greece has pressed its case for the return of these items, too, the campaign has focused on the British Museum. For Greece, the drive begun by Mercouri is a matter of national pride; for Britain, returning the marbles is out of the question. Still, Greeks hope that once the New Acropolis Museum opens, this will increase the pressure on the British Museum. In fact, Greek officials have tentatively broached the idea of a 'loan' for a temporary exhibition that would allow the world to see the Parthenon and all its friezes within sight of one another.

city of around 40,000, Athens has today over three million inhabitants – roughly one-third of the population of Greece. Metropolitan Athens extended as far as the topography of the Attica basin would allow until a few years ago, when the new airport and the Attiki Odos ring road encouraged the spread of the conurbation into the Mesogeia, on the east side of Mount Hymettos. Without the pressure of a population explosion as in previous building booms, this time planners had the opportunity to create properly zoned areas. But they failed to do so, resulting in yet more haphazard development, creating a pool of concrete that will no doubt soon be joined to the concrete sea that Athens already appears to be from the air.

'Look around and you'll see the ancient city, the modern city, and little else in between.'

One of the problems faced by the city is a lack of organic, continuous development over a period of centuries. Most of modern Athens was built in the relatively short period since the 1830s, when the city was limited to Plaka and a few surrounding scattered hamlets. Look around and you'll see the ancient city, the modern city, and little else in between. And it's precisely because its roots are so shallow – in terms of Greece's history – that they've been so easily pulled up by successive waves of development spurred by Greeks' desire to forge a modern identity. The process has been – and still is – one of trial and error, as Greeks struggle to balance what they proudly claim is an 'Eastern' perspective and temperament with a 'Western' orientation. A prime example is the huge controversy that erupted in 2007 over plans to raze a gorgeous art deco mansion – an architectural rarity in the city – because it partially obstructs the view from the New Acropolis Museum.

It's only since the 2004 Olympics that Greeks have felt able to measure up against what they've traditionally viewed as the more sophisticated 'Europeans' and begun to feel more comfortable and confident in their modern identity. Yet this neurosis about not being seen as 'backward' or being left behind continues to manifest itself in the ever-changing names of clubs, restaurants and other establishments that contribute to the feeling of a city that seems to be in a constant state of flux.

Where other European capitals often induce nostalgia for what has been, Athens is more likely to make one regret what might have been.

THE NEW ATHENIANS

Migrants have been a major force of change in Athens since it was established as Greece's capital in 1834. The first wave of migrants helped establish the city, either staffing its services or physically constructing it. Builders and craftsmen initially came for the work, intending to return to their villages and islands, then decided to stay. They started families and created neighbourhoods with the flavour of their natal lands: migrants from Iraklio, for instance, settled in one area; migrants from Santorini in another. Just as the city's population had stabilised, the city was engulfed by a second wave of migrants – an estimated 1.5 million refugees arriving in the early 1920s from Asia Minor (*see p20* **All change**). Their sudden influx stretched the city's resources and infrastructure as Athens absorbed their number. Again, the capital's population stabilised, only to swelled by a new wave of migration in the 1950s as the post-Civil War conservative government decided to weaken the Left by driving the population from the countryside into Athens.

In the '90s, Athens was hit by a new wave of migrants. But this time they were not Greeks, but foreigners. Albanians, Bulgarians, Russians, Filipinos, Pakistanis, Poles and Egyptians, as well as a host of Africans and, most recently, Asians. Their arrival created some tensions. However, in typical Greek fashion, the migrants' presence was loudly denounced in public debate, but has been generally accepted at the private level.

Settling in Athens, these newcomers followed the same patterns as the Greek migrants before them, coming 'temporarily' to seek work, then staying. They too carved small ethnic niches in the city and enriched it with an infusion of new foods, music and customs. Today, hummus is as much a part of the fabric of the city's life as the *mizithropitakia* (sweet cheese pies) and *paximadia* (rusks) introduced by early island settlers and the *rembetika* music introduced into urban culture by the Asia Minor refugees. In the street produce markets, or *laiki*, today, you'll find mangoes and lychees as easily as tomatoes and armfuls of rocket.

For every wave of migrants, Omonia has been the unofficial assembly point, the place where new arrivals go to get their bearings.

The smoke-filled *kafeneia* with geographical names reflecting the specific provincial origin of their patrons that once rimmed Omonia may have been supplanted by shiny department stores and hotels, but on the square itself, and in the tiny side streets around it, is where you can catch a glimpse of not just the Athens of today, but the Athens of tomorrow.

Hadrian's Library. *See p32.*

Architecture

Classic buildings, ancient and modern.

The first impression of the architecture of Athens is of a sea of 20th-century concrete, with a few neo-classical buildings squeezed into the gaps, and an island of ancient Greece in the shape of the Acropolis. Unlike Rome, which has developed more or less continuously since its golden age, Athens has few architectural remains from the period between its capture from the Romans by the Visigoths in AD 395 and 1834, when Athens became the capital of a liberated Greece.

ANCIENT ATHENS

The French poet Lamartine described the **Parthenon** (*see p65*) as 'the world's most perfect poem in stone.' Standing on the location of earlier temples, it is dedicated to Athena's incarnation as the virgin goddess (Parthenos). In 447 BC – 33 years after the Persians destroyed a previous temple on the site – Pericles gathered the best architects available, Iktinos and Kallikrates, under the supervision of the sculptor Phidias, and instructed them to draw up a plan for the reconstruction of the Parthenon. The architects were briefed to create

a temple worthy of the city's new-found cultural and political position. It was completed in only nine years, an astonishing achievement.

Though the Parthenon appears to be an ode to simplicity, it is the most technically perfect Doric temple ever built. The architects used mathematics to calculate the best way to create an impression of complete symmetry, even from a distance. Every measurement – the width and placement of columns, distances between them, volumes and angles – derived from the 'golden mean' ratio. Subtle modifications were used: the columns, for example, bulge slightly around the middle and lean somewhat inwards; the corner columns are slightly larger in diameter than the other exterior columns, since they are seen against the open sky; the *stylobate* (the base on which the columns are placed) has an upwards curvature towards its centre of six centimetres (2.3 inches) on the east and west ends, and of 11 centimetres (4.3 inches) on the sides. These adjustments counteract the illusion that straight lines, when seen from a distance, appear to bend. The effect of these calculations is a building that seems effortlessly natural and harmonious.

The temple stands on the conventional three steps. The *cella* (the area in the centre of the temple – it was the seat of the god and was left empty except for a sculpture) consists of two rooms end to end. Inside the colonnades, towards the end, stood Phidias' monumental gold and ivory statue of Athena Parthenos, representing the fully armed goddess with spear, helmet and *aegis* (shield), accompanied by a snake, and holding a statue of victory in her extended right arm. The ceiling was made of wood, painted and gilded. Light was let in, as was the norm in Greek temples, only through the doorway when the great doors were opened.

The Parthenon also had a hitherto unseen richness in quality and quantity of sculptures. The Parthenon had countless more *metopes* (panels above the columns) than other temples, all brilliantly sculpted. The Ionic frieze continues around the full perimeter.

The other buildings on the Acropolis are equally important in their influence on later architecture; one famous example is the Brandenburg Gate in Berlin, inspired by the **Propylaeum**. This gateway was the masterpiece of the architect Mnesicles. It was intended to give a feeling of passing from the mundane world to the sacred; from the outside, it also blocks the Parthenon from view, so that it appears all at once in its full glory. However, with work disrupted by the Peloponnese Wars, the Propylaeum was left uncompleted.

The **Erechtheum** (421-406 BC) is the most exceptional Ionic building on the Acropolis. While the Parthenon exudes elegant simplicity, the grace of the Erechtheum, composed of two adjoining temples, lies in its unique complexity. An exception to all the rules, it looks like a different building from each of its four sides. The last of the great works of Pericles to be completed, the Erechtheum was regarded with great respect and its site considered particularly sacred. It included, among other relics, the tomb of Cecrops, the legendary founder of Athens; the rock that preserved the mark of Poseidon's trident; and the spring that arose from it. The south porch, known as the Caryatid porch (a caryatid is a column shaped like a female figure), is the most famous, elevated by the alluring Caryae maidens.

The small, jewel-like **Temple of Athena Nike**, goddess of victory, is the earliest Ionic building on the Acropolis (424 BC), while on the slope of the Acropolis stands the cradle of ancient drama, the sixth-century BC **Theatre of Dionysus** (*see p66*), rebuilt in the fourth century by Lycurgus. This is where greats such as Aristophanes, Aeschylus, Sophocles and Euripides first presented their plays, and where the Festival of the Great Dionysia, a renowned drama competition, took place. In 334 BC one of the winners, Lysicrates, built a monument to commemorate the victory. The **Lysicrates Monument** (*see p71*) in Plaka is the only preserved choregic monument, and has been imitated by many neo-classical architects.

The achievements of these ancient architects of Athens' golden age stand as testament to one of the greatest legacies of classical Greece: 2,500 years later they're still among the most influential constructions in Western civilisation.

Neo-classical Athens

When Athens was made capital of the newly liberated Greece in 1834, influential foreign architects poured into the city. They were determined that the fledgling state's new buildings would reflect the glory of ancient Athens, and their work laid the foundations of the Athenian school of neo-classicism. The two who played the greatest role in the creation of neo-classical Athens were Danish brothers, Hans Christian and Theophilos Hansen. Both were involved in all three buildings of the **Neo-classical University Complex** (*see p81*) on Panepistimiou. The older of the two, Hans Christian, created the first fully developed example in the central **University** building, and Theophilos Hansen its *pièce de résistance*: the **Academy of Athens**. Considered to be one of world's finest neo-classical buildings, its central wing has the form of an Ionic temple with a colonnaded portico at each end, an obvious homage to the Erechtheum.

German architect Ernst Ziller, together with Theophios Hansen, was behind the third part of the trilogy – the **National Library**. Another of Ziller's masterpieces is the **Troy Mansion**, which is now home to the Numismatic Museum (*see p81*). His compatriot, Friedrich von Gärtner, was responsible for the **Old Palace**, which has become the Parliament Building (*see p81*), on Syntagma Square.

The most important Greek architect of the time was probably Lysandros Kaftandzoglou, who designed **Athens Polytechnic** (*see p88*). It would find its place in history much later, as the stage for the uprising against the Junta in 1973.

ROMAN ATHENS

The Romans captured and sacked Athens in 86 BC, razing the fortification walls and destroying a substantial part of its classical and Hellenistic monuments and artworks. Upon coming to power in 27 BC, Emperor Augustus embarked on a systematic reconstruction programme, showing respect and admiration for the local cultural heritage. In Rome, public buildings and monuments were built imitating Athenian models, while in Athens new ideas of planning and architecture were introduced. The **Roman Forum** (*see p74*) of Caesar and Augustus, with the impressive Gate of Athena Archegetis on its west side, was an open space intended as a market area. Just by the Roman Forum, the **Tower of the Winds** (*see p74*), also known as the Clock of Andronikos of Kyrrhos, was probably built in the mid first century BC. The tower was an early version of a meteorological station, which allowed nearby market merchants to know the time and wind conditions, enabling them to calculate the approximate arrival time of their deliveries by sea.

'Athens' temples, including the Parthenon, were converted into churches.'

During his reign, Hadrian implemented a large-scale building programme. The grandest of all Hadrian's projects was the **Temple of Olympian Zeus** (AD 132; *see p83*), the foundation of which had been laid more than 600 years earlier. The Corinthian temple is the largest ancient temple on the Greek mainland. In a move of confident self-aggrandisement, Hadrian placed a statue of himself next to the one of Zeus, in the sacred *cella*. **Hadrian's Arch** (*see p83*) was erected by the Athenians nearby, on the border between the old city and the new, to honour the imperial benefactor; the arch is now the starting point of Dionysiou Areopagitou, the pedestrianised walkway that connects the archaeological sites (*see p63* **Stepping stones to the past**). **Hadrian's Library** (*see p76*) was another of his grand works; its surviving walls, with their monumental Corinthian columns, stand just next to Monastiraki metro station.

The **Odeon of Herodes Atticus** (*see p66*) was built by the wealthy public benefactor as a memorial to his deceased wife. The theatre's semicircular auditorium is hewn out of the rocky southern face of the Acropolis hill. The 4,500 seat theatre, with its 30-metre-high (98-foot) arched façade, had a cedar roof when it was completed in AD 161. It is now the main venue of the annual Athens Festival.

BYZANTINE ATHENS

In the fourth century, paganism was quashed by Emperor Theodosius, and Athens' temples, including the Parthenon, were converted into Christian churches. Justinian I's decision to close down the schools of philosophy (AD 529) was the final nail in Athens' coffin, and the city started to decline. The so-called Dark Ages would last until around the ninth century, when the Byzantine Empire hailed a period of reconstruction and reorganisation that was to last until the 13th century.

Several small cruciform churches from this period still remain, scattered around the city. The interiors are usually heavily decorated with mosaics portraying religious figures and Byzantine emperors, as well as marble sculptural ornamentation.

The 12th-century **Panaghia Gorgoepikoos**, next door to Athens Cathedral and sometimes called the Little Cathedral, is built with material from ruins of older buildings. This is particularly evident in the upper part of the church's external walls, where fragments of classical marble friezes combine with contemporary reliefs to create a collage of Greek history. (*See also p19* **Traces of Byzantium**).

UNDER OTTOMAN RULE

Under Turkish rule (1456-1821), Athens was never much more than a garrison town and there are very few architectural traces still to be seen. The area of Plaka is built on the Turkish plan, but little is left from those days. The oldest Ottoman mosque in Athens is the **Fethiye Tzami**, built in 1458 on the Roman Forum, now used as an archaeological warehouse. Across the street from the Tower of the Winds stands another of the few Turkish remains, a gateway and a single dome from a madrasa, an Islamic school. The **Museum of Traditional Greek Ceramics** (*see p76*), just opposite Monastiraki metro station, is housed in the 18th-century **Mosque of Tzidarakis**.

MODERN TIMES

After Greece won its independence, many earlier buildings were unceremoniously demolished. This was partly out of rage against the Turks, but also because they had been built as extensions to classical monuments, and the classical revival demanded that monuments be stripped of the extra details that had been added over the centuries. The Acropolis is the most striking example: it has hosted the fortress of every power since Pericles, and has been altered accordingly. The Parthenon served as a Byzantine and Catholic church and as a medieval fortress under the Franks. Under Ottoman rule, it became a mosque and

CityLink: a much-needed boost for the city centre. *See p34.*

a gunpowder arsenal; in this latter role it sustained its worst damage to date, when the Venetians blew it up.

When Athens was appointed capital city of the newly independent Greece in 1834, a new city plan was proposed by Leo von Klenze. His idea was a small-scale, picturesque city, without grand boulevards or squares. Unfortunately this plan undermined the natural growth of the city, and didn't stand the test of the massive expansion that Athens would soon face.

POLYKATOIKIA

The first wave of the mass expansion of Athens took place between World War I and II as a result of the forced return of Greeks from Asia Minor. Some of the capital's finest architecture derives from this time. Apartment blocks from the 1920s and '30s took their inspiration from Cycladic architecture (plain, white stone walls) and modernist ideas. Architects like Dimitris Pikionis and Aris Konstantinidis were trying to define the Greek identity through modern architecture.

To solve the housing problems in Athens caused by the massive migration from the countryside in the 1950s, a system of part exchange called antiparohi *antiparochi* evolved. Developers acquired land for building in exchange for a certain number of apartments in the finished building. Concrete was the material of choice, easily available and easily handled by unskilled labourers. The system encouraged the standardisation of apartment blocks, the so-called *polykatoikia*. As investors strove to maximise their profits, the role of the architects

was taken over by engineers. The result was a rapid growth of new, practical housing, but with poor quality of design and construction and with a minimum of public space left between the buildings.

Although the artistic quality of pre-war architecture was far ahead of that of the post-war *polykatoikia*, the concept was more or less the same: derived from Le Courbusier's modernist ideal of a box-like construction that could fit all possible activities. In this sense, Athens exemplifies the functional model of modernism, in taking density to the extreme, and striving for the simplest, most non-decorative, most non-monumental architecture possible.

MONUMENTS OF MODERNISM

Another result of *antiparochi* is the almost total absence of monumentalism, except for the buildings on Leof Vas Sofias. One perfect example of these – and a benchmark in the modern architectural history of Athens – is the **US Embassy** (No.91, 1959-61), designed by Bauhaus architect Walter Gropius.

Also on a monumental scale is the **Athens Conservatory** (Rigillis & Leof Vas Konstantinou, 17-19 Vas Georgiou II), a fine example of the radical Bauhaus spirit. Finished in 1976, it was designed by the great visionary Ioannis Despotopoulos, who studied under Walter Gropius in Weimar. The Conservatory was, sadly, the only building to be completed in a planned Cultural Centre for Athens. The external marble colonnade is a dream of symmetry and a paradise for skate kids.

The **Athens Hilton** (*see p50*) caused a huge controversy at the time of its construction (1958-63). Accused of being both foreign and offensive, it is now considered one of the finest examples of post-war modernism.

THE OLYMPIC LEGACY

Although the 2004 Olympics was the major force behind recent regeneration in the city, the only public buildings of significant architectural value were created by Spanish architect Santiago Calatrava. He was invited to provide aesthetic unification to the main **Olympic Complex** (*see p98*) in Marousi, linking existing venues with new constructions. His identity is stamped all over the site: everything in the complex is white and many smaller constructions and buildings are covered in a broken ceramic-tile cladding, a homage to Gaudí's mosaics and a reference to Athens' ancient heritage.

The two main architectural features of the complex are the **Velodrome**, with its amazing glass-and-steel translucent roof, and the redesign of the main **Olympic Stadium**, with its even more famous roof, built in sections that were slid into place. The complex also features the **Agora Walkway**, covered by high arches that cast a fishbone shadow over the ground, as well as the 260-metre-long (853-foot) and 20-metre-high (65-foot) screen, the **Wall of Nations**.

Calatrava also designed the **pedestrian bridge** in Katehaki, crossing Mesogion Avenue from Katehaki metro station, which gives the illusion of hanging in the air on one side and of ramming into the apartment blocks on the other.

POST-OLYMPIC REGENERATION

The current buzz is around the once-grim Pireos Street, one of the city's least glamorous thoroughfares, stretching from Omonia Square to Piraeus. Against all odds the street is becoming an important destination for arts and nightlife. The Gazi area was the pioneer with **Technopolis** (*see p94*); the new annexe of the **Benaki Museum** (*see p94*), designed by architects Kokkinou and Kourkolas, is imaginative; and the new Keramikos metro station that opened in 2007 should ensure that development continues. In fact, regeneration is now spreading to the neighbouring areas of Rouf, Keramikos and Metaxourgio, and construction is set to begin soon on a new home ground for Panathinaikos Football Club in Votanikos.

In the city centre, the completion of the renovation of the historic Army Pension Fund building on Panepistimiou has given a much-needed boost. Rebranded as **CityLink**, it occupies the block bounded by Panepistimiou, Voukourestiou, Stadiou and Amerikis. Its main tenant is the upmarket department store Attica.

Designs on tomorrow

Major public buildings to look out for.

In 2000, the long-deserted Fix brewery on Syngrou Avenue was selected as the permanent new home for the **National Museum of Contemporary Art**. The planned renovation (due to finish in 2008) is a happy outcome for what had become one of Athens' saddest sights: a remarkable '60s industrial building – created by one of the true masters of modern Greek architecture, Takis Zenetos (also responsible for the Lycabettus outdoor theatre; *see p183*) – that had fallen into disrepair.

Another eagerly awaiting building project is the controversial **New Acropolis Museum** (*see p74 and p28* **If you build it, they will come**), designed by Bernard Tschumi. Some have criticised the large-scale design as being out of proportion with its surroundings – the building will occupy several blocks of the low-rise Makrygianni neighbourhood at the foot of the Acropolis. Others have welcomed the fact that Athens is finally implementing a

prestigious large-scale project by a big-name architect, providing a worthy permanent home for the Acropolis artefacts. The construction of the 20,000-square-metre glass and concrete structure – which includes a rectangular glass gallery to display the Elgin Marbles, should they be returned – has been delayed by long-running legal battles as well as new archaeological discoveries at the site.

In June 2007, the decision was taken to build a new **National Library** and **National Lyric Theatre** – the permanent home that the Greek National Opera has been waiting for for over half a century. These projects, along with an **Educational and Cultural Park**, will be handed over complete as a gift from the Stavros Niarchos Foundation to the Greek people. If inaugurated in 2015 as planned, this trio of major cultural projects will bring life not only to the Faliron Delta waterfront site, but be of huge importance to cultural Athens as a whole.

Statue of Zeus in the National Archaeological Museum.

Greek Myth & Legend

From the height of Mount Olympus to the depths of the underworld.

The Hellenic deities weren't exactly wonderful role models. They lied, cheated, squabbled and toyed ruthlessly with humans. Zeus, king of the gods, assumed various shapes – white bull, swan, golden cloudburst – to seduce unwilling women. His enraged wife Hera persecuted his mistresses, even chasing one pregnant rival with a giant python and transforming another into a pet cow.

The gods' main biographers were Homer, whose epic poems *The Iliad* and *The Odyssey* kick-started Western literature in the eighth century BC, and Hesiod, who wrote *The Theogony* in the seventh century BC. Ancient critics sometimes found fault with these saucy tales. 'Homer and Hesiod have attributed to the gods everything that is a shame and disgrace among men, stealing and committing adultery and deceiving one another,' Xenophanes later complained. Yet most Greeks didn't mind the bad behaviour, considering it just as instructive as a good example – and a far better yarn.

The Ancient Greeks believed deities took an active role in human affairs and destinies. They wooed the gods with lavish temples, prayers, offerings and games such as the Olympics. The sacrifice of animals was especially popular. Priests would slit the creatures' throats, sprinkle the altars with blood, burn the choice bits for the gods and foretell the future from the entrails.

People could worship any and all of the deities. Cities had patron gods, as did the trades. New divinities were borrowed freely from other cultures and then woven into local mythology. Oracles, such as Delphi, transmitted the gods' cryptic advice and prophecies.

Cults were a major force in Greek society. The most famous was based at Eleusis, the site of a sanctuary to the fertility goddess Demeter. The rituals known as the Eleusian mysteries were shrouded in secrecy, but rumours of drunkenness and orgies continue to this day.

These pagan rites gave way to Christianity in AD 324, but the power of the myths endured. The old tales were revived by the Romans, then again in the Renaissance.

THE GODS

One creation myth claims that the deities and living creatures sprang from the stream that encircled the world, Oceanus. In the most common version, Mother Earth emerged from the chaos and bore her son, Uranus (sky), while she slept. He showered her with fertile rain and she gave birth to flowers, trees, beasts, birds, the hundred-handed giants, the early gods (Titans) and the one-eyed Cyclops.

Family strife led the Titans to attack Uranus. The youngest of the Titans, Cronus, cut off his father's genitals with a flint sickle and became sovereign. He married his sister Rhea, but insisted upon devouring their children, as prophecy declared that a son would dethrone him. He swallowed five babies, then Rhea wised up. She gave birth to Zeus in secret.

'Zeus poisoned his father's drink, causing him to vomit up his elder siblings.'

Zeus grew to manhood and poisoned his father's honeyed drink, causing Cronus to vomit up his elder siblings – Hades, Poseidon, Hera, Hestia and Demeter (*see p38* **Gods almighty**). With their help, Zeus vanquished the Titans and became king of the gods and heaven. A dozen major deities dwelled high on Mount Olympus, while Hades brooded in the underworld and Poseidon ruled the ocean. Earth remained a neutral zone.

Supporting the 12 Olympians was a cast of thousands. The three Fates spun, measured and snipped the threads of mortal lives, the Furies punished evil-doers, while nine Muses inspired poets, artists and musicians. Trees contained beautiful female spirits (dryads), as did streams (naiads) and fields (nymphs). Lusty, goat-legged satyrs frolicked with wild women (maenads) in holy groves. Centaurs, skilled in sorcery and healing, raped and revelled. Other gods included Pan (shepherds), Asclepius (healing), Eros (love), Hypnos (sleep), Helios (sun), Selene (moon) and Nemesis (punishment).

THE GODDESS

The capital's name honours its patron, Athena, goddess of wisdom. This bold and brilliant divinity governed all knowledge – from weaving to astronomy and battle strategy. She stood for victory and noble defence, unlike Ares, the bloodthirsty god of war. Athena was also the goddess of wit, morality and clear air, and the protector of small children. The flute, yoke, trumpet and plough are among her inventions.

Her birth was extraordinary, even by Greek mythology's standards. In a fit of insecurity, worried that a son might surpass him, Zeus swallowed his pregnant first wife. Soon after, a horrible migraine gripped the king of the gods. The pain grew so severe that he begged for his skull to be chopped open with an axe. Out sprang Athena, fully grown and armed.

Despite the splitting headache, Athena was her father's favourite. Zeus refused her nothing, even allowing her use of his mightiest weapon, the thunderbolt. She remained a virgin, lofty and pure, but still managed to have a son. The smith god Hephaestus tried to ravage her. She fought him off, but some of his semen brushed her thigh and fell to earth, growing into Erichthonius, an early king of Athens.

Athena won the city in a contest against her uncle, Poseidon. He struck the cliff of the Acropolis with his trident, and a salt-water spring gushed from the rock. Athena produced an olive tree. The gods voted her contribution more useful to humans – as it brought food, oil and shelter – and awarded her Athens.

The ancients celebrated her each year at the Panathenea festival, when a grand procession would wind up the Acropolis, dominated by Phidias' majestic statues of the goddess. Her great temple, the mighty Parthenon (meaning 'virgin' in Ancient Greek) still stands today.

THE HEROES

Brave, handsome heroes obsessed with fame and glory star in many tales. More often than not, their ambition wreaked havoc.

Achilles is a prime example. Though he was a magnificent warrior, his 'destructive wrath' brought countless sorrows' to his people during the Trojan War, as Homer recounted in *The Iliad*. His arrogance finally outraged the gods: mid-battle, they directed an arrow to Achilles' only vulnerable spot – his heel. Hercules started poorly – with the murder of his wife and kids in a bout of madness – but redeemed himself through the Twelve Labours. Oedipus unwittingly murdered his father and married his mother. The great musician Orpheus played so sweetly, the gods allowed him to bring his bride back from death – on one condition: he couldn't look at her until they reached the surface. Riddled with doubt, he glanced back and lost her again. The heartbroken hero soon perished, torn apart by wild animals.

Pan and **Aphrodite** (sculpture in the National Archaeological Museum; *see p90*).

Jason, leader of the Argonauts, captured the coveted Golden Fleece, aided by the sorceress Medea. After ten years of happy marriage, he chucked her out. The vengeful woman murdered their children and his new wife, then fled in a chariot drawn by winged dragons. Medea reappeared briefly as Queen of Athens, stepmother to the hero Theseus. She attempted to poison him and was banished. Theseus went on to face the Cretan Minotaur, half man, half bull, imprisoned in the Labyrinth, who devoured young Athenian boys and girls. He killed the monster with the help of Princess Ariadne, then callously abandoned her on the way home. His comeuppance was swift: nearing Athens, Theseus forgot to hoist the white sail, a sign of victory for his worried father Aegeus. The grieving king leaped to his death.

Theseus was strong, but refined, smart and diplomatic, all qualities the ancient Athenians prized. He united the Attica region and laid the foundations of democracy. Perseus, on the other hand, was more of an action hero. He decapitated Medusa, the snake-haired gorgon, whose gaze turned flesh to stone.

Odysseus was celebrated as the cleverest Greek. The wily king fought in the Trojan War to reclaim Helen, the most beautiful woman in the world. His return trip took years, rather than weeks. Homer's *Odyssey* traces this epic journey, plagued by shipwreck, witches, sirens and giant man-eating Cyclops. Finally Odysseus reached his homeland, the island of Ithaca, to discover his faithful wife Penelope besieged by greedy, pushy suitors. He slew them with a great bow and reclaimed his kingdom – an unusually happy ending for ancient mythology.

THE HUMANS

The first generation was the 'golden race', who lived without care. They never grew old, lived off the fat of the land, and died contented. Next came the silver race, eaters of bread. They were so quarrelsome and ignorant that Zeus destroyed them. The insolent bronze race ate flesh and delighted in war. A more noble set, known as the race of heroes, followed. Sired by gods, with mortal mothers, the warriors who fought at Troy and the Argonauts were part of this age. The fifth and final race, known as the race of iron, is beset by unworthy descendants: cruel, unjust, lustful and treacherous. Hesiod wrote: 'I wish I were not of this race, that I had died before, or had not yet been born.'

Prometheus stole fire from the heavens and gave it to humans. Enraged, Zeus created the first woman: intelligent, lovely Pandora. The gods gave her a box, containing 10,000 curses. Curious, she opened it and released evil into the world. Pandora quickly slammed the lid, but hope alone remained inside.

The Greeks had a myth for every occasion, from the cradle to the grave. The countless stories tapped into universal themes – jealousy, infatuation, ambition and loyalty, to name a few. Perhaps this resonance explains their continued popularity, nearly 2,800 years after Homer first captured them in song.

Gods almighty

Aphrodite

Goddess of: Love.
Strengths: Born naked from the sea foam; also has a magic love-inducing girdle.
Flaws: Addicted to adultery.
Roman name: Venus.
Symbols: Rose, apple, swan.

Apollo

God of: Light.
Strengths: Bestowed enlightenment, governed music, medicine, oracles and crops.
Flaws: Cheated in a musical contest, then flayed his rival, Marsyas, alive.
Roman name: Apollo.
Symbols: Lyre, bow, tripod, laurel wreath.

Ares

God of: War.
Strengths: This natural born killer fathered Eros (Cupid) and Harmonia (Harmony).
Flaws: Lost twice to Athena.
Roman name: Mars.
Symbols: Spear, torch, armour.

Artemis

Goddess of: The hunt.
Strengths: Despite her bloodthirstiness, she protected pregnant women and small children.
Flaws: This eternal virgin turned a peeping tom, Actaeon, into a stag and hunted him.
Roman name: Diana.
Symbols: Bow and quiver, new moon and hind.

Demeter

Goddess of: The earth and fertility.
Strengths: Taught people about agriculture, civic order and wedlock.
Flaws: Starved humans when Hades stole her daughter, then created winter.
Roman name: Ceres.
Symbols: Corn, basket, poppy, serpent.

Dionysus

God of: Wine.
Strengths: Roamed the globe with drunken nymphs, satyrs and wild women.
Flaws: The portable party often spun out of control. Limbs were torn. Lives were lost.
Roman name: Bacchus (aka Liber).
Symbols: Ivy crown, wand, fawn, panther.

Hades

God of: The underworld and the dead.
Strengths: In milder moods, he bestowed wealth or an invisibility helmet.
Flaws: Kidnapped his bride Persephone, whose enraged mother invented winter.
Roman name: Pluto.
Symbols: Three-headed dog Cerberus, pickaxe, cypress tree.

Hephaestus

God of: Fire and metalworking.
Strengths: His fabulous jewellery earned him Aphrodite, the love goddess, as his wife.
Flaws: She cheated on him constantly.
Roman name: Vulcan.
Symbols: Hammer, tongs, a lame leg.

Hera

Queen of the gods, and goddess of marriage.
Strengths: Routinely renewed her virginity by bathing in a special spring.
Flaws: This jealous wife chased one rival with a python, kept another as a pet cow.
Roman name: Juno.
Symbols: Peacock, cuckoo, pomegranate.

Hermes

God of: Thieves, traders and messengers.
Strengths: Invented the lyre mere days after his birth (with gut from Apollo's stolen cows).
Flaws: Guided souls to the underworld.
Roman name: Mercury.
Symbols: Herald's staff, winged golden sandals, winged helmet.

Hestia

Goddess of: The hearth and civic harmony.
Strengths: Kept the home fires burning and avoided sexual intrigue on Olympus.
Flaws: Too dull to have one, really.
Roman name: Vesta.
Symbols: Sceptre, hearth.

Poseidon

God of: The ocean and flowing waters.
Strengths: Invented horses (or so he boasted).
Flaws: Caused storms and earthquakes.
Roman name: Neptune.
Symbols: Trident, chariot drawn by foam horses, dolphin.

Zeus

King of the gods, ruler of the sky.
Strengths: Saved his siblings by poisoning their cannibal father, the Titan Cronus.
Flaws: Raped his mother (who advised him not to marry his sister, Hera).
Roman name: Jupiter.
Symbols: Lightning bolt, clouds, eagle, oak.

Where to Stay

Where to Stay   40

Features

The best Hotels   43
A room with that view   47
Design central   53

Astir Palace Vouliagmeni. *See p55.*

Where to Stay

In the arms of Morpheus.

Athens can thank the 2004 Olympics for the improvement of its hotel infrastructure. Hotels upped their game with stunning new openings and radical renovations of existing premises. In the years that followed, as Athens attempted to establish itself as a city-break destination, even more new hotels have opened, most with an emphasis on design (*see p53* **Design central**); at the same time, big international hotel chains opened new branches.

These days, Athens offers plenty of choice when it comes to style, though budget hotels with shared facilities, and bed and breakfasts, are thin on the ground compared with luxury and boutique options. However, standards in every price category have improved dramatically, prices have stabilised, and features once found only in expensive hotels – like wireless or high-speed internet access – have trickled down to cheaper places. One great advantage of staying in Athens is the proliferation of roof terraces and roof gardens, many with spectacular views.

The area around Omonia Square has emerged as a popular location for new openings; Syntagma and Makrygianni are also being 'refreshed' in anticipation of the opening of the New Acropolis Museum.

Generally speaking, Athens hotel rates are now in line with most European countries – although far cheaper than London. Because of increased competition and the introduction of internet booking, pricing at Athens hotels is now a lot more transparent. Rates tend to vary throughout the year and are often negotiable: prices listed in this guide are the rates at which rooms were being sold during the summer high season. High season generally runs from Easter until October, with hotels offering discounts of around 25 to 35 per cent in low season. Competition for international clients is so strong that foreign travel agents often offer lower hotel rates than those available within Greece.

Acropolis & around

Expensive

Athenian Callirhoe

Kallirois 32 & Petmeza, Makrygianni, 11743 (210 921 5353/www.tac.gr). Metro Syngrou-Fix. **Rates** €160 single/double; €205 executive room; €265 junior suite. **Credit** AmEx, DC, MC, V. **Map** p251 E7 ①
A stylish hotel for those seeking contemporary-chic interior and a feeling of exclusivity in a convenient (if rather ugly) location on a busy avenue a few

Athenian Callirhoe.

minutes from Plaka and Syntagma. The decor is characterised by sleek, sharp-edged metal and glass, while rooms feature fluffy duvets, leather sofas and – in the upper price bracket – hot tubs. The Oyster Bar on the roof garden has stunning views and serves mainly seafood dishes prepared in an open kitchen, while the Merhaba bar on the ground floor is enlivened by an ethnic soundrack and belly-dancers. *Bars (3). Business centre. Concierge. Gym. Internet (high-speed, web TV, free). No-smoking floors. Restaurants (2). Room service. TV (games, pay movies).*

Divani Palace Acropolis

Parthenonos 19-25, Makrygianni, 11742 (210 928 0100/www.divaniacropolis.gr). Metro Akropoli or Syngrou-Fix. **Rates** €170 single; €180 double; €300 suite. **Credit** AmEx, DC, MC, V. **Map** p251 E7 ❷
Well-managed by a big Greek hotel chain, this classic luxury city hotel is ideally located for an evening performance at the nearby Herodeion (*see below*). There's a lot of gilt, mirrors and potted palms in the lobby, above a preserved, glassed-in portion of the Themistoclean Wall in the foundations. Rooms on the fourth to seventh floors enjoy Acropolis views; all rooms are big, with sleek bathrooms. Drinks and a great Greek buffet are served in the roof garden. *Bar. Business centre. Concierge. Internet (high-speed in business centre, €10.60/hr). No-smoking rooms. Pool (outdoor). Restaurants (2). Room service (6.30am-11pm). TV (pay movies).*

Electra Palace

Navarhou Nikodimou 18-20, Plaka, 10557 (210 337 0000/www.electrahotels.gr). Akropoli or Metro Syntagma. **Rates** (with breakfast) €180 single; €199 double; €225 triple. **Credit** AmEx, DC, MC, V. **Map** p249/p251 F5 ❸
With a stunning neo-classical façade, the Electra Palace provides the heart of Plaka with a smart, full-service hotel. Inside you'll find golden, creamy marble with inlaid designs, antiques with plenty of gold leaf, classic ceiling mouldings, gilded mirrors and dark-wood panelling, and a small, ethereally lit indoor pool/hot tub and spa. A ten-metre-long (33ft) rooftop pool is another attraction, as is the formal, attentive service and the good modern Greek restaurant. The only drawback is some loud motorbike noise from the otherwise quiet residential street – request a back-facing or garden-facing room. *Bar. Business centre. Concierge. Gym. Internet (wireless, €10/hr). No-smoking floors. Parking (€12/day). Pools (1 outdoor, 1 indoor). Restaurants (2). Spa. Room service. TV (pay movies).*

Herodion

Rovertou Galli 4, Makrygianni, 11742 (210 923 6832/www.herodion.gr). Metro Akropoli. **Rates** €142-€171 single; €169-€203 double; €210-€249 triple; €204-€245 junior suite. **Credit** AmEx, DC, MC, V. **Map** p251 E7 ❹
Under the same excellent management as the Philippos (*see below*), the Herodion shares its chief advantage – a location ideal for drooling at the

Acropolis. But it differs from its sibling in its decor, which is more subdued and traditional, gracefully integrating modern and classical elements. Rather uninspired though comfortable furniture dresses up the rooms, which have sumptuous marble bathrooms. Amenities include a green, atrium-like café, a cosy, elegant bar-lounge, and a modest roof garden with a view of the Acropolis that is as up close and personal as you can get. The location is just a few steps from the ancient Odeon of Herodes Atticus, venue for many cultural performances for the summer Athens Festival (*see p162*). Photo p42. *Bar. Business centre. Concierge. Disabled-adapted rooms. Internet (wireless, €3/hr). No-smoking floors. Restaurants (2). Room service (8am-1.30am). TV.*

Philippos Hotel

Mitsaion 3, Makrygianni, 11742 (210 922 3611/www.philipposhotel.com). Metro Akropoli. **Rates** €120-€134 single; €150-€174 double; €170-€194 triple. **Credit** AmEx, DC, MC, V. **Map** p251 E7 ❺
The Philippos is a good choice for those in search of a reliable four-star hotel within easy reach of the Acropolis. Its ground-floor lobby, reception, lounge and coffee bar have a pleasant decor, though the small bedrooms are less elegantly appointed. It attracts a mix of business and leisure travellers who are keen to avoid the 'copy and paste' mould of the giant international hotel chains and are looking for a hotel with some personality and good service. *Bar. Business centre. Internet (high-speed in business centre, €2/30mins). No-smoking rooms. TV.*

Moderate

Acropolis Select Hotel

Falirou 37-39, Makrygianni, 11742 (210 921 1610/www.acropoliselect.gr). Metro Syngrou-Fix. **Rates** (wit breakfast) €110 single; €130 double. **Credit** AmEx, DC, MC, V. **Map** p251 E7 ❻
Just a short walk from the Acropolis, the hotel's uninspired façade hides a renovated, elegant interior: the lobby, restaurant and bar are stylishly decorated with Italian furniture and original artworks. By contrast, the rooms are furnished in country style, with patterned bedspreads and curtains, and cramped bathrooms. Knowledgeable and professional staff have earned the hotel a fine reputation over the years. *Bar. Internet (shared terminal, wireless, €5.50/hr). No-smoking floors. Restaurant. Room service (7am-9.30pm). TV (pay movies).*

Adrian Hotel

Adrianou 74, Plaka, 10556 (210 322 1553/www.douros-hotels.com). Metro Monastiraki. **Rates** (with breakfast) €110-€125 single; €135-€150 double; €150 triple. **Credit** MC, V. **Map** p249/p251 E5 ❼

❶ Green numbers given in this chapter correspond to the location of each hotel on the street maps. *See pp248-252.*

Herodion. *See p41.*

In the thick of the pedestrian action on Adrianou, guests at the Adrian can watch all the neighbourhood animation from their balconies but still close the door on it with double-glazed windows (or avoid it altogether with a back-facing room). This mid-range hotel has comfortable – if dull – rooms (those with an Acropolis view are pricier), friendly and professional management, a comfortable lounge area, and a beautiful shaded roof garden with a view. *Breakfast room. Internet (wireless, shared terminal, €5/hr). No-smoking rooms. TV.*

Art Gallery Hotel

Erechthiou 5, Koukaki, 11742 (210 923 8376/ www.artgalleryhotel.gr). Metro Syngrou-Fix. **Rates** €75 single; €100 double; €120 triple; €140 quad. *Breakfast* €8. **No credit cards. Map** p251 E7 ❽
This small, family-run hotel is in a quiet residential area just outside the centre and within reasonable walking distance of the Acropolis. A mishmash of old family furniture, and paintings from a locally celebrated Impressionist artist (who used the house as a studio), decorate the interior. The renovated rooms have polished wooden floors and are flooded with light. The earnest service and a good top-floor bar-lounge with views of Philopappus Hill and the Acropolis complete the picture.
Bar. TV.

Hera Hotel

Falirou 9, Makrygianni, 11742 (210 923 6682/210 923 5618/www.herahotel.gr). Metro Akropoli. **Rates** €100-€130 single; €120-€155 double; €180-€220 junior suite. **Credit** AmEx, DC, MC, V. **Map** p251 E7 ❾
This recently refurbished boutique hotel has an ideal location – just a few minutes' walk to the Acropolis

and next to all imaginable forms of transport. Other pleasures of the Hera include good service, a pleasant circular indoor courtyard with a soaring 1920s-style iron and glass sun canopy where breakfast is served, and an elegant Acropolis-view rooftop café-restaurant. Rooms are a bit small, but on the whole the hotel is exceptionally good value for money. *Bars (2). Disabled-adapted rooms. Internet (high-speed in rooms, free; shared terminal, €6/30mins). No-smoking rooms. Parking (free). Restaurant. Room service (7am-midnight). TV (pay movies).*

Hermes Hotel

Apollonos 19, Syntagma, 10557 (210 323 5514/ 210 322 2412/www.hermes-athens.com). Metro Syntagma. **Rates** €120 single; €145 double; €165 triple. **Credit** AmEx, MC, V. **Map** p249/p251 F5 ❿
In an area that desperately needs more quality affordable hotels, this well-managed, comfortable property is most welcome. The location, on a fairly quiet but not unattractive street, is ultra-convenient – just two blocks from Syntagma Square and next to Plaka. The common spaces are not that welcoming; the only one worth mentioning is the simple rooftop terrace, which has excellent Acropolis views. Rooms are simple but efficient, if slightly cramped. *Bar. Internet (high-speed, €4/hr). TV.*

Magna Grecia

Mitropoleos 54, Plaka, 10563 (210 324 0314/ www.magnagreciahotel.com). Metro Monastiraki or Syntagma. **Rates** (with breakfast) €115 single; €130-€160 double; €160 triple. **Credit** AmEx, DC, MC, V. **Map** p249/p251 F5 ⓫
Housed in a 19th-century neo-classical building in a great location – right on Mitropoleos Square – this small, 12-room hotel retains its fine period features

Hotels

The best

For high-end design
Fresh Hotel (*p46*); Life Gallery (*p56*); Ochre & Brown (*p50*); Semiramis (*p57*); Twentyone (*p57*).

For mid-range design
Alassia (*p51*); Athens Art Hotel (*p51*); Eridanus (*p52*).

For sea views
Astir Palace Resort (*p55*); Divani Apollon Palace & Spa (*p55*); Poseidon Hotel (*p56*).

For eating
Premiere, **Athenaeum InterContinental** (*p52*); Milos, **Athens Hilton** (*p49*); Parea, **Eridanus** (*p52*); GB Rooftop Restaurant & Bar, **Grande Bretagne** (*p45*); St' Astra, **Park Hotel Athens** (*p49*); Vardis, **Pentelikon** (*p56*).

For concept
Periscope (*p50*); Semiramis (*p57*); Twentyone (*p57*).

For budget value
Athens Backpackers (*p43*); Fivos (*p49*).

For art
Athens Art Hotel (*p51*); Athenaeum InterContinental (*p52*); Baby Grand Hotel (*p46*); Semiramis (*p57*).

For history
Athens Hilton (*p49*); Hotel Grande Bretagne (*p45*); King George Palace (*p46*); Pentelikon (*p56*).

For nightlife on the doorstep
Hotel Arion (*p51*); Jason Inn (*p52*); Xenos Lycabettus (*p50*).

Where to Stay

– sky-high ceilings, French doors, elaborate original mouldings and hardwood floors. The 'boutique hotel' concept is somewhat strained by the odd mix of the neo-classical architectural elements, the boxy minimalism of much of the furniture and the island kitsch of the wall murals, but while it doesn't quite all come together, it's a novel effort. Rooms are individually decorated and vary quite a bit in terms of style, but all front-facing rooms have gorgeous Acropolis views, as does the pleasant rooftop bar. *Bar. Internet (wireless, free). No-smoking rooms. Room service. TV (CD, DVD).*

Plaka
Kapnikareas 7 & Mitropoleos, Plaka, 10556 (210 322 2096/www.plakahotel.gr). Metro Monastiraki or Syntagma. **Rates** €115 single; €145 double; €165 triple. **Credit** AmEx, MC, V. **Map** p249/p251 E5 ⑫
The banal façade hides a modern, decently priced city hotel with contemporary-chic decor in a convinient location near both Plaka and Ermou. Decor is minimal and sleek but by no means cold. Rooms are all comfortably and smartly furnished, quiet and spacious. A peaceful roof garden, which guests have at their disposal all day long, offers great views of the Acropolis – as do some of the rooms. *Bar (summer only). Internet (wireless, shared terminal, €4/hr). No-smoking rooms. Room service (7am-7pm, beverages only). TV.*

Budget

Acropolis House
Kodrou 6 & Voulis, Plaka, 10558 (210 322 2344). Metro Syntagma. **Rates** €87 double; €114 triple. **Credit** MC, V. **Map** p251 F6 ⑬

After more than four decades in business, the Acropolis House is still a place people either seem to love or hate: one traveller's faded elegance is another's old-fashioned shabbiness. The best and worst of the hotel is its long history: it's housed in one of Plaka's oldest buildings – a government-designated protected landmark – and retains all its original hand-painted frescoes, gilt-framed wall hangings, gloriously high ceilings and original fittings in the reception area. But the hotel has not been maintained well – the overall impression is dank, musty and somewhat shabby. Rooms are outmoded but practical, and management can be described in much the same way. *Breakfast room. No-smoking hotel (except lobby). TV.*

Hotel Adonis
Kodrou 3, Plaka, 10558 (210 324 9737). Metro Syntagma. **Rates** €63 single; €89 double; €115 triple. **No credit cards. Map** p251 F6 ⑭
In an excellent location next to the Acropolis House (*see above*), the Adonis has low room rates for a respectable hotel. The no-nonsense, experienced management serves breakfast on the rooftop, where decor is still cheap 1960s bar/taverna, but the few tables on the adjacent balcony have Acropolis views as good as posher places. Rooms are quite sparsely decorated but are functionally and inoffensively furnished with modern pieces. Tiny en suite bathrooms are balanced by large balconies in many rooms. *Bar. TV.*

Athens Backpackers
Makri 12, Makrygianni, 11742 (210 922 4044/www.backpackers.gr). Metro Akropoli. **Rates** €25 bed in 6-bed dorm with en suite bathroom. **Credit** AmEx, DC, MC, V. **Map** p251 F7 ⑮

Athens at its most relaxed

- **Peaceful Location:** at the foot of the Acropolis, in the new Acropolis museum neighbourhood, within an easy access to the main shopping, business areas and metro station.
- **Unique View of the Acropolis**
- **Comfort:** at the elegant and well equipped 90 guest rooms of Herodian Hotel and 50 rooms of Philippos Hotel, some ideally spacious for big families.
- **Taste:** Mediterranean cuisine at the Atrium Coffee Shop viewing the green back garden
- **Roof Garden:** 2 outdoor Jacuzzi's, olive garden, an impressive space, a enticing suggestion for private occassions, celebrations, dinners.
- **Conference and Banquet Facilities**

The friendly Greek-Australian staff do their best to make you feel at home in this earnest hostel: Athens Backpackers is like a fun university dorm right next to the Acropolis. The atmosphere is convivial, with DIY barbecues on site and affordable sightseeing and club/bar outings. An internet corner is available, and a casual, Acropolis-view bar on the roof is a great place to start the evening with sunset cocktails. Overall, a hostel to remember.
Bars (2). Internet (shared terminal, €3/hr). No-smoking hotel (except roof). TV room.

Hotel Dioskouros
Pitakou 6, Plaka, 10558 (210 324 8165/www. consolas.gr). Metro Akropoli. **Rates** €35-€40 single; €45-€60 double; €55-€75 triple; €65-€80 quad; €30 dorm bed. **Credit** AmEx, MC, V. **Map** p251 F6 ⑯
Much like the Student & Traveller's Inn (*see below*), the Dioskouros retains the spirit of a hostel while offering better standards. Guests won't get en suite bathrooms, spacious rooms or fancy furniture, but they will get a small, cosy hostel that's full of international independent travellers, a clean bed, air-conditioning in all rooms, friendly staff, a dorm-bed option, cooking facilities (October-May), a peaceful and partially covered garden set among lemon trees to socialise in, and a quiet and convenient location on the edge of Plaka.
Breakfast room. No-smoking rooms. TV room.

Student & Traveller's Inn
Kydathinaion 16, Plaka, 10558 (210 324 4808/ www.studenttravellersinn.com). Metro Syntagma. **Rates** €50 single (shared bath); €60 single; €55 double (shared bath); €70 double; €70 triple (shared bath); €85 triple; €17 dorm bed. **No credit cards.** **Map** p251 F6 ⑰

This long-time, low-cost traveller's favourite of a hostel enjoys a superb location on a pleasant pedestrianised street on the outskirts of the more tasteful part of Plaka, within walking distance of Syntagma Square. The inn has the clientele and casual, international camaraderie of a hostel, with four- and eight-bed dorm rooms with shared facilities. But it also has the convenient option of single, double and triple rooms. Rooms are basic but cheery enough, and en suite bathrooms have all been renovated. Internet access and a green courtyard for socialising are more advantages.
Bar. Internet (wireless, shared terminal, free). No-smoking rooms. TV room.

Historic Centre

Deluxe

Grande Bretagne
Syntagma Square, 10563 (210 333 0000/www. grandebretagne.gr). Metro Syntagma. **Rates** €280 single; €280-€320 double; €420 junior suite; €590-€14,000 suite. *Breakfast* €32. **Credit** AmEx, DC, MC, V. **Map** p249/p251 F5 ㊸
A manager at a competing five-star hotel has admitted that there's no question about it: the Grande Bretagne stands head and shoulders above every luxury establishment in town. Already a landmark steeped in history, the GB recently underwent a two-year, head-to-toe renovation that spared no expense in recapturing its turn-of-the-19th-century opulence. Antique furnishings, hand-carved architectural details, tapestried headboards, gold Bavarian cutlery and the like have all been painstakingly

More than just a hotel: the illustrious **Grande Bretagne** is a city landmark.

restored to their original glory. Extra touches like the 24-hour personal butler service add the final decadent finesse. Standard rooms, however, are not that spacious. If all this seems rather out of your price range, stop by for tea (served in hand-painted, gold-trimmed teacups) just to drink in the history. Another experience to remember – although not a cheap one – is dinner at the historic GB Corner bistro or the new GB Roof Garden restaurant and bar (see *p116*), with a panoramic view of the city.
Bars (2). Business centre. Concierge. Disabled-adapted rooms. Gym. Internet (wireless, high-speed, €10/24hr). No-smoking rooms. Parking (valet service). Pools (1 indoor, 1 outdoor). Restaurants (3). Room service. Spa. TV (pay movies).

King George Palace
Vas Georgiou A2, Syntagma Square, 10564 (210 322 2210/210 728 0350/www.classical hotels.com). Metro Syntagma. **Rates** €220-€260 double; €310-€360 junior suite; €400-€450 suite. *Breakfast* €25-€32. **Credit** AmEx, DC, MC, V. **Map** p249/p251 F5 ⑲
One of Athens' most historic hotels, the King George was closed for 14 years, under renovation for three, and finally reopened to reclaim its status at the luxury end of the market just before the Olympics. With 102 rooms, it is a personalised, upmarket residence with boutique hotel qualities. A marble 'carpet' is the backdrop to the glamorous cream and gold-toned lobby, where stately windows overlook Syntagma Square. Below, they've packed a surprising amount in to the gym, pool and mini spa. Rooms are individually designed, with hand-painted details, a mix of antiques and classy reproductions (but with incongruous contemporary elements thrown in), custom-made silk and satin upholstery, and soundproofing. The elegant seventh-floor restaurant terrace has wonderful views of the Acropolis.
Bar. Concierge. Disabled-adapted rooms. Gym. Internet (high-speed in rooms, wireless in common areas, shared terminal, free). No-smoking floors. Pool (indoor). Restaurants (2). Room service. Spa. TV (DVD, games, pay movies).

Expensive

Fresh Hotel
Sofokleous 26 & Klisthenous 2, 10552 (210 524 8511/www.thefreshhotel.gr). Metro Omonia. **Rates** €130 single; €155-€235 executive double; €385 suite. **Credit** AmEx, DC, MC, V. **Map** p249 E3/E4 ⑳
Like the Semiramis (*see p57*), the Fresh Hotel is not necessarily the kind of place you'd like to live in all the time, but a 'design experience' to savour for a stay of a few days. Electric hues are the design punctuation here, in the context of a straight-lined, minimalism that incorporates wood and 'natural' features like rock gardens. Rooms are small, but the space is used efficiently: armchairs open into extra single beds and electric blinds can be controlled from the bed. The poolside deck and lounge bar is the height of style.

Bars (2). Business centre. Concierge. Gym. Internet (wireless, free). No-smoking floors. Parking (€15 day). Pool (outdoor). Restaurants (2). Room service. Spa. TV (pay movies).

Moderate

Baby Grand Hotel
Athinas 65 & Lycourgou, 10551 (210 325 0900/ www.classicalhotels.com). Metro Omonia. **Rates** €120 double; €165 suite. *Breakfast* €10. **Credit** AmEx, DC, MC, V. **Map** p249 E3 ㉑
The old Athens Grand underwent a makeover in 2006 as a 'graffiti hotel' and, depending on where you look, the effects are impressive. Acid green mirrors and a stainless steel corridor lead past the frothy white Meat Me restaurant (with a small gym and pool visible through a glass floor) to the upstairs reception – where the desks are carved out of Mini Coopers – and spacious lobby bar. But stay in a room with just a few cartoonish characters on the wall and you'll feel like you're in a prefectly fine but not out of the ordinary place, with clean lines and comfortable, contemporary beds and furnishings. For the full effect, ask for a room where they've gone all out, and be surrounded by a Klimt-like forest or immersed in a village full of Smurfs. *Photo p49.*
Bar. Disabled-adapted rooms. No-smoking rooms. Internet (wireless, free). Restaurant. Room service. Spa. TV (pay movies).

Cecil Hotel
Athinas 39, Monastiraki, 10554 (210 321 7079/ www.cecil.gr). Metro Monastiraki. **Rates** €70 single; €100 double; €140 triple; €160 suite. **Credit** AmEx, MC, V. **Map** p249 E4 ㉒
This small friendly hotel, on one of the busiest streets in the city centre, is favoured by young travellers who want to explore the nearby nightlife of Psyrri. The building has a distinctive character, although the ordinary and rather cheap furnishing does not live up to it. However, when it comes to the things budget travellers really crave – clean, crisp, pleasant rooms and common areas; a convenient location for sightseeing; crucial amenities like air-conditioning, en-suite bathrooms, televisions, telephones; and a resident cat that gives the place a little personality – the Cecil really delivers.
Breakfast room. TV.

Grand O' Hotel
Pireos 2, Omonia Square, 10552 (210 523 5230/ www.classicalhotels.gr). Metro Omonia. **Rates** (with breakfast) €115 single; €125 double; €185 junior suite. **Credit** AmEx, DC, MC, V. **Map** p249 E3 ㉓
Overlooking Omonia Square, the Grand O' is well managed by one of the biggest Greek hotel chains. It's favoured by businessmen and youngish, mon-eyed travellers who are looking for something stylish, ultra-contemporary and luxurious. The hotel manages to carry off a modern, artful quirkiness alongside classic refinement. Front rooms, especially the corner ones, feature large windows with

A room with that view

In Athens, 'a room with a view' is invariably followed by 'of the Acropolis'. When the **Athens Hilton** (*see p49*) was built back in the 1960s many criticised its height because it had the cheek to compete with the Acropolis. Thankfully, more than four decades and dozens of roof-gardens later, the Acropolis still manages to surprise us by popping up in the least expected places. That means you don't necessarily have to stay in Plaka to enjoy a full-screen Parthenon view from your room.

If you do decide to stay in Plaka, check out the superior rooms in the **Electra Palace** (*see p41*): no.325 has one of the most stunning Parthenon views in the city. A cheaper option is the cosy **Adrian Hotel** (*see p41*) – three of its rooms (nos.304-306) have balconies from which you can almost touch the Acropolis. If money is not an issue, head to Syntagma Square, where the suites of the **King George Palace** (*see p46; pictured*) offer a wonderful

view of the Acropolis, as do most of the rooms of the **Hotel Grande Bretagne** (*see p45*) above the second floor. For a southern aspect, the front rooms of the **Divani Palace Acropolis** (*see p41*), between the fourth and seventh floors, bring the famous landmark to your bedside. If you're looking for space to linger over your view, opt for the junior suites at the **Hera Hotel** (*see p42*), complete with balconies; its upper-floor standard rooms are also good vantage points.

Further from Plaka, the Parthenon still pokes above the cityscape. At the **Eridanus** (*see p52*), opt for the smaller rooms on the third and fourth floors with large balconies that look straight to the Acropolis. In Kolonaki, stay on one of the upper floors of the **St George Lycabettus** (*see p50*), or at the **Athens Hilton**. With the National Gallery in the foregound, you'll enjoy a panoramic view of nearly all of Athens, including – guess what...?

Where to Stay

views over the busy square; those on the upper floors take in Lycabettus Hill as well.
Bar. Business centre. Concierge. Internet (wireless in common areas, high-speed in rooms, free). No-smoking rooms. Restaurant. Room service (6am-11pm). TV (pay movies).

Budget

Hotel Carolina
Kolokotroni 55, Monastiraki, 10560 (210 324 3551/ www.hotelcarolina.gr). Metro Monastiraki. **Rates** €45-€80 single; €54-€98 double; €60-€120 triple; €72-€150 quad. **Credit** MC, V. **Map** p249 E4 ❷

Located in one of the busiest streets of the historic centre of Athens, the Carolina is a good budget choice if you want to get a feel for the vibe of the city. The area is full of new trendy bars and Psyrri's nightlife is within walking distance. The pre-war building lends the premises a bit of the character and history lacking in so many Athens hotels. Brightly coloured matching sets of Greek island-style marine blue furniture not only make the smallish spaces more efficient but add a touch of warmth to the rather sterile feel of the hotel's spick-and-span, tile-floored rooms.
Bar. Internet (wireless, shared terminal, €3/hr). No-smoking rooms. TV.

THE SHORTLIST

WHAT'S NEW | WHAT'S ON | WHAT'S BEST

Fivos

Athinas 23, Monastiraki, 10554 (210 322 6657/
www.consolas.gr). Metro Monastiraki. **Rates** €40-
€45 single; €50-€65 double; €60-€80 triple; €70-€100
quad; €30 dorm bed. **Credit** AmEx, DC, MC, V.
Map p249 E4 ㉕
Under the same management as the Dioskouros
(*see p45*), the Fivos shares its strengths: dirt-cheap,
clean rooms with few amenities (though there's
wireless internet on some floors here) and few pre-
tensions. The location could hardly be more practical for visitors, within spitting distance of the
Monastiraki metro station and very close to all the
major central sites. The street on which the Fivos
stands, although it remains rather gritty and noisy,
has improved considerably since a recent facelift
that increased the pavement area and decreased the
amount of car traffic.
Breakfast room. Internet (shared terminal, wireless
on 1st & 2nd floors, €3/30mins). No-smoking hotel.
TV room.

Kolonaki & around

Deluxe

Athens Hilton

Leof Vas Sofias 46, Ilissia, 11528 (210 728 1000/
www.athens.hilton.com). Metro Evangelismos.
Rates €159-€349 single/double (€25 for 3rd person);
€870 junior suite. *Breakfast* €32.50. **Credit** AmEx,
DC, MC, V. **Map** p252 J5 ㉖

In Athens, the Hilton isn't just another standard
multinational hotel – it's an institution. Its building
design was a minor architectural milestone; scores
of famous visitors have spent the night here; it was
for years the only hotel offering five-star accommodation and service in the city; and the quality of its
pricey eateries and lounges is the subject of hot
debate. The Hilton is a city landmark – Athenians
call the whole surrounding district 'Heeltone'. The
results of the hotel's thorough renovation a couple
of years ago include a second swimming pool and
spa. Rooms, although not quite living up to the
hotel's history, are lavish, with prices to match. The
restaurants, cafés and roof-top Galaxy bar (*see p191*)
have once again become institutions. *Photo p51.*
Bars (2). Business centre. Concierge. Disabled-
adapted rooms. Gym. Internet (wireless, €9/hr,
€12/2hrs). No-smoking floors. Parking (€27/day).
Pools (1 indoor for children, 1 outdoor). Restaurants
(3). Room service. Spa. TV (DVD, pay movies).

Expensive

Park Hotel Athens

Leof Alexandras 10, Pedion Areos, 10682 (210
889 4500/www.athensparkhotel.gr). Metro Victoria.
Rates €145 single; €160 double; €200 suite.
Credit AmEx, DC, MC, V. **Map** p249 F1 ㉗
Situated on one of the city's central avenues, the
Athens Park Hotel is a well-organised and con-
stantly renovated city hotel just a three-minute walk
from the Archaeological Museum. In contrast to the

The **Baby Grand Hotel** is one of a kind. *See p46.*

somewhat dated aesthetic of the lobby and indoor restaurant areas, the attractive, spacious rooms (with a view of the Pedion Areos park across the street) are elegantly furnished and decorated in shades of royal blue. A rooftop swimming pool is good for cooling off on hot summer days, as is a drink from the Astra Café. Also on the rooftop, at the St' Astra lounge-bar and gourmet restaurant (see p119), you can dine with a panoramic view of Lycabettus Hill and the Acropolis.

Bars (2). Business centre. Disabled-adapted rooms. Gym. Internet (wireless in common areas, high-speed in rooms, €6/hr). No-smoking rooms. Parking (free). Pool (outdoor). Restaurants (2). Room service. TV (pay movies).

Periscope

Haritos 22, Kolonaki, 10675 (210 623 6320/www. periscope.gr). Metro Evangelismos. **Rates** €155-€195 double; €270 junior suite; €450 suite. **Credit** AmEx, DC, MC, V. **Map** p252 H4 ㉘

The Periscope is a concept hotel where the theme is surveillance: staying here is a little like living in an art installation. Bedroom ceilings are entirely covered with photographs of urban Athens landscapes shot from a helicopter, while the lobby bar broadcasts live images on huge flat-screen monitors from the hotel's rooftop periscope, which is controlled by loungers in the lobby bar. Rooms are all grey, and feature large beds with fine, fluffy linens. Bathrooms have industrial styling and are very sparse. Design-conscious travellers will love it, although the rest might find this total-grey look a bit unpleasant. The neighbourhood, a quiet street in Kolonaki, is arty with lots of high-end boutiques for browsing.

Bar. No-smoking rooms. Internet (wireless, free). Restaurant. Room service (7am-1am). TV (CD, DVD, free library).

St George Lycabettus

Kleomenous 2, Kolonaki, 10675 (210 729 0711/ www.sglycabettus.gr). Metro Evangelismos. **Rates** €155-€235 single; €165-€290 double; €300-€360 suite. **Credit** AmEx, DC, MC, V. **Map** p252 H4 ㉙

Nestled at the foot of pine-clad Lycabettus Hill, this intimate luxury hotel is just steps away from Athens' top designer shops and its museum row. Keep in mind, though, that the price of verdant surroundings in the centre is a steep hike or taxi ride up the hill. Your exertions will be rewarded by designer bedrooms in styles ranging from jewel-toned art nouveau to sleek black and white minimalism, and spectacular Acropolis panoramas from the rooftop pool bar, the Grand Balcon restaurant (see p119) and the hip new rock-baroque Sky Bar. Downstairs, the 1970s-themed lounge Frame (see p191), with gourmet food and excellent cocktails, is one of the trendiest spots in town.

Bars (3). Business centre. Concierge. Disabled-adapted rooms. Gym. Internet (wireless, €16/24hr; shared terminal, €5/30mins). No-smoking section. Parking (€20/day). Pool (outdoor). Restaurants (2). Room service (6.30am-midnight). Spa. TV (pay movies).

Moderate

Xenos Lycabetus Hotel

Valaoritou 6, Kolonaki, 10671 (210 360 0600/ www.xenoslycabettus.gr). Metro Syntagma. **Rates** (with breakfast) €90-€120 single; €110-€140 double; €120-€150 triple; €130-€170 suite. **Credit** AmEx, DC, MC, V. **Map** p249/p252 G4 ㉚

With just 25 rooms, this sleek, stylish boutique-style hotel puts the accent on personal service. The location – on a pedestrianised street filled with cafés and upmarket restaurants in a chic, central part of Kolonaki – is perfect for the fashion-conscious, and the hotel has its own popular café and restaurant. Rooms are not that big, but the pleasant contemporary furniture makes them feel uncluttered and there are large, marble-swathed bathrooms.

Bar. Internet (high-speed, free). Restaurant. Room service (7am-9.30pm). TV.

Budget

Hotel Orion & Dyrades

Emmanouil Benaki 105 & Dryadon 4, Exarchia, 11473 (210 382 7362/orion-dryades@mail.com). Metro Omonia then 15min walk. **Rates** €25 single (shared bath); €40 single; €35 double (shared bath); €55 double; €70 triple. **Credit** AmEx, MC, V. **Map** off p249 G2 ㉛

These quiet hotels are in a cul-de-sac on Strefi Hill in the arty Exarchia district. Both have renovated kitchens available for guest use, which makes them good options for travellers on tight budgets, though local tavernas also provide cheap dining options. Rooms in the Orion have shared bathrooms, while all rooms in the Dryades have en suite facilities. Both hotels are renovated, and the Orion in particular has been considerably upgraded with a more attractive lobby and rooftop. The very low room prices and the cool location draw a crowd that's young, international – and often attractive (foreign models on long stays seem to end up here).

Internet (wireless, free). No-smoking rooms. TV.

North of the Acropolis

Expensive

Ochre & Brown

Leokoriou 7, Psyrri, 10554 (210 331 2950/www. ochreandbrown.com). Metro Thissio. **Rates** €170-€190 double; €280 suite. **Credit** AmEx, DC, MC, V. **Map** p249 D4 ㉜

This new addition ticks all the boutique hotel boxes and, with just 11 gently minimalist rooms, service is personal. The simple façade doesn't blatantly announce itself among the scruffy frontages of a quiet street between Thissio and Psyrri. The interior is equally muted, in hues that reflect the name – yellow ochre walls and chocolate brown accents, punctuated by the odd splash of colour such as robin's-egg

blue chairs in the restaurant-bar or bright pink pillows and blinds in the chic contemporary rooms. Perks include flat-screen TVs, bathrobes, a turndown service and designer fixtures such as watering-can showerheads in the compact bathrooms.
Bar. Internet (wireless, free). No-smoking rooms. Parking (free). Restaurant. Room service. TV (DVD, pay movies).

Residence Georgio
Patision & Halkokondyli 14, Omonia 10677 (210 332 0100/www.residencegeorgio.com). Metro Omonia. **Rates** €150 double; €230-€245 suite. **Credit** AmEx, DC, MC, V. **Map** p249 F2 ㉝
An excellent five-star hotel attracting a monied Greek and Cypriot clientele. The hotel is big on both service and facilities, with a health club/spa and rooftop pool; the lobby has several living room-like 'pockets' to facilitate private conversation. Double rooms have enough space to spread out in and feature high-quality linens and pillows, attractive pearwood decor and jacuzzis in all bathrooms.
Bars (2). Business centre. Disabled-adapted rooms. Gym. Internet (wireless in common areas, high-speed in rooms, €8/hr). No-smoking floors. Pool (outdoor). Restaurants (2). Room service. TV (DVD, pay movies).

Moderate

Alassia
Socratous 50, Omonia, 10431 (210 527 4000/www. thealassia.com.gr). Metro Omonia. **Rates** €90 single; €120 double; €140 triple. **Credit** AmEx, DC, MC, V. **Map** p249 E3 ㉞

The orange-lit glass catwalk entry announces the Alassia's design intentions: in the lobby, the waist-high aluminium urns and tall, Cubist-style armchairs contrast with the underdeveloped environs around the corner from Omonia Square. The rooms are less impressive, but still provide a modern, minimalist environment for those allergic to the mass aesthetic of the big chain hotels.
Bar. Breakfast room. Internet (high-speed, €10/24hr). No-smoking rooms. Room service. TV.

Hotel Arion
Agiou Dimitriou 18, Psyrri, 10554 (210 324 0415/ www.arionhotel.gr). Metro Monastiraki. **Rates** €115 single; €145 double; €165 triple. **Credit** AmEx, DC, MC, V. **Map** p249 E4 ㉟
The Arion's draw is its position in the heart of Psyrri, one of Athens' more authentic – and tourist-friendly – nightlife areas. The sleek minimalist façade and lobby show signs of the hotel's effort towards creating a design profile, though the breakfast room is a little too stark. The comfortable bedrooms have small sitting areas and attractive, glass-encased bathrooms. A pleasant rooftop lounge has views of the Acropolis, as do many of the rooms.
Breakfast room. Internet (wireless, €5/hr). No-smoking rooms. Room service (breakfast, bottled drinks). TV.

Athens Art Hotel
Marni 27, Omonia, 10432 (210 524 0501/www. arthotelathens.gr). Metro Omonia. **Rates** (with breakfast) €79-€105 single; €89-€129 double; €105-€145 triple; €105-€160 suite. **Credit** AmEx, MC, V. **Map** p249 E2 ㊱

Athens Hilton. *See p49.*

The family-run Athens Art Hotel only re-opened in 2004 (its 1930s neo-classical façade retains the original marble details), but it has built up a reputation for good value. The rooms are each individually designed, but all feature pinewood floors, giant headboards, laptop-size safes, double-glazed windows, original paintings by Greek artists (or antique mirrors), and inspired lighting and fixtures. Personal service here isn't just an empty promise – every guest gets individual recommendations on sightseeing, dining, culture and nightlife from the staff, who keep up with Athens' cultural and entertainment scene. There are plans for a rooftop terrace bar. *Photo p54.*
Bar. Business centre. Internet (wireless in common areas, high-speed in rooms, free). No-smoking hotel (except lobby). Restaurant. Room service. TV.

Athens Imperial
Platia Karaiskaki, Metaxourgio, 10437 (210 520 1600/www.classicalhotels.com). Metro Metaxourgio. **Rates** €120-€140 single; €120-€180 double (€30 for 3rd person); €200-€240 junior suite. *Breakfast* €15. **Credit** AmEx, DC, MC, V. **Map** p249 D3 ③⑦
Since it opened a few years ago, the Athens Imperial has proved one of the most popular downtown hotels with visitors and Athenians too, as it regularly hosts exhibitions, congresses and social events. Its somewhat ugly location – in the up-and-coming but still dodgy area of Metaxourgio – is nevertheless convenient for sightseeing and clubbing, and the metro is on its doorstep. The rooms are big and attractive, the atrium-like restaurant is pleasant and the roof garden (with a pool) offers wonderful views.
Bars (2). Business centre. Concierge. Disabled-adapted rooms. Gym. Internet (wireless, free). Parking (€8/day). No-smoking rooms. Pool (outdoor). Restaurant. Room service. Spa. TV (pay movies).

Eridanus
Pireos 78, Keramikos, 10435 (210 520 5360/www.eridanus.gr). Metro Keramikos or Thissio. **Rates** €100-€160 double; €180 junior suite. **Credit** AmEx, DC, MC, V. **Map** p248 C4 ③⑧
The good-value Eridanus bills itself as a 'luxury art hotel', but it comes across as more of a sleek contemporary design hotel. Though on an unattractive, busy thoroughfare, it's in a regenerating area that's within easy walking distance of nightlife in Gazi, Psyrri and Thissio. The well-appointed rooms come with designer furnishings, gorgeous deep-green Indian marble bathrooms and original paintings, plus huge beds and high-tech facilities. Some have Acropolis/Philoppapus views. The service is personal, the management excellent. The hotel adjoins Varoulko (*see p124*), one of Athens' most celebrated gourmet restaurants; its owner-chef has recently opened a new restaurant, Parea, inside the hotel.
Bars (2). Gym. Internet (high-speed, €3/hr; web TV, €9.50/24hr). No-smoking rooms. Parking (free). Restaurants (2). Room service. TV (pay movies).

Budget

Jason Inn
Agion Asomaton 12, Psyrri, 10553 (210 520 2491/www.douros-hotels.com). Metro Thissio. **Rates** €85 single; €95 double; €120 triple. **Credit** MC, V. **Map** p248 D4 ③⑨
The hotel's structure may be unimpressive and the street it stands on nondescript, but the Jason Inn borders happening Thissio and Psyrri, with good access to the districts' excellent restaurants and bars. It's also handy for the ancient sites and the old central market. With standard-issue but pleasant rooms, an inviting rooftop garden restaurant and staff who thoroughly understand the needs of mid-range budget travellers, the Jason Inn is good value for money.
Bars (2). Internet (shared terminal, €5/hr). No-smoking rooms. Restaurants (2). Room service (7am-1am). TV.

King Jason Hotel
Kolonou 26, Metaxourgio, 10437 (210 523 4721/www.douros-hotels.com). Metro Metaxourgio. **Rates** (with breakfast) €70 single; €85 double; €105 triple; €128 quad. **Credit** MC, V. **Map** p249 D3 ④⓪
The King Jason has earned a good reputation thanks to the comfortable and well-equipped rooms and the efficient management (it's one of a small but reliable Greek chain). The lounge, breakfast area and bar are all sleek and cool. Staff are friendly and seem to have a sincere interest in helping guests. The hotel's only shortcoming is its decidedly unglamorous neighbourhood, which is often called 'up and coming' but has still a long way to go.
Bar. Internet (wireless, €5/hr). No-smoking rooms. Restaurant. Room service. TV.

Hotel Omega
Aristogeitonos 15, Psyrri, 11743 (210 321 2421/www.omega-hotel.com). Metro Monastiraki or Omonia. **Rates** (with breakfast) €55 single; €70 double; €80 triple. **Credit** AmEx, MC, V. **Map** p249 E4 ④①
A budget hotel right on Athens' central open-air fruit and vegetable market, which makes for a colourful, – but busy and noisy – location. The hotel rooms feel like large 1970s-era dormitories (they operate partly as dormitories for exchange students), with apathetic service to match. Most of the rooms have Acropolis views, as does the roof patio.
Breakfast room. No-smoking rooms. TV.

South Athens

Deluxe

Athenaeum InterContinental
Syngrou 89-93, Neos Kosmos, 11745 (210 920 6000/www.intercontinental.com). Metro Syngrou-Fix then 15min walk/tram Kasomouli/shuttle bus to city centre. **Rates** €260 single; €380 double; €800 junior suite. **Credit** AmEx, DC, MC, V. **Map** p250 D9 ④②

Design central

To read the hype about accommodation in Athens, you'd think that every second property is a design hotel. But the reality, in many cases, is rather more mundane. Often the 'design' ends at the reception area, as in the **Alassia** (*see p51*), or extends only partially through the hotel: the **Art Hotel Athens** (*see p51*) has original paintings by Greek artists in the common areas but in only some of the rooms; after its knock-out reception – with Mini Coopers as desks – some of the **Baby Grand Hotel**'s (*see p46*) rooms feel pretty standard for a 'graffiti hotel', unless you stay in a room with floor-to-ceiling murals.

In central Athens, only one hotel really lives up to the three buzzwords of design, style and concept. **Fresh Hotel**'s (*see p46*) design ethos permeates every aspect of the place, from the splashes of colour punctuating the façade, to the ground-floor bar-restaurant in a '70s shade of orange and the whimsical furnishings of the lobby, to the bedrooms themselves. If it's a minimalist fantasy you're looking for, the sleek white rooms certainly fit the bill, but the look is tempered by the holistic design approach, with clever touches such as coloured glass dividers between bedroom and bathroom that double as mood lighting.

More intimate and subtle, **Ochre and Brown** (*see p50; pictured*) is a recent and worthy competitor. Its 11 rooms place it firmly in the boutique hotel category, as does its personalised service and funky location on the fringe of the nightlife activity in Psyrri. Its name reveals the overarching colour scheme, a palette where yellow ochre and dark brown provide a warm touch to the sleek contemporary design, offset by splashes of vibrant fabrics. And like any good boutique hotel, it feels like your own personal pied à terre, and a central one at that.

For some of Athens' most interesting hotels, you'll need to head away from the centre. **Periscope**'s (*see p50*) witty theme of surveillance works well, especially in see-and-be-seen Kolonaki. Two of the capital's most exciting designs are in the northern suburbs, the traditional cool summer escape of wealthy Athenians. **Life Gallery** (*see p56*) impresses with its all-glass façade and the harmonious Japanese-style design in the rooms, but the talk of the town is still the day-glo slice of Miami style that is the **Semiramis** (*see p57*). Fans of the **W** hotels may want to check out that chain's first Greek property when it opens at the coastal **Astir Palace Vouliagmeni** (*see p55*) in 2008.

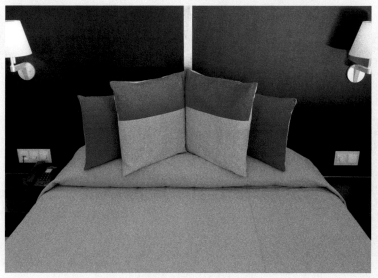

Athens' largest hotel (over 600 rooms and suites), specialises in efficient luxury. Its spacious rooms are furnished in cool white marble and blue and green fabrics, with extra touches like sunny sitting areas, double-headed showers and two or more phones per room. Executive suite floors have private check-in, and an Acropolis-view lounge with an all-day buffet. Café Zoe, the hotel's all-day restaurant, and gourmet Premiere with stunning views, are added attractions.

Bars (2). Business centre. Concierge. Disabled-adapted rooms. Gym. Internet (wireless, €20/24hr). No-smoking rooms. Parking (€16/day). Pool (outdoor). Restaurants (3). Room service. Spa. TV (pay movies).

North Athens

Moderate

Oscar Hotel
Philadelphias 25 & Samou, 10439 (210 883 4215/ www.oscar.gr). Metro Larissa Station. **Rates** €90 single; €105 double; €120 triple. **Credit** AmEx, DC, MC, V. **Map** p249 D1 ㊶

Don't be put off by the ugly monolith exterior and unexciting neighbourhood of the Oscar; it's across the street from a major Athens transport hub, with a metro station, train station and suburban railway to whisk guests to the foot of the Acropolis in ten minutes, to the airport in 30 minutes, or outside Athens altogether. 'A luxury you can afford' is how the Oscar describes itself, and while we can't quite muster the

enthusiasm to call the Oscar luxurious, its airy, cool, marble-and-brass lobby with stained-glass ceilings, and beautiful pool and rooftop bar with good city views are indeed impressive for a hotel in this price range. The somewhat uninspired rooms and neighbourhood are considerably less awesome.

Bars (2). Business centre. Concierge. Internet (wireless, high-speed, shared terminal, €5/hr). Parking (€7/day). Pool (outdoor). Restaurant. Room service (8am-1am). TV.

Budget

Hostel Aphrodite
Evnardou 12 & Michail Voda 65, 10440 (210 881 0589/www.hostelaphrodite.com). Metro Victoria or Larissa Station. **Rates** €14 dorm bed; €16 quad bed; €44 double. *Breakfast* €3.50-€5. **No credit cards.** **Map** off p249 E1 ㊹

Hostel Aphrodite, near Vathis Square, offers the young, convivial atmosphere you might expect from a hostel – without maddening detractions like lock-outs, overstuffed rooms and bare-minimum service. Beds are about as cheap as they come, extra services like travel and laundry are readily available, as are doubles and quads (some with private bath), and the multinational young staff create a kind of world-party atmosphere. The location is close to rail and metro stations, but the gritty neighbourhood should be seriously taken into consideration.

Bar. Internet (wireless, shared terminal, free). No-smoking hotel (except in common areas).

Inspired fixtures and fittings are a hallmark of the **Athens Art Hotel**. *See p51.*

Southern suburbs

Deluxe

Astir Palace Vouliagmeni

Apollonos 40, Vouliagmeni, 16671 (210 890 2000/ www.astir-palace.com). Bus A2, B2, E22 to Glyfada then bus 114/shuttle bus to city centre & airport. **Rates** *Arion Resort & Spa* €340-€370 single; €400-€430 double; €980 suite. *Westin Athens* €340-€430 single; €370-€460 double. **Credit** AmEx, DC, MC, V.

Recently acquired by Starwood, the somewhat aged prime resort of Athens is having a radical makeover, which had not been completed at the time of writing (meaning that marks of its age are still visible in some parts). However, the first impression of the new look is more than promising. The complex – actually made up of three hotels reachable only via a security-guarded access road – sprawls over a private, pine-clad peninsula 25km (16 miles) from Athens that offers magnificent sea views, private beaches and dozens of activities ranging from windsurfing, tennis and jet-skiing to private Pilates lessons. The first two properties – the Arion Resort & Spa and the Westin Athens – are now open, while the W Athens is due in 2008.

The Arion is the resort's flagship. Its luxury rooms and suites have en-suite closets and probably the best sea-view bathrooms in Athens. Its recently opened spa, while not huge, offers a range of therapies. At the Westin, the emphasis is on a more minimal look to attract a youngish clientele still looking for luxury and comfort. Its lobby features 'Unwind' events to introduce guests to different aspects of Greek culture: from wine-tasting to traditional Greek musical instruments seminars. The opening here of Galazia Hytra in summer, with consultant chef Maurizio Santin (of the famous modern Greek restaurant in Psyrri; *see p125*), is big news for gourmets.

Bars (4). Business centre. Concierge. Disabled-adapted rooms. Gym. Internet (wireless in common areas, high-speed in rooms, €10/24hr). No-smoking rooms. Parking (free). Pools (2 outdoor, 1 indoor). Restaurants (6). Room service. Spa. TV (pay movies).

Divani Apollon Palace & Spa

Agiou Nikolaou 10 & Iliou, Vouliagmeni, 16671 (210 891 1100/www.divanis.gr). Bus A2 from Panepistimiou to Glyfada, then bus 116, 117/ shuttle bus to Glyfada & city centre. **Rates** (with breakfast) €220-€290 double. *Divani Apollon Suites* €220 double; €250-€350 suite. **Credit** AmEx, DC, MC, V.

Part of a good local hotel chain, the Divani Apollon Palace & Spa offers the business or leisure traveller a true Athens beachside haven. The service is exceptionally good, as are the hotel amenities: a gorgeous location on Kavouri beach, verdant gardens, two large outdoor swimming pools with towering palm trees, a jacuzzi, a children's playground and tennis courts. The spacious rooms all have balconies with sea views. A romantic dinner can be had in the hotel's restaurant, Mythos tis Thalassas, with seafront tables and great seafood. Another major plus point is the extensive spa. A new 'sister' hotel, the Divani Apollon Suites, has just opened nearby.

Bars (3). Business centre. Concierge. Gym. Internet (wireless, €10/hr, €25/24hr). No-smoking rooms. Parking (€10/day). Pools (2 outdoor, 2 indoor). Restaurants (5). Room service. Spa. TV (DVD, pay movies).

Expensive

Margi

Litous 11, Vouliagmeni, 16671 (210 896 2061/www.themargi.gr). Bus E22 from Sina & Panepistimiou to Glyfada, then bus 114, 116. **Rates** €140-€260 single; €160-€280 double; €350-€600 suite. **Credit** AmEx, DC, MC, V.

The Margi seems inspired by a Moorish castle, with stone walls, distressed leather chairs, antique trunks, randomly placed candles and herbs in silver pots, and gauzy linens draped over outdoor arches. It's all deliciously atmospheric, though rooms still offer plenty of mod cons, including internet facilities and – in upper price brackets – hot tubs. And castle-dwellers never experienced such lavish American buffet breakfasts or elegant lounge bars offering sushi and tapas with their cocktails.

Bars (2). Business centre. Concierge. Gym. Internet (wireless, high-speed, €15/24hr). No-smoking rooms. Parking (free). Pool (outdoor). Restaurants (2). Room service. TV (DVD, pay movies).

Sun and sea at **Astir Palace Vouliagmeni**.

Metropolitan Hotel

Syngrou 385, Faliro, 17564 (210 947 1000/www.
chandris.gr). Bus A2, B2 from Panepistimiou. **Rates**
€155 single/double; €215-€250 suite. **Credit** AmEx,
DC, MC, V.

Situated on the major avenue connecting central
Athens to the beachfront, the 360-room Metropolitan
is ideal for business travellers, with most rooms featuring the necessary facilities. The hotel is also a
good choice for those heading to Piraeus, as it has a
relatively good link via Syngrou, or those with a car,
since the hotel has its own garage. The rooms are
comfortable, with big beds; those on the executive
floors have verandas with panoramic views.
Bars (2). Business centre. Disabled-adapted room.
Gym. Internet (high-speed, €10/hr, €30/24hr).
No-smoking floor. Parking (free). Pool (outdoor).
Restaurants (2). Room service. TV (DVD, games,
pay movies).

Moderate

Emmantina Hotel

Leof Posidonos 33, Glyfada, 11675 (210 898 0683/
www.emmantina.gr). Bus A2, B2 from Panepistimiou/
shuttle bus to airport & city centre. **Rates** €92 single;
€105 double; €125 triple. **Credit** AmEx, DC, MC, V.

A good-value hotel in the seaside suburb of Glyfada,
about 25 minutes from downtown Athens. Although
it mostly caters to business travellers, it can satisfy
those seeking a few days holiday. There is a large
public beach just 50m (150ft) from the hotel; the

main square of Glyfada, southern Athens' shopping
and dining centre, is just five or ten minutes' walk
away, and the hotel is near a popular golf course and
the south coast's summer nightlife. The rooms and
common areas have been pleasantly refurbished,
and there's a small pool on the roof.
Bars (2). Business centre. Concierge. Internet (wireless
in common areas, high-speed in rooms, €6/24hr).
No-smoking rooms. Parking (free). Pool (outdoor).
Restaurant. Room service (6.30am-2am). TV.

Poseidon Hotel

Leof Posidonos 72, Paleo Faliro, 17562 (210 987
2000/www.poseidonhotel.com.gr). Tram from
Syntagma, Edem stop. **Rates** (with breakfast) €110
single; €140-€155 double; €163 triple; €250 junior
suite. **Credit** AmEx, DC, MC, V.

With a tramline now connecting Paleo Faliro to central Athens, it can be a convenient place to stay –
relatively close to Piraeus port and marinas but with
easy access to the city. The Poseidon, right on the
coast, has its own private beach (separated by a
busy thoroughfare) and a pleasant café-taverna on
the sand. Alternatively, guests can opt for the nice
rooftop restaurant, which has great views of the
Saronic Gulf. There's a swimming pool if you don't
want to venture into the sea, and good cafés and
nightlife near the hotel during the summer.
Bars (2). Business centre. Concierge. Internet
(wireless in common areas, high-speed in rooms,
€5/hr, €7/24hr). No-smoking rooms. Pool (outdoor).
Restaurants (3). Room service (7am-midnight). TV.

Northern suburbs

Deluxe

Life Gallery

Thisseos 103, Ekali, 14565 (210 626 0400/www.
bluegr.com). **Rates** €260 single; €350 studio; €500
suite. **Credit** AmEx, DC, MC, V.

An exceptional boutique hotel aiming to attract business travellers who don't want their trip to be just
about business. The hotel promises no less than 'a
symphony of balance and a source of purity, reflecting the elements of life' and aims to 'embrace personal
and business life, body and soul satisfaction, providing the ultimate experience to the modern business
traveller'. As for body and soul, it offers a state-of-the-
art spa with a fitness centre, and yoga, meditation and
treatment rooms, in addition to a sauna, Turkish bath
and 'raindrop therapy'. Sleek rooms have a Japanese
style to them and high-tech features; bathrooms are
distinct in their Zen-like design.
Bar. Concierge. Gym. Internet (wireless, free). No-
smoking rooms. Parking (free). Pools (2 outdoor).
Restaurant. Room service. Spa. TV (DVD on request).

Pentelikon

Deligianni 66, Kifissia, 14562 (210 623 0650/
www.hotelpentelikon.gr). Metro Kifissia. **Rates**
€315-€380 single/double; €625-€3,150 suite.
Credit AmEx, DC, MC, V.

Semiramis. *See p57.*

The height of grand old luxury, the Pentelikon, built in 1929 and carefully preserving its belle époque style with constant renovations, seems less like a hotel than a country club or private estate. It is located in a residential neighbourhood in Kifissia just a short walk away from Platia Kefalari's fine restaurants. Vardis (*see p130*), its own gourmet restaurant, is one of the best in Athens. Grand staircases, ballrooms, silk curtains, and carefully kept, expansive gardens all preserve the feel of an age long departed. Many of Greece's famous politicians, artists and celebrities stayed during the hotel's 1930s heyday, and today a new generation of stars is regularly spotted here. The Pentelikon's sumptuous bedrooms are all individually decorated; suites in the two new wings offer extra luxury with a more contemporary-chic feel.
Bars (2). Business centre. Concierge. Internet (high-speed, free). Gym. No-smoking rooms. Parking (free). Pool (outdoor). Restaurants (2). Room service. Spa. TV.

Semiramis

Harilaou Trikoupi 48, Kifissia, 14562 (210 628 4400/www.semiramisathens.com). Metro Kifissia. **Rates** €180-€265 single; €230-€265 double; €260-€300 bungalow. **Credit** AmEx, DC, MC, V.
Athens' most famous design hotel is indeed one of a kind. The strength of the design ethic is readily apparent in every last detail of Karim Rashid's creation. The place feels positively futuristic. The hotel, aimed at art (not to mention hotel) enthusiasts, is positively daring, with a pink, green, orange and yellow colour scheme and a façade made of glossy white ceramic tiles. You can choose from the (not that) standard rooms, studios, garden bungalows and exquisite suites. T-1 internet connections on flat-screen monitors, remote-controlled curtains, cordless phones and digital locks in rooms just add to the futuristic feel of the Semiramis, while eccentric mini bars prove loyal to its unique pop personality. *Photo p56.*
Bar. Business centre. Concierge. Gym. Internet (wireless, web TV, free). No-smoking rooms. Parking (free). Pool (outdoor). Restaurant. Room service. Spa. TV (CD, DVD, free library).

Expensive

Twentyone

Kolokotroni 21 & Mykonou, Kifissia, 14562 (210 623 3521/www.twentyone.gr). Metro Kifissia. **Rates** €160-€190 single/double; €210-€240 suite. **Credit** AmEx, DC, MC, V.
A sleek design hotel in Kifissia's hip Platia Kefalari, which has scandalised the bourgeois local aesthetic with its industrial-chic grey tones and austere modern façade. Rooms are rather small, but feature designer furniture, fine linens and big glass-encased bathrooms. Split-level loft suites feature star-gazing sunroofs with electric blinds. Art installations in rooms and the bar add to the contemporary, design feeling. This is something of a 'scene' hotel, with a huge, fashionable outdoor café-restaurant at the

front, with tables sunk into the ground, and an all-black café-bar inside. Front-facing rooms are ideal for people-watching, while back-facing rooms are more private. Freebies like wireless internet access, quality toiletries and DVD/CD/MP3 players are nice extra touches. Guests can use the pool, gym and spa at the nearby Semiramis (*see above*) for free.
Bar. Business centre. Concierge. Disabled-adapted rooms. Internet (wireless, free). No-smoking rooms. Parking (free). Restaurant. Room service. TV (CD, DVD, free library).

Piraeus

Travellers on their way to or from the islands by ferry who want to stay in Piraeus overnight have limited options. The new **Piraeus Theoxenia Hotel** (Karaoli & Dimitriou 23, 210 411 2550, www.theoxeniapalace.com, €160 double), is the only five-star hotel in in Pireaus. The **Savoy** (Iroon Polytechniou 93, 210 428 4580, www.savoyhotel.gr, €120 double) is a typical, refurbished city-hotel in a '70s building in the port area. Other fairly reliable, smart digs within walking distance of the port include the **Park Hotel** (Kolokotroni 103, 210 452 4611, www.bestwestern.com, €80 double) and, for travellers on tighter budgets, the simple but efficient **Glaros Hotel** (Harilaou Trikoupi 4, 210 451 5421, www.glaros-hotel.gr, €65 double) or the **Anita Argo Hotel** (Notara 23-25, 210 412 1795, www.hotelargoanita.com, €65 double).

If you're seeking a pleasant location, you can taxi in from the **Mistral Hotel** (Alexandrou Papanastasiou 105, 210 411 7094, www.mistral.gr, €140 double), across town in the fashionable residential area of Kastella, with its good views and fish restaurants.

Attica region

Deluxe

Sofitel Athens Airport

Eleftherios Venizelos International Airport, Spata (210 354 4000/www.sofitel.com). Metro/suburban railway to the airport. **Rates** €250-€270 double; €300-€500 suite. **Credit** AmEx, DC, MC, V.
Since its opening alongside Athens' international airport, the Sofitel has been collecting lots of compliments. It's one of the nicer airport hotels in Europe; the main draw is its ideal location within walking distance of the airport itself. There are plenty of conference spaces in addition to its pleasant rooms and good restaurant.
Bars (2). Business centre. Concierge. Gym. Internet (wireless, €18/24hr). No-smoking floors. Parking (free). Pool (indoor). Restaurants (2). Room service. Spa. TV (DVD, pay movies).

Clean water. It's the most basic human necessity. Yet one third of all poverty related deaths are caused by drinking dirty water. Saying *I'm in* means you're part of a growing movement that's fighting the injustice of poverty. Your £8 a month can help bring safe water to some of the world's poorest people. We can do this. We *can* end poverty. Are you in?

shouldn't everyone get clean water? I don't think that's too much to ask for

Let's end poverty together.
Text 'WATER' and your name to 87099 to give £8 a month.

Standard text rates apply. Registered charity No.202918

oxfam.org.uk

I'm in

(x) Oxfam

Sarite Morales, Greenwich

Sightseeing

Introduction	**60**
The Acropolis & Around	**62**
The Historic Centre	**77**
Kolonaki & Around	**86**
North of the Acropolis	**91**
Greater Athens	**96**
Piraeus	**100**
Beaches	**103**

Features

Stepping stones to the past	63
Acropotips	64
Waifs and strays	67
An island in the city	70
Walk 1 Exploring the old Plaka	72
Demo-crazy	80
Walk 2 Gardens and monuments	84
Chic to cheek	89
It's a gas	95
The best Beaches	103

Maps

Piraeus	101
Beaches	105

National Gardens. *See p83.*

Introduction

There's more to Athens than the Acropolis.

Sightseeing in Athens, especially in summer, can be heavenly or hellish – which of the two depends chiefly on timing. Central Athens at noon in the white-hot sun of midsummer should be avoided at all costs. Do most of your active sightseeing in the morning and evening. Some archaeological sites stay open later than official closing times on summer evenings, while a few museums are initiating seasonal late-night hours – up to midnight – one day a week. And there's always a corner café or even the cinema to retreat to for a blast of revivifying air-con.

Spend early mornings wandering around and visiting museums. At noon, escape to the shady tavernas of Plaka for a leisurely outdoor lunch, followed by a visit to one of Athens' few properly air-conditioned museums. The Cycladic and Benaki museums stay well chilled, as does the National Archaeological Museum.

To save on walking, it may be worth buying a ticket for the **400 bus** (visit www.oasa.gr for a route map), a hop-on, hop-off public service that trawls past the major sites in the city centre in 90 minutes. Plan carefully, though, as it only runs hourly out of season (half-hourly 7.30am-9pm June-Sept); the €5 tickets must be purchased on the bus and are valid on most forms of public transport for 24 hours.

THE ACROPOLIS AND AROUND

Conveniently, most of Athens' significant ancient landmarks are close to each other, connected by a pleasant pedestrian promenade dotted with shady cafés. Dominating from on high, the **Acropolis** lies at the centre. The **Odeon of Herodes Atticus** and **Theatre of Dionysus** are on its southern slopes and the vast, verdant **Agora** is to the north-west.

Spread around the eastern edge of the Acropolis is picturesque but touristy **Plaka**. Its pedestrianised winding streets are full of ancient ruins, medieval churches, neo-classical museums and vine-covered tavernas. Behind the Agora lies the modern-day market area of **Monastiraki**, while to the west is revitalised **Thissio**, full of lively coffee shops and bars.

South-west of the Acropolis is the green expanse of **Philopappus Hill**, the highest point in southern Athens and a cool retreat from the bustling centre. Below Philopappus is **Makrygianni**, a quiet, residential district that is home to the massive, multimillion-euro New Acropolis Museum, due to open in 2008.

The **Erechtheum**'s Caryatid porch. See p66.

THE HISTORIC CENTRE

The modern city – the one constructed in the 19th century as capital of a newly independent Greece – evolved to the north and east of the Acropolis. Some of the handsome neo-classical structures of this period remain (most notably the University trio on Panepistimiou and the Royal Palace on Syntagma Square, now the Parliament building), but many were destroyed, making for today's juxtaposition of magnificent colonnaded mansions and grimy modern blocks.

Within the area known as the **Historic Triangle**, bounded by Mitropoleos (Plaka's northern border), Athinas and Akadimias (the two latter joining at the Omonia traffic circle; *see below*) is the commercial heart of the city, containing both the colourfully chaotic Central Market and the Stock Exchange. Situated at the head of the main shopping street, Ermou, **Syntagma Square** is probably the city's busiest *platia*. South and east of here lies the tranquil oasis of the **National Gardens**.

Sightseeing

KOLONAKI AND AROUND
Posh, pricey and some would say pretentious,
Kolonaki is home to countless designer shops
and some of the city's priciest cafés and clubs.
To the north-west is the grungy, characterful,
student quarter of **Exarchia**, while to the
north-east is heavily populated **Ambelokipi**.
All three neighbourhoods creep up the foothills
of **Lycabettus Hill**, home to acres of shrubs
and pines as well as a tiny sugar-cube chapel,
an acclaimed restaurant and an open-air theatre.

NORTH OF THE ACROPOLIS
North of Monastiraki is the formerly run-down
neighbourhood of **Psyrri**. For centuries, this
was a dark, seedy place. But in the late 1990s it
began to sprout edgy art galleries, restaurants,
bars with live music and strictly face-controlled
clubs, and now it's one of the hottest nightlife
zones in town. There's been a recent challenge
from the west though: in **Keramikos** and
Gazi, new galleries, cafés and nightclubs are
springing forth among the 19th-century ruins.
North of Psyrri is **Omonia Square**, a major
roundabout and traffic hub for several of
Athens' main boulevards. In the 19th century
Omonia was a genteel *platia*; today, it's still
a central point through which most visitors
will pass, but it's degenerated into a dodgy,
traffic-clogged meeting point for drug addicts,
prostitutes and down-and-outs. Most of the
area around Omonia also fits that description,
and is best avoided after dark.

GREATER ATHENS
Extending south along the Attica coast
are affluent suburbs such as **Glyfada** and
Vouliagmeni, home to some half-decent
beaches, glamorous seaside nightclubs,
and marinas full of extravagant craft.
North of central Athens, the vital artery of
Leof Kifissias flows up through **Marousi**, past
the Santiago Calatrava-designed main Olympic
complex, to the green and stately suburb of
Kifissia. This elegant district was where rich
Athenians built their holiday retreats – and so
it remains, to some extent – despite becoming
incorporated into Athens' urban sprawl.

PIRAEUS
Athens' sister city and main port has grown so
large that it's now pretty much joined up with
the capital, but still retains its own character,
filled with tavernas and old *rembetika* dives.

Guided tours

Private companies and travel agents can tailor
walks to specific themes or interests, while
guides provided by the Union of Official Guides
can lead you around the archaeological sites.

Standard package bus tours of Athens last
around four hours and include a guided tour
of the Acropolis and National Archaeological
Museum; they also drive by most other major
sites and finish up with lunch in a Plaka
taverna. Reservations can be made through
most hotels or any travel agency. The tours
run daily, year-round, and cost between €45
and €50. Reserve at least one day in advance.

CHAT Tours
*Xenofontos 9, Syntagma (210 322 2886). Metro
Syntagma.* **Open** 9am-7.30pm Mon-Sat. **Credit**
AmEx, DC, MC, V. **Map** p249/p251 F5.
Tours depart from just in front of the Hotel Amalia
(Leof Vas Amalias 10).

Hop In Sightseeing
*Syngrou 19, Makrygianni (210 428 5500/www.
hopin.com). Metro Akropoli.* **Open** 6am-10pm daily.
Credit MC, V. **Map** p251 F7.
Tours depart every morning from in front of the
McDonald's on Syntagma Square (or you can
arrange free pick-up from your hotel) and take in
most of the major sights of Athens, allowing passengers to get on and off for stops of up to an hour
(ticket valid for 24 hours). It's best to book in advance.

Key Tours
*Kallirois 4, Makrygianni (210 923 3166/www.
keytours.gr). Metro Akropoli.* **Open** 7am-8pm daily.
Credit AmEx, MC, V. **Map** p251 F7.
Tours depart from the head office, located on a major
thoroughfare south of the Temple of Olympian Zeus.
They will also pick you up at your hotel.

Other tours

Amphitrion Holidays
*Syngrou 7, Koukaki (210 900 6000). Metro
Akropoli.* **Open** 9am-5pm Mon-Fri. **Credit** AmEx,
DC, MC, V. **Map** p251 E9.
Offers four-hour tours of the city by minibus or taxi,
and individually tailored walking tours of Plaka and
the Acropolis with or without a guide.

Athenian Days
*210 864 0415/mobile 6977 660798/
www.athenian-days.co.uk.*
Personal guided tours for groups of up to six. Start
off with a one-hour talk on a subject chosen by the
group (Greek religion, everyday life in ancient
Athens) over cold drinks or a snack lunch, then a
professional guide will take you around related sites.
Pre-booking on the internet is recommended.

Union of Official Guides
*Apollonos 9A, Syntagma (210 322 9705/210 322
0090). Metro Syntagma.* **Open** 9.30am-3pm Mon-Fri.
Map p251 F5.
Provides licensed guides for individual or group
tours of archaeological sites within Athens and elsewhere in Greece, including Mycenae and Delphi.

Sightseeing

The Acropolis & Around

The many marvels within sight of the world's foremost classical landmark.

Looming in stately splendour over the higgledy-piggledy mix of sleek glass structures, pollution-stained offices, wedding-cake apartment blocks and crumbling neo-classical villas that make up the modern city of Athens, the temple-crowned Acropolis – one of the world's most famous sights – has survived occupation, civil war, fire, bombing, looting.

Attracting a crowd is nothing new for the 'Sacred rock'. Its strategic position – circled by the mountains of Hymettos, Penteli and Parnes, and, to the south-west, by the sea – made the sheer limestone plateau a natural site for defence, administration and religious worship, and as such it has been inhabited since the earliest days of human settlement.

The Acropolis ('high city') and the area around it, as the oldest continuously populated parts of Athens, are layered with the remains of all the civilisations that have existed here. The most impressive of these date from the fifth-century BC classical period, also known as the Golden Age of Athens, during which the Athenian leader Pericles initiated the building of the complex of temples and structures that now graces the top of the Acropolis, dominated by the **Parthenon** (*see p65*). Around its southern base are classical structures including the **Theatre of Dionysus** (*see p66*) and **Lysicrates Monument** (*see p71*). Lying in its south-western skirts of pines and scattered antiquities is the impressive **Odeon of Herodes Atticus** (*see p66*), added in the second century AD by the wealthy Roman of that name. To the north of the Acropolis is another Roman addition: the **Forum** (*see p74*), or central marketplace, ordered neatly around the unique eight-sided **Tower of the Winds** (*see p74*), which dates back to 50 BC.

The Byzantine era filled the area with dozens of tiny, frescoed churches. During the Ottoman occupation, Turkish rulers built mosques (like the one that remains in the Roman Forum) on the ancient sites. Relics of Ottoman daily life also appear in the form of structures like Athens' only remaining Turkish bath, the **Bathhouse of the Winds** (*see p71*).

THE NEIGHBOURHOODS

The best way to explore this most historic area of Athens is via the pedestrianised **Unification of Archaeological Sites walkway** (*see p63* **Stepping stones to the past**), which leads you past the key places on every visitor's itinerary. To discover the many fascinating neighbourhoods that have grown up around the Acropolis and its surrounding sites, just branch off the walkway wherever takes your fancy.

To the north and east of the pedestrian way lies the charming, if touristy, area of **Plaka** (*see p69*), where the cobblestone streets that wind around the base of the Acropolis are lined with ancient marble statues, Byzantine chapels, neo-classical houses, forgotten courtyards ablaze with bougainvillea, hole-in-the-wall shops festooned with leather sandals and strings of postcards, and tavernas exuding wafts of grilling meat and slow-baking vegetables.

In the area just north of the Acropolis lies the true heart of classical Athens: the sprawling Agora, where citizens haggled over the price of olive oil, bureaucrats hammered out the tricky points of the first democracy and the likes of Socrates paced among the stalls asking mind-bending questions. The marble ruins of the **Ancient Agora** (*see p75*) constitute the biggest, greenest and, some say, most fascinating archaeological site in Athens. On its northern boundary is vibrant **Monastiraki** (*see p75*), which since Ottoman times has taken over the Agora's mantle of the marketplace, playing host to Athens' most famous flea market (*see p146* **Following the (flea) market**).

To the south of the Acropolis is verdant **Philopappus Hill** (*see p68*), the highest point in southern Athens and the best place for outstanding views of the Acropolis. Surrounding the hill are the desirable residential districts of Philopappus and **Makrygianni** (*see p74*) to the east and working-class **Petralona** to the west. A

Stepping stones to the past

One of the few Olympic-era ventures that has proved an unqualified success, the **Unification of Archaeological Sites walkway** has made wandering through Athens' historic heart a real pleasure. The project links the city's most important sites and monuments by means of a four-kilometre (2.5-mile) paved walkway that begins opposite the Temple of Olympian Zeus (*see p83*) and follows Dionysiou Areopagitou and Apostolou Pavlou streets around the Acropolis and Ancient Agora, then crosses the train tracks and continues past **Keramikos** (*see p92*) down to **Technopolis** (the former gasworks, now a landmark cultural centre; *see p94*).

Until a few years ago, these streets were part of the main goods thoroughfare across Athens. Constantly congested with traffic and choked with exhaust fumes, they were hardly a good advertisement for the care the city was taking of its antiquities. But with the Olympic bid in mind, along with the concomitant effort to secure the return of the Parthenon Marbles, the Ministry of Culture turned its attention to improving the monuments and their environs – transforming sightseeing in central Athens into an altogether more relaxing experience.

In the years since Dionysiou Areopagitou and Apostolou Pavlou were pedestrianised, buildings along their length have slowly shaken off decades of grime and been restored to their former glory as magnificent neo-classical mansions (many now remodelled into contemporary cafés and restaurants) that command high prices. Meanwhile, the more recently tackled lower part of the walkway, leading from Thissio metro station to Gazi, is still evolving from a gritty industrial area, which was home to warehouses and the central bus depot, into an 'archaeological park' with manicured gardens and benches upon which to rest while gazing at the surrounding monuments.

One word of caution: vehicular use of this pedestrian route may be forbidden but don't assume you are safe from being run over – the walkway is seen as a convenient shortcut by many a cunning moped rider and delivery van driver, and is the sole means of getting to their home by car for some residents of Plaka and Thissio. In true Greek fashion, the policemen who are supposed to flag down and redirect vehicles on the pedestrian way themselves patrol in panda cars, rather than on foot.

Acropotips

- Hold on to your ticket. It will give you free entry (for five consecutive days) to all the other sites on the Unification of Archaeological Sites walkway. The sites are: Acropolis site and museum, Ancient Agora, Theatre of Dionysos, Keramikos, Temple of Olympian Zeus and Roman Forum.
- When you have your ticket checked, ask for a copy of the free bilingual guide to the site (in English and Greek). It's packed with information on the site and museum, but ticket-checkers usually don't bother to hand it out.
- Bring a bottle of water, sunscreen and a hat (and remember to take your empties and any other rubbish back down the hill with you when you leave).
- Go first thing in the morning to avoid the heat and the crowds, or in the early evening to watch the sunset from the temples. After 5pm the colours – particularly on Mount Hymmetos – are fabulous.

hotch potch of cement-block flats and restored neo-classical mansions, these areas are interesting for a stroll. They may lack the instant allure and abundant sightseeing of Plaka, but they are also free from touting taverna-owners and throngs of backpackers. Ano (Upper) Petralona, particularly, is becoming increasingly appealing, as interesting shops and unpretentious restaurants spring up, spilling over from neighbouring Thissio's overcrowded entertainment sector.

Thissio (see p76) has been transformed since the advent of the Unification of Archaeological Sites walkway. Where once it was almost entirely residential, and rather unattractive, it is now packed with dozens of cafés, bars and tavernas, which are surprisingly busy at all times of the week, and reach a raucous peak on sunny spring weekends and summer evenings. The houses on the walkway, **Apostolou Pavlou**, itself are now almost exclusively restaurants or cafés, but in the jumble of one-way streets behind are residential blocks, as well as derelict old houses being taken over by weeds, edgy galleries, a renovated 19th-century hat factory and the former royal stables, as well as countless chaotically parked cars and mopeds belonging to café customers.

Maps p250 & p251

Metro Akropoli or Thissio.

Acropolis

Dionysiou Areopagitou (210 321 0219/www. culture.gr). Metro Akropoli. **Open** *Apr-Dec* 8am-7pm daily. *Jan-Mar* 8.30am-2.30pm daily. **Admission** (incl entry to Temple of Dionysus, Ancient Agora, Roman Agora, Keramikos & Temple of Olympian Zeus) €12; €6 concessions; free under-18s, EU students, all Sun Nov-Mar. **No credit cards.**
Map p251 D6/E6.

Glimpsed between the forests of antennae on Athens apartment blocks, towering majestically at the end of central streets, spotlit against the night sky or glowing in the summer sunshine, the Acropolis is omnipresent. But nothing prepares the viewer for the breathtaking magnificence of this monument when seen up close. The awe it inspires comes from more than sheer beauty: the Acropolis temples are the greatest achievement of classical Greece, combining mathematical proportion with a glorious aesthetic to create an effect both human and sublime.

The Acropolis was a seat of royalty and a focus of religion as far back as Neolithic times. After the 11th century BC, however, Athena became the focus. Most of the myths surrounding the Acropolis are associated with the goddess of wisdom: it was on this rock that she battled Poseidon for control of Attica's greatest city. The god of the sea struck the rock with his trident and out gushed a spring, his offering to the people. Athena offered the olive tree (providing food, oil and shelter), and the citizens awarded her patronage of the city that still bears her name.

The earliest Acropolis temples to Athena date from 650 BC, but it was during the late fifth century BC, known as the Golden Age of Athens, that the Athenian general Pericles launched an ambitious programme of works by Greece's greatest artists and architects, producing the timeless monuments we see today. Though the temples' influence may be eternal, their physical state is not. The Acropolis has weathered invasions by the Spartans, Persians, Ottomans and Nazis, but its downfall may come from a more modern foe: the infamous Athenian smog is slowly eroding the marble. A team of international experts has been working for some 20 years to restore and protect the monuments, meaning that not only are some of the structures propped up with scaffolding, but the entire Acropolis rock is littered with huts and cranes – yet it somehow manages to maintain its majesty. (But go as early as possible, as the effect is diminished when there are coachloads of tourists.)

The Acropolis is entered through the **Propylaeum**. The work of the architect Mnesicles, this colossal gate obscures the view of the Parthenon and so stands alone on the horizon in all its grandeur, creating a theatrical passage from the profane to the sacred. The Propylaeum's north wing, known as the Pinakothiki (art gallery), was decorated with frescoes of scenes from Homer and filled with recliners where visitors could rest. Construction on the Propylaeum began in 437 BC, but was suspended five years later with the onset of the Peloponnesian Wars, and never finished.

On your right, as you stand before the immense Propylaeum, is the **Temple of Athena Nike**. Built in 424 BC, this tiny temple to the goddess of victory was demolished in 1686 by the Turks to make way for gun emplacements, then painstakingly reconstructed in the 1830s. The originals of its small but exquisite friezes showing battle scenes with Greeks, Persians and gods are displayed in the onsite Acropolis Museum until the New Acropolis Museum (*see p74*) is completed.

The main focus of the Acropolis is, of course, the **Parthenon**. The temple honours the incarnation of Athena as virgin goddess (Parthenos). Designed by the great sculptor Phidias, he also supervised its construction between 447 and 438 BC. It seems incredible that such a magnificent work could be completed in only nine years; the early second-century biographer and historian Plutarch commented, 'It is this, above all, that makes Pericles' works an object of such wonder to us – the fact that they were created in so short a span and yet for all time.' Despite its apparent simplicity, the Parthenon is the result of sophisticated calculations. Every measurement used in the construction of the temple is based on the golden mean: a geometrical system of proportion that still fascinates mathematicians today. And, to counteract the optical illusion that straight lines viewed from afar seem to bend, its columns bulge slightly and lean a few degrees inward (if their lines were extended,

they would eventually meet). The result of such intricate mathematical wizardry is to create a perfect structure, balanced in every way, that gives the impression of somehow being alive.

The Parthenon's decorations were no less marvellous than its structure. The metopes (part of the friezes) were sculpted with scenes of gods and celebrated mortals, their dynamism and detail surpassing everything the Greeks had created up until then. The pediment sculptures were the most magnificent: the east pediment showed the birth of Athena, springing fully formed from the head of Zeus, while the west pediment depicted Athena and Poseidon's battle for the city. Though many of these sculptures survive, you won't see them all in Greece. About two-thirds were removed from the Parthenon during the early 19th century – a frenzied period of antiquity acquisitions – by a team of agents for the seventh Earl of Elgin, Thomas Bruce, who was then British Ambassador to Constantinople. These pieces, which include the greater part of the frieze from within the Parthenon, 15 metopes and various sculptures from the triangular pediments, were bought by the British Museum for safekeeping, where they remain to this day on display in the Duveen Gallery, the subject of controversy.

Elgin was not the first to take treasures from the Acropolis, nor did the rock escape other forms of vandalism. A reportedly breathtaking 12-metre (40-foot) gold-and-ivory statue of Athena, by Phidias, disappeared after just a few centuries. The Byzantine emperors consecrated the Parthenon as a Christian church and the Ottomans later used it as a mosque. Under the Ottomans it also served as a gunpowder

Sightseeing

Cranes and scaffolding can't dim the glory of the **Acropolis**.

magazine; when the Venetians shelled the building in 1687 the powder ignited and blew the roof off. In the 15th century the Florentine rulers built a Frankish tower on the Acropolis, which is still visible in early to mid 19th-century etchings and watercolours of the rock. This structure was removed in 1875 by the archaeologist Heinrich Schliemann, an act considered vandalism by some, although purists were pleased to see it go. Nineteenth-century representations also show the low dwellings that once stood on the Acropolis, built by the Turkish settlers with stones 'borrowed' from the nearby temples.

The simplicity of the Parthenon contrasts with the fascinating complexity of the **Erechtheum** opposite. It was completed in 406 BC, on the spot where Athena and Poseidon are said to have battled for Athens. The structure unites two separate temples: the east porch once sheltered an olive-wood statue of Athena (now the goddess must make do with just a young olive sapling, growing in her honour on the western side of the temple), while the west porch was devoted to Poseidon. The most famous feature is the south porch, held up by six columns in the shape of voluptuous, drapery-clad maidens, known as the Caryatids, possibly after the women of Caryae, who were famed for their beauty and served as Athenian slaves. This latter fact may have been what inspired the Ottoman commanders to convert the temple to a harem during their occupation. Like the Parthenon, the Erechtheum survived its different uses relatively unscathed.

The Caryatids on the Erechtheum today are copies: one of the originals is in the British Museum, the other five are in the **Acropolis Museum** along with the friezes from the Temple of Athena Nike and the parts of the Parthenon series left by Lord Elgin, among other exhibits. This small museum, camouflaged in one corner of the sacred rock, is slowly shutting down, room by room, as its exhibits are transferred to the New Acropolis Museum.

The Acropolis has been open to wheelchair-users since Athens hosted the Paralympics in 2004. Previously, the disabled were kept out by the steep slopes, numerous steps and uneven, slippery ground, but there is now a lift at the side. Entrance is free of charge to those in wheelchairs, as well as to one able-bodied companion per chair. Bear to the left of the main entrance to the Acropolis (under the Propylaeum) and head through a large gate marked with a wheelchair sign. Continue left on a dust path through a wooded, shady glade in the shadow of the Acropolis until you come across what some Paralympic visitors rather unkindly, though aptly, described as a 'tin can on a stick'. It may look precarious, but it will take you straight up the northern face of the rock, depositing you just in front of the Erechtheum. An even path leads up to the Parthenon; from then on it's rather rocky going until you reach the museum, which is accessed by a small lift. Keep in mind that on very windy or rainy days, the wheelchair lift is out of action.

Disabled visitors have to leave the site the same way they came in (as will those who have checked bags), but others are recommended to exit by way of the **Theatre of Dionysus** (*see below*). Wander down through the sweet-scented pines, with the Parthenon towering above, admire the auditorium, then stroll out – passing the 19th-century **chapel of St George** on your left – on to the lower end of Dionysiou Areopagitou, opposite Acropolis metro station and the New Acropolis Museum (*see p74*).

Areopagus

Outside the entrance to the Acropolis. Metro Akropoli or Thissio. **Map** p251 D6.

Named after Ares, the god of war, this high, slippery limestone rock began life in officialdom as ancient Athens' highest court. According to myth, Orestes fled here after murdering his mother, Clytemnestra. Though the Furies had planned to kill him, Athena insisted on a jury trial (Orestes was acquitted), marking a transition from blood feuds to the rule of law. Athens' judicial council convened on the same spot from the eighth to the fifth centuries BC. In AD 51, when St Paul visited Athens; he delivered his famous 'Men of Athens' sermon here, converting Dionysus (a namesake, not the debauched god himself), who would later become the first bishop of Athens. The speech, recorded in the Bible (Acts 17:22-34), is carved on a bronze plaque at the bottom of the rock, often visited by pilgrims.

Odeon of Herodes Atticus

Dionysiou Areopagitou, near intersection with Propylaion (210 323 2771/www.culture.gr). Metro Akropoli or Thissio. **Open** during performances only. **Tickets** prices vary. **Map** p251 D6.

The most important theatre in Athens since Roman times, the Odeon of Herodes Atticus was built in AD 174 by the wealthy Herodes Atticus (friend of Emperor Hadrian and a benefactor to the city) in memory of his wife. Besides its marvellous acoustics, it also delights spectators with its beautiful backdrop of tiered Roman arches, behind which the soft bulk of Mount Hymmetos glows pinkish-purple in the dusk. More commonly called Herod Atticus or, in Greek, Irodio, the theatre is now the venue of the annual Athens Festival (*see p162*), hosting moonlit performances nightly every summer. Artists such as Placido Domingo and the Bolshoi Ballet have performed here, and the theatre is a regular host to interpretations and adaptations of the ancient Greek tragedies and comedies. Though the Odeon is only open for performances, you can appreciate its architecture and setting from the outside and look down on it from the Acropolis.

Theatre of Dionysus

Dionysiou Areopagitou (210 322 4625/www. culture.gr). Metro Akropoli. **Open** *May-Oct* 8.30am-7pm daily. *Nov-Apr* 8am-sunset daily. **Admission** €2; €1 concessions; free to holders of €12 Acropolis ticket. **No credit cards**. **Map** p251 E6.

This scrubby patch of land below the Acropolis saw the birth of drama as we know it: it was the site of the sixth-century BC Festival of the Great Dionysia,

Waifs and strays

They are an integral part of every Athens scene. Sit at a shady taverna and a posse of hungry cats will congregate. When a banner-carrying mob gathers for a demonstration, an excited pack of mutts leads the way. Each ancient site, each neighbourhood and each square has its own complement of stray dogs and cats – some sickly and scrawny, others plump and jolly.

There are an estimated 5,000 or more stray dogs in central Athens alone, along with an incalculable number of cats. The problem of unwanted former pets is not unique to Greece. The difference lies in the way the problem is tackled. In most western countries, authorities or welfare groups pick up abandoned animals, take them to a shelter and wait for them to be adopted. If not, they are put to sleep. But in Greece, a recent law requires municipalities to operate catch-neuter-release programmes for stray dogs, rather than putting them in shelters. Since there are some welfare groups that care for street animals, as well as plenty of individuals who leave out food for strays or happily let them snooze on their doorsteps, it might seem that the plan to let sleeping dogs lie would work.

However, only a handful of municipalities – Athens included – follows this humane population-control plan. And, sadly, even in those areas that have adopted the law, it's only practised sporadically (usually just before local elections), and never in combination with campaigns about responsible ownership.

Further, the law has no provision for puppies or other dogs unable to cope on the streets, and it simply ignores cats. In reality, most local authorities do nothing until the strays become a real problem, then resort to one of the cheapest, cruellest and least effective methods – poisoning – to 'clean up'.

Visitors to Athens generally have nothing to fear from the wandering dogs (nor from the cats that lurk in deserted buildings). They don't carry diseases transmittable to humans, and in most cases have been vaccinated, wormed and sterilised. More often than not, if dogs approach you it is for a stroke or a piece of your souvlaki rather than with any malicious intent. However, if you do feel intimidated (in areas where sterilisation is not commonplace, a pack of males surrounding a female in season can become aggressive), avoid eye contact and don't flap your arms about. Try to keep calm and walk away backwards very slowly, keeping your face and eyes averted from the dogs. If you have anything edible on your person, extract it slowly and drop it on the ground, again without making big, threatening movements.

Joggers and cyclists are tempting targets for some stray dogs that seem to see snapping at their heels (or wheels) as a merry pastime. If you don't share their idea of fun, slow right down or stop, at which point the dogs usually lose interest. If you plan on cycling or jogging regularly in areas where there are lots of dogs, it might be wise to invest in a water or lemon spray.

Cafés on **Adrianou**.

honouring the god with performances that led to the renowned fifth-century BC drama competitions. The tragedies of Sophocles and Euripides, as well as the comedies of Aristophanes, were first performed here. In its original state, the theatre seated 15,000. The best seats were reserved for the priests of Dionysus; you can still see the head priest's throne in the centre, carved with satyrs and adorned with lions' paws.

Philopappus Hill

Dionysiou Areopagitou & Apostolou Pavlou (www.culture.gr). Metro Akropoli or Thissio.
Map p250/p251 C7/D7.
The best spot for that picture-perfect shot of the Acropolis, this verdant landscaped park contains a wealth of archaeological finds and is home to a wide range of indigenous flora. In antiquity, it was known as the Hill of the Muses, and poets thronged its slopes for inspiration; in wartime, generals garrisoned themselves at its crest because of its sweeping views out to sea; now it attracts a daily crowd of local dog-walkers and joggers, as well as weekend brigades of smooching couples, families, and tourists. Beautiful all year round, with its pines and cypresses and its winding walks, Philopappus really comes into its own in spring, when the bulbs blossom and the grassy slopes are covered with poppies and daffodils. After Clean Monday (the first day of Lent), though, when it is traditional for families to drive up Philopappus and fly kites, the flowers are gone – plucked to wither and die in apartments throughout the city.

At the foot of Philopappus is the pretty, mosaic-tiled church of **St Dimitrios Loumbardiaris**, built in 1460 (*see p69*). Next to the church is the tourist pavilion, a scenic little wooden structure offering peerless views of the Acropolis. Opposite the church you will see a small cave said to be Socrates' prison, where the philosopher was held after being sentenced to death for corrupting the youth of Athens. One of these corrupted youths, Plato, wrote a version of his mentor's deathbed words in his *Phaedo*, a seminal work of Western philosophy.

Take a while to wander along the wonderfully peaceful, unevenly paved paths that wind around the hillside, shaded by trees and shrubs and provided with stone benches on which to rest and admire the panoramas across to Piraeus and the Saronic Gulf beyond. All this is the work of architect Dimitris Pikionis who, in the 1950s, landscaped the Acropolis and Philopappus area, linking the sites with characteristic pathways that use irregularly shaped stones and hundreds of indigenous shrubs and flowers. It was a massive and inspired project in which Pikionis creatively combined local natural stone, contemporary brick and antique fragments of every era found around the sites, fusing nature with culture, the past with the present.

At the peak of the hill is the AD 116 **Tomb of Philopappus**, a wealthy Syrian, grandson of a Hellenic ruler, who came to Athens after Romans occupied his homeland. He made enough lavish endowments to earn citizenship and the right to build this ostentatious tomb. On the way down the hill is Athens' **National Observatory**, Greece's oldest functioning research centre, housed in a beautiful neo-classical mansion. Further down the hill is a grassy, idyllic spot with some piles of stones and a few foundations. This is all that's left of the **Pnyx**, which could be considered the exact birthplace of democracy: when Athens converted from the rule of one governor to rule by the people in 594 BC, the Athenians built a 5,000-seat amphitheatre here, which was where the first voting by, of and for the people, for their own leadership, took place.

On the west side of the hill, cut into the green slopes, is the **Dora Stratou Garden Theatre** (*see p201*), which hosts regular performances of Greek folk dancing in summer.

When you've had your fill of Philopappus's winding tracks, shady benches and panoramic views, pop into the Culture Ministry's Acropolis Museum Shop in the coach park at the bottom of the hill. It's worth a quick once-over if you're looking for souvenirs such as postcards, clay replicas of pots and statuettes, and reproduction jewellery, as well as more imaginative items like puzzles of the Parthenon friezes and silk scarves with ancient patterns.

There was a furore when the ministry started constructing this shop before the Olympics, as it was part of a grand plan that included fencing off the entire hill as an archaeological site and constructing an open-air exhibition area in the old quarry where Athena's owls nest. Most of the fencing was pulled down by angry residents who believed an admission charge to the hill would be the next step; the exhibition space never progressed further than a pitifully ugly slick of concrete daubed with graffiti and pierced by a number of metal posts, but the shop and its adjacent grass-roofed toilet block turned out to be much less of a problem than the locals had feared.

Church of St Dimitrios Loumbardiaris

Philopappus Hill, off Dionysiou Areopagitou. Metro Akropoli or Thissio. **Open** during services. **Admission** free. **Map** p250 D6.

This church's scenic location and handsome interior mean it's highly popular for weddings and christenings, and you can barely approach it at Easter-time, when Athenians decked out in their finest clothes gather with candles and children outside the church for midnight mass. The peculiar name, 'St Dimitrios the Bombardier', is said to have been given because, in 1656, an Ottoman commander planned to attack the church with cannon on the feast day of St Dimitrios, but the saint intervened, striking the garrison with a bolt of lightning to foil the attack.

Plaka

Maps p249 & p251

Metro Akropoli, Monastiraki or Syntagma.
Clinging to the lower reaches of the Acropolis rock, Plaka is the capital's most touristy area – a maze of narrow, cobblestoned medieval streets that twist through ancient sites, packed squares and lovely Byzantine courtyards. (For a guided route through the labyrinth, *see p72* **Exploring the old Plaka**).

Peaceful and picturesque as it is, it's hard to believe that not long ago, Plaka was awash with brothels and seedy nightclubs. In the 1980s the Ministry of Culture, then under the redoubtable rule of *Never on Sunday* actress and Parthenon Marbles campaigner Melina Mercouri, set in motion a tide of change by refusing all applications for late-night entertainment licences and buying up uninhabited (and some inhabited) neo-classical buildings to renovate and turn into ministry offices and museums. Gradually, residents crept back, mansions were restored and dozens of more salubrious (if often overpriced) establishments opened up.

Plaka's tourist-packed main street, **Adrianou**, is aptly named after the Emperor Hadrian, since it starts (or ends) at the library he built in AD 132. Lined with shops selling leather handbags, cotton T-shirts, pots of olive oil and sachets of saffron, polished copper pots and gold necklaces, as well as 'traditional' tavernas with bouzouki music and persistent waiters reciting the menu, Adrianou is a hive of activity from dawn till dusk.

The most beautiful section of Plaka is the tiny village of **Anafiotika** (*see p70* **An island in the city**), a cluster of houses at the very base of the Acropolis.

Athens Cathedral (Mitropolis)

Platia Mitropoleos (210 322 1308). Metro Monastiraki or Syntagma. **Open** 6.30am-7pm daily. **Admission** free. **map** p249/p251 E5/F5.

The large, lavishly appointed Athens Cathedral, commonly referred to as Mitropolis, is one of the city's best-known landmarks. It is the seat of the Greek Orthodox archbishop (one of the nation's most influential – and controversial – figures) and is regularly packed with thousands of Greek grandmothers turn out to kiss touring holy relics, or when Athens' high society floods in for weddings, baptisms or funerals. One of the best times of the year to appreciate the cathedral is during the elaborate Easter celebrations: most of central Athens gathers here, shoehorned inside or spilling on to the marble forecourt, to light candles and say '*Christos anesti*' ('Christ is risen'), '*Alithos anesti*' ('Truly he is risen') to each other at midnight on Easter Saturday (*see also p164* **Rising to the occasion**). Though the icons and ecclesiastical objects are indeed impressive, the building's architecture is fairly standard. Of far greater artistic importance is the tiny Panagia Gorgoepikoos (also known as Mikri Mitropoli, Little Cathedral or Little Metropolis) next door. It was built in the 12th century, on the ruins of an ancient temple devoted to the goddess of childbirth, Eileithyia. What makes it unique are its building materials: the walls are made entirely of Roman and Byzantine marble relics, sculpted with reliefs depicting the ancient calendar of feasts.

An island in the city

A stone's throw from Plaka's bustling, touristy main street lies the tiny district of **Anafiotika**. Chiselled out of the rocks at the base of the Acropolis, this tiny settlement is all sugarcube dwellings, miniature courtyards edged with immaculate pots of geraniums and abrupt clotheslines of knickers and vests, narrow whitewashed alleys and Lilliputian flights of steps polished and rounded by decades of footsteps. Cascades of roses and jasmine are everywhere, and bright curtains hang across open doorways, from which emanate the blur of TV, the sounds of voices raised in familial dispute and the wafts of dinner stewing on the stove. It sounds just like the backstreets of an island town. Small wonder, because the area is in fact a lovingly recreated version of a Cycladic village. Stonemasons summoned from the island of Anafi (close to Santorini) to build King Otto's palace in the early 19th century were so homesick that they set out to reconstruct a copy of their home town in the foothills of the Acropolis (the word Anafiotika means 'Anafi-style').

To get right into the heart of Anafiotika, walk up Thespidos from Adrianou and turn right on to Stratonos. Then take a sharp left before the whitewashed St George of the Rock church (on Stratonos), where you will see a plaque dedicated to Konstantinos Koukidis, who fell to his death from the Acropolis, wrapped in the Greek flag, during the Nazi occupation. Climb the steps carved out of the rock, take the first left and keep ascending until you reach a rest spot with an unequalled view across the city, almost on a level with the Athens Cathedral and the lower slopes of Lycabettus. Then descend the white-edged steps and lose yourself in the maze of alleyways between the modest dwellings.

If you feel too intrusive (not to mention out of scale – backpack-wearers can barely squeeze through some of the passageways), head back up to the 'ringroad' that skirts the fence of the Acropolis site. But the residents, most of whom are descendants of the stonemasons who built the settlement, have long ago come to terms with their tourist-attraction status. The laundry still has to be hung out to dry and the evening meal prepared. And the scrawny cats rolling in the sunny courtyards no longer even bat an eyelid when camera-clutching strangers clatter by.

Bathhouse of the Winds

Kyrristou 8 (210 324 4340/www.culture.gr). Metro Monastiraki. **Open** 9am-2.30pm Mon, Wed, Thur-Sun. **Admission** €2; free-€1 concessions. **Map** p249/p251 E5.

Under Ottoman rule, every Athenian neighbourhood had one of these public baths, used not only for steams and scrubs, but also as essential meeting places. After Greece won independence, all Turkish baths (or hammams) in the city were destroyed – except this one, which has been recently renovated and reopened to the public. You can't actually bathe, but you can walk around the rooms and picture the languor of a lost era. Imagine being massaged on the marble slabs, dappled with pinpricks of light from the pattern cut in the high domes, with scantily clad attendants fetching tea and scented oils.

Centre of Folk Art & Tradition

Angelikis Hatzimichali 6 (210 324 3972). Metro Akropoli or Syntagma. **Open** 9am-1pm, 5-9pm Tue-Fri; 9am-1pm Sat, Sun. **Admission** free. **Map** p251 F6.

The rooms in the mansion of folklorist Angeliki Hatzimichali have been set up to depict the traditional Greek way of life, with housewares, ceramics and kitchen utensils from the 19th century. Museum exhibits include embroideries and family portraits.

Church of the Holy Trinity

Filellinon 21 (210 323 1090). Metro Syntagma. **Open** Sun mornings & during choir rehearsals. **Admission** free. **Map** p251 F5/F6.

Built in the 11th century, this church had some of its outer walls pulled down by the Turk Ali Haseki in 1780, for city fortifications. In later years, the chapel (also known as Agios Nikodimos) was sold to the Russian Orthodox Church, and in 1852 Tsar Alexander II had it restored with a new terracotta frieze and bell tower. It is still the stronghold of Russian Orthodoxy in Greece, and contains displays of ornate Russian embroidery. It is also famed for its chanters: stop by on Sunday to listen to them.

Church of St Catherine

Herephontos 14 & Lysikratous (210 322 8974). Metro Akropoli. **Open** *May-Oct* 8am-noon, 5-7pm daily. *Nov-Apr* 8am-noon, 4-6pm daily. **Admission** free. **Map** p251 F6.

This 11th-century church is built over the ruins of what some say is an ancient temple, while others believe it to be a sixth-century palaeo-Christian church; some of the columns still stand in the courtyard. Although the main body of the church – beautifully decorated with well-restored frescoes – is Byzantine, the two outer chapels were added in the first half of the 20th century. The church choir is reputed to be one of the best in the city.

Frissiras Museum

Monis Asteriou 3 & 7 (210 323 4678/www. frissirasmuseum.com). Metro Akropoli or Syntagma. **Open** 10am-5pm Wed, Thur, Fri; 11am-5pm Sat, Sun. **Admission** €6; €3 concessions. **No credit cards.** **Map** p251 F6.

A stylish recent addition to Athens' cluster of small museums and galleries, this collection of contemporary European paintings housed in two restored neo-classical houses is fresh and varied. Past exhibitions have included works by Francis Bacon and Lucian Freud, among many other illustrious names.

Jewish Museum

Nikis 39 (210 322 5582/www.jewishmuseum.gr). Metro Syntagma. **Open** 9am-2.30pm Mon-Fri; 10am-2pm Sun. Closed Sat. **Admission** €5; €3 concessions. **No credit cards.** **Map** p251 F6.

Archaeological digs have unearthed a synagogue in the Ancient Agora, evidence of the existence of a Jewish community in Athens as far back as the fifth century BC. Some 87 per cent of modern Greece's Jewish population were killed in the Holocaust, one of the highest percentages in Europe. This museum has excellent displays documenting the history of the country's Jews, including engravings, historical and religious artefacts, intricate carvings and works of art, and written records dating back 2,300 years.

Lysicrates Monument

Platia Lysikratou (www.culture.gr). Metro Akropoli. **Map** p251 F6.

Each year, winners of the Dionysian drama festival (who included Aristophanes, Sophocles and Euripides; *see p15* **Three wise guys**) were awarded a decorative tripod. In 335 BC Lysicrates, the producer of the winning play, built this marble public display for his prize: ostentatious, perhaps, but unbeatable PR. Six Corinthian columns are arranged around a circular base, carved with Dionysian emblems. In the 17th century the monument was incorporated into a Capuchin monastery, the foundations of which could be seen until recently in a pleasantly overgrown green space around the monument. However, in summer 2003 the whole area was paved over with gravel, an aesthetically unfortunate move that caused the area to be dubbed a 'giant litterbox'.

Museum of Greek Folk Art

Kydathinaion 17 (210 322 9031/www.culture.gr). Metro Syntagma or Akropoli. **Open** 9am-2pm Tue-Sun. **Admission** €2; €1 concessions; free under-18s, EU students. **No credit cards.** **Map** p251 F6.

The dimly lit, government-run building won't win any prizes for its looks, but inside are five floors packed with rich, beautiful folk art, including filigree jewellery, fine embroideries worked with gold and silver, Greek shadow puppets and highly skilled carvings in stone and wood. Don't miss the room of wall paintings by naive painter Theophilos Hatzimichalis, transported intact from his home on the island of Lesbos. Limited information in English.

Museum of Greek Musical Instruments

Diogenous 1-3 (210 325 0198/www.culture.gr). Metro Monastiraki. **Open** 10am-2pm Tue, Thur-Sun; noon-6pm Wed. **Admission** free. **Map** p251 F6/E5.

There's a lot more to Greek music than the bouzouki that plucked out the theme to *Zorba the Greek*. The

Sightseeing

Walk 1 Exploring the old Plaka

This walk wanders through colourful central streets into tranquil, flower-filled corners that still seem astonishingly removed from the passage of time. Sights range from 2,500-year-old ruins to incense-filled churches to modern-day museums. It shouldn't take you more than an hour and a half, unless you're dedicated enough to take the tour of all five museums mentioned (remember that most close at around 2pm).

Start the walk at the Russian Orthodox **Church of the Holy Trinity** (*see p71*). It was built as a small chapel in the 11th century, then, 800 years later, sold to the Russian government, which expanded it to its current size. Inside, Russian embroideries are on display and, if you're lucky, you may hear the renowned female chanters practising. Cross the street and turn right on to Kydathinaion. This is a quintessential Athenian moment: the turn takes you suddenly from a modern, traffic-filled artery on to a stone-paved walkway leading straight to the heart of the old city. Head down Kydathinaion, and on your right you'll pass the Byzantine **Church of the Transfiguration of the Saviour** (Kydathinaion 10, 210 322 4633), set in a shaded garden, around which neighbourhood men gather to play backgammon. Originally built in the 11th century, the church has been rebuilt and

added to many times; most of the current exterior dates from the 19th and 20th centuries. Opposite the church is the fine **Museum of Greek Folk Art** (*see p71*). Continue down Kydathinaion to pleasant, leafy **Platia Filomousou**. At some point everyone visiting Athens passes through this shady square lined with cafés and restaurants, both old-world and modern-day.

At the bottom of the square, turn left on to Farmaki, which will take you to the **Church of St Catherine** (*see p71*), then turn right on to Lysikratous, which leads to the **Lysicrates Monument** (*see p71*). In the 17th century the monument was incorporated into a Capuchin monastery, where Lord Byron stayed while writing the first canto of *Childe Harold*. The names of the branching streets reflect the guest: Vyronos (the Hellenised version of Byron) goes off to the south; to the north, Selley (Shelley) recalls Byron's Romantic buddy.

Have a look around the souvenir shops on Adrianou, which runs along the east side of the monument, and then turn left on to Thespidos, walking by the traditional taverna **Giouvetsakia** (*see p112*), with a history of over 50 years in Plaka. Walking straight along Thespidos will take you up to the base of the Acropolis. Turn right, following the rock to the whitewashed island-style **Church of St George of the Rock**. The church marks the entrance to **Anafiotika** (*see p70* **An island in the city**). Have a wander through this picturesque area, then head down on to Pritaniou, and turn right down the stairs of Mnisikleous. Cross Lysiou, then take the next left into Kyristou, to check out the steamy site of the old Turkish baths, the **Bathhouse of the Winds** (see p71).

At the end of Kyristou you meet the **Roman Forum** and the **Tower of the Winds** (*see p74*). On leaving, turn right on to Diogenous; immediately on your left is the **Museum of Greek Musical Instruments** (*see p71*), where

you can listen to recordings of regional folk music. Retrace your steps, then bear right around the Roman Forum and turn down Eolou, then take the first left on to Adrianou. On the right, you can look into the ruins of the once-luxurious **Hadrian's Library** (*see p76*). Follow the library on to Areos, where you'll turn right, passing multinational street traders on your way to Monastiraki Square.

The ancient library's next-door neighbour on this side is a mosque, home to the **Museum of Traditional Greek Ceramics** (*see p76*). Opposite is Monastiraki station, where you can hop on the metro to head anywhere in town.

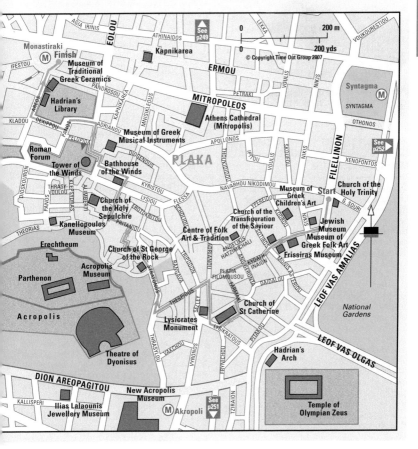

Sightseeing

displays in this unassuming but fascinating little museum trace how Asian, Middle Eastern and European influences filtered through the Hellenic sensibility to create instruments such as Byzantine lutes, the sitar-like *santouri* and the *gaida* (a Balkan take on the bagpipes). The instruments themselves are beautiful, intricately carved with precious metals, ivory and tortoiseshell; the displays are accompanied by headphones playing recordings.

Roman Forum & Tower of the Winds

Eolou & Pelopida (210 324 5220/www.culture.gr). Metro Monastiraki. **Open** *Apr-Oct* 8am-7.30pm daily. *Nov-Mar* 8am-sunset daily. **Admission** €2; €1 concessions; free to holders of €12 Acropolis ticket. **No credit cards. Map** p249/p251 E5.

One of Athens' most interestingly layered sites. Its earliest and most striking feature is the marvellous, eight-sided Tower of the Winds, built in 50 BC by Syrian astronomer Andronikos Kyrrhestas. The combination of sundial, weathervane and water clock was unlike any other building in the ancient world.

A century later, the Romans shifted Athens' central marketplace from the sprawling Ancient Agora (*see p75*), creating a smaller, more orderly one around the tower. The Ottomans made their mark by building a mosque on the same site. In the 20th century archaeologists used the Forum as a repository for unclassifiable smaller finds from all over Attica, which explains the presence of the odd Byzantine grave marker or garlanded sarcophagus.

Makrygianni & Koukaki

Maps p250 & p251

Metro Akropoli or Syngrou-Fix.

Two projects have irrevocably changed the neighbourhood directly to the south of the Acropolis, Makrygianni, in the last decade. The pedestrianisation of the area's main boulevard, **Dionysiou Areopagitou**, has unquestionably been a success. However, it has pushed a lot of traffic on to the surrounding residential streets, forming a daily gridlock.

On a far grander – national – scale, the construction of the **New Acropolis Museum** (*see p74*) has drastically changed the face of the neighbourhood: Makrygianni home-owners were forced out and their houses demolished to create space for the gigantic site; at the time of writing there was no end in sight to construction, and cranes continue to dominate the site. It remains to be seen what effect the museum will have on coach traffic, but the rapidly rising house prices seem to dictate that once-quiet, slightly seedy Makrygianni will soon be a district of deluxe new-build blocks.

Makrygianni is named after the Greek War of Independence hero General Yiannis Makrygiannis (the name translates as 'John

Long-John'), of whom a large bronze statue stands at the corner of Dionysiou Areopagitou and Vyronos. Vandals sometimes snap off the imposing general's sword, and his macho military image is often further compromised by a bouquet of flowers being placed in his hands.

South-west of residential Makrygianni is the lively district of **Koukaki**. Cheaper, more working-class than its neighbour, Koukaki is full of cars, souvlaki joints and corner shops trying desperately to compete against the inexorable surge of international chains that have already killed off a number of the area's hardware shops, grocers and corner stores.

Ilias Lalaounis Jewellery Museum

Karyatidon & Kallisperi 12, Makrygianni (210 922 1044/www.lalaounis-jewelrymuseum.gr). Metro Akropoli. **Open** 9am-4pm Mon, Thur-Sat; 9am-9pm Wed; 11am-4pm Sun. **Admission** €4; €3 concessions; free under-12s, all 3-9pm Wed, 9-11am Sat. **Credit** (shop only) AmEx, MC, V. **Map** p251 E6.

Located on a leafy residential street running parallel to Dionysiou Areopagitou, this museum displays the works of Ilias Lalaounis, the world-famous Greek-born jewellery designer who has haughty boutiques in New York, Paris and London. Admire decades of Lalaounis's work, ranging from reproductions of antiquities to minimalist, modern, molecule-inspired pieces, then visit the shop for some precious souvenirs.

New Acropolis Museum

Makrygianni & Hatzichristou, Makrygianni (www.culture.gr). Metro Akropoli. **Map** p251 E7.

It was hoped that this controversial, multi-million-euro, concrete and glass behemoth, designed by Bernard Tschumi, would be ready in time for the Olympics in summer 2004. But an inept building contractor and legal challenges (from residents whose houses were bulldozed as well as from archaeologists concerned at the harm construction would do to the ancient ruins beneath the site) constantly stymied the project. The building should now be completed by late 2007, but what with transferring the exhibits and setting up the displays, it is not expected to be open to the public before the end of 2008. When it finally opens its doors, visitors will be wowed by floor-to-ceiling windows giving a direct view of the Parthenon opposite, a state-of-the-art top-floor gallery housing the Parthenon friezes (with significant spaces left for those parts remaining in the British Museum), a glass floor exposing the ruins of an early Christian settlement beneath the museum and a hall of exquisite Archaic votive statues. The museum, which will house all the surviving artefacts from the Acropolis site, will contain a restaurant and café and be surrounded by landscaped gardens of olive trees.

An exhibition showing just a few of the ancient finds unearthed during excavation for the development – mosaic floors, clay utensils, coins and toys –

is running at the Acropolis Museum's neighbour, the Weiler Building (Dionysiou Aeropagitou and Makrygianni, 210 924 1043); scheduled to run until September 2007, dates may be extended.

Monastiraki

Maps p249 & p251

Metro Monastiraki or Thissio.
The vibrant heart of Athens' modern marketplace, **Monastiraki Square** is packed with carts of fruit, peddlers hawking mobile phones and knock-off sunglasses, stalls of knick-knacks, and trays of nuts and seeds. From this hub, spokes leading out in every direction are filled with a varied assortment of shops, each street with its own characteristic selection. Heading down towards Thissio is Ifestou, a brash alley of cut-price jeans, slogan T-shirts and trainers, interspersed with traditional stalls selling backgammon sets and copper coffee containers. Branching off from Ifestou are the antique streets – sleepy passages of tarnished silver, curling posters and old furniture. The area comes alive every Sunday with the renowned flea market (*see p146* **Following the (flea) market**), which has flourished since Ottoman times, centred on Platia Avyssinias and Ifestou.

Monastiraki Square provides one of the best vantage points on the layers of history that shaped the city. The square itself takes its name – 'little monastery' – from the tiny tenth-century church that stands in the square, alongside the

metro station. The church was destroyed and then rebuilt in 1678 as part of a large convent whose buildings, over the following 200 years, spread all around the surrounding areas, up to what is now the Central Market. Most of the buildings were destroyed during the late 19th century during archaeological excavations and railway construction. The little church is all that remains. Just behind the church is an 18th-century mosque, one of the most distinctive reminders of the Ottoman occupation (today the mosque is the **Museum of Traditional Greek Ceramics**; *see p76*). Next door, **Hadrian's Library** (*see p76*) is a monument to the city's Roman past. The classical temples of the Acropolis, rising above, give perspective to it all. And only a stone's throw from the square lie the ruins of the **Ancient Agora** (*see below*), one of the most important sites in the classical world.

Ancient Agora

Entrances on Adrianou & on the descent from the Acropolis (210 321 0185/www.culture.gr). Metro Monastiraki or Thissio. **Open** *May-Oct* 8am-7.15pm daily. Museum 10am-7.15pm Mon; 8am-7.15pm Tue-Sun. *Nov-Apr* 8am-5pm daily. Museum 8am-4.30pm daily. **Admission** €4; €2 concessions; free under-18s, EU students & holders of €12 Acropolis ticket. **No credit cards. Map** p249/p251 D5.
This market, founded in the sixth century BC, was the city centre for 1,200 years, witnessing the construction and destruction of overlapping stoas (colonnades fronting the market), temples and government

Traders and buyers converge on the **Monastiraki Flea Market**. *See p76.*

buildings. Far more than a place to shop, the market was the centre of all public life, including arts, politics, commerce and religion. A typical Athenian, for whom participation in such activities was as essential as breathing, would spend all day here, listening to the likes of Socrates, Demosthenes or St Paul holding forth among the oil and spice stalls, checking in at the circular tholos, where a council of 50 administrators was available 24 hours a day, and lighting a candle at the shrine to Hephaestus, which overlooked the whole scene. The latter is still the best-preserved classical-era temple in Greece – get up close and look at the friezes, which depict the adventures of Theseus and Heracles. The restored Stoa of Attalos, which functioned rather like an ancient shopping mall, today houses the excellent Agora Museum, focusing on artefacts connected to the incipient democracy.

Hadrian's Library

Dexippou & Areos (210 324 9350/www.culture.gr). Metro Monastiraki. **Open** 8am-7.30pm daily. **Admission** €2; €1 concessions. **Map** p251 E5.
The Roman Emperor Hadrian built this luxurious library in AD 132. Most of the space was a marble courtyard with gardens and a pool, but there were also lecture rooms, music rooms, a theatre and a small place for storing scrolls. The gate to the site is located between the handicraft stalls on Areos, just up from the Monastiraki metro station. However, most of the site is visible from adjoining streets.

Monastiraki Flea Market

Platia Avyssinias & surrounding streets. Metro Monastiraki. **Open** 8.30am-3pm Sun. **Map** p249 D5.
Platia Avyssinias comes to life on Sunday mornings, when Athens' best flea market fills the space and spills on to the streets around it. You can find anything here: cut-glass Turkish liquor sets, 100-year-old telephones, antique desks, gold-framed maps of the Balkans and sets of Russian nesting dolls. For a guided walk around the area, *see p146* **Following the (flea) market**. *Photo p75.*

Museum of Traditional Greek Ceramics

Areos 1 (210 324 2066/www.culture.gr). Metro Monastiraki. **Open** *Sept-June* 9am-2.30pm Mon, Wed-Sun. *July, Aug* hours vary. **Admission** €2; €1 concessions; free under-18s & EU students. **No credit cards. Map** p251 E5.
Built in 1789, this is the only Ottoman-era mosque in Athens still open to the public. After Greek independence, Athenians stripped the mosque of its minaret and turned it into a military barracks and then a jail. In 1918 it was turned into a government-run museum of ceramic art, against the wishes of many Greeks who would have preferred to see all remnants of the hated occupiers destroyed. The collection here is small and limited mostly to pieces from the second half of the 20th century – though many are beautiful, the main appeal of the museum is simply being inside the former mosque, in the heart of what was once the old Turkish bazaar.

Thissio

Maps p248 & p250

Metro Thissio.
Thissio takes its name from the best-preserved classical-era temple in Greece. Although the shrine, in the Ancient Agora (*see p75*), was built to the blacksmith god Hephaestus and is formally known as the **Hephaestum**, its most notable features include reliefs of Athenian hero and king Theseus carved on its metopes. It informally became known as the Theseion (Temple of Theseus), subsequently lending its name to the neighbourhood.

The construction of the paved walkway linking Thissio with the Acropolis and Keramikos has transformed the area from a low-rent neighbourhood – albeit with fantastic views of the Acropolis – into a buzzing destination. Old buildings have been renovated into cultural spaces (such as the **Melina Mercouri Cultural Centre**, *see below*), and Thissio has been inundated with galleries, cafés, restaurants and bars. The places to see and be seen at are mainly around the metro station, on bustling Iraklidon, and quiet, tree-lined Eptachalkou, home to an interesting gallery (Bernier/Eliades Gallery; *see p173*), homely ouzeries and a couple of small churches. The area is also home to one of the city's best-known churches, **St Marina** (*see below*), on the edge of Philopappus Hill.

Church of St Marina

Agias Marinas, off Apostolou Pavlou (210 346 3783). Metro Thissio. **Open** *Apr-Sept* 7.30am-noon, 5-7.30pm daily. *Oct-Mar* 7.30am-noon, 5-6.30pm daily. **Admission** free. **Map** p248/p250 C5.
This cheerful church honours the protectress of pregnant mothers and infants. St Marina's many domes are higher and narrower than those of most other Orthodox churches, giving it a sprightly, buoyant feel, definitely enhanced by the red-and-white peppermint-striped façade. This is one of the most popular churches in Athens, hosting a week-long festival to the saint every July.

Melina Mercouri Cultural Centre

Iraklidon 66 & Thessalonikis (210 345 2150). Metro Thissio. **Open** 9am-1pm, 5-9pm Tue-Sat; 9am-1pm Sun. **Admission** free. **Map** p248/p250 C5.
The original stone walls and airy spaces of this former hat factory have been retained as part of a clever conversion to create a fresh, modern venue for temporary art exhibitions. There is one permanent display: a nostalgic re-creation of a 19th-century Athenian street, complete with meticulously put-together shop windows of authentic paraphernalia like cigarette cards, food tins, elaborate hats and tin toys; a pharmacy where the chemist weighs out drugs on antique scales; and, of course, a *kafenio* with wrought-iron chairs, little cups on marble tables and overflowing ashtrays.

The Historic Centre

Athens' bustling commercial district and neo-classical heart.

The Historic Triangle

Maps p249 & p251

*Metro Monastiraki, Omonia, Panepistimio
or Syntagma.*

An incongruous jumble of distinguished neo-classical buildings and post-war apartment blocks, tiny Byzantine churches and designer boutiques, the heart of modern Athens nestles within just a few square miles of a rough triangle formed by Akadimias, Mitropoleos and Athinas streets. The capital's institutional and commercial centre for nearly two centuries, its mix of classical and post-modern aesthetics is the perfect introduction to the contrasts that characterise Athens. It's also oozing with history; it's home to some of the city's most remarkable public buildings, and nearly every street is named after a hero in Greece's resistance to Turkish occupation.

Just 180 years ago, however, this area was a sprawling, virtual wasteland, devastated by years of war and occupation. Visitors in the early 1800s described Athens as a city in ruins, with roofless houses, churches reduced to rubble and a population barely surpassing 6,000.

But the city's resonance with Greece's ancient glories – embodied by the magnificent Acropolis – made it the choice for the independent country's new capital, and modern Greece's first statesmen set about constructing a 19th-century neo-classical city worthy of the country's glorious past. A new king, Otto, was imported from Bavaria to introduce a monarchy to the fledgling state. Numerous ideas for his residence were submitted – including a blueprint for transforming the Parthenon and its surrounding buildings into a palatial complex – until eventually a plan for a building on Syntagma Square was settled upon. The handsome yet somewhat austere Royal Palace was constructed in 1836, since redesignated as Greece's **Parliament Building** (*see p81*).

The authorities invited Stamatios Kleanthis and Edouard Schaubert, a Greek and a German, to submit a plan for a brand new city. Expecting the population to mushroom, Kleanthis and Schaubert designed a city for 40,000 inhabitants – a modern European capital of wide boulevards, courtyards and ministries – on the plain to the north of the Acropolis. Their grid plan showed a marked rejection of the higgledy-piggledy Ottoman style of building, aiming to preserve Athens' ancient heritage while purging non-classical (Turkish and Byzantine) elements. Their plan was eventually modified by the architect Leo von Klenze, who favoured a more human-scale city. (For more on the birth of neo-classical Athens, *see p31*.)

The city shot up almost overnight, with stonemasons brought in from the Cycladic Islands and noted foreign architects arriving to make their mark. The German Friedrich von Gartner was responsible for building the rococo-style Royal Palace and planning the gardens behind; Hans Christian and Theophilus Hansen, two Danish brothers, built the complex of the **Academy of Athens**, **National Library** and **National University** on Panepistimiou (for all three, *see p81*), the Mint on Klafthmonos Square (demolished in 1939) and the **Hotel Grande Bretagne** on Syntagma Square (*see p45*). But Ernst Ziller, one of Hansen's students, had perhaps the greatest impact on the face of the new city. The German, who in 1868 settled permanently in Athens, built neo-classical masterpieces such as the **National Theatre** (*see p200*), the building that is now the **Presidential Palace** (*see p82*), a number of central hotels and the Stathatos Mansion on Vassilisis Sophias (now part of the **Museum of Cycladic Art**; *see p87*), and was responsible for restoring the ancient Panathenaic Stadium (*see p96*) for the 1896 Olympics.

With such talent involved in its creation, it's hardly surprising that Athens was once considered home to some of Europe's finest neo-classical architecture. City planners had the chance to work on an almost blank canvas, with the classical jewel of the Acropolis in the background as inspiration for elegant public buildings and intricately sculpted mansions.

Sightseeing

Browsers throng the pedestrianised stretch of **Ermou**, home to big-name shops.

By the 1920s, with the influx of more than a million refugees from Asia Minor, the city had exploded. Some 12,000 homes were hastily constructed in 1923, and in the post-World War II years, as Greeks flocked to the city from outlying regions, neo-classical villas were hacked down to make room for faceless modern blocks. And the destruction continues. Anything built in the last two centuries is still regarded as fair game by rapacious property developers. A pre-Olympics facelift restored the façades of some 1,000 old buildings in the city centre and along the so-called Olympic routes, but most pre-war houses are being eyed by real estate firms. Even an ancient site is at risk: developers are allegedly eyeing the site of the Temple of Agrotera, opposite the Temple of Zeus, as the government drags its feet about the area's expropriation.

A good place at which to start your neo-classical Athens experience is on **Platia Klafthmonos**, a famous gathering point for politicians who would come here to commiserate over electoral defeats. The **City of Athens Museum** (*see p79*), located here, has a scale model of the city in 1842, its early days as the Greek capital. A walk down Stadiou will bring you to Greece's first modern Parliament building, today the **National Historical Museum** (*see p79*). Then head up to Panepistimiou, home to the **Neo-Classical University Complex** (*see p81*) and what is now the **Numismatic Museum** (*see p81*). The latter was originally Heinrich Schliemann's house, designed by Ziller.

On nearby Akadimias, the **Cultural Centre of Athens** (*see p79*) houses a comprehensive collection of theatrical mementos.

The 19th and 20th centuries also saw the commercial needs of the city addressed, with restaurants, banks and shops springing up. The **Central Market**, built at Platia Varvakeios, off Athinas, in 1870, has remained the capital's most vital and vibrant market-place. Every Athenian neighbourhood has its weekly street market, but the Central Market is open daily. The open stalls offer an impressive array of cold cuts, nuts and fruit and vegetables. But it is the covered fish and meat markets that really deserve a visit. The fish market showcases a bewildering range of seafood on ice, and the blood-spattered meat market is not for the squeamish. For an original Athens experience, visit the meat market after 3am, when Athens clubbers cram into a handful of all-night restaurants specialising in tripe soup (*patsas*), supposedly a hangover cure.

In stark contrast to the seedy underbelly of Greek nightlife, the heart of Athens also accommodates some of the city's oldest, and smallest, churches, including the **Church of the Saints Theodore**, an 11th century structure and one of Athens' oldest remaining Byzantine monuments. Another Byzantine gem is the **Kapnikarea** (*see p79*) in the middle of Ermou shopping street. Ancient Athens makes an appearance too, whether in the remains of the **Themistoclean Wall** (sometimes

Good old-fashioned blood and gore at the **Central Market**'s meat and fish stalls.

surprisingly well preserved, like the section in the foundations of the National Bank of Greece, on Eolou), or in the little sixth-century **Church of St John of the Column**, which is built around an ancient Corinthian pillar.

Church of St John of the Column

Evripidou 72 (no phone). Metro Omonia. **Open** mid morning-early evening daily. **Admission** free. **Map** p249 E4.

Locally known as Agios Ioannis Kolonastis, this quirky little church is located at the intersection of Omonia's migrant community, Evripidou's spice market and Psyrri's gritty old workshops and edgy new nightlife. The tiny chapel, dating from about the sixth century, was built around an ancient Corinthian column that protrudes incongruously from the roof.

City of Athens Museum

Paparigopoulou 5-7, Platia Klafthmonos (210 324 6164). Metro Panepistimio. **Open** 9am-4pm Mon, Wed-Fri; 10am-3pm Sat, Sun. **Admission** €3; €2 concessions. **No credit cards. Map** p249 F4.

Otto, Greece's first king – a teenager brought over from Bavaria – lived here while waiting for construction of his first palace (now the Parliament Building) to finish. Most of the museum consists of re-creations of the rooms as they were when the king and his bride Amalia lived in them, including a throne room. There's a lot of pink and gilt rococo – perhaps to remind them of home. Don't miss the collection of paintings of Athens from the early 19th century, when it was little more than a village, and the absorbing model of the town as it was in 1842.

Cultural Centre of Athens

Akadimias 50 (210 362 9430/www.culture.gr). Metro Panepistimio. **Open** *Theatre Museum* 9am-2pm Mon-Fri. **Admission** free. **Map** p249 F3.

The pretty Cultural Centre is fronted by several statues of Greek notables, but everyone looks at only one sculpture: the woman whose robe seems to magically evaporate around her gravity-defying breasts. She's the famous Greek actress Kiveli, second wife of the former prime minister, George Papandreou. Inside the centre there's a theatre museum, with exhibits on the ancient Greek stage, lots of memorabilia from the likes of Melina Mercouri and Maria Callas, and a gallery that shows new works by Greek artists. At the back, you can join Athens' students and intellectuals in its popular café.

Kapnikarea

Kapnikarea & Ermou (210 322 4462). Metro Monastiraki or Syntagma. **Open** 8am-1pm, 5-7.30pm. Mon, Wed, Fri; 8am-7.30pm Tue, Thur, Sat, Sun. **Admission** free. **Map** p249 E5.

This beautiful 11th-century church appears suddenly and felicitously, smack in the middle of the bustling shopping strip of Ermou. The church, dedicated to the Virgin Mary, was built over the ruins of an ancient temple dedicated to a goddess, possibly Athena or Demeter. It is laid out in the typical Byzantine cross-in-square plan. Inside, it is decorated with a mix of medieval mosaics and paintings by renowned 20th-century Greek artist Fotis Contoglou. *Photo p81.*

National Historical Museum

Stadiou 13, Platia Kolokotroni (210 323 7617/www.culture.gr). Metro Panepistimio or Syntagma.

Demo-crazy

Public demonstrations are a way of life in Athens, where most citizens prize their right to protest as an inalienable aspect of their democratic freedoms. In 2006, police recorded a staggering 890 rallies in the city, more than two a day. As a result, the city centre frequently grinds to a halt as crowds of protestors choke the main arteries of the commercial district. The protests rarely affect public transport – unless they coincide with strike action, which Greeks are similarly fond of – but driving through the centre can become a nightmare. Protests also create havoc for shoppers. City-centre shop owners often close up early on protest days – either because they know business will be slow as shoppers avoid the city centre, or in fear of vandalism.

Violence is not usually a problem, but that's not to say it never happens, especially when members of left-wing or anarchist groups hijack demonstrations. There was an extended spate of such trouble in 2006 and early 2007, as students protested proposed reforms to the higher education system. Cars were vandalised and storefronts smashed as suspected anarchists clashed with police.

One of the main bones of contention was a proposed law to loosen the ban on police entering university grounds. The concept of police on campus has been anathema since 1973, when the military Junta bloodily suppressed a student rebellion at the Athens Polytechnic (*see p88*). As police are currently still forbidden from entering university

grounds, anarchists use university buildings as a base for their operations, manufacturing petrol bombs and then emerging to hurl them at police, usually in the evenings after official protest marches have ended. There are no reports of bystanders being injured during demos, but it's wise to avoid the entrances to university faculties on protest days.

Anarchist groups are also believed to be responsible for occasional attacks against foreign, usually US, targets and on big business interests (the branches of major banks, luxury car showrooms, the occasional Starbucks). Unlike the well-planned hits of terror group November 17 (which was broken up by the government in 2003 just in time for the 2004 Olympics), the aim of these attacks is not to kill or injure, but to express the protestors' objections to the actions of imperialist powers and the ills of capitalism.

The protest tradition is not confined to the ranks of anarchist extremists and students. Teachers, police officers, street cleaners and even pensioners regularly take to the streets to demand higher salaries, more benefits, and better treatment by the state in general. Even prostitutes and nuns have been known to march through the city, with the average Athenian barely raising an eyebrow. Despite the disruption, most city dwellers are tolerant – if not supportive – of demonstrations. Opinion polls show that 75 per cent of Greeks regard street rallies as an acceptable form of protest.

Open 9am-2pm Tue-Sun. **Admission** €3; €1.50 concessions; free under-18s, to all Sun. **No credit cards**. **Map** p249 F4.

The heroes of Greece's War of Independence were essentially bandits who lived in a network of mountain hideouts during the rebellion. Their paraphernalia, displayed here, includes lavishly engraved weapons and embroidered outfits galore. There are also paintings and engravings of key battles, personal items belonging to war hero Lord Byron, and the embalmed heart of war hero and Greek president Constantine Kanaris. The building itself was Greece's first Parliament, whose chamber is still preserved intact. The plumed bronze statue out front is of Theodoros Kolokotronis, a lowly mountain bandit who became the war's greatest general.

Neo-Classical University Complex

Panepistimiou, between Ippokratous & Sina (University 210 361 4301/Academy 210 360 0209/ Library 210 338 2541/www.culture.gr). Metro Panepistimio. **Open** *Library Sept-June* 9am-8pm Mon-Thur; 9am-2pm Fri, Sat. *July* 9am-2pm Mon-Sat. **Admission** free. **Map** p249 F4.

Though the formal name of the street is Eleftherios Venizelos, it's known to everyone – and even written on maps – as Panepistimiou ('University') thanks to these buildings, which are among the most impressive structures in Athens. These models of neo-classical design were all built in the years after Greece gained independence, and exemplify what the new state hoped it would become: a blend of its classical heritage and modern, Western-style statesmanship.

The central building housed Athens' first National University. It was designed by the Danish architect Hans Christian Hansen and built in 1842. The Ionian entryway columns are replicas of the columns of the Propylaeum, the entrance to the Acropolis. Inside the portico, there are colourful frescoes depicting Greece's first king, Otto, sitting on his throne surrounded by ancient Greek gods and heroes.

To the right of the University is the ornate, marble Academy of Athens, designed by Theophilus Hansen (brother of Hans Christian) and built in 1859. Its marble entry is based on the columns of the Acropolis temple Erechtheum, and its classical-style friezes are modelled after those on the Parthenon. In front, the building is flanked by seated statues of Plato and Aristotle, while on either side rise high columns topped by statues of Apollo and Athena. On the far left is the National Library. It was built in 1902, also designed by Theophilus Hansen. Its entrance has Doric columns and is modelled after the Temple of Hephaestus in the Ancient Agora. The library itself is open to the public, but the stacks are not.

The façades of these three buildings were recently renovated after one of the most passionate and protracted student protests to take place in recent years resulted in their vandalism (*see also p80* **Democrazy**). Although it's very rare to see students entering and leaving these buildings – which are

rarely used for teaching – they are often to be seen milling outside Athens University, a traditional starting point for protest marches by disgruntled social groups. *Photo p82.*

Numismatic Museum

Panepistimiou 12 (210 364 3774/www.culture.gr). Metro Panepistimio. **Open** 8.30am-3pm Tue-Sun. **Admission** €3; €2 concessions. **No credit cards**. **Map** p249 F5.

It's worth taking a look at this small museum, even if you're not interested in coins, just to walk around the mansion of Heinrich Schliemann, the famed German archaeologist who fulfilled his lifetime obsession when he discovered the rich Mycenaean kingdoms believed to be those described in *The Iliad*. The mansion is decorated with wonderful Pompeii-style frescoes and mosaics, carved marbles and moulded ceilings. It's a gorgeous showcase for the display of ancient gold, silver and bronze coins, many engraved with gods and mythical symbols.

Parliament Building & Tomb of the Unknown Soldier

Syntagma (no phone/www.culture.gr). Metro Syntagma. **Open** *Parliament Library* 9am-1.30pm Mon-Fri. **Admission** free. **Map** p249/p251/p252 G5.

Once the domain of royalty, later a shelter for starving refugees, and today the seat of government, Greece's Parliament Building has many stories to

Pocket-sized **Kapnikarea** church. *See p79.*

Sightseeing

tell. It was built in 1842 to house Otto, Greece's first king. Over the next 70 years, the palace swung between opulence and neglect as various kings were exiled and returned. In 1922, after thousands of Greeks were forced to flee Asia Minor during the Greek-Turkish population exchange (*see p20* **All Change**), the building acted as a shelter to the newly homeless. All this left it in a very sorry state and, after the return of a national parliamentary government in 1926, the building was gutted, renovated and reopened as a single-chamber council for the parliament. Today, it is the scene of lively parliamentary debates, broadcast live on state television. Most of the building is closed to the public, although its elegant library is open to researchers.

In the square below the building is the Tomb of the Unknown Soldier, erected in 1929, a monument to Greece's fallen. Carved on the tomb is a dying soldier, based on a fifth-century BC sculpture from Aegina, and an excerpt from Pericles' 430 BC funeral oration, given in honour of the Athenians who died in the Peloponnesian Wars. The tomb is guarded by the kilt- and stocking-clad elite presidential guards, or Evzones, who perform a ceremonial changing of the guard every hour.

Platia Klafthmonos
Metro Panepistimio. **Map** p249 F4.
The Platia Klafthmonos once played an important role in modern Greek politics. The name translates as the 'Square of Wailing', and it's where politicians who had lost office traditionally went to console each other after the elections. The sculpture in the centre is called *National Reconciliation.*

Maps p251 & p252
Metro Akropoli, Evangelismos, or Syntagma.
Once part of the Royal Palace and located south-east of the Historic Triangle, the National Gardens (*see p83*) are a godsend, particularly in summer: beautiful, shady, and dead in the city centre. Unsurprisingly, the real estate around them is among the city's most desirable. This is easy enough to see if you take a stroll down Irodou Attikou (*see p84* **Walk 2**), where you will pass the pristine **Presidential Palace**, designed by Ernst Ziller (the Bavarian architect who created many of modern Athens' most important buildings), and, on the corner of Leof Vas Georgiou, the stately **Maximos Mansion**. The official residence of the prime minister, the Maximos is frequently surrounded by reporters haranguing visiting ministers. They quickly withdraw when the high-kicking Evzones ceremonial guards march up the street – and the whole scene, set against the backdrop of the park, makes for a great modern Athenian moment.

Byzantine Museum
Leof Vas Sofias 22 (210 721 1027/www.culture.gr).
Metro Evangelismos. **Open** *June-Oct* 8am-7.30pm
Tue-Sun. *Nov-May* 8.30am-3pm Tue-Sun.
Admission €4; €2 over-65s; free students.
No credit cards. Map p252 H5.
The Byzantine Museum has a world-renowned collection of icons, mosaics, sculptures and religious art. Renovation has more than doubled its permanent

Neo-Classical University Complex. *See p81*.

exhibition space and its collection has been enriched with new features including rare illuminated manuscripts. In addition, archaeologists have discovered the site of Aristotle's Lyceum on the grounds, which are open to the public. At the time of writing only the museum's left wing was open.

Hadrian's Arch
Leof Vas Amalias & Dionysiou Areopagitou (no phone/www.culture.gr). Metro Akropoli. **Open** 24hrs daily. **Admission** free. **Map** p251 F6.
To thank the Roman Emperor Hadrian for finally completing the Temple of Olympian Zeus (*see below*), Athenians built this arch in his honour in AD 131. Hadrian also saw to it that the arch clarified his own sovereignty. He had its west side inscribed: 'This is Athens, the ancient city of Theseus'. The east side was inscribed: 'This is the city of Hadrian and not of Theseus'. Nearby is some more honorific masonry: the statue of Byron at the corner of Amalias and Olga.

National Gardens
Leof Vas Amalias 1 (210 721 5019). Metro Syntagma. **Open** 7am-sunset daily. **Admission** free. **Map** p251/p252 G5/G6.
The lush National Gardens were originally planted in 1839 as a private sanctuary adjoining the Royal Palace (now the Parliament). Amalia, Greece's first queen, had over 15,000 domestic and exotic plants brought in from Genoa, the coastal resort of Sounio and the island of Evia. Many of these trees still remain. The garden was opened to the public in 1923, and is now a welcome deep-green – sometimes even jungly – oasis in the parched city centre. Winding paths lead past statues, fountains and trellised promenades with such mock-natural abandon that it's actually possible to get lost. There is also a botanical museum, children's library, duck ponds, a depressed collection of caged wildlife, a playground and a café.

National War Museum
Leof Vas Sofias & Rizari 2 (210 725 2974/www. culture.gr). Metro Evangelismos. **Open** 9am-2pm Mon-Fri; 9.30am-2pm Sat, Sun. **Admission** free. **Map** p252 H5.
Admittedly, three sprawling floors on the history of Greek warfare – from Alexander the Great's battle plans through to the Balkan conflicts – might not be everyone's cup of tea; but a certain stripe of visitor will be in heaven. Meanwhile, anyone should enjoy a brief foray into the Saroglos Collection, which includes suits of armour, Three Musketeers-style foils and engraved Turkish scimitars. Outside there are real tanks and warplanes, which visitors can climb up into. Avoid weekday mornings in term-time, when busloads of kids are deposited to run riot among the planes. Most labels are in English.

Temple of Olympian Zeus
Leof Vas Olgas & Leof Vas Amalias (210 922 6330/ www.culture.gr). Metro Akropoli. **Open** *Summer* 8am-7.30pm daily. *Winter* 8am-3pm daily. **Admission** €2; €1 concessions; free to holders of €12 Acropolis ticket. **No credit cards**. **Map** p251 F6.

In a city infamous for bureaucracy and construction delays, this colossal temple still holds the record for the longest tie-up – nearly 700 years. The tyrant Pisistratos commissioned the largest temple in Greece in 515 BC, ostensibly to honour Zeus, but mainly to keep his subjects occupied. After he was overthrown, the citizens of the new democracy refused to complete what they saw as a monument to tyranny. And so the temple languished for centuries, until the Roman Emperor Hadrian recognised the opportunity it presented. He finished the temple in seven years, fitted out with a gigantic gold-and-ivory sculpture of the god, and, for good measure, added a similar one of himself. Today, only 16 of the original 104 columns remain, but their majesty still overwhelms.

Zappeion
Leof Vas Amalias (210 323 7830). Metro Syntagma. **Open** *Garden* 24hrs daily. *Exhibition Hall* varies. **Admission** free. **Map** p251/p252 G6.
On the south side of the National Gardens are the orderly Zappeion Gardens, centred on the stately Zappeion Exhibition Hall, built in 1888 by Theophilus Hansen, the Danish neo-classical architect who also designed parts of the University complex on Panepistimiou. Hansen combined an entrance reminiscent of an ancient temple with a main body that referenced contemporary Mediterranean buildings. The building hosts conferences and exhibitions, the latter open to the public; it was also the first headquarters of the Olympic organising committee. The area in front hosts outdoor concerts and events, while the complex of buildings to the east of the hall includes a restaurant, a café, Aigli (*see p135*), an outdoor cinema and a summer-only nightclub.

Evzones at the Parliament Building.

Sightseeing

Walk 2 Gardens and monuments

This three-hour route, ideal for an afternoon stroll, takes you through lush greenery, past some handsome historical sites and through one of the few central Athens districts to have preserved its traditional flavour.

The **National Gardens** (*see p83*), a cool sanctuary during the sweltering summer months, is the best place to start from. Enter the grounds next to the Parliament Building on Leof Vas Amalias and lose yourself in a refreshing set of towering palm trees, pines and cypresses, dotted with little bridges over brooks and shaded corners. At your exit, on the east side, a café with an ivy-covered terrace serves rather rough and ready fare, but is a nice shady place at which to have a rest and enjoy a cool drink.

Emerging from the park on to the immaculate Irodou Attikou – one of the most heavily policed streets in Athens thanks to its high-ranking residents – is an abrupt reality check. Directly opposite the exit, on your right, are the **Maximos Mansion**, the prime minister's official residence, and the **Presidential Palace** – both neo-classical structures. The latter – home to Greece's kings until Constantine left in 1967, and now used mainly for entertaining visiting dignitaries – is guarded by Evzones, who march solemnly towards each other at regular intervals.

At the south end of Irodou Attikou you will be arrested by the breathtaking vision of Athens' marble **Panathenaic Stadium**,

known as the Kallimarmaro (*see p96*). A 19th-century reconstruction of the ancient Olympic Stadium, it was the site of the first modern-day Olympics in 1896 as well as the 2004 Olympics archery competitions and the finish of the marathon.

To the left of the stadium (as you face it) you will find some steps leading upwards. Climb these and follow Agras around to the right until you reach the back entrance to the stadium. The more athletic can run around a gravel track tracing the fringe of the ancient stadium. Others can explore the maze of paths weaving through the lush greenery of pine-covered **Ardittou Hill**, whose summit offers sweeping views of Athens, reaching as far as the sea on a clear day. It's allegedly haunted by the ghosts of those murdered during the Nazi occupation of Athens, who were hastily buried here.

Emerging again from the stadium's back entrance, turn right and follow Archimidous. Turn right on to the stairs of Klitomachou to get a taste of one of Athens's oldest surviving neighbourhoods, **Mets**. Here are rows of pre-1940s houses, with tiled roofs and flower-covered balconies on ascending levels of an uphill slope, connected by little staircases. Klitomachou leads to Trivonianou, which will bring you to the striking Bauhaus-style entrance of the **Athens First Cemetery** (*see p96*). This graveyard, with its huge monuments to famous Greek writers, actors and politicians,

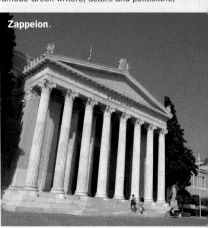

Zappeion.

National Gardens.

also houses the works of Ianoulis Halepas, the famous belle époque sculptor from the Aegean island of Tinos. His masterpiece, *I Koimomeni* (*Sleeping Girl*), is around 300 metres (330 yards) in on the right.

Leaving the cemetery, drop down a block, then turn right and walk along Evg Voulgareos until you reach Markou Moussourou, one of the most beautiful and historic streets in the neighbourhood. Walk down Markou Moussourou until you reach Ardittou; cross it and adjoining Leof Vas Olgas to reach the southern edge of the park. Take a moment to look to your left and admire from a distance the **Temple of Olympian Zeus** (*see p83*) – the largest temple ever constructed

in Greece, which now retains only a few of its columns. On the same site, but in a somewhat better state of preservation, is **Hadrian's Arch** (*see p83*).

Unless you have the urge to explore these ancient landmarks, turn right into the park, where, around 150 metres (165 yards) further on, you will see the elegant **Zappeion** exhibition hall. Next door to the Zappeion is the **Aigli Bistro Café** (*see p135*), a favourite with politicians and their entourages. It also pulls in its fair share of aspiring actors, students and families on a weekend stroll. It's the perfect place at which to stop, rest and enjoy a good iced coffee and some people-watching.

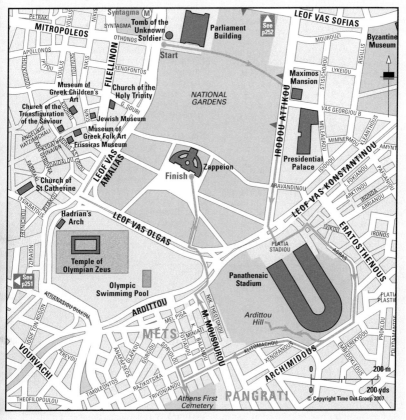

Kolonaki & Around

Lycabettus Hill looks down equally on the fashionable cafés and chic designers of Kolonaki, and the scruffy students and artists of boho Exarchia.

Sightseeing

Rising above the varied neighbourhoods of Kolonaki, Ambelokipi and Exarchia, taller even than the Sacred Rock of the Acropolis, **Lycabettus Hill**, topped with its little white chapel dedicated to St George, appears to have been transported from a distant Greek island. Indeed, its origins are garlanded with myth – it's said to have had a violent start to life as a rock thrown by the goddess Athena. Once the wilderness home to the wolves (*lykoi*) from which it probably got its name, it remains a forested outcrop, with paths winding to its summit 277 metres (908 feet) above sea level. It's also the stunning setting for the outdoor **Lycabettus Theatre** (*see p183*), with its summer festival lineup of world-class contemporary music, dance and theatre events, as well as a pricey restaurant and a café. Most visitors, however, come simply to take in the breathtaking panorama across the bustling city to the port of Piraeus, the Saronic Gulf and beyond. All this is accessible by road and on foot, but many opt for the **funicular** (210 722 7065), which runs every 30 minutes, 9am-3am daily, from the corner of Aristippou and Ploutarchou (€5.50 return). For walkers, the easiest route leads up from the ring road where Rogakou becomes Sarantapichou.

Since the mid 1800s, **Kolonaki**, which meanders around and up the southern slopes of Lycabettus, has indisputably been the tip-top address in Athens. The nobles and dignitaries who first settled near the Royal Palace (today's Parliament; *see p81*) and Embassy Row gave it its foreign, aristocratic air. Today it's home to the city's top designer shops and most fashionable cafés, as well as block after block of neo-classical mansions and gracious apartment buildings housing all manner of wealthy people,

from diplomats to pop stars. This is the place in which to people-watch and spend money – though it's possible to enjoy Kolonaki just by strolling along its tree-lined streets, browsing its art galleries and window shopping.

Kolonaki

Map p252

Metro Evangelismos or Syntagma.
Kolonaki's hub is **Platia Kolonaki** (*see p89* **Chic to cheek**). This small square hums with activity generated by the cafés and shops lining its edges. Radiating off the square are some of Athens' best streets for shopping and socialising: start on Tsakalof, Anagnostopoulou or Patriarchou Ioakim for boutiques, and Milioni or Skoufa for cool places at which to imbibe caffeine or cocktails. In the midst of the designer stores, the **Greek Costume Museum** (*see p87*) is devoted to what the locals of yesteryear were wearing.

Heading uphill (and we do mean up) towards Lycabettus, you'll reach the quieter **Platia Dexamenis** – home to a couple of café-restaurants, the swish **St George Lycabettus** hotel (*see p50*), a playground, plus one of Athens' best outdoor cinemas, the **Dexameni** (*see p170*). Several art galleries line its perimeter. If you're here on a Friday morning, walk up Xenokratous to visit one of Athens' oldest produce markets, where immigrant housekeepers and pearl-wearing old ladies bargain together at the stalls – a reminder that even in this most genteel of neighbourhoods, the old-fashioned village *laiki agora* (peoples' market) still thrives. North of Platia Dexamenis is the stately **Gennadius Library** (Souidias 61, 210 721 0536, www.ascsa.edu.gr/gennadius), the largest private collection of anything written in Greek. Only bona fide researchers may use its reading room, but its free lectures (November-May) on Greek history and the history of art are open to the public.

To the south, Kolonaki is bordered by the boulevard of Leof Vas Sofias, home to Athens' Museum Row: from west to east, you'll first come across the **Benaki Museum** (*see p87*), then the **Museum of Cycladic Art** (*see p87*), and the **Byzantine** (*see p82*) and **National War** museums (*see p83*). Finally, around the corner on Leof Vas Konstantinou, you'll reach the **National Gallery** (*see p96*).

Benaki Museum

Koumbari 1 & Leof Vas Sofias (210 367 1000/ www.benaki.gr). Metro Syntagma. **Open** 9am-5pm Mon, Wed, Fri, Sat; 9am-midnight Thur; 9am-3pm Sun. **Admission** €6; free Thur. **No credit cards**. **Map** p252 G5.

Housed in the gorgeously restored mansion of the wealthy 19th-century Benakis dynasty, this pre-eminent collection of Greek art and artefacts spans the eras from antiquity to the 20th century. Don't miss the sumptuous gold Hellenistic jewellery, the Byzantine shrines or the intricate re-creations of Ottoman-era sitting rooms. There are temporary exhibitions as well. The gift shop is a destination in itself, offering exquisitely reproduced ceramics and jewellery.

Greek Costume Museum

Dimokritou 7 (210 362 9513). Metro Syntagma. **Open** 9am-2pm Mon-Fri or by appointment. Closed Aug. **Admission** free. **Map** p252 G4.

This boutique-sized museum devoted to the history of clothing and fashion is located in the midst of Kolonaki's designer clothing shops. The 25,000 dresses and accessories include centuries-old folk costumes from every region of Greece, and copies of Minoan, Byzantine and classical Greek fashions.

Museum of Cycladic Art

Neofytou Douka 4 & Irodotou (210 722 8321/ www.cycladic-m.gr). Metro Evangelismos. **Open** 10am-4pm Mon, Wed-Fri; 10am-8pm Thur; 10am-3pm Sat. **Admission** €5; €2.50 Sat. **No credit cards**. **Map** p252 H5.

The world's largest collection of Cycladic art is one of Athens' must-sees. While Greek sculpture reached its pinnacle with the Parthenon Marbles, the first seeds in that tradition had been sown some 2,000 years earlier in the Cycladic Islands of the Aegean. There, between 3200 BC and 2200 BC, a matriarchal culture flourished that produced a unique art form featuring elegant, angular marble female figures – forms that inspire even today's artists. The museum also owns a collection of classical pottery, and the adjoining Stathatos Mansion, a Bavarian-style neo-classical building designed by Ernst Ziller, where contemporary exhibitions are held. The gift shop sells exceptionally fine reproductions.

Exarchia & beyond

Maps p249 & p252

Metro Victoria or Omonia.

Bohemian **Exarchia**, for all its grit and grime, holds a place in the heart of every Greek, as evinced by its frequent mention in songs, novels and films. Situated between the university and the polytechnic, the district has drawn students and intellectuals to its cafés since the mid 19th century (*see p89*

Chic to Cheek). The headquarters of left-wing parties and anarchist groups followed, establishing Exarchia as the perennial epicentre of progressive thought and political ferment. Most significantly in recent history, it was here, in 1973, that the students of the **Athens Polytechnic** (*see p88*) rose up against Greece's hated military dictatorship. Many of those students went on to become prominent left-wing politicians. While the front of the polytechnic is often filled with students and demonstrators passing out leaflets against the latest Western imperialist offence, its neighbour is usually fronted by shiny tour buses disgorging hundreds of people, all there to see one of the essential sights of Greece: the **National Archaeological Museum** (*see p90*), home to the mythical treasures of Mycenae, the sculptures of classical masters and much more.

A good street at which to see life in action in Exarchia is **Kallidromiou**, where you'll find a cluster of small cafés favoured by locals and intellectuals. Saturday mornings see this narrow thoroughfare transformed into one of Athens' busiest outdoor markets. Rising above Kallidromiou is **Strefi Hill**, a pocket (though

National Archaeological Museum. *See p90.*

Market stall on **Kallidromiou**. *See p87.*

hardly pristine) woodland with a couple of summertime tavernas where you can feel magically transported from concrete to forest. On pedestrianised **Valtetsiou**, especially in the evening, you have your pick of lively cafés, bars, all manner of eateries or a film at the open-air **Riviera** cinema (*see p170*).

Walking east towards Lycabettus you come to **Neapoli**, the 'new city' that grew up (literally) in the early 1900s to accommodate the faculty and students of the university. There are some pretty niches but, sadly, its charming beaux-arts, neo-classical and village-style houses continue to be razed for apartment blocks. It does, however, offer some venerable tavernas, art cinemas, experimental theatres and *rembetadika*.

Further along, sprawling east of Lycabettus Hill, is **Ambelokipi**, a bustling, densely packed district. Its name, meaning 'grape arbours', betrays its rural origins; it was once full of vineyards supplying Athenians with wine. Ambelokipi has no tourist sights or museums, but it does have a number of good restaurants, tavernas and cinemas, as well as several trendy nightspots.

North of Exarchia, across Leof Alexandras, is **Pedion Areos**, Athens' largest park. Its proximity to Exarchia makes it frequently the site of political rallies, book fairs and free concerts. However, its location in a slightly run-down area means that the park has a growing number of homeless people and a decreasing number of maintenance workers;

definitely not the place for an evening stroll. That said, it's still spacious and green, decidedly welcome qualities anywhere in town.

Athens Polytechnic

Patision & Stournari. Metro Victoria. **Map** p249 F2.
The date that resonates most deeply in the heart of Greeks is 17 November 1973, when thousands of students at the Athens Polytechnic rose up in protest against Greece's military junta. The colonels countered with guns and tanks, killing at least 33 students. Though the day was one of the darkest in modern Greek history, it was also the turning point leading to the overthrow of the dictatorship the following year. The students' bravery is commemorated with a monument in the courtyard, which Greeks of all walks of life turn out to cover with flowers each year on that date. The anniversary is also marked by a mass, union-organised march and demonstrations (*see also p80* **Demo-crazy**) – often ending in exchanges of Molotov cocktails and tear gas between anarchists and police.

Epigraphical Museum

Tositsa 1 (210 821 7637/www.culture.gr). Metro Victoria. **Open** 8.30am-3pm Tue-Sun. **Admission** free. **Map** p249 F2.
Located on the ground floor of the National Archaeological Museum (*see p90*), with a separate entrance from the pedestrian street that runs between the museum and the polytechnic, this collection of inscriptions includes a 480 BC decree by the Assembly of Athens to flee the city before the Persian invasion; a sacred law concerning temple-worship on the Acropolis; and a stele with the Draconian laws on murder.

Chic to cheek

Nothing betrays Athens' origins as a collection of villages more than the neighbourhood square, or *platia* – the hub around which all local life revolves. The city *platia* is the place in which to talk business and current affairs but, mostly, to just linger. One glance at the café-sitters tells you all you need to know about the nature of the place and its people, and nowhere is this more obvious and striking than in two of the city's foremost *platias*. Though barely a mile apart, Platia Kolonaki and Platia Exarchia are worlds apart in style and attitude. What they do have in common, aside from passionate devotees, is a spirited parallel past and a unique enduring present. Both also underwent Olympic-era reconstruction, much to residents' dismay.

Platia Kolonaki (whose official name, Filikis Etairias, is known only to postmen and historians) is now a neo-kitsch sampler of concrete nooks and crannies and (mostly out-of-order) fountains and waterfalls. The design has not been improved with the addition of portrait busts of historical figures. Fortunately, its live inhabitants are among the best turned-out in Europe. Tucked under the trees on the square's southern edge is the unassuming 'little column' for which the district is named; the British Council stands opposite. During the day, Platia Kolonaki is where business deals are made, the morning's papers perused, the latest scandal discussed and tomorrow's media stars discovered. After dark, it's flooded with young execs and singles eager for action. You'll see some elegant elders too, faithful patrons of the landmark cafés and their vintage waiters.

When you've had your fill of chic and long for a bit of cheek, head for Platia Exarchia, about 20 minutes away. To best experience the transition from glam to grit, head north-west towards Exarchia on **Skoufa**, which changes names a couple of times along the way (to Navarinou, then to Tzavella). Glittering cafés soon give way to sombre bookshops, and pristine façades become poster-plastered and covered with defiant graffiti. When you can go no further, you'll be at Themistokleous, which runs along the south-east edge of **Platia Exarchia**; turn right, grab a souvlaki at Kavouras and check out the *platia* scene. Its cafés and bars are filled with students and old-time lefties, but you're just as likely to see businessmen or taxi drivers having a drink. Don't worry if you're approached by down-and-out figures asking for change or a cigarette; they're harmless and won't mind if you say no.

Platia Exarchia's colourful streetlife happily overcomes the square's recent facelift, which looks like it might have been designed by an Iron Curtain planner on a good day. Overlooking the square, the Bauhaus-style building housing the Floral café looks a bit tatty, but this was Athens' first apartment block, the 'blue apartment house', built in 1932-33 in the new spirit of communal living. During World War II, it served the Greek Resistance.

Off the square is a mix of scenically decrepit neo-classical houses, apartment blocks daubed with graffiti and scores of shops, artisanal book binderies, purveyors and makers of musical instruments, home-style tavernas and some of the best places to hear *rembetika*, the Greek blues.

National Archaeological Museum

Patision 44 (210 821 7717/www.culture.gr).
Metro Victoria. **Open** *Apr-15 Oct* 1-7.30pm Mon;
8am-7.30pm Tue-Sun. *16 Oct-Mar* 10.30am-5pm
Mon; 8.30am-3pm Tue-Sun; 8.30am-3pm holidays.
Admission €7; €3 concessions; free some Sundays.
No credit cards. Map p249 F2.

This is one of the world's major collections – so plan
to spend the greater part of the day here to properly
appreciate its astounding array of treasures. If you're
pressed for time, you can hire an English-speaking
guide for a one-hour tour of the highlights (from €50
for groups of five or less; book in advance).

The best way to tackle the museum is chronolog-
ically, starting on the ground floor in the narrow
Gallery 5, at the left of the central hall (Gallery 4).
Here you will find Neolithic artefacts from 6800 to
3300 BC, the time of the first documented settlements on the Acropolis. Exhibits include pottery
and household objects, clay figurines, tools and a
hoard of fabulous gold ornaments confiscated from
plunderers in the late 1990s.

Then head across the central hall to the Early
Cycladic room (Gallery 6), to survey the remarkably
contemporary-looking female figurines. The most
impressive of these is the girl on the right of the door,
at 1.52m (5ft) the largest known example, preserved
complete from around 3200 BC.

Next, enter the central gallery (no.4), home to some
of the museum's most celebrated finds, the
Mycenaean antiquities. Renowned warriors who
fought the Trojans with the aid of Athena in *The
Iliad*, the Mycenaeans flourished between 1600 and
1100 BC. Homer described their citadel, overseen by
King Agamemnon, as 'well-built Mycenae, rich in
gold.' This was thought to be myth until German
archaeologist Heinrich Schliemann unearthed their
settlement in 1876. The astonishing hoard he found
included a gold death mask (originally believed to
be Agamemnon's but later dated to the 16th century
BC, long before the king's lifetime), a perfectly
preserved 16th-century BC gold diadem and the
15th-century BC golden Vaphio cups.

When you've had your fill of gold, make for the
sculptures in the outer circle of the museum's maze.
Galleries 7 to 13 (left) are full of *kouroi* from the seventh to fifth centuries BC. These statues of youths and
maidens were the first monumental works in Greek
art. The earliest are stiff and stylised, but following
the forms through the centuries, you can see artists
learning to depict the body more naturalistically.

Galleries 14 to 28 contain some of classical Greece's
greatest sculptural achievements. Most classical
sculptures were made in bronze, and later melted
down and used for tools and weapons. Among those
that survive – mostly thanks to shipwrecks – is the
famous 460 BC sculpture of either Poseidon or Zeus,
poised to hurl (depending on who it is) a trident or
thunderbolt. There are also several later marble
copies of bronze originals, such as the athlete bind-
ing his hair, a 100 BC copy of a bronze made by the
renowned sculptor Polycleitos in the fifth century BC.

These galleries also include an impressive array of
funerary sculptures. These became so sumptuous, as
families competed to create showier monuments, that
they were eventually banned in 317 BC. In the midst
of all this marble, is perhaps the most celebrated
exhibit in the museum: the bronze Artemision race-
horse and its child jockey. Made around 140 BC and
retrieved in pieces from a shipwreck off Cape Artemis
on Evia, its sculptural detail is so lifelike that the animal's straining muzzle appears almost damp with
sweat. Whether the boy actually belongs with this
horse is the subject of debate.

The final sculpture galleries (29 to 33) contain
Hellenistic statuary dating from the second century
BC to the first century AD. Having started your tour
of Greek sculpture viewing stiff, archaic monuments,
here you can see how far the discipline has come, with
sculptures full of movement and sensuality.

Before going upstairs, make a detour left through
the Bronze Collection (galleries 36 to 39) to trace
the course of metalworking in antiquity from 3000
BC to the first century BC. The majority of bronzes –
statuary of all sizes and themes, vases and tripod
cauldrons – were dedications in the major Greek sanctuaries that, like Olympia, were multipurpose centres
for worship, healing and athletic competition. This
also explains the assortment of medical instruments
and commemorative weaponry. Especially fascinating is the famous Antikythera Mechanism (80 BC); its
workings and function are still under scrutiny, but
scientists believe it was a calendrical device. The
collection culminates with the Helenistic 'Lady of
Kalymnos' (second century BC), whose discovery in
1994 and restoration is documented in detail.

The upper floor hosts the vase collection, a vast
chronological survey of ancient pottery production
and trade from the 11th century BC to the Roman era.
From fine, angular, geometric patterns to curvilinear
motifs, followed by the incised detail of the Archaic
black-figure style and the naturalistic red-figure ware
of the Classical period – nothing tells us more about
ancient Greek life and thought than vase painting.
In addition to providing narratives of mythology,
warfare, worship, sport and daily activity, classical
potters also signed their work, enabling today's
archaeologists to track ancient trade routes. Classical
Athenian vase painters were highly skilled at endow-
ing their figures with mood, character and action.

Finally, climb the short flight of stairs to marvel at
the superb display of wall paintings and artefacts
from prehistoric (16th century BC) Akrotiri, on Thera
(present-day Santorini). Videos show the early excavations of the site and the restoration of the famous
frescoes whose entombment under volcanic ash preserved them in near-perfect condition. The scenes of
boxing children, antelopes and crocus gathering are
remarkable for their innovative imagery, spirited
design, naturalistic representation and rich colours.

For sustenance after this visual feast, the museum
has just opened a café-restaurant overlooking the
sculpture garden. Next door, the gift shop sells cards,
replicas of statues and jewellery. *Photo p87.*

North of the Acropolis

Ancient roads lead to the city's latest hotspots.

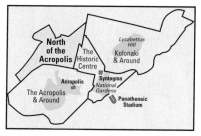

Described by the historian Thucydides in 430 BC as 'the most beautiful quarter outside the city walls', ancient **Keramikos** was a tranquil, cypress tree-filled area in the valley of the Eridanus river. It was divided roughly in half by the fifth-century BC Themistoclean Wall: the inner zone was where potters produced the famous ceramics for which the region was named, while the outer edge was the site of the state cemetery, the burial ground for the dead of the Persian wars and notable Athenian males.

The wall's two key portals were the Dipylon, which led to Plato's Academy, and the Sacred Gate, which led to Eleusis. The gated sections fronted two important roads, the Panathenaic Way that leads to the Acropolis, and the Sacred Way (or Iera Odos), along which worshippers of Demeter and Persephone would pass to hold secret initiation rites on Eleusis. The neighbourhoods around the roads took on a more rough-and-tumble identity typical of the edge of a town: prostitutes made alfresco assignations with soldiers; moneylenders, wine sellers and other shady dealers gathered to do business. More recently, it became home to a chaotic flea market, humble workshops and hashish dens.

Now this area and its surrounding neighbourhoods are emerging as the hippest entertainment districts in Athens, thanks to new high-end restaurants, trendy cafés, hip artists' studios and clubs. The new Keramikos metro stop, which opened in late spring 2007, has also been a huge boon to the area, making public transport exceptionally convenient.

The hub of this renaissance is known as **Gazi**, after the former gasworks that once powered the city, which has now been refashioned as the multi-use **Technopolis** arts complex (*see p94*). The Gazi effect is reaching out to include the gritty but regenerating neighbourhoods of **Metaxourgio** (once home to the city's silk factories), Keramikos and **Rouf**. Metaxourgio and Keramikos are multi-ethnic – a small Chinatown lies between the two, for instance – but some patches also recall a bygone Athenian era of grand neo-classical residences and cobblestoned streets. Now, developers and artists are buying up decrepit old buildings and remodelling them into lofts, theatres, shops and chic ethnic restaurants.

The area immediately around Technopolis, home to workers from the gasworks at the beginning of the 20th century, has also bloomed since the mid 1990s. Along its signature street, Persefonis, are some of the city's most modern, always-busy restaurants. The main thoroughfare of Pireos is rapidly transforming itself from industrial wasteland into a hot entertainment strip. Further along Pireos to the south-west is the revitalised neighbourhood of **Rouf** and its cultural anchor, the Benaki Museum's excellent **Pireos Street Annexe** (*see p94*), with intelligent, erudite exhibits of mainly contemporary art.

To the south-east of Keramikos is **Psyrri**, which for years was a dark, scruffy quarter of workshops and craftsmen's studios. Some of these are still active, but even before Gazi became popular they were being joined by innovative galleries, restaurants, nightspots and hole-in-the-wall music joints, making this one of the centre's hottest places to go out.

Psyrri

Map p249
Metro Monastiraki or Thissio.
Wander around **Psyrri** in the daytime, and you'll see glimpses of an Athens of yesteryear: elderly, black-clad women shuffle along, hunched over bags of shopping from grocery shops that exude the scent of mothballs; old men in suits sit outside crumbling, once-fine neo-classical houses overrun with stray cats; hawkers carry poles festooned with fluttering lottery tickets; street vendors sell feather dusters or fresh fruit, and roasted chestnuts from barrows. Tiny corner stores tend to specialise heavily – one sells just plastic flowers, another carnival costumes, and a third walking sticks and little leather animal

Sightseeing

Cultural remains from the on-site museum at **Keramikos**.

harnesses. As the streets approach the main thoroughfare of Evripidou, things start to get more multicultural: Sikhs gather to exchange news at pavement curry houses; Chinese traders sell bargain clothing from hastily set-up shops festooned with red lanterns.

By night Psyrri is entertainment central, with everything from traditional Greek *bouzoukia* to fashion-police-patrolled clubs and tiny, jazzy, smoky bars. Much of the action centres on the three squares of Iroon, Agion Anargyron and Agion Asomaton (home to the **Benaki Museum of Islamic Art**; *see below*), where cheery tavernas, hipster-filled outdoor cafés and sleek DJ bars cluster around old churches.

Benaki Museum of Islamic Art

Agion Asomaton & Dipylou (210 325 1311/www. benaki.gr). Metro Monastiraki. **Open** 9am-3pm Tue, Fri-Sun; 9am-9pm Wed. **Admission** €5; €2.50 concessions; free Wed. **No credit cards**. **Map** p248 D4.

In two gloriously restored neo-classical mansions on the edge of Psyrri is this world-renowned collection of Islamic art. Antonis Benakis (also founder of the outstanding Benaki Museum; *see p87*) spent much of his life in Egypt, where he painstakingly amassed this 8,000-piece collection, now displayed over four floors. Exhibits hail from regions of the old Islamic world as diverse as Spain and India, and date from the early days of Islam up until the 19th century. Items include an impressive collection of ceramics – ranging from 11th-century Fatimid pieces from Egypt to a colourful 16th-century Ottoman bowl from Iznik in modern Turkey, decorated with the then mega-fashionable tulip. From the early Islamic period a stand-out piece is a pair of carved doors

from eighth-century Mesopotamia. Don't miss the exquisitely detailed tenth-century gold belt from Samarra, in modern Iraq; a 14th-century universal astrolabe, the only known surviving piece of medieval astronomical equipment of its kind; and a series of 19th-century Iranian daggers in gem-encrusted or painted ceramic cases that manage to make even such deadly instruments look beautiful. The café on the top floor has magnificent views not only over Keramikos, but also of the Acropolis, Philopappus and its observatory, the hills surrounding Athens and the sparkling Saronic Gulf.

Keramikos

Map p248

Metro Keramikos or Thissio.

Until recently, Athens' tranquil classical cemetery was bounded on two sides by hectic, polluted thoroughfares. Visitors to Keramikos had to venture at their peril down the narrow pavement of roaring Pireos before, thankfully, slipping through the gate into the quiet oasis.

Since the Olympics, the Unification of Archaeological Sites walkway (*see p63* **Stepping stones to the past**) has made the approach to Keramikos a lot more pleasant, and the area itself is transforming from a lonely-after-dark dud to a vibrant urban centre. Wander down from the Acropolis on the cobbled promenade, passing cafés full of lively young people, cross the train tracks at Thissio metro station, then, keeping the beacon of Technopolis ahead, follow the railings around the edge of the Keramikos site along Ermou until you reach the entrance, usually guarded by a few stray dogs.

The art of sustenance: the café at the **Benaki Museum, Pireos Street Annexe**. *See p94.*

Keramikos

Ermou 148 (210 346 3552/www.culture.gr). Metro Keramikos or Thissio. **Open** *Oct-Mar* 8.30am-3pm daily; *Apr-Sept* 8am-7.30pm daily. **Admission** €2; €1 concessions; free to holders of €12 Acropolis ticket. **No credit cards. Map** p248 C4.

Peaceful, green Keramikos, with its daisies, grassy hillocks, butterflies and tortoises, has been many things during its long life: shrine, city gates, hang-out of prostitutes and soldiers, artists' quarter and the oldest and largest cemetery in Attica. What these uses had in common was that they were all suited to a site on the edge of the (ancient) city. The site's name derives from the prevalence of potters' work-shops on the grassy banks of the river Eridanus, which cut through the site and marked the north-west boundary of ancient Athens. In 478 BC that boundary was built in stone with the construction of the Themistoclean Wall around the entire city (the wall's foundations still mark the outer edges of Keramikos). Despite being built in haste, in fear of a sudden enemy attack, the walls were studded with grand gates. At the south-west edge of the site are the remains of the Dipylon Gate, the main entrance to Athens and the largest gate in ancient Greece. The roads from Thebes, Corinth and the Peloponnese led to this gate, and many ceremonial events were staged here at important arrivals and departures.

To the south-east is the Sacred Gate, reserved for priestesses to pass through on the Sacred Way (Iera Odos) to Eleusis, to perform ancient Greece's most important religious rites, the mysteries of the god-dess of agriculture, Demeter, and her daughter Persephone. Along the sides of the sacred road grew Athens' main cemetery, resting place for war heroes and wealthy statesmen; it was definitely prestigious to be buried here, as shown by the many elaborate tombstones. The earliest tombs are probably the seventh-century BC tumuli – high, round burial mounds built to honour great warriors. But 200 years later, the classical Athenians decided they wanted a lot more than just mounds of dirt, hence the showy monuments. The most distinctive of these is the fifth-century BC marble bull on the tomb of Dionysios of Kollytos, a man praised for his good-ness, who died unmarried, mourned by his mother and sisters. The tomb of Dexileos, who died in 394 BC, shows a sculpture of the young man astride a rearing horse, while the lovely fifth-century BC stele of Hegeso shows the departed woman, seated on the right, taking a trinket from a box held by her maid.

As on the Acropolis, many of the sculptures that are exposed to the elements are copies, with the orig-inals displayed in the small but fascinating on-site Oberlander Museum. The museum also contains other fabulous cultural remains like pottery shards depicting erotic scenes, used in a brothel once on the site, and bits of marble carved with curses, which people would slip into the graves of their enemies.

Gazi & beyond

Map p248

Metro Keramikos or Thissio.

The area known as Gazi has its roots in the 1857 opening of a French gas firm's Athenian factory. The gasworks operated until the 1980s, often spewing black exhaust into the surrounding area, coating buildings and leaving a pervading stench. But in the 1990s the municipality helped redesign the premises into an arts centre called **Technopolis**, located at the crossing of Ermou and Pireos streets. Today the gasworks' chimneys are a landmark, illuminated with red coloured lights that draw arty types to the complex's concerts and galleries. The revival of the once-sooty surrounding streets has been complete: Persefonis, Technopolis's southern border street, is home to some of Athens' sleekest restaurants, and the smaller roads off it are full of theatres, arts spaces and cool bars.

Pireos, the long avenue leading from Omonia Square towards Piraeus, has enjoyed a new lease of life. Among its highlights are the new **Benaki Museum, Pireos Street Annexe** (*see below*), in the district of Rouf, and the **Foundation of the Hellenic World** (*see below*), housed in a converted factory on the edge of Rouf. Arts space **Athinais** (*see below*), also a converted industrial space, lies further west. South of Rouf are the vast old factories of **Tavros**. Though not easy to get to, their sheer size seems to have inspired several transformations into nightclubs and party spaces.

To the north-east of Gazi, in **Metaxourgio**, modish ethnic restaurants and restoration projects are replacing the junk shops and brothels around Dourouti Square. One of the most interesting developments in the area is **Metaxourgeio** (Akadimou 14-16, 210 523 4382, www.metaxourgeio.com), a beautiful complex – instigated by Greek actress Anna Vagena and her singer-songwriter husband Loukianos Kilaidonis – with a theatre, an Edward Hopper-themed bar, a music studio and a bistro.

Athinais

Kastorias 34-36, Rouf (210 348 0000/www.athinais. com.gr). Metro Keramikos. **Open** *Exhibition hall* 9am-10pm daily. **Admission** free. **Map** p248 B3.
Athinais exemplifies the best of the industrial-to-arts conversions that are transforming the area's landscape: the former silk factory on the outskirts of Rouf is now a sophisticated arts complex housing Greece's only Museum of Ancient Cypriot Art, with treasures dating from the ninth century BC, as well as gallery spaces, a concert hall, a theatre and a cinema. It also has two excellent restaurants – the lush Red and the more affordable brasserie Votanikos – and the sleek Boiler Bar. Unfortunately, the complex, which is still swathed in its original 1920s stonework, has yet to have a knock-on effect on its run-down, out-of-the-way surroundings.

Benaki Museum, Pireos Street Annexe

Pireos 138 & Andronikou, Rouf (210 345 3111/ www.benaki.gr). Metro Keramikos. **Open** 10am-6pm Wed, Thur, Sun; 10am-10pm Fri, Sat. **Admission** varies. **No credit cards. Map** p248 A5.
The Benaki Museum's younger sibling was built to accommodate temporary exhibitions, but it also acts as an arts space for cultural events, from film screenings and theatre performances to poetry evenings

and concerts. There's a focus on photography, as seen in the massive exhibition in 2006 on the work of Greek photographer Voula Papaioannou, who meticulously documented the country during its tumultuous World War II and post-war years. Shows in 2007 have included a retrospective on the work of iconoclast Greek painter and sculptor Nonda, the post-war surrealist-symbolist sculptor Dimitras Armakolas, and a multimedia performance based on the myth of Prometheus. Designed by Maria Kokkinou and Andreas Kourkoulas, the building itself – a rust-red marble structure covering an entire block and housing an atrium lined with wooden blinds and steel mesh – is an architectural gem. The café is also very good. *Photo p93.*

Bios

Pireos 84, Keramikos (210 342 5335/www.bios.gr). Metro Keramikos or Thissio. **Open** *Café-bar* Oct-May 9am-2.30am daily. June-Sept 11.30am-2.30am daily. Call for performance & screening times. **Admission** free. **No credit cards. Map** p248 C4.
An art-grunge venue in a former Bauhaus building that serves as a brilliant showcase for the latest in cutting-edge music, digital and electronic art, Bios has become one of the only spaces for truly experimental artists in Athens. Its concerts, films and exhibits regularly attract crowds who want to explore the latest emerging talent, both Greek and international. *See also p192.*

Foundation of the Hellenic World

Pireos 254, Tavros (212 254 0000/www.fhw.gr). Metro Kallithea then 10min walk. **Open** *Mid June-mid Sept* 9am-4pm Mon, Tue, Thur, Fri; 9am-9pm Wed; 10am-3pm Sun. *Mid Sept-mid June* 9am-2pm Mon, Tue, Thur; 9am-9pm Wed, Fri; noon-6pm Sat; 10am-4pm Sun. **Admission** free.
This vast, multi-purpose space is a fantastic use of a converted factory; it's now a cultural centre that is devoted to multimedia and virtual reality exhibits on ancient Greece. These take you through sound-and-light tours of ancient Miletus, the Temple of Olympian Zeus (*see p83*) and the ancient Olympics. There's also abundant theatre and gallery space, which is often used for educational programmes.

Technopolis

Pireos 100, Gazi (210 346 0981/www.culture.gr). Metro Keramikos. **Open** 9am-9pm daily. **Admission** free. **Map** p248 B4.
The City of Athens bought this abandoned gasworks and helped finance its conversion into a huge, multi-purpose arts and performance space: an attractive urban landmark. The Technopolis buildings preserve their original industrial lines, and make an excellent home for everything from exhibitions of cartoon art to avant-garde theatre to rave concerts. The one permanent exhibit is the Maria Callas Museum, a small collection of the diva's personal items, including a handful of photos, mementos and costumes. If you visit the museum during the day, you'll need to find someone in the central office to let you in.

It's a gas

On any given weekend, you'll find gritty-chic Gazi packed with Dior-dressed diners, arty bohemians lingering over ouzo and mezedes after a trip to the Benaki Museum's **Pireos Street Annexe** (*see p94*) or to the **Breeder** gallery (*see p173*), and adrenalised revellers gyrating to revved-up music at bars and clubs such as **GazArte** (Voutadon 32-34, 210 345 2277), **Glam Bar** (Elasidon & Dekeleon 40, 210 342 2554), **Mad** (Persefonis 53, 210 346 2027) and other venues. For Athenians who have grown weary of the crowds at Psyrri and the pretentiousness of Kolonaki, Gazi and its surrounding area have become the new hotspot for arts, music, dining and let-your-hair-down fun. And the new Keramikos metro station has made access to the area simple.

Gazi's new identity only came together in the last few years, after a combination of public, private and artistic forces resurrected what had been one of the most forlorn corners of the capital: a sooty, dirty and crumbling expanse of pockmarked old buildings, abandoned warehouses, gloomy blocks of badly built flats and weed- and rubble-filled lots that were home to starving stray cats.

The nucleus of the area is the gasworks that opened in 1857. By the early 20th century, a settlement had grown up in the surrounding area to house workers from the plant that became known as Gazohori or 'Gas Land'.

When the city finally closed the works in the 1980s, the neighbourhood seemed destined for a life of obscurity. Eerily empty after dark, it represented everything that had gone wrong

in Athens in the 1970s and '80s: as much of the city centre became increasingly polluted, unattractive and uninhabitable, Athenians fled for the suburbs. Much of central Athens was virtually ignored by planners until the city began preparing for the 2004 Olympics and started to worry about its image. At this point, the City of Athens, the Greek state and several plucky entrepreneurs and artists put their money into Gazi and its environs.

The most telling sign of that transformation is the former gasworks itself, which has been revamped as arty **Technopolis** (*see p94*). It has caused a ripple effect in Gazi and beyond: developers are building luxury loft apartments, drafting plans for shopping centres and rehabilitating neo-classical houses. In the meantime, artists are taking advantage of still-reasonable rents to run thriving contemporary art spaces such as **Bios** (*see p94 & p192*).

Polite company once shunned the adjoining artery of Pireos, which for decades was a drab drag populated mainly by lorries lugging industrial supplies. Flanked by ugly warehouses and car workshops, the only entertainment was to be found in strip clubs and the gaudy bouzouki clubs known as *skyladika*, (literally, 'the place of the dogs', because of the singers' predilection for howling into the microphone). The most visible sign of the thoroughfare's change of fortunes is the **Pireos Street Annexe** of the Benaki Museum (*see p94*), an architectural landmark, with interesting contemporary art, a shop showcasing Greek design and a fantastic café. Further signs of a brighter future include Lefteris Lazarou's Michelin-starred restaurant **Varoulko** (*see p124*), which has swapped Piraeus for Pireos, moving in next to the sleek **Eridanus** hotel (*see p52*).

Appropriately, given the area's rising reputation for nightlife, it's after dark, when Technopolis's defunct smokestacks glow crimson, illuminating an area once considered the most bedraggled in Athens, that you can see just how far Gazi's star has risen.

Sightseeing

Greater Athens

The bigger picture.

Greater Athens sprawls across a central plain, often referred to as the Attica Basin, which is surrounded by mountains. This geographical position is partly responsible for the city's temperatures and high pollution levels. But even this crowded city has oases – spots perfect for relaxation, quiet walks and enjoying the Mediterranean sun. With the herb-scented, flower-filled rambles of Mount Hymettos, the soothing, medicinal waters of Lake Vouliagmeni, the people-watching possibilities of Kifissia's posh, tree-lined streets and the seaside promenade that overlooks the glittering Saronic Gulf, greater Athens offers a whole new insight into Athenian life and leisure.

East Athens & eastern suburbs

Maps p251 & p252
Metro Akropoli, Evangelismos or Syngrou-Fix.
To the east of central Athens, just beyond the Zappeion Gardens and the Temple of Olympian Zeus, the ground starts to rise into the foothills of **Mount Hymettos**. The elevated eastern suburbs run along most of the 16-kilometre (ten-mile) length of the mountain. Most of these are fairly ordinary residential neighbourhoods, with **Pangrati**, the district closest to central Athens, the most interesting to visitors. Further up the mountain, you can take a break from smoggy central Athens with a walk on trails scented with wild herbs.

Pangrati

Within a 15-minute walk from Syntagma Square, Pangrati is one of Athens' oldest areas. For most Athenians, it is somewhere to enjoy shopping or a frappé at one of the numerous cafés along **Ymittou**. But there is an important ancient site here too. Pangrati's dominant feature is the huge, marble **Panathenaic Stadium**, rebuilt in the 19th century. To the south-west of the stadium is the steep but lovely street of **Markou Mousourou**, shaded by flowering trees and filled with the scent of jasmine and bougainvillea from the balconies of the surrounding neo-classical buildings. Markou Mousourou borders **Mets**, one of Athens'

prettiest residential neighbourhoods. Heading up Markou Mousourou and then turning right on Trivonianou, you'll reach the entrance of the tranquil, shady and fascinating **Athens First Cemetery**. *See also p84* **Walk 2**.

Athens First Cemetery
Anapafseos & Trivonianou (210 922 1621). Metro Akropoli or Syngrou-Fix, then 10min walk. **Open** sunrise-sunset daily. **Admission** free.
A walk in the city's largest cemetery is like a tour through modern Greek history. Athens' most famous are buried here, many in lavish tombs. They include actress, culture minister and national heroine Melina Mercouri, War of Independence hero Theodoros Kolokotronis and Nobel laureate George Seferis. Sculptor Yiannoulis Chalepas created the *Sleeping Beauty* statue on the tomb of Sophia Aphentaki.

National Gallery
Leof Vas Konstantinou 50 (210 723 5937/ www.nationalgallery.gr/www.culture.gr). Metro Evangelismos. **Open** 9am-3pm, 6-9pm Mon, Wed; 9am-3pm Thur-Sat; 10am-2pm Sun. **Admission** €6.50; €3 concessions. **No credit cards.** **Map** p252 J5.
The highlight of Greece's finest art gallery is a collection of El Greco's masterpieces. In 2007 the museum hosted international exhibitions showcasing Botero, Cézanne and Picasso, among others.

Panathenaic Stadium
Leof Vas Konstantinou (210 752 2986/www. culture.gr). Metro Akropoli or Evangelismos.
Open phone for details. **Admission** phone for details; free to holders of €12 Acropolis ticket. **Map** p252 G7/H7.
Note: At time of writing, the stadium could only be seen from the outside. It is expected to be open to the public by late August 2007. Opening hours should be the same as for other archaeological sites.
This enormous marble stadium, which boasts a seating capacity of around 50,000, was originally built in 330 BC to host the first Panathenaic Games. It later fell into ruins, and much of its marble was used for the construction of other buildings. In the 19th century it was rebuilt to host the first modern Olympics (1896). The reconstruction used marble from nearby Mount Penteli, famed for its beauty – hence the stadium's nickname, Kallimarmaro, meaning 'beautiful marble'. The marble was meticulously cleaned and restored for the 2004 Olympics, during which the stadium hosted the archery competition and marathon finish. The shady path around the top of the stadium is popular with local joggers, especially on cooler summer evenings.

Athens Olympic Sports Complex. *See p98.*

Mount Hymettos

A magnificent natural backdrop to the creeping suburbs of eastern Athens, Mount Hymettos is the nearest and arguably the most pleasant place to escape Athens' urban jungle. Its gentle slopes are traced with paths that wind through pine forests, dells of flowering bulbs and acres of scrubland dotted with indigenous herbs and wandering tortoises. But even if you never set foot on it, you can enjoy one of Hymettos' most famed qualities: at sunset, a spectacular display of rosy hues illuminates the mountain, starting off a soft pink and deepening to a vivid purple as the evening wears on. This phenomenon has been admired since antiquity, with the fifth-century BC poet Pindar describing the hill as '*iostephanos*' or violet-crowned.

The ancient Greeks believed the mountain was the original source of honey. It's not hard to see why. Honey from the mountain's abundant wild herbs – fragrant thyme, sage and lavender scent the air and make any walk up here a treat – is still considered among the finest in Greece.

Kaisariani Monastery

Ethnikis Antistaseos, Kaisariani (210 723 6619). Bus 223 or 224, then 20min walk. **Open** 8am-3pm Tue-Sun. **Admission** €2; €1 concessions. Free to all Sun Oct-Mar. **No credit cards.**

It's a mere 20-minute drive from Athens following the mountain road known as Ethnikis Antistaseos, but this Byzantine monastery on pine-clad Mount Hymettos feels a world away from the city. The monks still hold services in the two chapels, one built in the 11th century, the other 500 years later.

Have a wander around the fresco-filled sanctuaries and feel free to taste the spring water gushing from the ram's-head fountain (it's said to boost fertility). Then, setting off through the picturesque 11th-century olive grove, follow one of the many mountain trails to get unrivalled views over the Attica basin and to breathe in the fresh, thyme-scented air.

Northern suburbs

Metro Irini, Kifissia, Marousi or Neratziotissa.
Heading north out of Athens, the boulevards of Leof Kifissias and Mesogeion run through increasingly expensive, spacious and leafy suburbs. Not that one could tell while driving on either road, though – they are filled with a huge, ugly build-up of randomly set shopping malls, business centres, supermarkets, neon signs and advertising hoardings. But behind this façade are neighbourhoods like **Paleo Psychiko**, with graceful neo-classical buildings, old flowering trees and diplomats' residences, and **Papagou**, which is mainly populated by former military officers.

Athens' northern suburbs are framed by mountains – Tourkovounia to the west, Penteli to the north, Hymettos to the east. That means the wealthy residents who get to live in their foothills have space, clean air, greenery and a different climate from the denizens of central Athens – in winter, these districts may see up to 30 centimetres of snow, while downtown sees nary a flake. The bowl created by the mountains is also the reason that the city's infamous pollution ends up trapped in the lowland city basin.

The two suburbs of most interest to tourists are **Kifissia**, 16 kilometres (ten miles) from central Athens, and **Marousi**, 12 kilometres (7.5 miles) from the city. The former is an attractive, wealthy, tree-lined district full of parks, cafés, posh shops, outstanding restaurants and two museums. Marousi is home to the Santiago Calatrava-designed **Athens Olympic Sports Complex**, the 2004 Olympics' main venue.

Kifissia

Formerly a cool summer resort for Athens' wealthiest citizens, who built airy neo-classical holiday homes along its neat, tree-lined streets, the prestigious northern suburb of Kifissia still retains the same qualities that made it so appealing to its earlier inhabitants.

By far the easiest way to get to Kifissia is on the Line 1 metro, which terminates here. Walking out of the metro, you'll head up Adrianou, which flanks a pretty park filled with cafés. Continuing up the street, you'll pass Leof Kifissias to enter the commercial centre of the area. This is focused around Kassaveti, Kolokotroni, Kyprou and Georganta streets, all lined with prestigious shopping malls, restaurants, nightclubs, expensive designer shops and the chicest people-watching cafés.

Gaia Centre

Othonos 100 (210 801 5870/www.gnhm.gr). Metro Kifissia. **Open** 9am-2.30pm Mon-Sat; 10am-2.30pm Sun. **Admission** €5; €3 concessions. *Gaia Centre & Goulandris Museum of Natural History* €7; €4 concessions. **No credit cards.**
The Gaia Centre is part environmental research lab, part edutainment. The Centre, affiliated with the

Glyfada.

Museum of Natural History (*see below*) down the street, has three floors of well-made displays on ecosystems and the environment, including plenty of interactive video, computer and tactile displays. There's an exhibition on solar power, where you can cover and reveal the sun with varying degrees of cloud to see how fast it will run an engine; a touch-screen game where you can try to make your organic crop succeed on its own or by using pesticides; and a laser-light rotating-globe show every hour. The exhibits, designed in association with London's Natural History Museum, are well made and a hit with children, but most of the information is in Greek.

Goulandris Museum of Natural History

Levidou 13 (210 801 5870/www.gnhm.gr). Metro Kifissia. **Open** 9am-2.30pm Mon-Sat; 10am-2.30pm Sun. **Admission** €5; €3 concessions. *Gaia Centre & Goulandris Museum of Natural History* €7; €4 concessions. **No credit cards.**
The extensive, excellently researched exhibition on Greece's rich natural wildlife makes the Museum of Natural History a fitting stop in leafy Kifissia. The displays include insects, mammals, birds, reptiles, shells, rocks, minerals and fossils. The botanical collections have over 200,000 species of Greek plants, 145 of which have been discovered and recorded only recently, thanks to the museum's research.

Marousi

One of the twelve Athenian municipalities during classical times, Marousi has always been overshadowed by Kifissia. It wasn't until the end of the 20th century that the residential area was transformed, with the development of the **Athens Olympic Sports Complex** and the other big Olympic projects. Construction continues, with vast new shopping centres like the gigantic **The Mall Athens** (35 Andrea Papandreou), plus low-rise, high-rent office buildings, and entertainment parks. Proximity to the Sports Complex has also brought more prominence to the nearby **Museum of 20th Century Design**.

Athens Olympic Sports Complex

Leof Kifissias 37 & Spiros Louis (210 683 4777). Metro Irini. **Open** 8am-8pm daily. **Admission** free.
The main, multi-stadium complex for the 2004 Olympics has long been Athens' biggest venue for sports and music events. Dating from 1979, it was given an extensive facelift for the Games, including the famous glass and steel roof designed by Spanish architect Santiago Calatrava, and completed in the nick of time. *Photo p97.*

Museum of 20th Century Design

Patmou 4-12, Design Plaza (210 685 0611/ www.designplaza.gr). Metro Irini. **Open** 9am-6pm Mon, Wed; 9am-8pm Tue, Thur, Fri; 10am-3pm Sat. **Admission** free.

This may once have been the most random museum in Athens: a stylish collection of furniture, lamps and interior design pieces by distinguished figures of art and architecture of the 20th century (Salvador Dalí, Le Corbusier, Philippe Starck and Antoni Gaudi), located next to a football stadium in a far-flung suburb of the city. But now that the stadium is a landmark Olympic monument by Santiago Calatrava, it's all beginning to make some weird kind of sense. If you're at the stadium and inspired to see some more good design, it's a worthwhile place to visit.

Syngrou & southern suburbs

Metro Faliro or Piraeus; tram from Syntagma; buses A2, E2, E22 from Panepistimiou.

Syngrou runs from central Athens south to its coastal suburbs and beaches. It can be pretty ugly – home to a haphazard smattering of big-box buildings, abandoned or run-down blocks of flats (many built to house Greek refugees when they fled from Asia Minor in 1923; *see p20* **All change**) and commercial centres – though more recent developments including hotels, a conference centre and a multiplex cinema have given it a bit of polish.

A lot of those big-box structures are home to some of the largest nightclubs and *bouzoukia* in town. As with much in Athens, there's a quirky appeal to making your way through an arbitrarily gritty area, then suddenly finding yourself in one of the most wildly posh nightclubs in the Mediterranean.

Once the road hits the coast, things improve. The busy Leof Posidonos, named after the god of the sea, runs along the coast through the wealthy seaside suburbs of **Faliro**, **Glyfada**, **Voula** and **Vouliagmeni**. The locals have taken to calling this area the 'Athenian Riviera'. It's lined with clean, well-maintained public and pay-per-visit beaches (*see pp103-106*), all invariably full of the requisite topless, thong-clad bathing beauties.

Between the beaches are huge, luxurious seaside nightclubs (*see p190* **Summer clubbing**), which entertain Athens' party people during the summer. Like their city-centre equivalents, these spots are huge, seasonal, pricey and trendy, but have the added advantage of open-air beachfront locations. Some are open all day, to lounge and have coffee in their stunning settings. Many have decks that go right up to the water, pools, gauzy draperies and model-perfect waiting staff. All heat up after midnight, when long lines of designer-clad wannabes wait for admission from the fashion police at the doors.

Before the Olympics, major changes were made to this coastal area. Of most importance was the opening of a tram line from central Athens branching off to Neo Faliro and Glyfada,

meant to shorten and ease the trip from the city to the seaside and the Olympic venues at Faliro and Helliniko. Although the tram earned lots of complaints in its early days, mainly about its slow speed, and the annoyance of vehicles obstructing the lines, it is nowadays a real benefit to permanent residents of the southern suburbs as well as to beach-goers.

Battleship Averoff

Trocadero Marina, Paleo Faliro (210 983 6539/ www.bsaveroff.com). Tram from Syntagma (Trocadero stop)/metro Piraeus, then bus 909 to Oulen stop. **Open** *Oct-May* 9am-1pm, 3-5pm Mon-Fri; 10am-2pm Sat, Sun. *June-Sept* 9am-1pm, 6-8pm Mon-Fri; 10am-2pm, 6-8pm Sat, Sun. **Admission** €1.50. **No credit cards**.

The 10,200-ton steel-plated armoured battle cruiser *Averoff* famously played a decisive role in the Balkan Wars as well as in both World Wars, before being decommissioned in 1958. In 1983 the Hellenic Navy undertook the decision to restore it and declared the ship a national monument. It is moored at the Trocadero Marina, restored to its original state and operating as museum. Berthed next to the *Averoff* is the reconstructed trireme that was used to bring the Olympic flame into Piraeus in summer 2004. This vessel, a handmade replica of a 2,500-year-old Greek warship, is powered by 170 oarsmen. She has toured the Greek islands and even been as far as London.

Evgenidio Planetarium

Syngrou 387 (entrance from Pentelis 11), Paleo Faliro (210 946 9600/www.eugenfound.edu.gr). Bus 126 from Sina & Panepistimiou. **Open** 5.30-8.30pm Wed-Fri; 10.30am-8.30pm Sat, Sun. **Admission** *Feature film presentation* €8; €5 concessions. *Digital presentation* €6; €4 concessions. **No credit cards**. Completely refurbished, the Evgenidio Planetarium shows documentary films on stars and planets on its overhead domed screen. Commentaries for the films and exhibitions are in Greek, but earphones with English translations are often available.

Lake Vouliagmeni

Leof Posidonos, Vouliagmeni (210 896 2239). Bus E22 from Sina & Panepistimiou, Limni stop. **Open** *June-Sept* 7am-7.30pm daily. *Oct-May* 8am-4.30pm daily. **Admission** €7. **No credit cards**. Vouliagmeni (meaning 'sunken') is a fascinating geophysical phenomenon as well as a beautiful lake. Set inside a huge jutting rock on the inland side of the coast road, its blue-green mineral-infused waters come partly from the nearby sea and partly from a deep, but still unknown, freshwater source. What is known is that the water stays at around 24°C (75°F) year round, making this a popular spot for winter bathing. The waters are said to have positive effects for conditions such as rheumatism, which explains the preponderance of genteel, elderly, bathing-capped crowds. They also appreciate the small spa facilities, attractive landscaping and old-fashioned café on one bank.

Piraeus

The liveliest port in the Mediterranean.

The gateway to hundreds of Greek islands, Piraeus is not only the busiest port in the Mediterranean but one of the busiest in the world. The chaotic central harbour of yore has been scrubbed up and organised, but it remains active from dawn until dusk as thousands of passengers and hundreds of ships come and go. During the morning rush hour, cars, taxis and scooters vie to reach the quayside and crowds of passengers besiege ticket offices. For some, this frenzied hubbub is invigorating. For others, the port is not really somewhere to linger in – just long enough to down an iced coffee while waiting for your ship to start boarding. But if you do find yourself stuck here for a few hours, waiting for the next boat, the port – and its environs – have a lot to offer.

Thousands of years ago, Piraeus was an island. Even after the thin channel that separated it from the rest of Greece dried up and Piraeus rejoined the mainland, it took another 1,000-odd years before the great Athenian general Themistocles recognised the peninsula's potential as Attica's best-situated natural harbour in the fifth century BC. Until

then, Athenians had moored in the bay of Faliro, today a wealthy seaside suburb.

Themistocles had his new port built up to accommodate Athens' many ships, but his most impressive accomplishment was the construction of the **Long Walls** in 478 BC. The fortifications, which surrounded the entire port and ran all the way back to the city of Athens, are still the most striking remains in Piraeus today; walking around, you are likely to come upon the fenced-off foundations of the walls.

In medieval times, the port became known as 'Porto Leone', after the colossal stone lion that guarded its entrance. The lion was removed in 1688 and taken to Venice, where it remains.

By the 19th century, Piraeus was a busy, fast-growing city. In 1923 it grew even more, as the Greek-Turkish population exchange brought thousands of refugees from Asia Minor to Greece, many settling in Piraeus. The port became known as a colourful but seedy place, full of hashish dens and dives where the Greeks from Turkey sang gritty *rembetika*, a type of music developed in the 1920s and '30s whose lyrics describe the joys and sorrows of society's

Kastella and Mikrolimano harbour.

poor and dispossessed. This image persisted into the mid century, immortalised in Jules Dassin's movie *Never on Sunday*, in which feisty blonde star Melina Mercouri (who later became minister of culture and remains a national heroine) plays a lively prostitute with a heart of gold who loves to swim in the harbour. These days, however, the murky waters of Greece's main port are anything but inviting.

Today, Piraeus has grown in size and has acquired a character distinct to that of Athens. Pireots consider themselves a world apart from their stressed-out Athenian counterparts.

The streets surrounding the railway station at Piraeus are an incongruous mix of shipping firms' offices, pawn shops and food outlets of varying quality. On Sundays, you will find the **Piraeus Flea Market** sprawled out along the streets of Alipedou and Skylitsi. A walk through this proletarian district, with many post-war building and storefront signs still preserved, will eventually lead you to Piraeus's must-see **Archaeological Museum**, housing the bronze sculptures of Athena and Artemis that graced the port in Themistocles' day.

South of the museum are Piraeus's two smaller and more scenic harbours, **Zea Marina** and **Mikrolimano**. The larger of the two is Zea Marina, also known as Pasalimani; this is the harbour for yachts plying the Saronic Gulf islands. It is lined with buzzing cafés and bars, and is also home to the **Hellenic Maritime Museum**. The fish tavernas of atmospheric

Mikrolimano (also known as Tourkolimano) attract the most tourists, and with good reason. For coffee, cocktails and good food, Istioploiko (Akti Koumoudourou, 210 413 4084), next to the Yachting Club on the southern arm of the bay, is a lively place. Behind Mikrolimano rises the pretty neighbourhood of **Kastella**, Piraeus's most fashionable district, lined with attractive, narrow streets and pastel-hued neo-classical mansions. Its bars on Leof Vas Pavlou offer great views; Don Quixote, at no. 68 (210 413 7016), is one of the most popular.

Archaeological Museum of Piraeus

Harilaou Trikoupi 31, Zea Marina (210 452 1598/ www.culture.gr). Metro Piraeus. **Open** 8.30am-3pm Tue-Sun. **Admission** €5. **No credit cards**.
This museum is home to some of the most magnificent works of classical Greek art in existence. The greatest pieces by the Greek classical sculptors were generally made in bronze, but few survive, as most were melted down for weapons or tools in the intervening centuries. Some, however, were lost in the waters of Piraeus, where they stayed, perfectly preserved, for centuries, until they were found during an underwater excavation in 1959. The marvellous bronze statues of Athena, Apollo and Artemis are among the most stunning finds showcased at the museum, which has recently undergone renovation.

Highlights of the collection include a brilliantly sculpted and perfectly intact bronze of Athena, believed to date either from the fourth century BC or from a first-century BC sculptor imitating the earlier classical style. Either way, it is a masterpiece,

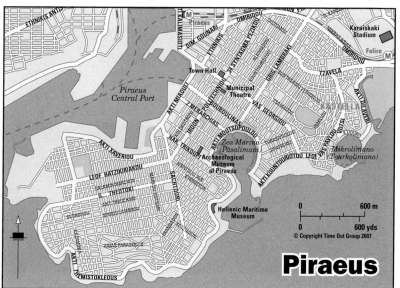

with a noble, helmeted head and a sash made of writing snakes, and bearing the head of Medusa. Another must-see here is a well-sculpted bronze of Apollo, believed to date from around the sixth century BC, two lovely bronzes of Artemis and a perfectly intact fourth-century BC bronze tragic mask, with a wild, snaky beard, sunken cheeks and dramatically dismayed eyebrows.

Don't miss a large fourth-century BC shrine to the mother of the gods, with the goddess seated on a throne with a lion next to her. The museum also contains what may have been the largest funerary monument in ancient Greece. Built by a merchant from Istria for his son, the piece is the size of a small temple, with larger-than-life sculptures of the merchant, his son and their servant surrounded by friezes of Greek heroes. It was the lavish ostentation of pieces like this that led to the banning of funerary monuments in Athens in 317 BC.

Hellenic Maritime Museum

Akti Themistokleous & Freatidas, Zea Marina (210 451 6264/www.culture.gr). Metro Piraeus, then bus 904. **Open** 9am-2pm Tue-Sat; 9.30am-2pm Sun. **Admission** €3; €1.50 under-18s. **No credit cards.**

From Odysseus to Aristotle Onassis, the nautical world has always been fundamental to Greece's psyche. The 2,500 exhibits at this museum begin with models of prehistoric ships, and include sophisticated ancient navigation equipment, paintings, maps, flags, guns and models galore.

Getting there

For the main port of Piraeus, take metro Line 1 (ISAP). For Zea Marina, take the metro to Piraeus, then bus 904. For Mikrolimano, take the metro to Piraeus, then trolleybus 20.

Cafés and fish tavernas line pretty **Mikrolimano** harbour. *See p101.*

Beaches

The sea and sand draw overheated, overstressed Athenians to the southern shores – and not only in summer.

Most international visitors head to the islands for some beach life, but few are aware that just south of Athens lie kilometres of clean coastline perfect for bathing – the nearest just half an hour or so from the city centre. What better antidote to a hot climb up the Acropolis than to hop on a tram or bus and set off for the seaside?

The mild Greek climate means water temperatures are fairly temperate most of the time and many locals are year-round swimmers, swearing by regular dips as a way to stay fit.

The beaches closest to Athens fall into two categories: publicly maintained free beaches, which are open all year, and privately managed beaches, open from mid May to mid September and charging an entrance fee. Private beaches make up the great majority, and have the advantage of providing amenities like umbrellas and sunloungers, changing cabins, WCs and a cold rinse-off shower. Some private beaches are almost like sports clubs, with tennis courts or watersports facilities; many have a snack bar or mini market, and often a children's playground.

While private beaches are the most comfortable option, there are so many nooks and crannies along this line of coast that it is possible to escape the fenced-off enclaves and find a spot to call your own for the day.

Athens' beaches are at their most crowded on summer weekends. It's no use coming out later thinking the masses will have moved off. These days many avoid peak hours and head for a swim after 6pm in summer, while others prefer a dip before noon. This guarantees huge vehicle congestion along the coastal road of Leof Posidonos all day, almost every weekend in summer. Buses or trams are a slow but sure transport option, while taxis will often refuse to go down the coast for fear they may get stuck in a traffic jam.

Beaches usually close at sunset regardless of their stated 'official' hours. Sadly, midnight dips aren't an option except on public beaches; privately managed beaches are closed (and usually locked up) at night. Crime of any sort is still unlikely, but common-sense precautions like keeping an eye on your belongings apply. Your biggest problem is likely to be getting socked by a tennis ball from 'rackets' games, which are ubiquitous on all beaches.

The best...

The following beaches are listed in geographical order, from north (Faliro) to south (near Varkiza). For beaches further from the city, see p206 **Drive-by beaches**.

Edem Beach
Leof Posidonos, Paleo Faliro. Tram from Syntagma ('Edem' stop)/bus A1, B1, B2, E1, E2, 101, 217, X96. **Open** 24hrs daily. **Admission** free. ❶
Athens' most urban beach may not be its best, but it is certainly the most convenient. Set in the seaside suburb of Faliro, Edem is skirted by an attractive promenade running between the coast and Leof Posidonos. The long beach, which is mostly sandy but has a few pebbles to contend with, is flanked at one end by a couple of tavernas, while the other end stretches towards the rather seedy Flisvos area (the redeeming feature of which is a very pleasant open-air cinema). Since the beach is publicly managed, it is free of charge and largely a self-service experience. But the Hotel Poseidon (which is actually located over the road but operates the Poseidon taverna and beach bar on the sand) offers private beach facilities (with sunbeds, drinks service, changing room, shower and a lifeguard), while the nearby Edem taverna serves reasonably priced meals to hungry beachgoers. If driving, be aware that parking is notoriously difficult in the Paleo Faliro area. You're much better off taking the tram from Syntagma: it stops right at the entrance to the beach.

The best Beaches

For a beach-side temple
Astir Beach, see p106.

For long stretches of sand
Attica Vouliagmeni Beach, see p106.

For peace & quiet
Agios Kosmas, see p104.

For sports & facilities
Asteria, see p105.

For style by the sea
Varkiza Beach, see p106.

Agios Kosmas

Off Leof Posidonos, Elliniko (next to the Ethniki Athlitiko Kentro/National Athletic Centre, turn off at the sign marked 'Agios Kosmas beach'). Tram from Syntagma ('2nd Agios Kosmas' stop)/bus A1, A2, B1, E1, 140. **Open** *Mid May-mid Oct* 9am-9pm. **Admission** free. ❷

Slightly off the beaten track, but worth it, and actually quite easy to get to by tram, Agios Kosmas hit the news in spring 2007, when the mayor of the municipality went on a hunger strike to force the formerly privately run beach to open to the public. Greek law gives the right of free access to the sea, and the mayor argued that this stretch of coast had no access. One of Athens' smallest, most tasteful and peaceful beaches, it feels in some ways more like a sleepy island resort than an Athens 'scene' beach. The water is clean and boosted by an extra filter and barrier in place to deal with environmental pollution. Facilities, and the beach itself, are generally well maintained, but it has yet to be seen how well public maintenance will work. The toilets are especially

Astir Beach. *See p106.*

modern and clean; the outdoor showers less so. A small garden is available for a little shade, and there is also a snack bar. Next door, the vast expanses of concrete are reminders of the 2004 Olympic sailing events. This was where crews launched their vessels and viewers sat to watch the action.

Asteria

Entrance on Leof Vas Georgiou B, between Platia Katraki Vasos & Platia Kritis, Glyfada. Tram from Syntagma (get out at Glyfada on Metaxas then walk down to the sea, or at 'Palia Dimarhio' stop then walk along the coast)/bus A1, A2, E2, 114, 116, 149, X96. **Open** *Beach* Mid May-mid Sept 8am-9.30pm daily (last entry 8pm). Lifeguards on duty until 8pm. *Pool area* Mid May-mid Sept 10am-7pm, 9pm-3am daily. Closed mid Sept-mid May. **Admission** *Mon-Fri* €7; €3.50 concessions. *Sat, Sun* €10; €5 concessions. *Parking* €5 cars; €2 motorbikes. ③

With door staff who act like bouncers, landscaped gardens and a nightclub, Asteria feels like an exclusive beach club. And although it isn't a private members club, it is the priciest Athens strand, and encompasses a giant complex and huge beach on a bay in Glyfada, with easy access from Athens city centre. With immaculate WCs, extensive dressing rooms, huge gardens, a playground, a volleyball court, a pool complex, a few shops, watersports (water volleyball, inner tubes and blow-up teetertotters) and several cafés, the Asteria is particularly popular with scensters and well-off families. Which is not to say the beach has a really refined or restrained quality about it; it can be as rowdy as any other beach and at high season can become a virtual sea of people. One of its unique features is the elegant pool area, surrounded by cabanas, which transforms into a combination of cocktail bar, café, lounge, disco and restaurant at night.

Voula A & Voula B

Leof Alkyonidon, Voula. **Open** *Early May-mid Sept* 7am-9pm daily. Closed mid Sept-early May. **Admission** €5; €3 concessions.
Voula A *Opposite Asklipeo Voula Hospital complex. Bus A1, A2, E1, E2, E22, 114, 116, 149.* ④
Voula B *Close to the Voula Dimarhio (town hall). Bus A1, A2, E1.* ⑤
Under the same management and just a couple of kilometres apart on the same thoroughfare, these two private beaches are nearly identical. Both are on the cheaper side, and tend to be less crowded than some of the other beaches. Both have generous grounds with gardens, generic snack bar and shops, plus facilities for sports such as beach volleyball. Voula A is directly next door to a large, pleasant beachside bistro-café, Palmie (meals around €20), while Voula B has tennis courts and has just finished building seven cute, one-room bungalows that can be rented out on a short-term basis during the summer. Surrounded by palm trees and looking out over the glittering sea, these little guesthouses are idyllic at sunset and sunrise when the beach is closed, but not so peaceful during the heat of the day.

Kavouri-Vouliagmeni

Parallel to Iliou, near Agios Nikolaos church, in the Kavouri district of Vouliagmeni. Bus E1, E2, 114, 116, 138, 149. **Open** 24hrs daily. **Admission** free. ⑥
The incredibly popular Kavouri-Vouliagmeni is a long stretch of sand near the Divani Apollon Palace hotel (*see p55*). This public beach is packed throughout the summer; if you can't find a patch of sand, join the others and play 'rackets' by the sea. Though this is a strictly self-service resort, there is a string of fish

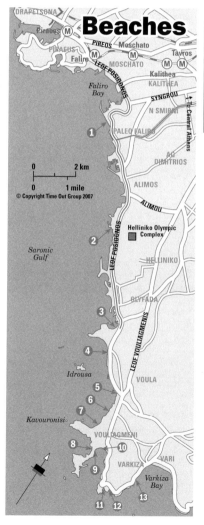

Sightseeing

tavernas (all rather upmarket) beside the beach, and some pleasant places for strolls amid them. The main problem here is space, so if there isn't enough, head to nearby Megalo Kavouri (*see below*).

Megalo Kavouri

Off Leof Kavouriou, in Kavouri district of Vouliagmeni. Bus 114 (get off at Strofi Kavouriou, a leafy square). **Open** 24hrs daily. **Admission** free. ❼
Although set in the middle of one of the most expensive areas in the Athens area, Megalo Kavouri has a casual, downmarket feel. The large beach includes a view of an ancient temple ruin on a tiny island opposite. Shallow waters mean it's a good place for swimmers who are less than proficient, which is probably why swarms of families flock here. Besides several nondescript, inexpensive cafés, no basic beach services are available (not even changing cabins or outdoor showers), but a shady, tree-dotted area just next to the beach makes for a great do-it-yourself picnic site. Parking is readily available.

Astir Beach

Entrance via Platia Aiglis, on Apollonos, Vouliagmeni Bay. Bus 114, 116 from Platia Glyfada. **Open** 8am-9pm daily. **Admission** *Mon-Fri* €11; €7 concessions. *Weekends* €17; €9 concessions. ❽
Open all year round, this popular though pricey private beach (also known as Asteras) attracts keen racket-players, winter swimmers and sunseekers. Set in a sheltered bay – with an ancient temple devoted to Apollo and the gourmet fish restaurant Ithaki on one flank, the Astir Palace Vouliagmeni (*see p55*) on the other – the beach gets an extensive range of watersports, beach volleyball and racketball areas, a bar and shop. And you might just spot Paris Hilton's one father-in-law-to-be jogging down the beach, as he's a regular and the town mayor. Parking in July and August is extremely difficult. Easy access for the disabled is a positive distinguishing feature. *Photo p104.*

Attica Vouliagmeni Beach

Opposite Platia Aiglis & next to Apollonos, Vouliagmeni Bay. Bus 114 from Glyfada. **Open** 24hrs daily. **Admission** free. ❾
Opposite the private Astir Beach (*see above*), this is the free part of Athens' largest beach. It may not boast an ancient temple, sports facilities or even sunbeds and umbrellas, but it does have a gorgeous view. The narrow stretch of sand definitely attracts a younger, alternative crowd, so if that doesn't sound like your thing, continue on to the privately managed section (*see below*), which, although virtually the same beach, has a separate entrance.

Attica Vouliagmeni Beach

On Vouliagmeni Bay. Entrance where Leof Athinas becomes Leof Posidonos, next to the Dimarhio (town hall) at Platia 24 Iouliou, Vouliagmeni Bay. Bus 114, 116. **Open** *Mid May-mid Sept* 8am-9.30pm (last entry 8pm) daily. **Admission** €5. ❿
Excellent value, and stylish to boot, the privatised part of Attica Vouliagmeni Beach is perhaps the best compromise between the high-frills Astir (*see above*)

and the free-for-all public Attica Vouliagmeni (*see above*). This well-organised beach is set on an enormous stretch of sand on Vouliagmeni Bay, perhaps the most beautiful part of the Athens' coastline. A low-ish admission fee offers visitors an elegant chaise longue and umbrella, snack bars, two small children's playgrounds, volleyball, tennis and basketball courts, and the usual amenities like changing rooms, WCs and open showers.

...and the rest

While not exactly proper beaches, **Agnanti** and **Lambros** (named after the eateries they are adjacent to), two mini-beaches opposite Lake Vouliagmeni, deserve a mention. These beaches, a stylish café and taverna flanking them, tend to be very windy, so are great for extra-hot days. However, they practically disappear in high tides. Both have shallow waters, making them good alternatives for those with little confidence in their swimming abilities. The beaches have no closing hours, and can be reached via bus 114 or 116 from Glyfada.

Limanakia A & Limanakia B

Between Vouliagmeni & Varkiza. Bus 116, 149, E2. **Open** 24hrs daily. **Admission** free. ⓫ ⓬
Resting on an otherwise nondescript stretch of Athens coastline that winds along to Sounion, these two are easy to miss, but well worth a stop if only to gape at the stunning bays, which are beautifully lit up at night. Descend one of the small dirt paths leading steeply downhill towards the rocks. Limanakia B (just a short walk from A) leads down directly towards a quiet, rather private area of the rocks. A section of this beach is a well-known gay nudist haven (*see p178*). The steep rocky path at Limanakia A descends towards a café built into the rocks, which offers access to the water below. There's a bona fide scene at the rocks, and the café-bar is bursting with teenagers and twentysomethings, and is host to all-day parties throughout the summer, as well as the local scuba club.

Varkiza Beach

Varkiza Bay. Bus 116, 125, 171. **Open** *Mid May-Sept* 8am-8pm daily. *Closed Oct-mid May.* **Admission** €12; €3 concessions. ⓭
You can't miss the vast, multicoloured modern 'Do It' beach bar-restaurant that marks the entrance to the recently renovated private part of this sprawling bay. Drop in for a cold coffee and to admire the orange Perspex walls and geometric white sofas straight from the pages of a design magazine, then join the beautiful people sunning themselves on the beach. Lifeguards, watersports, drinks service – you name it, they've got it at this hip and happening beach, which belongs to the Grecotel chain. Otherwise, head next door to the public part of the beach, where on windy days you can watch kitesurfers whisking perilously from one edge of the bay to the other.

Eat, Drink, Shop

Restaurants	**108**
Cafés	**133**
Shops & Services	**140**

Features

The best Restaurants	111
Taverna tips	114
Eating up the sights	116
Modern Greek	121
Fast food	124
The menu	126
Greek wines	130
The best Cafés	134
Café society	135
Beyond baklava	138
Where to shop	141
Walk 3 Following the (flea) market	146
Get the Athens look	150
Nature's beauty	158

Cellier Le Bistrot. *See p115.*

Restaurants

Whether you're looking for mama's cooking or the latest culinary twist, Athens goes down a treat.

Eating out – and eating outside – is an integral part of Greek culture; it's hard to overestimate the pleasure of a meal in a leafy garden or overlooking the moonlit sea on a summer evening. If you want to dine with the locals, make your reservation for late evening – Greeks hardly ever go out for dinner before 10pm.

The last decade or so has seen a renaissance on the Athens restaurant scene, with fine Greek dining coming into its own, star chefs making waves, and ethnic cuisine – everything from sushi to Indian – becoming the stuff of weekly outings for urban Greeks. More and more Greek chefs have trained abroad, and more and more are experimenting with the roots of their native cuisine, forging a new Greek culinary vernacular with exciting food based on traditional, regional ingredients. That's not to say, though, that tried and true traditional taverna fare still isn't a part of Greek dining; in fact, in recent years, even the taverna has been reinvented, with many places modern in look, traditional in menu, and always modest in price. Finally, as if to attest to the country's newfound culinary pride, four Athens restaurants, **Pil Poul et Jérôme Serres** (*see p111*), **Spondi** (*see p127*), **Vardis** (*see p130*) and **Varoulko** (*see p124*), have been awarded a Michelin star for their high standards.

TIMES AND PRICES

Making a table reservation is an absolute necessity, especially from Thursday to Sunday afternoon, in club-restaurants and in most upmarket restaurants in general. If you are in town around Orthodox Easter (*see p162*), or especially in the days surrounding 15 August, phone ahead, as most restaurants outside the touristy areas shut down for the holiday.

Your tip should be around 10 to 15 per cent on top of the bill (but check whether service is included). Be warned that the combination of good food and a great eating environment doesn't come cheap in Athens – although the comparatively high restaurant prices in these places don't seem to deter people. Seafood, in particular, is surprisingly expensive, and if it seems cheap, it's probably cooked from frozen.

TAVERNA TALENT

Eating at traditional tavernas and *mezedopolia* (*see p109*) is one of the best experiences Greece has to offer. Both serve the hearty, deeply flavourful dishes based on the precepts that have governed Greek cooking for centuries: fresh, seasonal ingredients, lots of extra virgin olive oil, local cheeses and a few fragrant herbs and spices. These are assembled sometimes with a wonderful simplicity – like *horta* (wild greens) with lemon. At other times there is an inspired creativity in the combination of ingredients – a hallmark of peasant cooking, where ingenious cooks must make the best of a limited range of foodstuffs. The winter classic, *stifado*, is a good example of striking combinations; in this traditional dish, rabbit is stewed with dark Mavrodaphne wine and dozens of tiny onions.

Tavernas are friendly, cheap and informal. They usually have cosy interiors, sometimes lined with wine barrels, outdoor gardens draped in bougainvillea and grape trellises, and cats winding their way around your chair legs. Many have no written menus, and even when they do, you'll often find that there's plenty of discrepancy between what's on the menu and what's in the kitchen. Usually, the waiter will just reel off what's cooking today, and you'll pick from his list.

There are three main types of dishes available: the first course, often shared, which includes *salates* (salads) and mezedes (small plates); grilled foods, mainly meats, such as ribs, chops, and Greek burgers and, of course, fish; and casseroles, called *mageirefta*, which comprise a whole list of classic one-pot dishes, often vegetarian, and baked dishes such as moussaka and *briam*, a baked summer vegetable medley. Salads tend to be seasonal, so expect the tomato-feta-cucumber trio known as *horiatiki*

Price guide

€ up to €20
€€ €21-€35
€€€ €36-€50
€€€€ over €50
For a meal for one including starter, main course and dessert.

Try **Kuzina** for playful, contemporary twists to traditional Greek cuisine. *See p112.*

(village salad) in summer; shredded cabbage and carrot salad in winter; and romaine lettuce and dill salads in the spring. Mezedes include the whole range of Greek dips, from the yogurt-garlic combo tzatziki to *fava* (a purée of yellow split peas topped with raw onions and often capers), and roasted aubergine spread). Vegetable fritters, such as those made with aubergine or tomatoes, crisp fried vegetables, small filo pies, *saganaki* (pan-fried cheese), small mint-flavoured meatballs, savoury bean dishes prepared with *gigantes* (Greek giant beans), black-eyed peas, chick peas and more are also standard fare. All this is accompanied with carafes of *hima* (local barrel wine) and, in the more touristy locales, with the serenades of strolling musicians. For advice on choosing a good taverna, *see p114* **Taverna tips**.

MEZEDOPOLIA AND OUZERIE

If you're in the mood to sample dozens of dishes in one sitting – and to drink a lot – head to a **mezedopolion**. These places serve mezedes, lots of small dishes, rather than large main courses, meant as an accompaniment to wine, ouzo and gossip. In some *mezedopolia*, ordering couldn't be easier. The waiter will come out with a large tray of all the dishes that are available, and you make your choice from those. In other establishments, you might pick from a menu or in the kitchen.

> ❶ Purple numbers given in this chapter correspond to the location of restaurants on the street maps. *See pp248-252.*

The best guides to enjoying London life

(but don't just take our word for it)

'More than 700 places where you can eat out for less than £20 a head... a mass of useful information in a geuinely pocket–sized guide'

Mail on Sunday

'Armed with a tube map and this guide there is no excuse to find yourself in a duff bar again'

Evening Standard

'I'm always asked how I keep up to date with shopping and services in a city as big as London. This guide is the answer'

Red Magazine

'Get the inside track on the capital's neighbourhoods'

Independent on Sunday

'A treasure trove of treats that lists the best the capital has to offer'

The People

Rated 'Best Restaurant Guide'

Sunday Times

Available at all good bookshops and timeout.com/shop from £6.99

100% Independent

Though the focus is ostensibly on nibbles to accompany your meal, most *mezedopolia* serve dishes just as well made and delicious as you'll find at a taverna. If it turns out this is your favourite way of eating – and it certainly has the advantage of allowing you to try everything – you can also turn your taverna experience into a meze feast. Simply order one of each of the salads and appetisers.

Mezedopolia are also known as *ouzerie*, as ouzo, the aniseed-flavoured spirit distilled from the remains of grapes from the wine press, is the traditional accompaniment. You'll also come across other members of the ouzo family: *raki* (the basic drink with or without the aniseed flavouring), *tsipouro* (smoother than ouzo) or *tsikoudia* (Cretan *raki* without aniseed). All are served with water and ice.

MAGEIRION
One last category of casual Greek dining establishments is the **mageirion**, where the classics of the home kitchen, especially the wonderful array of vegetable specialties, are the focus. In these low-key, informal restaurants, typically frequented at lunch by locals of all walks of life, you are expected to walk back to the kitchen where an open counter displays the day's specials, which you point to and choose. Wine is often siphoned straight from the barrel.

Acropolis & around

Creative

Pil Poul et Jérôme Serres
Apostolou Pavlou 51 & Poulopoulou, Thissio (210 342 3665/210 345 0803/www.pilpoul.gr). Metro Thissio. **Open** 8pm-12.30am Mon-Sat. **Average** €€€€. **Credit** AmEx, DC, MC, V. **Map** p248/p250 C5 ❶

All stately and classic, Pil Poul, arguably the most beautiful restaurant in Athens, with a million-euro view of the Parthenon, found its soul in the able, delicious, very haute cuisine of one-star Michelin chef Jérôme Serres. Serres creates a menu of Franco-Med delights, drawing on the best Greek ingredients but also on a considerable palette of raw materials from around the broader Mediterranean. Signature dishes include a stunning smoked foie gras crème brûlée with orange sauce, sea bream perfectly prepared and playfully presented with a few ouzo-spiked bonbons, and partridge risotto complete with an olive branch.

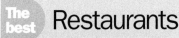

Restaurants

For contemporary Greek food
Humble taverna staples are treated with creative flair at **Apla** (*see p131*). **Hytra** (*see p125*) is a pioneer of Greek haute cuisine. **Rififi** (*see p119*) serves smart Greek dishes at palatable prices.

For old-school taverna food
Old-fashioned **Philippou** (*see p121*) offers great value for Kolonaki. There's top-notch taverna food at rock-bottom prices at **Nikitas** (*see p125*).

For ouzo
Ouzadiko (*see p119*) has dozens of varieties – and gorgeous Greek dishes to go with it.

For seafood
Thalatta's (*see p125*) location – in gritty Gazi – may seem incongruous, but the seafood is superb. **Milos** (*see p122*) uses the minimum of fuss and the freshest of ingredients. Simplicity is key at **Trata** (*see p127*), too, where fish is grilled to perfection. Athenians rush to the waterside to **Diasimos** (*see p132*) as soon as the sun comes out, or to **Varoulko** (*see p124*), considered by

foodies to be the most artful seafood around; while **Papadakis** (*see p119*) has made a name for itself as a place for elegant but homespun seafood, fish and traditional Greek food with a modern twist.

For top cuisine
There's a distinctive haute Franco-Med flair to the dishes prepared by Frenchman Jérôme Serres at **Pil Poul et Jérôme Serres** (*see p111*). Mezedes reach heights of gourmet splendour at **Pasaji** (*see p114*), and a superb wine collection goes with innovative Greek dishes at **48 The Restaurant** (*see p118*). Delicate and daring combinations rule at **Spondi** (*see p127*), while **Vardis** (*see p130*) has classic quality. Lefteris Lazarou demonstrates innovative skill with seafood at **Varoulko** (*see p124*).

For vegetarian food
Quirky **To Kouti** (*see p112*) has plenty to tempt vegetarians, as do traditional and modern tavernas of all stripes. **Aneton** (*see p130*), in the northern suburb of Marousi, is worth the trip for some of the most skillfully prepared veggie dishes in all of Athens.

Greek contemporary

Kuzina

Adrianou 9, Thissio (210 324 0133). Metro Thissio.
Open 1pm-12.30am Mon-Thur, Sun; 1pm-1am Fri,
Sat. **Average** €€. **Credit** DC, MC, V.
Map p248/p249 D5 ❷
Kuzina is the baby of one Athens' original bad-boy
chefs, Aris Tsnaklides, who brought Asian and
Pacific Rim flavours to this then-provincial scene
almost 20 years ago and lived through each and every
one of its fads until finally he, too, settled on what
mama knows best: Greek food, artfully presented,
authentic in spirit but playful in execution. Kuzina, a
bustling all-day restaurant in the heart of ancient
Athens, is the *mezedopolio* reborn. Tsnaklides takes
long-lost traditional dishes and transforms them,
magician-like, into the stuff of iconoclastic modern
Greek cuisine. His fig and ouzo pâté – for lack of a
better word for it – takes its cue from an old rural
Corfu dish. He marries ginger with Greek octopus
and produces one of the best Greek pasta dishes in
town, with lobster tail or langoustines piled over
Greek noodles that have been swathed in browned
butter, but now hug a cold hub of mascarpone in their
tangled embrace. Enjoy the bustle, the jars of preserves, and the new spin on old-world ambience and
cuisine that he has managed to pull off with verve.
Reservations are essential for dinner. *Photo p109.*

To Kouti

Adrianou 23, Monastiraki (210 321 3229).
Metro Monastiraki or Thissio. **Open** noon-1am
daily. **Average** €€. **Credit** AmEx, MC, V.
Map p249/p251 D5 ❸
All the restaurants along Adrianou have breathtaking views of the Acropolis and the Ancient
Agora, but most serve faux-Greek fodder. This boho
haunt painted in pretty pastels stands out from the
crowd. From the menus handwritten in picture
books to the rose petal ice-cream, this offbeat spot
is unabashedly romantic. If there is a moon rising
over the Acropolis, it's even more magical. Quirkily
named dishes are a bit hit-and-miss, but there are
lots of great vegetarian options like mushroom pie,
fluffy leek soufflé and pasta with gorgonzola sauce.
One specialty to look for is the beef braised in honey.

Greek traditional

Café Abyssinia

*Kinetou 7, Platia Avyssinias, Monastiraki (210 321
7047). Metro Monastiraki.* **Open** 11am-midnight
Tue-Sat; 11am-7pm Sun. Closed July, Aug. **Average**
€€. **Credit** MC, V. **Map** p249/p251 D5 ❹
Among the dusty china and antique furniture
strewn about Platia Avyssinias, the heart of the
Monastiraki flea market, Café Abyssinia has the
bohemian feel of a 1950s cabaret. Tiny tables are
squeezed among the market stalls, crowded with
locals tucking into mussels pilaf, northern Greek
stuffed cabbage leaves, cumin-scented ground meat

sausages, kebabs, dips, and the star dessert, large
Greek prunes filled with pastry cream. Starters are
generally better than main courses, though the giant
beefburger with red pepper relish is a crowd-pleaser.
For a quieter tête-à-tête, book a window seat on the
mezzanine, with dreamy views of cats prowling the
tin roofs, crowned by the Parthenon.

Giouvetsakia

Adrianou 144 & Thespidos, Plaka (210 322 7033).
Metro Akropoli. **Open** 10am-2am daily. **Average** €.
Credit MC, V. **Map** p251 F6 ❺
There is still a handful of authentic eateries in sou-
venir- and souvlaki-infested Plaka. This traditional
taverna, run with courteous service by the same family since 1950, is postcard pretty with its red-checked
tablecloths and ivy-covered walls. At the bustling
junction of Kydathinaion and Adrianou, it is the perfect spot for people-watching while you guzzle fried
aubergines dipped in tzatziki, Greek salad, tasty
stuffed tomatoes or classic moussaka. Giouvetsakia
is named after the house specialty, *giouvetsi* – a clay-
pot baked, tender hunk of lamb with *orzo* (small
pieces of pasta shaped like rice) and tomato sauce.
Try the home-made baklava for dessert or settle on
the complimentary fruit dusted with cinnamon.

Ikonomou

*Troon 41 & Kydantidon, Ano Petralona (210 346
7555). Metro Ano Petralona.* **Open** 8pm-1.30am
Mon-Sat. **Average** €. **No credit cards.**
Map p250 B6 ❻
If you want a glimpse of old Athens, a bit off the
beaten track but well known to city insiders (especially of a certain age and social standing), then this

Café Abyssinia.

is it. This taverna hasn't done much to its simple, homelike decor (or lack thereof) in decades, but that is part of the charm. Concentrate instead on the delicious traditional cuisine, as expressed in dishes like *stifado*, a meat stew fragrant with cinnamon and rich with dozens of whole, small onions; and lamb cooked in a thick, equally fragrant, tomato sauce. If rabbit's on the menu, grab it.

Therapeftirio

Kallisthenous & Kydantidon 41, Ano Petralona (210 341 2538). Metro Petralona. **Open** noon-1.30am daily. Closed Aug. **Average** €€. **Credit** MC, V. **Map** p250 B6 **7**
The residential neighbourhood of Petralona is full of unpretentious restaurants serving super home-style nosh. As well as plenty of seasonal vegetables and meat casseroles, Therapeftirio is well known among local gourmets for very fresh fish at friendly prices. Home-made taramasalata, *garides saganaki* (prawns sautéed with tomato and cheese) and pan-fried red mullet go down a treat with a steaming bowl of *spanakorizo* (rice with spinach and tomato) and an ice-cold beer. With cooking this good and service with a smile, it is easy to overlook the drab interior, especially if you can nab a table on the pavement under the orange trees.

To Paradosiako

Voulis 44A, Syntagma (210 321 4121). Metro Syntagma. **Open** noon-1am Mon-Fri; 11am-10pm Sat, Sun. **Average** €. **No credit cards.** **Map** p249/p251 F5 **8**
It would be easy enough to walk right past this hole-in-the-wall on the fringes of Plaka, with just a handful of tables squeezed on the pavement beside the parked cars. But it would be a shame to miss this great-value lunch spot smack in the centre of town but a world apart from the tacky tourist traps that litter the neighbourhood. Pull up a chair and tuck into delicious traditional dishes, like leek and carrot pilaf, baked chickpeas and whole grilled calamari.

To Steki tou Ilia

Thessalonikis 7, Thissio (210 342 2407). Metro Thissio. **Open** 8pm-1am Tue-Sun. **Average** €. **No credit cards.** **Map** p248/p250 C5 **9**
Situated on a peaceful pedestrian street that's only a few blocks away from the bustling cafés of Thissio, this home-spun grill-house is a mecca for thrifty carnivores, who keep coming back for the pièce de résistance: enormous platters of *paidakia*, char-grilled 'lamb chops' served with grilled bread drizzled in olive oil and oregano. The dish is best enjoyed with a simple salad of wild greens, garlicky aubergine purée, and a slab of feta. A second location, further down the street towards Thissio metro station, at Eptachalkou 5 (210 345 8052), is open Monday rather than Sunday.

Japanese

Furin Kazan

Apollonos 2, Plaka (210 322 9170). Metro Syntagma. **Open** noon-11pm Mon-Sat, 2-11pm Sun. **Average** €€€. **Credit** AmEx, DC, MC, V. **Map** p249/p251 F5 **10**
Furin Kazan is Athens' 'cult' sushi place, where locals come to read the paper, linger over lunch and savour some of the best sushi in town at some of the most affordable prices. There's also a selection

Taverna tips

There are hundreds of tips for finding a good Greek taverna, but only one vital piece of advice upon which your life, or at least your stomach, depends: go where the Greeks go.

Walk past a taverna where you don't understand a word being spoken by the people eating outside and you've found your place. Local Greeks invariably choose the best tavernas – by taste, value for money and atmosphere. Don't worry, entering a taverna full of Greeks is nothing like going into a tightly knit English pub.

Ninety-nine percent of the battle for a good meal is won before even entering the taverna. Once in, many tourists will be too polite to leave, however bad their meal. And there's little room for surprise. Tavernas tend to be uniformly bad, uniformly reasonable or uniformly excellent. Avoid places where someone outside is trying to drag you inside. Nearly always it's standard tourist fare – and possibly worse. Good tavernas let their cooking do the talking.

Recommendations from hotels are not always to be trusted, as staff may have a particular place to plug. If you're here for a few days, one option is to go for a small snack and see how you get on in a taverna before committing yourself fully. The strong-willed can take up the invitation of many tavernas, good and bad, to look at food in their kitchens, then leave without ordering.

Ignore set meals. They're not good value and, in some places, the food has already been served up on dozens of plates, waiting for people like you. Several outfits cater to the plate-breaking, bouzouki-dancing Greek stereotype. Have a good time by all means, but keep an eye on the bill.

To avoid being ripped off in tavernas, you must have a menu to see the prices. Fresh fish can be extremely expensive, as can bottles of wine. The taverna's own wine (ask for '*hee-ma*'), sometimes still served out of a barrel, is cheaper and usually perfectly acceptable. But when it's bad, it is bad.

Should you have a reasonable complaint, speak quietly with the waiter or, if still not satisfied, with the owner. Greeks don't like being confronted in front of others. If you're getting nowhere, seek the help of fellow Greek diners. They will very likely back you up. There's nothing like a good argument to end a nice meal.

of noodles, soups and other Japanese classics. This is somewhere best visited at lunchtime to feel the pulse of the city; unfortunately, it can be a little dowdy and dead at night.

Historic Centre

Creative

Pasaji
CityLink, Stoa Spyromiliou, Syntagma (210 322 0714). Metro Syntagma. **Open** 1pm-1am daily. **Average** €€. **Credit** MC, V. **Map** p249 F4 ④

This contemporary *mezedopolio*, with its gorgeous mosaic work and its enviable location in one of the city's most walked-through pedestrian stoas, is a newcomer to the city-centre restaurant scene. Here you will find decidedly upmarket versions of the Greek meze palette, from delicious, velvety *fava* (purée of yellow split peas) topped with caramelised onions and Santorini capers to tiny dried apricots filled with *kaimaki*, a thick cream made with buffalo milk that's a speciality of Anatolian Greeks. Delicately spiced, hand-made sausages, aromatic beef or lamb cooked in fragrant tomato sauce and served with creamed charred aubergine, hand-made pies and more make up the haute meze menu. It's the brainchild of one of Athens' only woman chefs, Nena Ismirnoglou, who takes her elegant home cooking to another level at Pasaji. For dessert, don't miss the strawberry semifreddo.

Tudor Hall
King George Palace, Vassileos Georgiou A3, Syntagma Square (210 322 2210). Metro Syntagma. **Open** 12.30-4.30pm, 7pm-midnight Mon-Sat. **Average** €€€€. **Credit** AmEx, DC, MC, V. **Map** p249/p251 F5 ⑫

Despite its pompous name, this grand restaurant on the top floor of the King George Palace hotel has nothing remotely medieval about it. Greek columns, fake chandeliers and gold brocade drapes provide the backdrop for middle-aged couples speaking in hushed tones. Professional waiters in bow ties and white jackets cruise the room (they should ditch the name tags – a giveaway that this is part of a hotel chain). In contrast with the decor, the excellent French cuisine is exquisitely unpretentious; the tone of the menu was set by the team of famed French chef Alain Ducasse. Specialties include lamb and rosemary fillet cooked *en croute* in a chick-pea coating; duck souvlaki with balsamic glazed onions served over parmesan polenta. A dense chocolate trilogy is an indulgence that should ease the pain of the *très haute* bill that is sure to follow.

French

Cellier Le Bistrot
Panepistimiou 10 (in the arcade), Syntagama (210 363 8525). Metro Syntagma. **Open** *Sept-May* 10am-2am daily. *June-Aug* 10am-6pm Mon-Sat. **Average** €€€. **Credit** AmEx, DC, MC, V. **Map** p249 F4/G4 ⑬
This stylish bistro could be in Paris. Waiters in waistcoats attend to bon viveurs surrounded by vintage French posters, giant mirrors and chandeliers. The exceptional wine list contains around 250 Greek and international labels, many available by the glass, plus special offers on top-quality bin-ends that change every couple of months. The food is equally excellent, from traditional dishes of the day to caviar, oysters, and superior salads. Don't miss the grilled halloumi cheese finished with brandy and the duck leg confit. Meals can end on a cool note, with a scoop of Madagascar vanilla ice-cream, or more typically Greek *kaimaki* ice-cream, flavoured with mastic and topped with sour cherry spoon sweets. *Photo p118.*

Greek traditional

Athinaikon
Themistokleous 2, Omonia (210 383 8485). Metro Omonia. **Open** 11.30am-12.30am Mon-Sat. **Average** €. **No credit cards. Map** p249 F3 ⑭
A stone's throw from hectic Omonia Square, Athinaikon is a favourite among the journalists and lawyers who work in the area and who know value for money when they see it. This longstanding meze palace offers authentic dishes in marvellously old-fashioned surroundings. The dark wood interior, with its marble-topped tables and black

and white chequerboard floor, bustles day and night. Waiters handle the constant turnover with brisk good humour, while cooks in white hats churn out dishes from a four-page menu featuring excellent prawn fritters, fried mussels with garlicky *skordalia*, mussels or shrimp *saganaki* in tomato sauce with feta, seafood pasta, and grilled sardines. End with a plate of cinnamon-scented semolina pudding, *halva*, a wedge of chocolate *karydopita* (walnut cake), or a simple bowl of cool, thick Greek yoghurt and spoon sweets.

Diporto
Theatrou & Sokratous, Central Market (no phone). Metro Monastiraki. **Open** noon-6pm Mon-Sat. **Average** €. **No credit cards. Map** p249 E4 ⑮
Duck down into this grungy basement lined with wine barrels, where blood-spattered butchers and suit-clad brokers have been savouring Barba Mitsos's pot-luck lunches and potent wine for as long as anyone can remember. If it's crowded (and it usually is) he will sit you at any table with empty seats, so be prepared to mingle with the market traders for a lunch of chickpea soup, fried whitebait and the freshest Greek salad, all sourced from the market across the street.

Doris
Praxitelous 30, Platia Klafthmonos (210 323 2671). Metro Panepistimio. **Open** 8am-6.30pm Mon-Sat. **Average** €. **No credit cards. Map** p249 E4 ⑯
Doris has been dishing up delicious Greek grub in its cheerful pink space, serviced by polite staff in white coats, since 1900. It's one of the few places where you can get a traditional Greek breakfast of rice pudding and *loukoumades* (baby dough fritters

Pasaji.

dunked in honey, walnuts and cinnamon). The lunch menu, with dishes of the day chalked up on the blackboard, is incredibly cheap and as close as it gets to home cooking. Try the stuffed tomatoes and peppers, the spinach-rice or cabbage-rice pilaf, the baked giant beans, and the whole host of seasonal specialities cooked in olive oil, known as *ladera*.

Tzitzikas kai Mermigas

Mitropoleos 12-14, Syntagma, (210 324 7607). *Metro Syntagma.* **Open** 1pm-1am Mon-Sat. **Average** €. **Credit** MC, V. **Map** p249/p251 F5 ⑰
Tzitzikas kai Mermigas, the Greek translation of Aesop's fable of the cricket and the ant, was a long-time suburban favourite that decided to bank on its success and open up a second shop in the centre. The interior is modern rustic, and so is the food. Ordering a large array of excellent mezedes, from the small house cheese pies called *mastihato* to the shrimp with ouzo and cream, is the way to go. Don't miss the goat braised with rosemary and the Greek grape distillate, *tsipouro*. The two favourite desserts are *ekmek pagoto*, a syrup-soaked thin sponge cake topped with mastic-flavoured ice-cream, and *kazantipi*, which roughly translates as 'burnt' cream and is delicious.

Mediterranean

Cibus

Zappeion Gardens (210 336 9364). Metro Syntagma or Akropoli then 10min walk/tram to Zappeion stop. **Open** 8.30pm-12.30am daily. **Average** €€€. **Credit** AmEx, DC, MC, V. **Map** p251/p252 G6 ⑱
This Athenian landmark trades on its enchanting setting in the Zappeion gardens. The elegant terrace is ideal for a light lunch (served from sister café Lallabai, still known by its historic name Aigli; *see p134*), while the formal dining room, with picture windows overlooking the park, is atmospheric after dark. The lunch menu focuses on bistro-style standards, while the Italian-Med dinner menu is more refined (with prices to match): treat yourself to sea bream with asparagus and coriander, followed by cheesecake with date compote and kumquat coulis. *Photo p120.*

GB Roof Garden

Hotel Grande Bretagne, Syntagma Square (210 333 0766). Metro Syntagma. **Open** 1pm-1am daily. Closed Nov-Apr. **Average** €€€€. **Credit** AmEx, DC, MC, V. **Map** p249/p251 F5 ⑲

Eating up the sights

Summer in Athens is all about escaping to the seaside. For those stranded in the centre, the alternative is rooftop dining. It doesn't come cheap, though: at many restaurants where the view is the main draw, prices can be sky-high, and tables are by reservation only. But there are a few places not content to rest on the laurels of their location, where good food complements the glamour.

On the summit of Lycabettus Hill, the 360-degree view from **Orizondes Lykavitou** (210 722 7065, noon-2am daily, average €€€€) stretches as far as the sea. Accessible only by cable car or a sweaty slog up pine-forested footpaths, this glitzy restaurant used to be the showpiece of TV celebrity chef Yannis Geldis, but these days lower-key chef Petros Kalevrosaloglou is at the helm. The food is still competent but nowhere near as glorious as the vista or the room. Further down the hill, **Le Grand Balcon** (*see p119*), atop the St George Lycabettus Hotel, has equally panoramic views from its silver leather seats, and haute cuisine prepared under the tutelage of popular Corfu chef Hector Botrini. Resident DJs occasionally spice up the funky terrace decked with Swarowski chandeliers and see-through plexiglass chairs.

The liveried waiters at the **Pil Poul et Jérôme Serres** (*see p111; pictured*) reckon this is the most popular spot in town to pop the question. The marble roof garden of this fancy restaurant is certainly hard to beat for romance, with its jaw-dropping vistas of the moonlit Acropolis. The posh nosh, like foie gras crème brûlée, steak with truffles and grouper in champagne sauce, will set you back the cost of a Tiffany diamond. The chic **GB Roof Garden** (*see p116*) is a great place to linger over classic Euro fare. One caveat: it's booked days in advance.

At **Varoulko** (*see p124*), seafood master Lefteris Lazarou serves up his sea urchin risotto and wine-sweetened octopus on a rooftop with a view of the Acropolis and car headlights whizzing along Pireos.

The Athens Hilton is a double hitter when it comes to views: **Milos** (*see p122*), above the pool, has a panoramic view of all Athens' major sites; up on the roof, **Galaxy** (*see p191*) is a bar that also serves a full menu of finger food, barbecue and 'Mediterasian' affectations. This is the watering hole favoured by Athens' glamorous nightlifers – who can afford its galactic prices.

You don't have to pay astronomical prices to dine under the stars, though. Right on the

The swanky rooftop restaurant of the Hotel Grande Bretagne has unbeatable bird's-eye views of the National Gardens, the Parthenon and Parliament – a quintessentially Athenian vista with the Greek flag fluttering in the breeze. Posing on plush sofas and elegantly laid tables under the pergola, Athenian socialites graze on standard five-star hotel fare, such as tartare of yellow-fin tuna, pan-fried tiger prawns and rocket salad. The Wagyu steaks imported from Japan are worth the hefty price tag. For a cheaper taste of the high life, go for a champagne cocktail at the small bar. It's essential to book in advance.

Kolonaki & around

Bar-restaurants

Balthazar

Vournazou & Tsocha 27, Ambelokipi (210 644 1215). Metro Ambelokipi. **Open** *May-Oct* 9pm-1.30am daily. *Nov-Apr* 9pm-1.30am Mon-Sat. **Average** €€€€. **Credit** AmEx, MC, V.

Balthazar has been the place to see and be seen in since it opened two decades ago in one of the grandest 19th-century mansions in the capital. Its greatest asset is the walled garden canopied by palm trees and swaying Chinese lanterns, where advertising executives schmooze over cocktails at the long outdoor bar. The restaurant suffers somewhat from an excess of style over substance, but reliable dishes on the menu include warm foie gras with bergamot compote, pumpkin purée with sour cream and sweet chilli, ravioli with spinach and truffle oil, and knock-out espresso ice-cream with hot chocolate and orange fondant.

Mommy

Delfon 4, Kolonaki (210 361 9682). Metro Panepistimio. **Open** *May-Sept* 7pm-1.30am daily. *Oct-April* noon-1.30am daily. **Average** €€€. **Credit** AmEx, DC, MC, V. **Map** p249/p252 G3 ⑳

This groovy bar-restaurant on a pedestrian street packed with cafés is a hit with the fashion and media tribes. All mismatched armchairs, printed lampshades and arty photos, it can get noisy indoors as the night goes on – but the wooden deck scattered with wicker armchairs and floral cushions is magical on hot summer nights. Pretty young things nibble tuna tartare, beef carpaccio and chicken satay, while their beefy beaux dig into seafood risotto and banoffi pie.

walkway ringing the Acropolis, the pretty roof terrace of **Filistron** (*see p134*) is a serene spot at which to quaff palatable house wine as you share *bekri meze* (pork stew), grilled potatoes with smoked cheese, and char-grilled haloumi. On a less frequented side street nearby, **Greek House Attikos** (Garivaldi 7, 210 921 5256, 7.30pm-1am daily, average €€) is where performers at the Herodes Atticus outdoor theatre come to unwind over tasty salmon crêpes and schnitzel after the show. (You can watch the performance for free from the front tables.) And above the atmospheric antique market of Monastiraki, **Brachera** (Platia Avyssinias 3, 210 321 7202, May-Oct 8.30pm-2am daily, Nov-Apr 8pm-1.30am Tue-Sat, 1pm-8pm Sun, average €€) is a mellow bar-restaurant popular with locals for its close-up Acropolis views, great cocktails and decent Mediterranean dishes.

Eat, Drink, Shop

Cellier Le Bistrot brings fine wines and a little bit of Paris to central Athens. *See p115.*

Ratka

Haritos 32, Kolonaki (210 729 0746). Metro
Evangelismos. **Open** 9am-2am Mon-Fri; 1-5pm Sat.
Closed June-Sept. **Average** €€€. **Credit** AmEx,
DC, MC, V. **Map** p252 H4 ㉑

Ratka doesn't need to advertise. This chic Kolonaki
bolthole is a cross between a bistro and a bar, and
nothing has changed since it opened 30 years ago.
Yet it is still as fashionable as ever, especially
among fortysomething movers and shakers, from
ministers to movie directors. The multi-ethnic
menu ranges from spaghetti al pesto to steak siz-
zled right at your table on a hot griddle plate, snails
and surprisingly good sushi.

Creative

48 The Restaurant

Armatolon & Klefton 48, Ambelokipi (210 641
1082). Metro Ambelokipi. **Open** 9pm-1am Mon-
Sat. **Average** €€€€. **Credit** AmEx, DC, MC, V.

All brushed concrete, green glass and light sculptures that change colour, 48 was last year's hottest
meal ticket. Chef Christoforos Peskias, who trained
at El Bulli, twists classic Greek dishes into surprising new variations: intense mackerel tartare,
tomato sushi, feta ice cream, battered cod with a
trio of garlic sauces, rare Charolais fillet of beef in
caper sauce served with a cone of hand-cut chips,

and an array of dishes that speak of new cooking techniques from foam to slowly-roasted *sous vide* shanks that melt like butter on the tongue. The clued-up sommelier oversees an outstanding wine list, showcased in the scarlet cellar downstairs. Desserts are deadly: limit yourself to refreshing tangerine sorbet or succumb to honeyed halva ice-cream, cinnamon tart, or the Chocolate Theme – a chocoholic's downfall.

Le Grand Balcon

St George Lycabettus Hotel, Kleomenous 2, Kolonaki (210 729 0712). **Open** 8.30pm-1am Tue-Sat. **Average** €€€€. **Credit** AmEx, DC, MC, V. **Map** p252 H4 ㉒
Restaurants with a great view, which this one has – stretching from the Parthenon to the Saronic Gulf on a clear night – all too often don't have menus that stand up to their world-class vistas. Though the Grand Balcon suffered from hotel-kitchen syndrome for a long time, the last year has seen a marked improvement. Greek-Italian consulting chef Hector Botrini, whose Corfu restaurant is a landmark among the food-loving intelligentsia of Greece, was brought in to jazz up the menu. And he has, with dishes like fennel soup with shrimp and ouzo jelly, foie gras with vanilla oil and apricot preserves, and sea bream with roasted aubergine mousse. Botrini makes some of the best risotto this side of the Adriatic, so don't miss his Greek-inspired herb and red mullet version or the risotto with baby squid and parsley cream. Reservations essential.

St' Astra

Park Hotel Athens (rooftop), Leof Alexandras 10, Pedion Areos (210 889 4500). Metro Victoria. **Open** 8pm-12.30am Mon-Sat. Closed July, Aug. **Average** €€€. **Credit** AmEx, DC, MC, V. **Map** p249 F1 ㉓
Chef Hervé Pronzato (previously at Michelin-starred Spondi; *see p127*) now oversees the menu at this glamorous glass box of a restaurant on the top floor of the Park Hotel. A bamboo bar, cowhide rugs and Murano chandeliers provide a suitably snazzy backdrop for innovative dishes like shrimp grilled inside a linguine blanket and served with tomato marmalade, lobster ravioli with baby vegetables, and pork fillets stuffed with ricotta cheese and served with fried aubergine and honey-sweetened fig sauce. Pronzato's imaginative and well-executed style extends to the desserts, with intoxicating concoctions such as strawberries marinated in mastika liqueur and ouzo sorbet. The food is good here, the atmosphere snazzy but impersonal (as are most hotel restaurants); the small portions and big prices are not quite so appetising.

French

Prunier

Ypsilantou 63, Kolonaki (210 722 7379). Metro Evangelismos. **Open** 8pm-12.30am Mon-Sat. Closed July, Aug. **Average** €€€. **Credit** AmEx, DC, MC, V. **Map** p252 J4 ㉔

This cosy French bistro – accented with antiques, copper utensils and tasteful art nouveau touches – exudes romance. The repertoire comprises solid French standards such as coq au vin and snails bourguignonne, and original concoctions like quail *salmnis* (with oregano and lemon) and *délice des amoureux* (sautéed seafood laced with cognac in a vol-au-vent). Reservations essential.

Greek contemporary

Ouzadiko

Karneadou 25-29 & Alopekis 28-30, Kolonaki (210 729 5484). Metro Evangelismos. **Open** 12.30pm-5.30pm, 8pm-midnight Tue-Sat. **Average** €€. **Credit** AmEx, DC, MC, V. **Map** p252 H4/H5 ㉕
Despite its unpromising location in a deserted shopping mall, Ouzadiko has been packed every night since it first opened its doors a decade ago. Once inside, the atmosphere is cosy and the conversation lively, but it's the outstanding food prepared by chef-owner Stella that keeps connoisseurs coming back time and again. Choose from one of the largest selections of ouzo anywhere in Greece, accompanied by dozens of delicious Greek dishes with a twist – spinach and cumin patties, taramasalata made with smoked trout, cheesy chickpea fritters, and stewed octopus with black-eyed peas. The smoked aubergine salad and flat-bread sticks with nigella seeds are house signatures. Stella's bean cookery, talent with aubergines, and casserole dishes are all outstanding.

Papadakis

Voukourestiou 47 & Fokylidou, Kolonaki (210 360 8621). Metro Syntagma. **Open** 1.30pm-1.30am Mon-Sat. Closed 2-3wks Aug. **Average** €€€. **Credit** AmEx, DC, MC, V. **Map** p252 G4 ㉖
Papadakis is owned and operated by star daytime TV chef Argyro Barbarigou. She had a popular taverna on Paros for years before closing down and reopening in one of the most demanding neighbourhoods in Greece: upmarket Kolonaki. Today, her restaurant is the place to come to for some of the most elegant home cooking around. In a pared down, simple but chic space, Barbarigou serves mostly seafood specialities, such as caramelised octopus and skate salad. Her chickpea soup served with taramasalata is brilliant, but so is the mastika-flavoured crème caramel served in a martini glass. The people who love Papadakis are the ones who know that the best food is the simplest, but are also partial to pleasing aesthetics, good service and a tireless hostess-chef. *Photo p123.*

Rififi

Emmanouil Benaki 69A & Valtetsiou, Exarchia (210 330 1369). Metro Omonia. **Open** 1pm-1am Mon-Sat. Closed Aug. **Average** €. **No credit cards.** **Map** p249 G2 ㉗
On a corner that was once home to one of Athens' most renowned tavernas, Rififi, which roughly translates as 'robbery', is a favourite little place

Eat, Drink, Shop

Cibus. *See p116.*

among the writers, editors, publishers and other bookish types who live and work in Exarchia. The Greek cuisine served here, in a light, wood-cast setting that recalls the grocery-tavernas of yore, might best be described as contemporary traditional. Try the walnut and mushroom soup, which looks terrible but tastes great, the light-as-air greens fritters, and the cabbage and dried fruit salad moistened with a light buttermilk dressing. Desserts are aptly simple: the best is the semolina halva. Vegetarians will love this place.

Greek traditional

Alatsi
Vrassida 13, Ilissia (210 721 0501/mobile 6979 800203). Metro Evangelismos. **Open** 1pm-1am Mon-Sat. Closed Aug. **Average** €€. **Credit** DC, MC, V. **Map** p252 J5 ❷❽
Alatsi, which means 'salt' in the Cretan dialect, was opened three years ago to instant success by a well-known TV and print journalist, and has become the place to see and be seen in for those in the worlds of politics, media and theatre. The chef, Dimitris Skarmoutsos, uses Cretan produce – from olive oil to cheese, meat and vegetables – to present Crete's traditional cuisine in a sleek, upmarket manner. You'll still find the tried and true island classics, though, from braised Cretan rabbit with tiny green olives to meat and vegetable stews enriched with *avgolemono*. Cretan wedding pilaf, made by boiling rice in rich meat broth, and topped off with a sheep's-milk butter called *staka*, makes the richest risotto pale in comparison. The menu changes with the seasons. *Photo p128.*

Dexameni
Platia Dexamenis, Kolonaki (210 723 2834). Metro Syntagma. **Open** *May-Oct* 10.30am-1.30am daily. *Nov-Apr* 10.30am-10pm daily. **Average** €. **No credit cards. Map** p252 H4 ❷❾
An Athenian landmark, Dexameni reopened in summer 2004 under new management. Regulars may be nostalgic for the old rickety chairs and quick-witted waiters, but this outdoor oasis in a small park is still blissful. Passers-by parade down the sloping walkway lined with tables, watched by leisurely diners knocking back jugs of house wine and simple snacks like bite-sized filo pastries, 'mum's' meatballs, traditional spinach and cheese pies, pickled octopus, courgette croquettes, and rocket and tomato salad. Dessert is simple – typically just a small glass plate with a spoonful of fruit preserves and a tall glass of chilled water.

Kafeneio
Loukianou 26 & Patriarchou Ioakim, Kolonaki (210 722 9056). Metro Evangelismos. **Open** noon-midnight Mon-Sat. Closed Aug. **Average** €€. **Credit** DC, MC, V. **Map** p252 H4 ❸⓿
Distinguished gents, ladies who lunch and yuppie couples all love this Kolonaki classic, where waiters in black jackets and starched white shirts have been dishing up superior Greek staples for years. The consistent quality, faithfulness to the classics and immaculate service make Kafeneio extremely foreigner-friendly. There are lots of great things to try: house salad of cucumber, avocado and spring onions; creamed leeks with bacon; stuffed squash; lamb fricassé; artichokes à la polita, with chopped carrots and potatoes; little aubergine 'shoes', called *papoutsakia*; aubergine baked with feta; and roast

suckling pig. Puddings are classics too, the likes of Greek walnut cake, apple pie and the now long-adopted chocolate soufflé. The dark wooden interior is reassuringly old-fashioned. In summer, lunch can last for hours at one of the pavement tables.

Philippou
Xenokratous 19, Kolonaki (210 721 6390). Metro Evangelismos. **Open** 1-5pm, 8pm-midnight Mon-Fri; 1-5pm Sat. Closed 2wks Aug. **Average** €. **Credit** MC, V. **Map** p252 H4 ③

This old-school taverna (founded back in 1923) is one of the best-value spots in an area where fancy design tends to prevail over fine food. A good lunch venue, this low-key local specialises in *mageirefta*, traditional casseroles like *arakas* (pea, potato and dill stew), *hirino lemonato* (pork with lemon) and *briam* (slow-roasted vegetables). Though the dining room is rather dowdy, you can admire the doodles by famous Greek artists who have dined here over the years. On summer nights, the tables creep up the steps outside and spill on to the pavement opposite – a mellow place at which to while away an evening with a jug of red house wine.

Vlassis
Pasteur 8, Platia Mavili (210 646 3060). Metro Ambelokipi or Megaro Moussikis. **Open** Sept-June 1-5.30pm, 8.30pm-midnight Mon-Sat;

1pm-5.30pm Sun. *July* 1pm-5.30pm Mon-Fri. Closed Aug. **Average** €. **No credit cards**.

Housed in an old townhouse on a quiet dead end near the American Embassy, Vlassis is one of the longest-standing popular tavernas in the city. Run by an extended family where aunts, cousins and sisters cook, Vlassis is where you will find all the home-cooked specialities Greeks used to enjoy at the hands of grandmothers a generation ago: fat stuffed cabbage or grape leaves, depending on the season, served with lemon sauce; meat stews; artichoke and fava bean casseroles in a lemon and dill sauce; great Greek fries; and a whole array of classic taverna appetisers that are still the heart and soul of the cuisine. Once upon a time, Vlassis was the place to be for the young, hip, artsy and literary crowd. They were loyal customers: they're still regulars but a lot greyer now.

Italian

Il Postino
Grivaion 3 & Delphon, Kolonaki (210 364 1414). Metro Panepistimio. **Open** 1pm-1am Mon-Sat; 1.30pm-12.30am Sun. **Average** €. **Credit** MC, V. **Map** p252 G3 ②

Antonio has run a string of successful Italian restaurants in Athens. His latest venture is a cosy *osteria* where you can savour home-style Italian cooking at

Eat, Drink, Shop

Modern Greek

Tried and trusted trad Greek food – from mezedes (small plates with big flavours) to grilled meats and fish to the whole bevy of healthy, olive-oil-based vegetable and bean stews – is as popular as it always has been. But there have been stirrings on the dining scene in the past few years, as innovative chefs have begun to reinvent local cuisine.

The decade leading up to the Olympics witnessed the first glimmer of change: there were signs that local chefs were getting over their love affair with all things foreign (from wasabi to wonton wrappers to radicchio). Traditional Greek ingredients and regional dishes began to resurface on menus, albeit shaped by contemporary culinary trends. The city's cutting-edge cooks, it seemed, had begun to turn to their own culinary history for inspiration.

A few chefs led the pack: Lefteris Lazarou (**Varoulko**; *see p124*) almost singlehandedly changed the way Greek diners of a certain depth of pocket viewed the fruits of the sea, making once lowly creatures like the monkfish and gar fish the stuff of gourmet dining; Yiannis Baxevannis (**Galazia Hytra**; *see p125*)

took the roots of his native Cretan cuisine, applied his French training, and created a whole new vernacular. Arguably the most iconoclastic of the new generation of chefs is Christoforos Peskias (**48 The Restaurant**; *see p118*), a Cypriot-born, American-educated protégé of Spanish culinary genius Ferran Adria, who brought the whipped-cream canister to staid Greek staples such as tzatziki. He also turned stuffed tomatoes inside-out – creating something called Greek sushi – and generally applied previously unknown techniques and ingredients (agar agar among them) to the gamut of Greek traditional food, becoming the darling of restaurant-savvy Athenians in the process.

Today, contemporary Greek food has become a fascinating potpourri of modern techniques applied to traditional, ages-old recipes and ingredients. At the same time the Greek capital has also seen a mini regional renaissance. Crete is at the top of the list but tavernas specialising in the foods of the Mani, Kassos, Ikaria and other small, distant locales have brought yet more diversity and complexity to the Athens restaurant scene.

surprisingly affordable prices almost any time of the day or night. Neapolitan love songs welcome you into a narrow space lined with photos of Italian movie stars, laminated newspapers and old postcards. Choose the *vitello tonnato* (veal with tuna) and marinated anchovies from the tray of starters; follow that up with fresh tagliatelle with porcini mushrooms, and rabbit and rosemary stew.

Pecora Nera
Sevastoupoleos 158, Ambelokipi (210 691 4183).
Metro Panormou. **Open** 1pm-2am Mon-Sat.
Average €€. **Credit** AmEx, DC, MC, V.
Owned by an actor, this split-level trattoria has a touch of theatre about it. Good-natured young waiters, funky music and first-rate cocktails create a lively setting for casual dining. The big communal table by the bar is fun for birthday parties and other get-togethers, and the cute conservatory lined with sofas is ideal for dinner à deux, but the mezzanine can be noisy. Excellent appetisers include crunchy bruschetta with gorgonzola and pears; the pork with polenta and the bona fide spaghetti carbonara are similarly accomplished.

Japanese

Freud Oriental
Xenokratous 21, Kolonaki (210 729 9595).
Metro Evangelismos. **Open** 8pm-1am Mon-Sat.
Closed mid July-mid Aug. **Average** €€€.
Credit MC, V. **Map** p252 H4 ⓺
Sushi masters sharpening their knives behind an oval cut-out counter greet diners on entry to this upmarket Japanese restaurant. The minimalist interior – all low, cream sofas and exposed stone – contrasts strongly with the glitzy clientele. Start with some melt-in-the-mouth tuna *tataki* and special *temaki* (hand-rolled shrimp, avocado and asparagus), followed by *kurodai* tempura teriyaki – exquisitely light sea bream tempura on a bed of crispy noodles. Choose carefully from the impressive but expensive saké selection – a small carafe can set you back as much as €80. For a clandestine rendezvous, bag one of the handful of tables in the tiny, candlelit garden at the back.

Kiku
Dimokritou 12, Kolonaki (210 364 7033).
Metro Panepistimio. **Open** 1.30pm-1am Mon-Sat (sushi not served 5.30-8.30pm). Closed Aug.
Average €€€€. **Credit** AmEx, DC, MC, V.
Map p252 G4 ⓸
The best Japanese restaurant in Athens, Kiku introduced Athenians to sashimi and tempura long before the current sushi fad kicked in. Although the minimalist interior is discreetly screened from the street by white blinds, that's where discretion ends: this is where moneyed Athenians come to flash their cash and show off their skills with chopsticks. But genuine lovers of Japanese cuisine also visit to enjoy authentic and unusual dishes like *tori tsukune*, *yakisoba* and exquisite udon noodles.

Mediterranean

Bakaliko de Toute Façon
Skoufa 48, Kolonaki (210 362 5700). Metro Panepistimio. **Open** 11am-1am Tue-Sat. Closed Aug. **Average** €€. **Credit** AmEx, MC, V.
Map p252 G4 ⓹
Hellenic chic meets French gastronomy courtesy of Gallo-Greek owner Eric Artigault, whose impeccable sense of style pervades this deli-café. Pick up organic olives and olive pâté in the grocery, then head up to the loft to brunch with local bon viveurs on smoked swordfish, spinach and courgette tart or spinach and bacon salad with goat's cheese. Ask about the dishes of the day, which change with the seasons. It is also worth checking in to sample the excellent pastries, which taste great with sour cherry cordial from the island of Chios.

Middle Eastern

Alexandria
Metsovou 13 & Rethymnou 7, Exarchia (210 821 0004). Metro Victoria. **Open** 8.30pm-midnight Mon-Sat. Closed Aug. **Average** €. **Credit** MC, V.
Map p249 F1 ⓺
Located behind the Archaeological Museum, this is an excellent Middle Eastern restaurant, surprisingly not on the tourist trail. The cosy interior, with its mellow light and antique floor tiles, is separated into two spaces – opt for a table on the left, lined with aromatic herbs and spices. Authentic treats include fresh *fatoush* salad (diced tomato, cucumber and mint with crispy pitta croutons), *koubepia* (lamb rissoles with pine nuts and raisins) and Om Ali, a creamy Egyptian pudding studded with dates, nuts and sultanas. The pretty courtyard is equally seductive. Booking is essential at weekends.

Seafood

Milos
Athens Hilton, Vas Sofias 46, Ilissia (210 724 4400). Metro Evangelismos. **Open** 12.30-4.30pm, 7.30pm-midnight daily. **Average** €€€ lunch; €€€€ dinner.
Credit AmEx, DC, MC, V. **Map** p252 J5 ⓷
Costas Spiliades singlehandedly rebranded Greek cuisine at his restaurants in Montreal and New York. Now he's brought the Milos phenomenon home, to a lean, spare space in the Athens Hilton (*see p49*). Opt for the chef's table in winter, which is bordered on three sides by the open kitchen; or outdoors on the deck, which is pure Greek summer magic when the light is right and the weather warm. Spiliades sources the freshest ingredients from fishermen and farmers around the country. These raw materials – piled high in a dazzling array of colours around the sizzling open kitchen – are handled with the minimum of fuss, letting the flavours speak for themselves. Flash-fried slivers of aubergine and courgette with yoghurt sauce are as light as tempura, and hand-picked *horta* from

Eat, Drink, Shop

Papadakis. *See p119.*

Crete is barely wilted and dressed in nothing but purest olive oil and a squirt of lemon. His Greek salad is the best in town, with a price tag to prove it, and one bite of Spiliades' whole bream baked in sea salt will transport you. Traditional Greek pastries like *galaktoboureko* (custard cream oozing between sheets of syrup-soaked filo) are equally well handled.

North of the Acropolis

Bar-restaurants

Soul
Evripidou 65, Psyrri (210 331 0907). Metro Monastiraki. **Open** 9.30pm-1.30am daily. Closed 10 days Aug. **Average** €€. **Credit** MC, V. **Map** p249 D4/E4 ❸
A mojito in Soul's back garden – with palm trees and red walls – feels like a trip to the tropics. The fairly priced dinner menu is limited but tasty: opt for Mediterranean rather than Asian dishes, like mixed leaves with manouri cheese, chicken stuffed with goat's cheese and sun-dried tomatoes, and pasta with smoked salmon. In the stylish dining area indoors the music can muffle conversation as the bar gets busy. Later, head upstairs to the small, smoky Stereo club to work off your dinner on the dancefloor. *See also p192.*

Taki 13
Taki 13, Psyrri, (210 325 4707). Metro Monastiraki. **Open** 12.30pm-late Mon, Wed-Sun. *Kitchen* 12.30-3pm, 7.30pm-1am Mon, Wed-Sun. **Average** €€. **Credit** MC, V. **Map** p249 D4 ❸

Taki 13 was a groundbreaker when it first opened about 15 years ago in the then-industrial area of Psyrri, which was just at the beginning of its transformation into Athens' bar and meze mecca. The small, exposed stone interior with its cosy mezzanine and cool music also operates alfresco across the street in the summer months. The menu is a melange of Greek and international classics. Try *hiouniar*, a luscious veal stew that comes with rich, smoky aubergine cream; baked mushrooms are another well-liked dish here. There's live music on Fridays and Saturdays.

Creative

Kitrino Podilato – Koukoumavlos
Keramikou 116-118 & Iera Odos, Gazi (210 346 5830). Metro Keramikos. **Open** 8pm-12.30am Mon-Sat. Closed mid May-Oct. **Average** €€€. **Credit** AmEx, MC, V. **Map** p248 C4 ❹
This sprawling post-industrial warehouse space has been transformed into a restaurant and nightclub. Kitrino Podilato, which means yellow bicycle (after the one that hangs on stone wall inside), was one of the first places to open its doors in the now-hip district of Gazi. Of late, Santorini chef Nikos Pouliasis has spearheaded the contemporary kitchen here, turning out unusual dishes such as grilled tuna with sweet aubergine mousse, Greek spring rolls with filo, pasturma and kasseri cheese, lots of dishes seasoned with ginger and saffron, and one of the most unusual Mediterranean-style desserts around: a grecified tiramisu with sweet aubergine cream and cocoa.

Varoulko

Pireos 80, Keramikos (210 522 8400). Metro Keramikos or Thissio. **Open** 8.30pm-12.30am Mon-Sat. **Average** €€€€. **Credit** AmEx, DC, MC, V. **Map** p248 C4 ❹

Greece's most famous chef, Lefteris Lazarou, made his name for his extraordinary way with seafood, from pesto calamari to his legendary poached monkfish. Lazarou recently relocated from Piraeus to this lofty, multi-level space with glass floors and see-through kitchen window, beside the Eridanus hotel (where he's just opened a new restaurant, Parea; *see p52*). The food is better than ever, with the addition of innovative meat dishes. Goat and chocolate risotto, or wedding pilaf with marrow may sound unappetising to some, but are fantastic. Still, the sea's bounty remains the real star, especially Lazarou's light and refreshing marinated fish carpaccios, his myriad ways with monkfish, his caramelised octopus with *mavrodafne*-sweetened *trahana* cream, and his famous braided gar fish. For dessert, try the subtle pineapple, orange and passionfruit soup. Lazarou likes to surprise his customers with an endless parade of dishes, though you can order à la carte if you like (safer on the wallet). Whatever you do, be sure to book well in advance. *Photo p129.*

Fast food

For most Athenians, breakfast is typically a cappuccino and *koulouri* (sesame-studded bread ring) wolfed on the hoof. Street vendors sell *koulouria* and sugary 'donats' (a steal at €0.50); but for the freshest snacks, head straight to the source: the all-night **Koulouria Bakery** in Psyrri (Karaiskaki 23, 210 321 5962, 24hrs daily), full of red-eyed ravers.

Athens is littered with *fastfoudadika* – fast-food joints à la grecque. These holes in the wall serve *tost* (toasted sandwiches), *piroski* (a stodgy sausage roll) and all kinds of *pittes* (pies). At **Ariston** (Voulis 10, Syntagma, 210 322 7626, 7.30am-5pm Mon, Wed, Sat, 7.30am-9pm Tue, Thur, Fri), the humble *tyropitta* (feta pie) has been elevated to an art form. There's always a huddle of customers outside this pie shop, which has been churning out flaky pastries since 1910. Try the *spanakopitta* (spinach), *prassopitta* (leek) or *kolokythopitta* (courgette). The tomato-filled *tyropitta* from **Takis** bakery (Misaraliotou 14, 210 923 0052, 7am-8pm Mon-Fri, 7am-4pm Sat, closed Aug), a few blocks below the Acropolis, has an equally devoted following.

Souvlaki is every Greek's illicit treat – hot pitta bread full of grilled meat, raw onion, tomato, tzatziki and chips. There are several variations of this post-pub staple: the standard souvlaki is stuffed with hunks of skewered meat; *gyro* (pronounced 'yee-roh') with shavings of pork or lamb; and kebab with minced beef mixed with onions, garlic and spices. Follow the smell of sizzling fat to Monastiraki Square, where three souvlaki joints sweat it out. Legend has it these meatmeisters made more money than anyone else during the Olympics. The grub is as tasty – and service as gruff – at **Savvas** (Mitropoleos 86, 210 324 5048, 8.30am-3am daily) and **Bairaktaris** (2 Platia Monastiraki, 210 321 3036, 10.30am-late daily), but **Thanasis** (Mitropoleos 67-69, 210 324 4705, 8.30am-3am daily; *pictured*) is the favourite.

Greek contemporary

Hytra

Navarchou Apostoli 7, Psyrri (210 331 6767).
Metro Monastiraki or Thissio. **Open** 8.30pm-
midnight Tue-Sat; 1-5pm, 8.30pm-midnight Sun.
Closed May-Oct. **Average** €€€. **Credit** AmEx,
DC, MC, V. **Map** p249 D4 ②
The uncluttered space – white linen tablecloths, red
banquettes and stark prints of cooking utensils –
suggests this is a place for people who take food
seriously. The menu showcases the finest Greek
ingredients but with a Greek and Mediterranean
flair, as executed by presiding chef Maurizio Santin.
The tiny cumin and orange scented meatballs with
aubergine purée alone make a trip here worthwhile.
Sweets are beautifully presented; try the *tiganites*
(doughnuts) with chocolate and orange or the
caramelised dried fruit souvlaki served with a tart
yoghurt and coffee mousse. The restaurant operates
as the Galazia Hytra at the coastal Astir Palace
Vouliagmeni *(see p55)* from May to October.

Greek traditional

Chryssa

*Artemisiou 4 & Keramikou, Keramikos (210 341
2515). Metro Keramikos.* **Open** 8.30pm-1am Mon-
Sat. **Average** €€. **Credit** MC, V. **Map** p248 C4 ③
This sedately stylish restaurant was housed for eons
in a lovely old house, but recently moved to the
nightclub-buzzing neighbourhood of Keramikos,
where an otherwise austere, formerly industrial space
is offset with plants and feminine touches; mellow
music, soft lighting and creamy colours create a
seductive mood. The attentive owner, Chryssa
Protopapa, is a cult hero on the Athens dining scene
and one of the longest-operating restaurateurs in
town, with a loyal and steady clientele who love her
personal service. Chryssa starts your night with a
basket of warm rolls with white *tarama* (fish roe) and
red pepper purée while you browse the short but creative menu. Stand-out dishes include chicken and
prawns in a prawn reduction, sardines with Greek
couscous and fennel, and mussels steamed in Greek
wine. Salt cod with fennel, capers, and lemon purée is
a knockout, as is her signature chocolate-banana pie.

Ineas

*Aisopou 9, Psyrri (210 321 5614). Metro
Monastiraki.* **Open** 6pm-1.30am Mon-Fri; noon-
2am Sat, Sun. **Average** €€. **Credit** DC, MC, V.
Map p249 D4 ④
With pistachio walls covered in vintage ads, antique
tins and colourful bottles, Ineas combines cheerful
style with fresh flavours. The lively crowd of locals
and tourists share out-of-the-ordinary appetisers like
fried feta in a light honey and black sesame batter,
spinach salad with warm goat's cheese in a walnut
crust, and grilled portabello mushrooms with lash-
ings of garlic. Friendly waiters add to the easygoing
vibe, though things can get frantic at weekends.

Mamacas

*Persefonis 41, Gazi (210 346 4984). Metro
Keramikos.* **Open** 1.30pm-1.30am daily. **Average**
€€. **Credit** AmEx, DC, MC, V. **Map** p248 B4 ④
A modern spin on the old-time taverna, Mamacas
pioneered the Gazi neighbourhood revival back in
1998. With whitewashed walls and pared-down
chic, it may have become a little too trendy for its
own good. It still serves Greek grub, but not as
wholesome as mama's, and the service has an attitude problem – perhaps because the hoi poloi just
aren't as exciting as the various models and pop
stars who tuck into meatballs in tomato sauce, calamari and spinach stew, and Cretan rusks topped
with sheep's cheese, capers and tomatoes. Waiters
in tight white T-shirts and starched aprons are
equally mouth-watering, even if their job performance is wanting. Mamacas is also a stylish place
to sip cocktails later in the evening *(see p192)*.

Nikitas

*Agion Anargyron 19, Psyrri (210 325 2591).
Metro Monastiraki.* **Open** 11am-6.30pm daily.
Closed Aug. **Average** €. **No credit cards.**
Map p249 D4 ④
Just about the last old-time taverna in the Psyrri
neighbourhood, this unpretentious little joint is now
hemmed in by bars and gimmicky music-and-meze
joints. But Nikitas has preserved its friendly character and still turns out top-notch taverna food at
rock-bottom prices throughout the day. Order the
souvlaki, *fava* (split-pea purée), *horta* (stewed
greens), and that increasing rarity, hand-cut chips,
plus extraordinary baked quince for pudding.

Tellis

*Evripidou 86, Psyrri (210 324 2775). Metro
Monastiraki.* **Open** 8am-2am Mon-Sat. **Average** €.
No credit cards. Map p249 D4 ④
There is really only one thing that people order at
this cult meaterie: giant-sized portions of pork
chops and chips. Who cares about the neon lights,
greaseproof paper tablecloths and uncomfortable
chairs, when you can stuff yourself with prime
meat for peanuts? Go the whole hog and have a
huge cabbage salad and baked feta with tomato
and chilli peppers on the side. Punters range from
artists to lawyers to bouzouki singers.

Seafood

Thalatta

*Vitonos 5 & Pireos 105, Gazi (210 346 4204).
Metro Keramikos.* **Open** *Mid Nov-Greek Easter* 8pm-
midnight Mon-Sat; 1-5pm Sun. *Greek Easter-mid Nov*
1pm-midnight Mon-Sat. Closed Aug. **Average** €€.
Credit AmEx, DC, MC, V. **Map** p248/p250 B5 ④
This fancy fish restaurant on an unlikely backstreet
behind Pireos is for people who are serious about
seafood. The nautically themed interior borders on
kitsch, but the courtyard strung with fairy lights is
peaceful and pretty. The expansive chef-owner,
Yiannis Safos, makes a point of visiting every table

Eat, Drink, Shop

The menu

Avgolemono: a sauce made out of lemon, egg yolks, and chicken, fish or meat stock. Also used for a soup made with rice, chicken stock, lemon and egg yolks.

Baklava: a pan-Middle Eastern sweet made from sheets of filo pastry layered with nuts.

Barbouni: red mullet, usually selected by the customer, grilled and served with olive oil.

Bekri meze: cooked pork marinated in wine, sometimes topped with melted cheese.

Briam: a vegetarian casserole of aubergines, courgettes, tomatoes, potatoes, bay and spices, similar to ratatouille.

Dolmades: young vine leaves stuffed with rice, spices and (usually) minced meat.

Fasolia plaki or pilaki: white beans in a tomato, oregano, parsley and garlic sauce.

Fava: a dip made of puréed yellow split peas, usually topped with chopped red onions.

Garides: large prawns, fried or grilled.

Gemista: tomatoes or peppers stuffed with a combination of rice, mince, herbs, pine nuts and raisins.

Gigantes or gigandes: white beans baked in tomato sauce; pronounced 'yigandes'.

Halloumi or hallumi: a cheese traditionally made from sheep's or goat's milk, but increasingly from cow's milk. Best served fried or grilled. Primarily a Cypriot speciality.

Horiatiki: 'Peasant' salad of tomato, onion, cucumber, feta and sometimes green pepper, dressed with extra virgin olive oil.

Horta: salad of wild greens.

Htipiti: tangy purée of feta cheese, flavoured with red peppers.

Kalamari, kalamarakia or calamares: small squid, usually sliced into rings, battered and fried.

Kataifi or katayfi: syrup-soaked 'shredded-wheat' dessert rolls.

Keftedes or keftedakia: herbay meatballs made with minced pork or lamb (rarely beef), egg, breadcrumbs and possibly grated potato and mint.

Kleftiko: paper-wrapped, slow-roasted lamb on the bone (often shoulder), flavoured with oregano and other herbs.

Kokkinisto: chunks of meat – usually lamb or beef – baked with tomatoes and herbs in an earthenware pot, which seals in the juices and flavours.

Loukanika or lukanika: spicy coarse-ground sausages, usually made with pork and heavily herbed.

Loukoumades: tiny, spongy doughnuts dipped in honey.

Loukoumi: Turkish delight, made with rice flour, syrup, rosewater and pectin, often studded with nuts.

Mageirefta: cooked vegetable dishes such as casseroles and stews. (This is a useful word to know in restaurants that do not have menus, where the waiter might say, 'We have such-and-such for salads, such-and-such for meats and such-and-such for mageirefta.' It can also be a useful word for vegetarians or people who don't want to eat hunks of grilled meat or fish at every meal.)

Marides: picarel – small fish best coated in flour and flash-fried.

Melitzanosalata: purée of grilled aubergines.

Meze (plural mezedes): a selection of appetisers and main dishes that can be either hot or cold.

---

to explain dishes and make recommendations. Besides an impressive selection of shellfish, Safos re-invents Greek classics with outstanding results: mousaka is made with seafood instead of ground meat; courgettes are filled with rice and seafood; grilled octopus comes served over *fava* and sun-dried tomatoes; and salmon, an adopted Greek fish, is cooked in champagne sauce.

Thai

Bar Guru Bar

Platia Theatrou 10, Psyrri (210 324 6530). Metro Monastiraki. **Open** 9pm-1am Mon-Thur; 9.30pm-1.30am Fri, Sat. Closed mid July-late Aug. **Average** €€. **Credit** AmEx, MC, V. **Map** p249 D4/E4 ⓭

Still hotter than a green chilli after seven years, this Thai bar-restaurant never goes out of style, partly because the menu changes often. A postmodern pagoda presides over architects and architects swapping gossip over real Thai food. The hot *tom yam goong* soup (shrimps, lemongrass, chillies and coriander), *goong tod* (fried baby shrimps with sweet and sour peanut sauce) and *gean gai rama* (Burmese chicken curry with caramelised onions and coconut milk) are especially delicious. The dimly lit mezzanine is like an upmarket opium den, perfect for a secret rendezvous. After midnight, the bar (*see p189*) is swamped with beautiful people fighting for the fantastic frozen margaritas and Thai martinis. The top-floor jazz club, where local bands jam with a great line-up of international guests, is less of a crush.

Moussaka(s): a baked dish of minced meat, aubergine and potato slices and herbs, topped with béchamel sauce.
Oktapodi: octopus, usually grilled fresh and served with lemon and olive oil.
Papoutsaki: aubergine 'shoes', slices stuffed with mince, topped with sauce, usually béchamel or similar.
Pastourma(s): dense, dark-tinted, garlicky cured beef.
Saganaki: fried cheese, usually *kefalotyri*; also means anything (mussels, shrimp, spinach) made in a shallow, two-handled skillet, often with wine, ouzo or tomato sauce and with added cheese.
Skordalia: garlic and breadcrumb or potato-based dip, used as a side dish with fried fish and boiled beets.
Soutzoukakia: baked meat rissoles, often topped with a tomato-based sauce.
Souvla: large cuts of lamb or pork slow-roasted on a rotary spit.

Souvlaki: chunks of meat quick-grilled on a skewer (known to British takeaways as kebab or shish kebab). For variations, and where to find them, *see p124* **Fast food**.
Spanakopitta: small turnovers, which are traditionally triangular, stuffed with spinach, dill and feta.
Spetsofai: a stew of sausages and peppers cooked with wine and bay leaf.
Stifado: a rich meat stew (often rabbit) with small, whole onions, red wine, tomatoes, vinegar, cinnamon and bay.
Tarama, properly taramasalata: fish roe pâté, originally made of grey mullet roe (*avgotaraho* or *botargo*), but now more often cod roe, plus olive oil, lemon juice and breadcrumbs.
Tyropitta: cheese-filled filo pastry, like spanakopitta, but usually without spinach and with more feta.
Tzatziki: a dip of shredded cucumber, yoghurt, garlic, lemon juice and mint.

East Athens & eastern suburbs

French

Spondi
Pyrronos 5, Platia Varnava, Pangrati (210 752 0658/210 756 4021/www.spondi.gr). Trolleybus 2, 4 or 11 from Syntagma. **Open** 8pm-midnight daily. Closed Sun in Aug & 1wk mid Aug. **Average** €€€€. **Credit** AmEx, DC, MC, V. **Map** off p252 H7 ⑤
Year after year, Michelin-starred Spondi is cited as Athens' best restaurant, and two years ago, it also became a member of Relais & Châteaux. The revamped interior is more colourful, but the stone courtyard shaded with bougainvillea creates a surprisingly low-key backdrop to the chef's elaborate creations. His signature dishes include sea bass in rose petal sauce; hare and truffle millefeuille, and sweetbreads with truffles, chestnuts and salsify. Don't miss the daring desserts, created in collaboration with Paris-based pâtisserie Bristol, like banana-pineapple purée in a basil-saffron sauce. The excellent wine list is a revelation.

Seafood

Trata
Platia Anagenniseos 7-9, Kaisariani (210 729 1533). Bus 223, 224 from Akadimias. **Open** noon-1am daily. **Average** €€. **Credit** DC, MC, V.

Alatsi. *See p120.*

Simple grilled Greek fish is the trademark at Trata, by far the best of the seafood restaurants lining this lively square in Kaisariani, where Greek families flock for Sunday lunch. Intensely flavoured fish soup and battered prawns are delicious. Consistently fresh seafood is complemented by fast, polite service, essential for a restaurant that is always jammed to the gills.

Southern suburbs

Greek contemporary

Bakaliko Ola Ta Kala
Gianitsopoulou 1 & Kyprou, Platia Esperidon, Glyfada (210 898 1501). Bus A3, B3 from Panepistimiou. **Open** 9.30am-6pm Mon; 10.30pm-2am Tue-Sat; 5.30pm-1.30am Sun. **Average** €€. **Credit** MC, V.
This chic little deli-café stocks traditional specialities sourced from artisans and co-operatives all over Greece. Sample great home-made treats like smoked cheese from Metsovo, Santorini's famous fava beans and swordfish carpaccio. Delicious dishes of the day, such as cuttlefish and spinach stew, summer vegetable 'crumble' or lentil soup with yoghurt are written up on the blackboard. For dessert, don't miss the *masourakia* from Chios, crispy filo rolls oozing nuts and honey, delicious with a Greek coffee served with a slice of Turkish delight. Prettily packaged goodies from the grocery make great gifts.

Greek traditional

Louizidis
Ermou & Iasonos 2, Platia Vouliagmenis, Vouliagmeni (210 896 0591). Metro Dafni, then bus 171. **Open** *Mar-Nov* 12.30pm-midnight daily. *Dec-Feb* 12.30-5pm daily. **Average** €. **Credit** AmEx, DC, MC, V.
Kyria Athina calls the shots at this family-owned taverna. She runs a tight ship, turning out classics like moussaka, *pastitsio* and octopus macaroni. Baked dishes and seasonal vegetable stews, called

lathera, for which this taverna is well known, often run out later in the day, but you can always make do with grilled meat. The flower-filled veranda is a blissful oasis in this posh coastal suburb.

Pandelis
Naiadon 96, Paleo Faliro (210 982 5512). Tram Panagitsa. **Open** 7.30pm-1am Tue-Fri; 12.30-5pm, 7.30pm-1am Sat; 12.30-5pm Sun. Closed 1st 3wks Aug. **Average** €. **No credit cards**.
Greeks consider the regional cuisine of Poli, brought by Greek emigrés and refugees from Contantinople (Istanbul) in the early part of the 20th century, to be the finest Greek regional fare, and Pandelis is the standard bearer, located in the heart of the area where many refugees settled. The simple decor, long tables and sometimes gruff service don't make a dent in the food experience, which includes an array of aubergine dishes to wax poetic about; grilled meats *yiaourtlou*, with spicy tomato and yogurt sauce; and *pita kaisarias*, an irresistible pie filled with spiced pasturma meat, tomatoes, kasseri cheese and a cardiologist's nightmare portion of butter. The roasted aubergine salad is one of the best around.

Tria Asteria
Melitos 7 & Plastira 77, Nea Smyrni (210 935 8134). Tram Agias Fotinis. **Open** *Sept-mid June* 8pm-1am Mon-Sat; 12.30pm-midnight Sun. *Mid June-Sept* 8pm-1am Mon-Sat. Closed 10 days mid Aug. **Average** €. **Credit** AmEx, DC, MC, V.
One of the first kebab places to open in Athens, Tria Asteria, off a main square in the suburb of Nea Smyrni, is still going strong after more than 20 years. The decor may be nondescript – right down to the synthetic tablecloths – but there are tables on the square in summer and the spiced-up Anatolian fare will tempt even a diehard vegetarian. Excellent marinated grilled meats aside, one of the best things on the menu is *pita kaisarias*, a classic savoury pie made with soft, buttered, homemade filo pastry wrapped around an irresistible filling of mild kasseri cheese,

pasturma and tomatoes. The classic shredded-wheat pastry dessert, *kiounefe*, filled with soft cheese and sweetened with a light syrup, is a perfect finish.

Zevkin
Leof Eleftherias 46, Alimos (210 985 5795). Tram Achilleos. **Open** 8pm-2am Tue-Sat; noon-2am Sun. **Average** €. **No credit cards.**
This slightly out-of-the-way taverna serves food that is a homage to the island of Ikaria, birthplace of the young owner, the waiting staff and no small percentage of the customers. Food here is meant to be shared: simple, robust dishes like *soufico*, a rustic, layered vegetable dish, scream out for communal bread dipping. Vegetable fritters and island goat are other typical crowd-pleasers. Sunday lunch is when things really happen; festivities begin around 3pm and last well into the early evening, with live music and singing from the tables. If you get lucky, you might find yourself dancing.

Italian

Vincenzo
Gianitsopoulou 1, Glyfada (210 894 1310). Bus A3, B3 from Panepistimiou. **Open** 1pm-1.30am daily. **Average** €. **Credit** MC, V.
This cosy pizza place caters to jazz aficionados with regular gigs. The pizzas are the next best thing to the genuine Italian article: a perfectly thin crust is topped with a couple of simple ingredients – prosciutto and rocket, or crushed cherry tomatoes and mozzarella. Finish with a decadent profiterole and a shot of frangolino mulberry liqueur. The back garden brimming with basil plants is quieter than the buzzing terrace at the front.

Mediterranean

Aioli
Artemidos 9, Platia Esperidon, Glyfada (210 894 0181). Bus B3 from Panepistimiou. **Open** 7.30pm-1.30am Mon-Fri; 12.30pm-1.30am Sat. Closed Aug. **Average** €€. **Credit** DC, MC, V.
A favourite date venue, this little restaurant feels like a corner of Provence. The cute, candlelit space is decorated in pastels, with flower-print wallpaper and rose-patterned plates. Start with delicious walnut bread and a bowl of smooth aïoli. Then make eyes over goat's cheese soufflé, cannoli filled with parmesan and rocket, fetuccine with crabmeat, fillet steak with rocket and capers, and, most romantic of all, pavlova with fresh strawberries.

Malabar
Margi Hotel, Litous 11, Vouliagmeni (210 967 0924). Bus A2 from Panepistimiou to terminus, then bus 114, 116 to Apollonos stop. **Open** noon-2am daily. **Average** €€€. **Credit** AmEx, DC, MC, V.
Despite the animal prints and ambient music, the colonial dining room at the Margi Hotel feels rather formal, but the candlelit terrace is quietly exclusive.

The lunch menu, which focuses on bistro standards like rocket and parmesan salad, char-grilled vegetables and grilled salmon, is unadventurous but perfectly good. The expensive dinner menu features more exciting options like marrow and peanut butter ravioli or a perfectly poached grouper in an earthy sauce of shiitake mushrooms, fennel and ruby port. You can also sample the sushi menu as you show off your tan on loungers by the pool.

Northern suburbs

Creative

Semiramis
Hotel Semiramis, Harilaou Trikoupi 48, Kifissia (210 628 4500). Metro Kifissia. **Open** noon-midnight daily. **Average** €€. **Credit** AmEx, DC, MC, V.
Cheekily kitsch or awfully pretentious? Whatever. Since opening last summer, this retro-futuristic bar-restaurant designed by Karim Rashid is always packed. Granted, it looks a lot like Barbie's play house, with squidgy pink sofas and amoeba-shaped tables that interconnect to accommodate unexpected dinner guests. Jeff Koons' porno portraits stare down at you while you nibble on finger food at the bar, and fresh-faced waiters in pastel flares and silver sneakers are eager to please. The chef, Yiannis Loukakos, has not been swayed by the flashy surroundings. The food, a blend of fresh Asian and

Set for top cuisine at **Varoulko**. *See p124.*

Mediterranean flavours, is straightforward but accomplished: tuna steak in a pepper crust with a dollop of caponata, or sweet and sour lobster with mango salad. A dense fig tart makes a good finish.

Vardis

Hotel Pentelikon, Diligianni 66, Kifissia (210 623 0650/6/www.pentelikon.gr). Metro Kifissia/ bus 550 from Kallimarmaro, A7 from Platia Kaningos. **Open** 8pm-12.30am Mon-Sat. Closed Aug. **Average** €€€€. **Credit** AmEx, DC, MC, V.
This Michelin-starred restaurant in the old-fashioned Hotel Pentelikon is the epitome of gastronomic grandeur. In a classic dining room lined with Venetian mirrors, attentive waiters dance around tables set

with Riedel crystal, starched linen and porcelain tableware. Chef Betrand Valegeas has created some outstanding dishes like Solea Solea (sole meunière with gnocchi), côte de veau with morel risotto, lobster salad, roast duck à l'orange with potatoto soufflé, and cauliflower couscous with grilled red mullet. The frothy chocolate 'grand cru' is a sublime finale.

Greek contemporary

Aneton

Str Lekka 19, Marousi (210 806 6700). Metro Marousi. **Open** 8.30pm-midnight Mon-Sat. Closed Aug. **Average** €€. **Credit** AmEx, MC, V.

Greek wines

Only a decade ago, mentioning the words 'Greek' and 'wine' in the same sentence would most likely bring hoots of derision. Memories of sunny evenings spent choking over jugs of retsina that was as harsh as drain-cleaner were about the extent of the average consumer's relationship with Greek wine. But, in recent years, a growing number of boutique wineries have been producing wines that scoop up international awards and win accolades from illustrious wine critics for their originality, style and quality.

Better equipment and training (many Greek winemakers now study in Australia or France) have contributed to this turnaround in fortunes for the industry. But Greece's first Master of Wine, Konstantinos Lazarakis, points out that these facts alone don't explain the explosion of interest in the region. 'Greek wines have seen a lot of improvements in quality over the years, but this is true for other countries as well. What really has changed is that wine consumers around the world are much more open to alternatives; they are getting increasingly bored with another merlot, another chardonnay, and they are starting to look for wines that are different.'

This opening up of the global market spelled hope to struggling Greek wineries. Although Greece was an important wine producer in classical times, in the modern state there had been little incentive to keep low-yield vineyards rather than turning over the land to holiday homes or crops such as olives that received heftier EU subsidies. The locals are not particularly avid wine-drinkers, and attempting to break into a global market dominated by low-priced, mass-market New

World wines was almost unthinkable to the average Greek vineyard owner with a couple of lines of an indigenous grape variety that got watered if and only if the heavens opened.

If bored consumers and wine writers searching for novel alternatives helped get Greek wines into specialist magazines and adventurous off-licences, the change in vogue from heavy, high-alcohol wines to lighter ones lifted easygoing Greek wines out of obscurity and into mainstream consumption. 'Choosing a wine that partners well with food is much more popular now than opening a big, high-alcohol wine that is so rich it almost becomes a meal on its own,' says Lazarakis. 'Greek

This tiny, out-of-the-way restaurant has managed to acquire a cult following in the two years since it opened, mainly because chef-owner Vassilis Kalydis is one of the most vibrant young talents around – and arguably the best overall vegetable chef in Athens. Proof of his talents lies in simple but delicious dishes like fried courgette fingers served with white *tarama* (fish roe) sauce; runner beans, tomatoes and parsley pesto; cooked greens in tomato sauce with pistachio pesto; and sautéed purslane with grated myzithra cheese and walnuts. Another hallmark is his taking of clichéd Greek ingredients and putting them to new use, such as making retsina the basis for sauces, or for steaming fresh clams. The decor pays homage to the past too: Kalydis outfitted the restaurant to look like a period piece from Greece circa 1960, right down to the orange wallpaper and bathroom *chatchkas*, which he hand-picked at flea markets.

Apla

Harilaou Trikoupi 135 & Ekalis 39, Nea Erythrea (210 620 3102). Metro Kifissia, then bus 561. **Open** *Oct-May* 8pm-midnight Mon-Fri; 1pm-1am Sat; 1pm-6pm Sun. *June-Sept* 8pm-midnight Mon-Thur; 8pm-1am Fri, Sat. Closed 2wks mid Aug. **Average** €€€. **Credit** DC, MC, V.
The understated interior – stripped wooden tables in a light space walled with shattered glass – belies the extraordinary, if often inconsistent, Greek food

wines are ideal to be enjoyed with food: they have been made with that purpose in mind for centuries, if not millennia.'

While Greece cannot compete in the bargain basement sector because of the small-scale production, Lazarakis believes that the cost of what actually goes into making a bottle of €10 Santorini wine from a small, historic, family-run producer is much higher than for a €10 Australian wine from a vast, bland, mechanised estate. 'You pay more money for what you get; that goes into the wine rather than for branding, marketing, etc,' he says. 'Greece can propose some excellent wines at moderate prices. I believe that wine over a certain price cannot be seen as a plain commodity – it has a cultural element that cannot be overlooked.'

Perhaps the highest profile wine producers in Greece today are the Gerovassiliou and Alpha estates. The former, which is based near Thessaloniki, was picked as one of the top 100 wineries in the world in 2006 by *Wine & Spirits* magazine, while *Decanter* magazine selected its 2005 Viognier as Best Old World White in 2006. Gerovassiliou's sibling winery, Biblia Chora, has also been widely praised for its polished whites, particularly the Biblia Chora Estate, which blends sauvignon blanc with indigenous assyrtiko grapes. Prestigious Alpha Estate, in northern Greece, won *Decanter*'s Best Old World Red in 2005 for its Alpha Estate red (a blend of syrah, merlot and local xinomavro).

Don't miss a chance to visit Greece's key wine-producing areas to see the vineyards and sample the vintages. Just over an hour from Athens, Nemea (in the Peloponnese; *see p215*) is where more than 40 producers, including such top names as Papaioannou and Gaia, grow their acres of bold red agiorgitiko (among other grapes). Koutsi village, within the Nemea appellation, is Greece's front-runner for *cru* status. The island of Santorini, meanwhile, combines breathtaking beauty with high-quality wine production: the crisp indigenous grape assyrtiko thrives in the volcanic soil. In the north of Greece, Naoussa, where tasty red xinomavro flourishes, is described by Lazarakis as the Burgundy of Greece, not just for its resemblance in style but for its low-tech, small volume wineries. 'There is little tourism, so not much English is spoken, but take a Greek speaker with you and you will have a wonderful time, visiting the vineyards, tasting the wines and eating excellent food in the local tavernas,' he says.

To get a real taste of Greece, at tavernas or restaurants, you should choose wines made from indigenous grapes. Lazarakis recommends the assyrtiko from Santo Wines (Santorini), Lafazanis' agiorgitiko (Nemea), Antonopoulos' moschofilero (a scented, acidic, pinky-white variety from Mantinea), the xinomavro from Karydas (Naoussa), and Meditera's Peza Nobile, which uses the ancient Cretan variety vilana.

And if you want to exorcise any recollections of paint-stripper retsina, order a bottle of Ta Dakrya tou Pefkou (The Pine's Tears) by Kechri & Co. Beautifully presented and eminently drinkable, this classy retsina won Grand Gold at the Thessaloniki International Wine Competition in 2006, and is credited with bringing resinated wine out of the swill bucket and into the cellars of snooty oenophiles.

● *For wine shops in Athens, see p154.*

Eat, Drink, Shop

cooked up by Chrysanthos Karamolegos. Sure, he is able to turn humble taverna staples into a gourmet affair, with dishes like courgettes stuffed with crab and drizzled with *avgolemono* sauce, battered baby calamari with harissa sauce, tempura of sardines with fig vinaigrette and lemon paste, and lamb fillet marinated in honey, mustard, lemon and mint. But his liberal use of spices from every corner of the globe sometimes blurs the line between Greek, Greek-inspired and confused. Karamolegos has an unmistakeable flair for sweet dishes, and his take on the classic Greek custard-filled *galakto-boureko*, in this case prepared with mascarpone and prunes, is unique. Service is friendly, but slow and sometimes ill informed. Prices are not much higher than an upmarket taverna.

Gefseis me Onomasia Proelefsis

Leof Kifissias 317, Kifissia (210 800 1402). Metro Kifissia/bus 550 from Kallimarmaro, bus A7, B7 from Platia Kaningos. **Open** *Mid Sept-May* 8pm-12.30am Mon-Sat; 1-5pm Sun. *June-mid Sept* 8pm-12.30am Mon-Sat. Closed 2wks mid Aug. **Average** €€€. **Credit** AmEx, MC, V.

Vintner Panos Zoumboulis (who owns the Vinifera wine shop next door) has converted the rambling villa where he grew up into a gourmet Greek restaurant, serving ingredients sourced from small producers and artisans nationwide. From Dinos, the impeccable maître d', to cheerful chef Nena Ismirnoglou, who takes time to explain new dishes, there is no doubt that the people who run this place are passionate about what they do – and it comes across in the cooking. Peasant dishes like *fava* (split-pea purée) are tarted up with caramelised beetroot chips; marinated anchovies with shavings of apple, purslane and celery have the subtlety of sushi; goat baked between layers of aubergine and tomato in a yoghurt crust is a wonderfully earthy main dish. The intense chocolate tart with delicate praline crust is ingenious.

Turkish

Tike

Kritis 27 & Harilaou Trikoupi, Kifissia (210 808 4418, 210 801 4584). Metro Kifissia, then bus 525. **Open** 1pm-12.30am Mon-Thur, Sun; 1pm-1am Fri, Sat. **Average** €€. **Credit** AmEx, DC, MC, V.

This outpost of the award-winning Istanbul restaurant chain has won over the locals, who can't get enough of the brilliant kebabs in a setting that could be a modern-day harem girl's dream house. The glass-walled space sits pretty in a vast garden with a mosaic fountain. The decor is inspired by the Orient, with a buzzing red-and-black interior, round tables and bejewelled lampshades. The two dining areas are divided by an impressive grill and wood oven that turns out fantastic *tavuk adana* (tender chicken kebab served with paper-thin bread) and *fındık lahmacun* (spicy minced meat on a crisp pitta base). Try not to wolf the puffy pitta breads with garlic butter before the arrival of such starters as

velvety *mütebbel* (char-grilled aubergine with yoghurt), and tomato and onion salad dressed with pomegranate juice. Finish with *helva*, – a warm, crumbly semolina pudding studded with pine nuts that conceals a heart of vanilla ice-cream.

Piraeus

Seafood

Diasimos

Akti Themistokleous 306-308 (210 451 4887/ 210 453 1418). Metro Piraeus, then bus 904. **Open** 10am-1am daily. **Average** €€. **Credit** AmEx, MC, V.

With the first hint of summer, locals flock to the waterfront for a taste of the sea. You'll spot Diasimos among the many (mostly tacky) fish restaurants along the coastal strip of Freatida by the sign outside ordering you to STOP! The entrance is adorned with octopus hung out to dry and crates of cockles, shrimps and fish. This is the place for a quintessentially Greek supper: a whole grilled fish simply dressed in olive oil and lemon. The spaghetti with shrimps is also delicious, and the service is fast and friendly.

Kollias

Stratigou Plastira 3 (Kalokairinou & Dramas), Tabouria (210 462 9620). Metro Piraeus, then bus 843 to Tabouria stop. **Open** 1pm-1am Mon-Sat; 1-6pm Sun. Closed Aug. **Average** €€. **Credit** AmEx, DC, MC, V.

Although way off the beaten track in an unpromising apartment block, Kollias is a landmark for local gourmets. Fish fetishist Tassos Kollias will take you on a tour of his kitchen so you can choose your supper from ice boxes bulging with clams, oysters and all manner of obscure sea creatures from around the country. You'll also get to choose from the impressive, colourful array of seafood starters. As soon as you sit down on the flower-filled terrace decked with nautical paraphernalia, you're presented with a shot of heavenly fish soup. Follow that with squid cooked in its own ink, sea urchin salad, seafood beggars' purses and the catch of the day. The wine list is extensive, Greek and very reasonably priced. The restaurant may be moving to Paleo Faliro in late 2007, so call before setting out.

Plous Podilatou

Akti Koumoundourou 42, Mikrolimano (210 413 7910/210 413 7790). Metro Piraeus, then bus 915; or Metro Faliro, then 10min walk. **Open** 12.30pm-12.30am daily. **Average** €€€. **Credit** AmEx, DC, MC.

Of all the seafood restaurants squeezed along post-card-perfect Mikrolimano – otherwise known as the Athenian Riviera – Plous Podilatou has the most elegant decor and inventive menu. As a full moon rises above the tinkling masts and star-spangled sea, indulge in ouzo-seared crabmeat served over spinach salad, or Greek salad served in pitta bread, grilled aubergine with smoked octopus and red pepper flakes, and lemon sole with shrimps and capers.

Cafés

Get hooked on Athens' café culture.

Athinaion Politeia is great for both people-watching and Acropolis-watching. *See p134.*

Athenians love coffee, especially when they can spend at least a couple of hours savouring it at their favourite café. It's not the coffee itself that drives them to spend hours in cafés, but the ritual attached to drinking it and enjoying it with friends. Greeks use cafés as their *stekis*, or hangout, where they can talk, watch crowds, discuss the latest business deal, or simply enjoy being seen in the latest cool place in town. In Athens, where a frenetic city life is fuelled by copious doses of caffeine, the kind of coffee you drink and where you drink it can say a lot about you. To unravel the complexities of who drinks what where, *see p135* **Café society**.

Everyone derives great pleasure from the coffee ritual: old men sipping loudly at cups of thick *elliniko* (traditional Greek coffee), hipsters nursing tall glasses of icy *frappé* (Greece's very own concoction of Nescafé, cold water, sugar and an optional shot of condensed milk), and young things swirling their straws around *freddos* (iced cappuccinos or espressos). Many café owners take pride in their product, paying attention to flavour (specify if you want a weak brew) and presentation (a little cookie often comes tucked

between spoon and saucer). Even the ever-popular instant coffee – or 'nes', as it's known – comes with an appealingly frothy head.

When it's warm, people take their coffee outside: in summer it's hard to find a free table outside one of the popular cafés in the central neighbourhoods of Thissio, Kolonaki or Plaka.

Acropolis & around

Amaltheia

Tripodon 16, Plaka (210 322 4635). Metro Akropoli.
Open 10am-1am Mon-Thur, Sun; 10am-2am Fri, Sat.
No credit cards. Map p251 E6 ❶
This small, traditional pastry café specialises in dairy-based sweets, and while few in variety, they are certainly good. It's well known for its yoghurt – which comes topped with honey and walnuts, chocolate sauce, dark cherry or quince compote, or diced fruit – and is a classic spot for savoury crêpes.

> ❶ Pink numbers given in this chapter correspond to the location of each café on the street maps. *See pp248-252.*

aPLAKAfe
*Adrianou 1, Thissio (210 325 5552). Metro
Thissio.* **Open** 9.30am-late daily. **Credit** MC, V.
Map p248/p250 D5 ❷
In one of the most accessible spots under the
Acropolis, aPLAKAfe, at the junction of Apostolou
Pavlou and Adrianou pedestrian walkways, is a good
spot to rest after a few hours of sightseeing. Be sure
to try a plate of *loukoumades* topped with warm
honey and ice-cream. The selection of special coffees
includes double espresso with cream in a caramel and
truffle-frosted glass, and 'coffee time' espresso, with
vodka and Cointreau, topped with orange peel.

Athinaion Politeia
*Apostolou Pavlou 33 & Akamantos, Thissio (210
341 3795). Metro Thissio.* **Open** 8am-2am daily.
Credit AmEx, DC, MC, V. **Map** p248/p250 D5 ❸
An old mansion has been transformed into a café
with a great view of the crowds on Apostolou Pavlou
and the Acropolis beyond. There's a super range of
coffees on offer, from basic Greek coffee to the likes

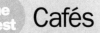

The best Cafés

For classic frappés
Athinaion Politeia (*see above*) and
Ionos (*see right*) froth it up nicely.

For cappuccino freddos
Clemente VIII (*see p135*) and **Queen's Tea
& Coffee** (*see p137*) make the best in town.

For a cup of real Greek coffee
Aigli Bistro Café (*see right*) and **Ethnikon**
(*see p135*) make coffee the traditional way.

For location, location, location
Athinaion Politeia (*see p134*) has a
prime view of the Acropolis; **Dioskouri**
(*see right*) has the Agora in its sights;
Aigli Bistro Café (*see p134*) is in the
tranquil National Gardens.

For fashion and style
Kolonaki's coolest hang out at **Tribeca**
(*see p138*) and **Da Capo** (*see p137*).

For the sweet and lovely
Amaltheia (*see p133*) is famed for its
yoghurt, topped with sour cherry or quince;
Petite Fleur (*see p137*) has the best hot
chocolate in Athens. For yummy pastries,
see p138 **Beyond baklava**.

For cool treats
Savour ice-cream at **Dodoni** (*see p139*)
or the amazing gelato at **Pagotomania**
(*see p139*).

of espresso corretto, an explosive mix of espresso
and sambuca. The Terpsichori crêpe with chocolate
and fresh fruit is an indulgent treat. *Photo p133*.

Dioskouri
*Dioskouron 13 & Mitroou, Plaka (210 321 9607).
Metro Monastiraki.* **Open** 9am-1am daily. **Closed**
Nov-Feb. **No credit cards. Map** p249/p251 E5 ❹
While the frappé isn't anything to write home about,
the tables here have a magnificent view of the
Agora, with Gazi and Keramikos fading into the
urban background. It's best avoided at summer
lunchtimes, as there's very little shelter from the sun.

En Athinais
Iraklidon 12, Thissio (210 345 3018). Metro Thissio.
Open 8.30am-3am Mon-Thur, Sun; 9am-4am Fri, Sat.
No credit cards. Map p248/p250 C5 ❺
Housed in a restored neo-classical building, En
Athinais has a splendid view of the Acropolis
through its large windows. Outside, the tables on the
pedestrianised street are a great place to people-
watch with a good cup of coffee or a light meal.

Filistron
*Apostolou Pavlou 23, Thissio (210 342 2897/210 346
7554). Metro Akropoli or Thissio.* **Open** *Sept-mid
June* noon-1.30am Tue-Sun. *Mid June-Aug* 6pm-2am
Tue-Sun. **Credit** DC, MC, V. **Map** p250 D5/D6 ❻
A pleasant, if often crowded hangout for light meals
and good coffee. Its best asset is its terrace, which is
lush with climbers and flowers and has a lovely view
across the city. For indulgence, try their alternative
frappé with a ball of vanilla ice-cream instead of milk.

Ionos
*Angelou Geronta 7, Platia Filomousou, Plaka (210
322 3139). Metro Akropoli or Syntagma.* **Open** 8am-
2am daily. **Credit** AmEx, MC, V. **Map** p251 F6 ❼
Ionos is one of the best places for a frappé in Plaka.
Alternatively, try the ice-cold 'special' chocolate
milkshake. There are also backgammon boards.

Tristrato
*Angelou Geronta & Dedalou 34, Plaka (210 324
4472). Metro Akropoli or Syntagma.* **Open** 10am-
1am daily. **No credit cards. Map** p251 F6 ❽
A blast of cool air hits you as soon as you push open
Tristrato's wooden door. Several herbal teas are
available, such as Greek mountain tea, as well as a
broad selection of coffees to go with the home-made
baklava or cheesecake with cherries.

Historic Centre
Aigli Bistro Café (Lallabai Café)
*Zappeion, National Gardens (210 336 9363).
Metro Akropoli or Syntagma.* **Open** 9am-4am daily.
Credit AmEx, DC MC, V. **Map** p251/p252 G6 ❾
An all-time classic spot for Greek coffee, Lallabai
(still known by most Athenians as Aigli) is located
in a picture-perfect setting among the trees and fountains beside the Zappeion exhibition hall. It's an
ideal shady refuge from the sizzling summer heat.

Café society

No matter that a cup of coffee costs a small fortune since the advent of the euro, there's still a café on every corner of Athens – and it's always packed. Coffee can be roughly divided into three categories: *ellinikos* (Greek), *frappé* (chilled and frothed Nescafé) and *freddo* (iced cappuccino). Whatever your poison, it can be ordered *sketo*, *metrio* or *glyko* – plain, medium or sweet.

Sludgy *ellinikos* is an acquired taste, favoured by the grizzled patrons of *kafenia*, nicotine-stained coffeehouses where many an elderly gent idles away an afternoon as the slam of backgammon and click-clack of worry beads beat time. The number of *kafenia* in downtown Athens is dwindling, but some self-consciously old-school enterprises now serve Greek coffee brewed the traditional way in a tiny copper beaker heated over hot ash (or *sti hovoli*). It is usually served with a wedge of Turkish delight or a cinnamon biscuit and always with a glass of cold water. **Aigli Bistro Café** (*see p134*) is the perfect place at which to savour a Greek coffee with a dash of panache.

Ouzo may be a Greek cliché, but the national drink is, in reality, frappé – a frothed-up blend of Nescafé, sugar, cold water and condensed milk (one even inspired a book, *Frappé Nation*). Most Athenians are devoted to frappé, be they anarchic college students, middle-aged office workers or ageing taxi drivers. Those who like to be seen will usually sip it at a modern café (*kafeteria*) like **Athinaion Politeia** (*see p134*), on the scenic pedestrian walkway circling the Acropolis. Since the drink is cool and refreshing, it goes down a treat in the hot Greek summer, when it becomes ubiquitous.

These days, though, the hipster's coffee of choice is a freddo, to be sipped slowly at landmark cafés like **Da Capo** (*see p137*) or at low-key gems like **Queen's Coffee & Tea** (*see p137*), both in Kolonaki. So far, the **Starbucks** behemoth hasn't had too much impact on the city's café culture, although there are now several branches (probably the only cafés in town where smoking is forbidden).

Every neighbourhood square retains its couple of rival cafés with their own faithful regulars (there was a time when patrons of *kafenia* were strictly divided according to their political affiliation, though this is no longer so). Athenians plan their day around (multiple and leisurely) coffee breaks. Even midweek at noon, you'll have a hard time finding a free table at one of the crammed cafés along Skoufa in Kolonaki, Adrianou in Plaka or Iraklidon in Thissio. And Athenians don't just come to cafés for a caffeine fix; they swap gossip, seal deals and break hearts. So when a local suggests '*Pame gia kafe?*' ('Shall we go for a coffee?'), be prepared for anything.

Aiolis

Eolou 23 & Agias Irinis (210 331 2839). Metro Monastiraki. **Open** 10am-2am daily. **No credit cards.** Map p249/p251 E5 ⑩

Though jam-packed during the day, the pedestrianised shopping strip of Eolou can be quite deserted at night. But the small tables of the Aiolis café are hardly ever empty. This former local café, housed in an attractive neo-classical building, attracts thirtysomethings who call in for an espresso, a chocolate soufflé or even a mojito.

Clemente VIII

CityLink, Voukourestiou 3 (210 321 9340). Metro Panepistimio or Syntagma. **Open** 7.30am-11.30pm Mon-Sat; 10am-11.30pm Sun. **No credit cards.** **Map** p249 F5 ⑪

On an exclusive pedestrianised street near some of the most expensive shops in the city, the chic Clemente VIII, opened in October 2006, is a place to catch a glimpse of some of the city's celebs. It stands on the site of one of Athens's most famous old cafés, Brazilian. The cappuccino freddo is among the best in Athens. Fresh and inventive sandwiches, salads and cakes accompany the drinks. *Photo p136.*

Ethnikon

Syntagma Square (210 331 0576). Metro Syntagma. **Open** 6am-2am daily. **Credit** MC, V. **Map** p249/p251 F5 ⑫

The glamour set flocks to **Clemente VIII** for its superb cappuccino freddos. *See p135.*

Ethnikon has a great location in the paved, tree-shaded heart of Syntagma Square, right in the middle of downtown Athens. Be sure to try Greek coffee served the traditional way, in a *briki* with a bronze base, and accompanied by a complementary sugary *biskotoloukoumo* sweet. Other popular desserts include a sumptuous chocolate cake with layers of melted chocolate and a strawberry garnish.

Flocafé

Stadiou 5, Syntagma (210 324 3028). Metro Syntagma. **Open** 7am-midnight Mon-Fri; 8am-midnight Sat; 10am-midnight Sun. **No credit cards.** **Map** p249 F4
This home-grown café chain is standing up to the competition from Starbucks. It offers a huge number of coffee options, and also serves up great snacks. As in most Greek cafés, the music and the conversation can get loud, especially in the evening. **Other locations**: throughout the city.

Krinos

Eolou 87, Athens Central Market (210 321 6852). Metro Monastiraki. **Open** 7.30am-4pm Mon, Wed, Sat; 7.30am-9pm Tue, Thur, Fri. **No credit cards.** **Map** p249 E4
Open since 1922, this old-style pâtisserie is known for its excellent *loukoumades* and its reliably good Greek coffee. Add walnuts and ice-cream to the *loukoumades*, or order other traditional sweets such as rice pudding or sweet *boughatsa* (a pastry filled with cream and dusted with powdered sugar and cinnamon). The place is packed with locals, especially older Athenians out for a late-morning break after shopping at the Central Market.

Nikis Café

Nikis 3, Syntagma (210 323 4971). Metro Syntagma. **Open** 7am-2am daily. **No credit cards.** **Map** p249/p251 F5
Ideal for a quick coffee stop when you're out shopping or strolling along nearby Ermou, this crowded but cosy little hole-in-the-wall café-bar also offers light meals and snacks.

Polis

Pesmazoglou 5, Aithrio Stoas Vivliou (210 324 9588). Metro Panepistimio. **Open** 9am-2am Mon-Sat; 5pm-1am Sun. **No credit cards.** **Map** p249 F3
A cool café-bar in the hidden-away courtyard on top of the Stoa tou Vivliou – the historic book arcade between busy Stadiou and Panepistimiou – Polis serves a range of coffees, cocktails, sandwiches and light meals.

Kolonaki & around

Cafeina

Kiafas 6 & Zoodochou Pigis, Exarchia (210 384 1282). Metro Omonia or Panepistimio. **Open** Oct-May 10.30am-late Mon-Fri; noon-late Sat, Sun. June-Sept 10.30am-late Mon-Fri; noon-late Sat. **No credit cards.** **Map** p249 F3
You will be hard pressed to discover a smaller café than Cafeina, a cosy yet avant-garde hangout in bohemian Exarchia. Its plush, comfortable sofa is ideal for long conversations with a group of friends, the coffee is good, the hot chocolate's even better, and the speakers normally pump out a wicked selection of freestyle and deep house beats.

Da Capo: the place to be seen in see-and-be-seen Kolonaki.

Cake

Irodotou 13 & Kapsali, Kolonaki (210 721 2253).
Metro Evangelismos. **Open** 9am-10pm Mon-Fri;
11am-8pm Sat; 11am-6pm Sun. **Credit** AmEx, MC,
V. **Map** p252 H5 ⑱

Kolonaki has a wealth of cafés, but this tiny
one, serving a good selection of beverages and
all kinds of fragrant cakes, stands out from the rest.
Pop in and try to grab one of the three stools for
a slice of the heavenly chocolate fudge cake, the
rich but not too sweet American-style cheesecake,
or a sinful dark chocolate and biscuit creation
called the Hedgehog.

Da Capo

Tsakalof 1, Platia Kolonaki, Kolonaki (210 360
2497). Metro Syntagma. **Open** 7am-2am daily.
No credit cards. Map p252 G4/H4 ⑲

Renowned for its cappuccino freddo, Da Capo is also
known for its elite clientèle (not to mention its rather
limited seating). There's a selection of sweets and
cakes to go with the coffee.

Filion

Skoufa 34, Kolonaki (210 361 2850).
Metro Panepistimio. **Open** 7am-1am daily.
No credit cards. Map p252 G4 ⑳

One of the oldest café hangouts in Athens,
this lovely place was known as Dolce until recently. It remains one of the top coffee spots for the
city's artists, writers, painters, scholars and, of
course – this being Kolonaki – lots of shoppers.
There's a range of beautiful handmade chocolates
as well as delicious apple-pie and *galatopita* (a kind
of milk pudding).

Petite Fleur

Omirou 44, Kolonaki (210 361 3169). Metro
Panepistimio. **Open** 11am-11pm daily. Closed Sat
& Sun in July and all Aug. **No credit cards.**
Map p252 G4 ㉑

An adorable little café that specialises in chocolate,
Petite Fleur also features savoury and sweet crêpes,
inventive salads, and a relaxing, nostalgic atmosphere enhanced by old jazz and blues records on the
turntable. The hot chocolate is smooth, creamy and
decadent; giant mugfuls of it are served with a
spoonful of chestnut or sour cherry preserves. The
coffee is also outstanding, especially the mocha.

Queen's Coffee & Tea

Ploutarchou 18, Kolonaki (210 729 2522).
Metro Evangelismos. **Open** *Apr-Oct* 7.30am-late
Mon-Fri; 9am-late Sat; 10am-6pm Sun. *Nov-Mar*
7.30am-9pm Mon-Fri; 9am-10pm Sat; 10am-6pm
Sun. **Credit** AmEx, DC, MC, V. **Map** p252 H4 ㉒

This small café supplies a wealth of gourmet
coffees and teas to the denizens of this posh neighbourhood, but it also makes what may be the best
cappuccino freddo in Athens. On a sunny day, grab
one of the few tables and enjoy a frothy iced-coffee
drink, a smooth filtered brew, a thick milkshake
or one of a selection of herbal teas in flavours such
as apple and cinnamon, pear and camomile.
The baked goods, notably the berry or apple pies,
are also excellent.

Rosebud

Skoufa 40 & Omirou 60, Kolonaki (210 339 2370).
Metro Panepistimio. **Open** 9.30am-2.30am daily.
Credit AmEx, DC, MC, V. **Map** p252 G4 ㉓

This café-bar is a regular meeting point for arty types and cinephiles. The decor is mainly a cute combination of wood and velvet, and the speakers put out a pleasant mixture of jazz and soul.

Sofia's Valaoritou Café
Valaoritou 15, Kolonaki (210 361 1993). Metro Panepistimio or Syntagma. **Open** *May-Sept* 8am-10pm Mon-Fri; 8am-7pm Sat. *Oct-Apr* 8am-10pm Mon-Fri; 8am-10pm Sat. **Credit** AmEx, DC, MC, V. **Map** p249/p252 G4 ㉔
A welcome addition in December 2006 to the famous Valaoritou Brasserie, this café is a gem. Alternatives

to coffee include vanilla rooibos tea or a glass of Vinsanto sweet wine. Food is fresh and beautifully prepared – the cafe's version of *galaktoboureko*, made with creamy camembert instead of the more traditional custard, is genius – and the atmosphere elegant and comfortable.

Tribeca
Skoufa 46 & Omirou, Kolonaki (210 362 3541). Metro Panepistimio. **Open** 9am-4am daily. **No credit cards. Map** p252 G4 ㉕
This café-bar might be the size of a dolls' house, but it still manages to attract the coolest crowd in

Beyond baklava

Nothing enlivens a cup of coffee like a rich, buttery, syrup-drenched Greek pastry. Spiced with Near Eastern flair and often made with scented honey, Greek sweets are celebrated delicacies in the capital, where the best pastry chefs use top-grade ingredients and cherished family recipes. Favourites include baklava (layers of sugared walnuts, buttered filo pastry, clove and cinnamon), *galaktoboureko* (fresh custard in filo), *diples* (fried coils of dough smothered in honey syrup and sprinkled with ground walnuts), *karidopita* (a fragrant, delightfully syrupy walnut cake), *melomakarona* (walnut cookies soaked in orange-scented syrup), *kourabyedhes* (crumbly butter cookies covered in powdered sugar) and *kataifi* (logs of walnuts, sugar and spices wrapped in shredded filo and soaked with honey).

Greeks from Istanbul introduced a mouth-watering selection, including *kazan dipi* (a crème brûlée-like dessert made with buffalo milk cream), *kaimaki* ice-cream (flavoured with aromatic mastic – resin from the lentisk tree from the Aegean island of Chios) and *ekmek* (an Anatolian cake soaked in rich syrup). Fresh *loukoumia*, also known as Turkish delight, imbued with flavours such as rose, pistachio and mastic, also has its roots in Asia Minor. Even something as simple as yoghurt can be decadent, when it's the traditionally thick and creamy Greek kind, served with thyme-scented honey or *glyka tou koutaliou* 'spoon sweets' such as baby walnut, bitter orange, lemon blossom or quince preserves.

Another Greek classic is an aromatic bread called *tsoureki*, traditionally served at Easter but now a year-round staple. Flavoured with mastic and *mahlepi* (crushed Persian cherry pits), *tsoureki* is a breakfast favourite, served warm with butter.

You probably won't find the best *galaktoboureko*, baklava or *loukoumia* in cafés. Instead, you'll need to visit a *zacharoplasteio*, or pâtisserie. The best *galaktoboureko* in Athens is to be found at **Kosmikon** (Leof Ionias 104, Agios Nikolaos, North Athens, 210 864 9124), a *zacharoplasteio* founded in 1961, where fresh, hot and unbelievably creamy *galaktoboureko* comes in round pans. For an alternative version, made with camembert, try **Sofia's Valaoritou Café** (*see above*). For the best baklava, go to **Karavan** (Voukourestiou 11, Historic Centre, 210 364 1540), which has a wide selection of classic nutty and syrupy pastry, including versions with chocolate, dates, pistachios and hazelnuts; Karavan also has excellent *loukoumia*. For a taste of Istanbul baklava, stop by **Karaköy Güllüglou** (Nikis 10 & Ermou, Syntagma, 210 321 3959), an excellent Turkish pâtisserie that has opened several branches in Athens. **Hara** (*see p139*) has dreamy *kazan dipi* and *kataifi*.

A prime spot for the best *melomakarona*, *diples* and *kourabyedhes* is **Varsos** (*see p139*), a pâtisserie and café in the leafy northern suburb of Kifissia. Loukoumades, the simple but delectable fried fritters drenched in honey syrup, are best enjoyed at **Krinos** (*see p136*). A few pâtisseries, such as **Agapitos** (Voulis 7, Syntagma, 210 325 8110, www.agapitos.gr) make *tsoureki* filled with chocolate, a decadent northern Greek speciality.

In recent years, Greeks have also begun to favour non-Greek sweets such as millefeuille, best made at **Despina** (Patriarchou Ioakim 56, Kolonaki, 210 729 5582) and cheesecake (we reckon the city's best is at **Cake**; *see p137*).

super-chic Kolonaki, who let their hair down to the accompaniment of a wide variety of tunes, ranging from '80s new wave to R&B.

Wunderbar
Themistokleous 80, Exarchia (210 381 8577). Metro Omonia. **Open** 9am-4am daily. **No credit cards.** **Map** p249 F2 ❷⑥
Earthy colours reign here, and colourful sofas (which spill out onto the square) seat a young, stylish crowd. Stop by for a good cappuccino in the daytime; in the evening a clubby atmosphere pervades.

North of the Acropolis

A Lier Man
Sofroniou 2, Gazi (210 342 6322). Metro Keramikos. **Open** noon-3am Mon-Thur, Sun; noon-late Fri, Sat. **No credit cards.** **Map** p248 B4 ❷⑦
An aesthetically pleasing café-bar in the newly hip neighbourhood of Gazi, A Lier Man serves a range of coffees, light Mediterranean food and drinks.

Pagotomania
Taki 21 & Aisopou, Psyrri (210 323 0001). Metro Monastiraki. **Open** 10am-2am Mon-Thur, Sun; 10am-4am Fri, Sat. **No credit cards.** **Map** p249 D4 ❷⑧
Dreamy *gelato* rules at this sunny café, which has branches around the city. Swirls of chocolate and hazelnut are sweet inspiration, as are fruity flavours such as mango. The espresso also gets top marks. **Other locations**: throughout the city.

Ta Serbetia tou Psyrri
Eschylou 3, Psyrri (210 324 5862). Metro Monastiraki. **Open** 10am-1am daily. **No credit cards.** **Map** p249 D4 ❷⑨
There's a folk-arty feel to the hand-decorated furniture and yet more artistry in this café's kitchen, which produces home-made delicacies such as *galaktoboureko* custard pie and preserves (raspberry, cherry, grape, bergamot, quince), served either with yoghurt or the northern Greek sweet *kazan dipi*.

Voutadon 48
Voutadon 48, Gazi (210 341 3729). Metro Keramikos. **Open** 10am-midnight Mon-Thur, Sun; 10am-1.30am Fri, Sat. **No credit cards.** **Map** p248 B4 ❸⓪
French-inspired cuisine, coffee to match, and amazing desserts such as rose-flavoured sorbet make this café-bistro one of the best new spots in trendy Gazi.

East Athens

Dodoni Ice Cream
Ymittou 95, Pangrati (210 751 4445). Metro Evangelismos, then 15min walk. **Open** 8am-2am daily. **No credit cards.**
Greece's premier ice-cream parlour chain is a must for sweet-toothed coffee drinkers. You can combine a cappuccino or freddo with one of the many heavenly ice-cream flavours on offer, including gourmet almond caramel choco, mango sorbet or tiramisu. **Other locations**: throughout the city.

Northern Suburbs

Da Luz
Harilaou Trikoupi 157, Kifissia (210 625 3065). Metro Kifissia. **Open** 8am-3am daily. **Credit** AmEx, DC, MC, V.
This modern café opens for coffee in the morning and later in the day transforms into a cool bar attracting a young and trendy crowd. The very good Mediterranean food served here is another of Da Luz's attractions.

Hara
Patission 339, Ano Patissia (210 201 5009). Metro Ano Patissia. **Open** 9am-2am daily. **No credit cards.**
A sweet, old-style café founded around 1929 by a Greek from Istanbul, Hara specialises in traditional Greek coffee and Anatolian-tinged desserts such as *ekmek*, *kaimaki* ice-cream and *kataifi*.

Varsos
Kassaveti 5, Platanos Square, Kifissia (210 801 2472). Metro Kifissia. **Open** 7am-1am Mon-Fri; 7am-2am Sat; 7am-midnight Sun. **No credit cards.**
A pâtisserie-café founded in 1892, Varsos is a great place at which to sample Greek coffee and mouth-watering baked goods such as *tsoureki*, *melomakarona*, strawberry pie and meringues. The yoghurt is also superb.

Southern Suburbs

Cafe Brasil
Eleftherias 4, Glyfada (210 894 2124-6). Tram Kolimvitirio. **Open** 9am-midnight daily. **Credit** AmEx, MC, V.
This café-bistro is part of Brasil Suites, a boutique hotel in Glyfada, but anyone can pop in to savour the array of outstanding coffees and Brazilian and Greek sweets and food. Staff are polite and helpful and the atmosphere is elegantly cosy.

Chocolat
Zissimopoulou 9, Glyfada (210 894 3442). Tram Kolimvitirio. **Open** 9am-1.30am daily. **Credit** MC, V.
The sandwiches here are delicious, and a meal in themselves; desserts are dreamy; coffee and chocolate drinks are excellent. And all within spitting distance of the promenade for a seaside stroll.

Piraeus

Love Café
Akti Koumoundourou 58, Mikrolimano, Piraeus (210 417 7778). Metro Piraeus, then trolleybus 20 or metro Faliro, then 15min walk. **Open** 10am-2am daily. **No credit cards.**
Sip your fancy coffee drink or, by evening, your fancy cocktail, and watch as yachts fill the scenic Mikrolimano harbour. The decor is warm and the atmosphere relaxing; light dishes, such as sandwiches, are also served.

Shops & Services

The Athens of the Ancient Agora is now a modern marketplace.

Shopping may not be high on everyone's list of relaxing holiday actitivies, particularly in temperatures pushing 40 degrees Celsius. But in Athens, even the most reluctant of consumers can be tempted by the fact that all the capital's main shopping areas are within easy walking distance of each other. It also helps that shops here tend to congregate like with like.

As a general rule, Greek shops are open from morning to mid afternoon on Monday, Wednesday and Saturday, and morning until dusk on Tuesday, Thursday and Friday. Family-owned corner shops and pharmacies still close for an afternoon siesta on those late-opening days, but the majority of stores stay open all day. Shops in tourist areas are allowed to open all day every day, including Sunday.

Sales periods are strictly limited to a couple of weeks in January/February and again in August, but you will find that some shops have signs announcing *prosfores* (bargains) at other times of the year. Although eastern-style haggling is frowned upon in consciously 'European' Athens (markets aside), in tourist areas you may well find shop owners giving you a 'special price' for your purchases.

One-stop shopping

Department stores & malls

Attica

CityLink, Panepistimiou 9, Historic Centre (211 180 2500/211 180 2600). Metro Syntagma. **Open** 10am-9pm Mon-Fri; 10am-8pm Sat. **Credit** AmEx, DC, MC, V. **Map** p249 F4/F5.
Housed in a landmark building (formerly King Otto's stables, then the Nazi headquarters during World War II), Attica has some 300 shops within the shop, selling more than 800 different brands of clothing, accessories, cosmetics and homewares. International fashion labels include Missoni, Joseph, Sonia Rykiel, Burberry, Diesel and Adidas. Parents in search of trendy togs for their tots can find a great selection, sports fanatics can browse happily in the athletics section, and makeup junkies love the gleaming cosmetics hall on the ground floor, which includes shops of Jo Malone candles and local brand Korres's natural-based skincare. The shop windows are the most admired in Athens, with constantly changing theatrical displays that, more often than not, feature spectacular one-off creations by jewellery designer Katerina

Psoma. The CityLink complex to the rear hosts stand-alone stores of such luxury brands as Hermes, Cartier, Ferragamo and Dolce & Gabbana.

The Mall

Andrea Papandreou 35, Marousi, Northern suburbs (210 630 0000/www.themallathens.gr). Metro Nerantziotissa. **Open** 9am-9pm Mon-Fri; 9am-8pm Sat. **Credit** AmEx, DC, MC, V.
One of the largest retail centres in south-eastern Europe, this eight-storey development has more than 200 shops selling everything from laptops to lingerie, as well as a 15-screen multiplex, a food hall with snack stops, coffee shops and diners, and many other diversions. French bookstore Fnac, household furnishings chain Zara Home and electronics giant Mega Kotsovolos (owned by Dixons) are the main draws, along with cheap clothing from Zara, Bershka, Mango, Accessorize, Koton and Sfera.

Notos Galleries

Eolou 99 & Lykourgou 2-6, Historic Centre (210 324 5811). Metro Omonia. **Open** 9am-9pm Mon-Fri; 9am-6pm Sat. **Credit** AmEx, DC, MC, V. **Map** p249 E3.
Seven floors of clothing, perfumes and cosmetics, swimwear and suncreams, children's fashions and more. The international labels represented are fairly generic – Benetton, Lacoste, Bostonians, Trussardi Jeans – but the sixth floor is dedicated to trendy items for teens and twentysomethings, with names such as Custo Barcelona, Nolita and Michiko Koshino. At the top floor café you can enjoy a cold drink or snack while admiring the view. Around the corner on Platia Kotzia, Notos Home (210 374 3000) can fulfil all your home furnishing needs.

Markets

The Sunday morning flea market that sprawls between Monastiraki and Thissio metro stations (with a fringe element stretching down to Gazi of enterprising individuals selling off their old clothes, DVDs and mobile phones of dubious origin) is hugely popular with collectors hunting down that elusive ancient coin or exotic stamp, designers and artists in search of inspiration, and bargain-hunters after retro shoes and unusual furnishings for their home. To get started, *see p146* **Walk 3**.

Each neighbourhood of Athens boasts its own weekly farmers' market (*laiki*). Residents clear their cars – reluctantly – from the designated street the night before, and by daybreak the lorries and pick-up trucks are

Where to shop

ATHINAS
Shopping heaven for foodies, with a meat and fish market and satellite stalls selling cheeses, nuts, olives and herbs. Perpendicular to Athinas is spice street Evripidou. From the fragrant sacks that line the pavement, you can pick up a surprisingly affordable handful of vivid saffron threads from Kozani and a bouquet of dried *rigani* (oregano).

SYNTAGMA SQUARE
Books, music and clothing are the focus here, although there are still a few deli-type shops from which you can purchase vivid green olive oil, sun-warmed pistachio nuts and almond biscuits flavoured with mastic resin (rumoured to heal everything from mouth ulcers to, believe it or not, rabies).

ERMOU
This central shopping drag attracts global high-street brands such as Zara, Marks & Spencer and Sephora. Posses of teenagers descend on it to snap up the newest trends, while families come to buy basics. As you get further away from Syntagma Square, Ermou transforms briefly into a snack area of mouthwatering souvlaki stalls before becoming a strange mix of dusty old antique shops, hardware stalls and too-cool-for-school streetwear shops.

MONASTIRAKI
A fertile hunting ground for antiques lovers and souvenir-hunting tourists. Looking for a second-hand *bouzouki*? Want a handpainted backgammon set? Or perhaps a Guns 'n' Roses T-shirt or a pair of Converse trainers? Wander the winding alleys and you will find all these and much more. *See also p146* **Walk 3**.

PLAKA
Labyrinthine and atmospheric Plaka is similarly tourist-focused, with lots of menu-touting restaurateurs, stalls of handcrafted leather sandals and satchels, and souvenir shops with museum replica statuettes, cheesecloth dresses and olive oil soaps.

KOLONAKI
This upmarket area is home to branches of most global designer brands (Gucci, Giorgio Armani, Burberry, to name just a few) and fancy cafés at which to flaunt your new finery.

THE SUBURBS
Similarly high-end fashion boutiques can be found in the leafy northern district of **Kifissia**, with shops congregated in the area around Kolokotroni and Levidou streets. On the south coast, **Glyfada** has a mix of street brands and classy designer labels. The main coastal avenue of shops, with the tram line running along it, is Metaxas.

Eat, Drink, Shop

starting to rumble in, laden with fresh fruit and vegetables. Some stalls sell just one, seasonal, product, such as freckly apples from Tripoli, whereas others offer a cornucopia of wild greens, glossy olives, earthy potatoes and imported bananas. For the best organic produce, visit the Friday market in **Platia Dexameni**, an offshoot of the main Kolonaki market.

Books & magazines

International newspapers and magazines are sold at certain larger kiosks (*periptera*), such as those on Syntagma and Kolonaki squares. **News Stand**, near the Acropolis (Athanasiou Drakou 2, 210 922 5146; another 40 branches throughout the city) stocks a vast array of international periodicals, ranging from *Wallpaper** and *Collezione* to *Newsweek* and *Decanter*, as well as newspapers from Britain, France, Italy, the US, Turkey and elsewhere. Most European papers arrive on the morning of publication; German and US newspapers can be purchased later in the afternoon.

Eleftheroudakis

Panepistimiou 17, Historic Centre (210 325 8440/ www.books.gr). Metro Panepistimio. **Open** 9am-9pm Mon-Fri; 9am-6pm Sat. **Credit** AmEx, DC, MC, V. **Map** p249 F4.
Whether you have left your map of the Peloponnese behind, want to brush up on Homer, get some tips on which Greek wines to buy, or just need an easygoing bestseller for the beach, this is the place to look. The ground floor has tempting display tables of the staff's top picks from each of the seven floors above, which offer novels and classics (in English and Greek), cookery and travel books, guidebooks, interiors and art volumes, and children's books. For a break from browsing, pop up to the sixth-floor café.
Other locations: Nikis 20, Syntagma (210 322 9388); Lazaraki 27, Glyfada, Southern suburbs (210 894 3892); Kifissias 268, Kifissia, Northern suburbs (210 623 6677).

Children

Fashion

The Little Baby Shop

Spefsippou 10, Kolonaki (210 724 5640). Metro Evangelismos. **Open** 10am-3pm Mon, Wed, Sat; 10am-3pm, 5-8pm Tue, Thur, Fri. **Credit** AmEx, MC, V. **Map** p252 H4.
Decorated like an old-fashioned English nursery, complete with Beatrix Potter pictures and pastel-painted walls, this charming shop is stocked with carefully chosen pieces by British and Greek labels. The smock-fronted floral frocks by Greek design duo Aesthetic Theory are top-sellers for little girls; the hand-decorated T-shirts by local designers Any

Wish, the slogan babygros from London and the personalised pillows are favourites for newborns.

Mouyer

Kanari 8, Kolonaki (210 361 7714). Metro Syntagma. **Open** 9.30am-3.30pm Mon, Wed; 9.30am-9pm Tue, Thur, Fri; 9.30am-4pm Sat. **Credit** AmEx, DC, MC, V. **Map** p252 G5.
Greek children take their first steps in Mouyer shoes. The brand has been equipping the nation's tots with anatomically supportive footwear since 1900, when the first Mouyer shop opened in Athens. It now has more than 30 stores throughout Greece, selling quality leather shoes made in Italy and France for children aged between four months and 12 years old. As well as Mouyer's own label, you'll find imported shoes from cult brands like Camper, Stones and Bones, and Babybotte.

Toys

Jack in the Box

Haritos 13, Kolonaki (210 725 8735). Metro Evangelismos. **Open** 10am-3.30pm Mon, Wed, Sat; 10am-8.30pm Tue, Thur, Fri. **Credit** AmEx, DC, MC, V. **Map** p252 H4.
Traditional wooden toys and puzzles, cuddly soft toys, board games, musical boxes, wind-up tin cars, carousels and other carefully chosen toys from a bygone era line the shelves (and floor) of this treasure trove of a shop.

Neverland

Solonos 18, Kolonaki (210 360 0996). Metro Syntagma. **Open** 9am-3pm Mon, Wed; 9am-3pm, 5-8.30pm Tue; 9am-8.30pm Thur, Fri; 9am-3.30pm Sat. **Credit** DC, MC, V. **Map** p252 G4.
An Aladdin's cave of goodies for youngsters (and for parents with an eye for quality collectibles). On display here are furry animals, micro-scooters, board games and dolls, as well as detailed sets of furniture and crockery for old-fashioned doll's houses.

Electronics & photography

Computer purchase & repairs

Apple Store

Akadimias 32, Historic Centre (210 364 1211/www.applestore.gr). Metro Panepistimiou or Syntagma. **Open** 9.30am-3.30pm Mon, Wed, Sat; 9.30am-8.30pm Tue, Thur, Fri. **Credit** MC, V. **Map** p252 G4.
Need first aid for your Mac or iPod, or some funky accessories? Although a mere shadow of the temples of tech that are the Apple stores in London and New York, this small branch can provide a quick fix – though you may need to open an account with them.

Plaisio

Voulis 3 & Kolokotroni, Historic Centre (210 325 8000/hotline 800 11 12345/www.plaisio.gr). Metro Syntamga. **Open** 9am-9pm Mon-Fri; 9am-4.30pm Sat. **Credit** AmEx, DC, MC, V. **Map** p249 F4/F5.

This electronics superstore sells the latest models from Hewlett Packard, Acer, Sony and Toshiba, and lots of other gadgets to keep techies happy for hours. Unfortunately, Plaisio only provides a repair service for its own-brand Turbo-X computers, but the staff will put you in touch with those catering for the other makes.
Other locations: throughout the city.

Photography

Giagtzoglou & Sons
Christou Lada 5-7, Historic Centre (210 324 1780). Metro Panepistimiou. **Open** 8am-4pm Mon-Fri. **No credit cards. Map** p249 F4.
Handily located between Syntagma and Omonia squares, just behind the Old Parliament building, this small shop offers speedy, efficient and helpful service. As well as printing your photos (from digital or film), staff can do enlargements and touch-ups and even construct an artistic album of your holiday snaps. Whatever your photographic needs, the owner, Leonidas, will try his best to please. The shop also stocks camera accessories.

Picopoulos Camera Service
3rd floor, Lekka 26, Historic Centre (210 322 5650/210 323 5409/nicpico@acsmi.gr). Metro Syntagma. **Open** 9.30am-5.30pm Mon-Fri. **No credit cards. Map** p249 F5.
Don't be put off by the unpromising entrance – take the lift to the third floor and you will be greeted by walls of photographic equipment and helpful staff who can undertake repairs for all types of cameras.

Fashion

Designer

Bettina
Pindarou 40 & Anagnostopoulou 29, Kolonaki (210 339 2094). Metro Syntagma. **Open** 10am-3.30pm Mon, Wed, Sat; 10am-8.30pm Tue, Thur, Fri. **Credit** AmEx, DC, MC, V. **Map** p252 G4.
This simple, white, minimalist gallery stocks the collections of Greece's home-grown fashion talents Sophia Kokosalaki and Angelos Frentzos, as well as pieces from such revered international labels as Comme des Garçons, Junya Watanabe and Martine Sitbon. Find the prices a bit steep? Then check out the Bettina stock shop, which carries a selection of last season's pieces (Voukourestiou 4, Syntagma, 210 323 8759).

Free Shop
Voukourestiou 50, Kolonaki (210 364 1308). Metro Syntagma. **Open** 10am-4pm Mon, Wed, Sat; 10am-9pm Tue, Thur, Fri. **Credit** AmEx, DC, MC, V. **Map** p252 G4.
It started out in the '70s as a hippie hangout of Indian clothing, patchouli and trippy LPs. In the '90s it stocked Paul Smith and Gap. Now, in its latest incarnation to suit the spirit of the times, Free Shop sells a fresh and innovative combination of conceptual Comme des Garçons and Martin Margiela, sculptural Balenciaga, Midas-touched Lara Bohinc accessories and vertiginous Pierre Hardy heels. The character of the shop is still evolving, as young buyer (and part-owner) Melissa

Eat, Drink, Shop

Vassilis Zoulias Old Athens pays homage to '50s and '60s style. *See p152.*

Metaxas experiments and explores, picking up Fair Trade trainers or beaded necklaces here, an extravagant icon bag or a simple jersey tunic there.
Other locations: Dim Vasileou 15, Neo Psichiko, Northern suburbs (210 675 4308); Botsari 1, Glyfada, Southern suburbs (210 968 0123).

Occhi
Sarri 35, Psyrri (210 321 3298/www.occhi.biz).
Metro Thissio. **Open** noon-5pm Mon, Sat; noon-9pm Tue-Fri. **Credit** AmEx, MC, V. **Map** p249 D4.
This open-plan art space/concept clothing store exhibits designs by up-and-coming talents from Greece and further afield. The collection of handmade clothes and accessories, which are all based on the idea of fashion as a wearable art form, includes loom-woven wool and Lurex clutchbags by Joanna Louca (a Cypriot designer picked out by Louis Vuitton for the magazine *Percorsi di Creatività 4* as a top talent to watch in 2007), easily elegant dresses from Copenhagen's Sarah Heartbo, jersey tops and baggy harem pants by Portuguese label Aforest, American Apparel T-shirts, and KrvKurva Tyvek bags with limited edition graphics.

Discount
For discount shoe stores, *see p149*.

Factory Outlet
Athens Airport retail park (210 354 1800). Metro Airport. **Open** 10am-9pm Mon-Fri; 10am-8pm Sat. **Credit** AmEx, DC, MC, V.
Looking for a bargain? Then check out the airport's discount shopping terminal. In this appropriately hangar-like building, you can find more than 400 brands of discounted clothes and accessories. Ranges include sportswear by Adidas and New Balance, designer clothing and accessories from Luella, See by Chloe, Joseph and Missoni, streetwear from Energie and Von Dutch, and shoes from Camper and DKNY.

General

.LAK
Skoufa 10, Kolonaki (210 628 3260/www.lak.gr).
Metro Syntagma. **Open** 10am-4pm Mon, Wed, Sat; 10am-8.30pm Tue, Thur, Fri. **Credit** AmEx, DC, MC, V. **Map** p252 G4.
Under the direction of Greek fashion entrepreneur Lakis Gavalas – of the nearby eponymous emporium (Voukourestiou 50, 210 362 9782), and the man behind a one-off Kelly bag for Hermès, emblazoned with the Greek flag – young fashion students produce this line of cool, casual separates complete with quirky detailing. Stock includes unisex graphic T-shirts and leather sandals, cute towelling dresses and jersey hoodies for girls, easy chinos and sweatshirts for boys.
Other locations: A Metaxa 24-26, Glyfada, Southern suburbs (210 628 3203); Androutsou 153, Piraeus (210 628 3207).

Shop
Ermou 112A, Monastiraki (210 323 1683). Metro Thissio. **Open** 10am-9pm Tue, Thur, Fri; 10am-5pm Wed, Sun; 10am-6pm Sat. **Credit** AmEx, DC, MC, V. **Map** p249 D4/D5.
This trendy lifestyle store sells an eclectic selection ranging from slouchy Pepe jeans, psychedelic GSUS shirts, vintage YSL shades and printed swimwear for girls and guys, to Cowshed cosmetics and Italian toothpaste. Don't miss the diffusion line of softly tailored trousers and jackets by Greece's Yiorgos Eleftheriades, called Collage Social, or the colour-block dresses by Cyprus-born, Paris-based Erotokritos. When you're all shopped out, relax with a chilled coffee at the upstairs café.
Other locations: Patision 52 (210 882 6054).

Shocking Pink
Benizelou Palaiologou 4, Plaka (210 322 6554).
Metro Monastiraki or Syntagma. **Open** 10am-8pm daily. **Credit** AmEx, DC, MC, V. **Map** p249 E5.
Graphic and fashion designer Kelly Michaloudaki wanted to open a shop that offered something rather more creative than the usual tourist tat to visitors wandering Plaka. So she designed a bright, white marble-floored store and filled it with racks of colourful kaftans and printed T-shirts, display cases of cheerful beaded necklaces and hot-hued heels, plexiglass chandeliers and capacious handbags. The result is feminine, fun, mood-enhancing and certainly creative. Even if you're not clothes shopping, check out Kelly's imaginative Athens fridge magnets adorned with evil eyes (a steal at just €2.50 each).

Underground
Skoufa 35, Kolonaki (210 364 0734). Metro Syntagma or Panepistimio. **Open** 9.30am-4pm Mon, Wed, Sat; 9.30am-9pm Tue, Thur, Fri. **Credit** AmEx, DC, MC, V. **Map** p252 G4.
Visiting this off-beat basement store is rather like going round to a trendy friend's house and rummaging through her wardrobe. The clothes and accessories, picked out by super-stylish owner Katerina Gouma from both Greece and abroad, are effortlessly cool and unusual, and the friendly staff are skilled at picking suitable items for you from the rails and, with a mere twist of the fabric, displaying an innovative new way in which each could be worn. Fashionistas love the line designed for Underground by avante garde designer Apostolos Mitropoulos: skinny pants, layered vest-tops and multi-usage dresses in his signature hues of black and yellow.
Other locations: Kyriazi 14-16, Kifissia, Northern suburbs (210 801 6144).

Used & vintage

Amerikaniki Agora
Sofokleous 19, Historic Centre (210 321 7051).
Metro Omonia. **Open** *Sept-July* 9am-2.30pm Mon, Wed, Sat; 9am-2.30pm, 5-8pm Tue, Thur, Fri; *Aug* 9am-2.30pm daily. **No credit cards**. **Map** p249 E4.

Eat, Drink, Shop

Elixirion. *See p153.*

Walk 3 Following the (flea) market

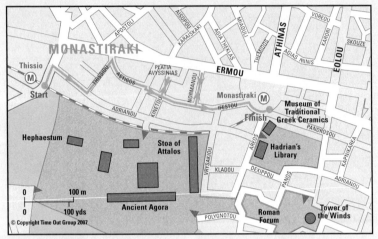

Located next to Athens' Ancient Agora, where traders from all around the Mediterranean once peddled their wares, Monastiraki's colourful, crowded flea market has become the meeting place for sellers of everything, from antique furniture and rare books to clothes, kitsch and junk. Sunday, when the rest of the city shuts down completely, is the liveliest market day, when dealers from all over converge on the area to hawk their choicest and cheapest offerings. Keep in mind that haggling is expected – indeed, de rigueur – no matter how low the initial price may seem. And remember to start fairly early. Stalls and shops open at about 8.30am and close around 3pm.

Begin the walk at Thissio metro station, going down pedestrianised Adrianou. Take note on your right of the sprawling ruins of the Ancient Agora (*see p75*), where fifth-century BC vendors once told riff-raff like Socrates (*see p15* **Three wise guys**) to move along and stop scaring away customers. Continue down Adrianou, turning left on to Thissio, lined with stir-crazy caged songbirds and sawdusty carpenters' workshops. Have a poke around **Erato** (Thissio 9, 210 331 1991), a favourite bookstore of Athenian literati, full of old hardback foreign-language books, leather-bound rare editions, old prints and Greek newspapers dating back to the 1860s. Continue down Thissio, then right on Astigos,

which will take you past a row of shops selling old records and books. At the end of Astigos, dog-leg right then immediately left on to frenetic Ifestou, then take the first left up sleepy Kinetou, which leads you into Platia Avyssinias, the heart of the market, where dealers sell old lamps, musical instruments, crockery, mirrors, painted trunks, cut-glass Turkish tea sets and other such treasures.

On your left as you enter the square is **Café Abyssinia** (Kinetou 7, 210 321 7047), an excellent place for a coffee or snack break. A family-run institution, its Arabic and French takes on Greek classics burst with flavour. A little further down is **Kougianos** (Platia Avyssinias 6, 210 321 2473), which has old periscopes and other instruments, wooden signs from the early 1900s and upholstered furniture. On the other side of the square, Platia Avyssinias 3 can yield some good finds: at street level, **Costas Alexandros** (210 321 1580) has antique desk sets with ink bottles and working quills, battered, marble-topped rococo writing tables, 1920s typewriters, Victrolas and old Greek toys. Downstairs, **Motakis** (210 321 9005) is one of the few stores in Athens licensed to carry certified antique furniture.

Leave the square along Ifestou, a street full of shops selling cheap clothes and trinkets, but keep your eyes peeled for the small entrances that lead downstairs into dusty storehouses of junk and treasure. Be sure not to miss Normanou, a sunny alley on the left of Ifestou. Here you'll find shops selling maps, prints, old photos and everything else for your walls. Try **Darousos Theotokis** (Normanou 7, 210 331 1638) for prints of old Greek ads and cinema stills. Back on Ifestou, look for **Vavas** (Ifestou 30, 210 321 9994). Barely even a hole in the wall, this stand has been selling carved *tavli* (backgammon – the national pastime of Greece's café-sitters) sets for decades. The handpainted sets make unusual gifts, while the pocket editions (prices start from €10) are ideal for passing the hours on the island-bound ferry. At Ifestou 24, duck into the arcade of stores selling old Greek records. On the edge of the arcade is **Nasiotis** (Ifestou 24, 210 321 2369), where bibliophiles can get lost in the stacks of second-hand holiday reading, rare and first editions, old magazines and Greek movie posters. Follow Ifestou to Monastiraki metro station, just opposite which is **Kiritsis** (Areos 1, 210 324 0544), a stall full of coins, stamps and wartime paraphernalia.

Poised over the central meat market, with potent aromas wafting up through the open windows in summer, this second-hand clothing outlet attracts every variety of the style-conscious from students on a budget to designers searching for inspiration. If you're prepared to spend hours sifting through the kilos of bulk-bought clothes from the States, you might just be lucky enough to chance upon a glamorous 1930s gown or a recent piece by Calvin Klein or Donna Karan.

Borell's

Ypsilantou 5, Kolonaki (210 721 9772/mobile 6942 271667). Metro Evangelismos. **Open** 10am-3pm Mon, Wed, Sat; 10am-2pm Tue, Thur, Fri. **Credit** DC, MC, V. **Map** p252 H5.
Ccostume jewellery aficionados should be sure to visit this antique emporium. It is packed with genuine 1930s, '40s and '50s pieces, many signed by such luminaries of the jewellery world as Miriam Haskell, Trifari and Kenneth Lane. Pieces are collected by the shop's owner during her regular trips to antique fairs in Britain.

Le Streghe son Tornate

Haritos 9, Kolonaki (210 721 2581). Metro Evangelismos. **Open** 10.30am-3.30pm Mon, Wed, Sat; 10.30am-8.30pm Tue, Thur, Fri. **Credit** AmEx, DC, MC, V. **Map** p252 H4.
With its classic Chanel suits, flamboyant designer gowns and leopardskin coats, this colourful boutique stands firmly in the category of 'vintage' rather than 'second-hand'. Prices are high, but the selection, by Athens' celebrated thrift expert Riana Kounou, is first class.

Fashion accessories & services

Dry cleaning & laundry

5 a Sec

Xenokratous 40, Kolonaki (210 721 5914). Metro Evangelismos. **Open** 8am-8pm Mon-Fri; 9am-4pm Sat. **No credit cards**. **Map** p252 H4.
Cheap, quick dry-cleaning and laundry services, but don't expect individual attention – this is a chain and staff just want to get the job done. Jumpers cost between €2.50 and €3.50, trousers about €4 and leather jackets and coats from €40.
Other locations: throughout the city.

National Dry Cleaners & Laundry

Apollonos 17, Historic Centre (210 323 2226). Metro Syntagma. **Open** 8am-5pm Mon, Wed; 8am-8pm Tue, Thur, Fri. **No credit cards**. **Map** p249/p251 F5.
This friendly, family-run dry-cleaners is particularly good at cleaning suede and leather items. Staff also offer a leather-dyeing service, a point worth bearing in mind if you spill a glass of red wine down your pale leather jacket.

Hats

Katerina Karoussos

Dorylaiou 17, Ambelokipi (210 645 5821). Metro Megaro Mousikis. **Open** 9am-8pm Mon-Fri; 10am-3pm Sat. Bespoke service before 3pm. **Credit** AmEx, DC, MC, V.

Using top-quality fabrics and feathers, the capital's best-known milliner creates elaborate headgear for theatrical performances, made-to-measure masterpieces for weddings and special occasions, and a line of simple but chic summer straw boaters and soft fabric everyday caps. As well as producing her renowned hats, Karoussos recently launched a nostalgic, '50s-inspired prêt à porter clothing collection with designer Vassilis Zoulias, available at Zoulias' Old Athens store (*see p152*).

Jewellery

Elena Marneri Creative Gallery

Agathoupoleos 3, Patissia, North Athens (210 866 8195). Metro Victoria. **Open** 10am-3.30pm Mon, Wed, Sat; 10am-2.30pm, 5.30-9pm Tue, Thur, Fri. Closed Mon in July & Aug. **Credit** AmEx, DC, MC, V.

It might be slightly off the beaten track, but a visit to this gallery will give you an instant snapshot of the contemporary Greek jewellery scene. Carefully stowed away in its glass cases and drawers are the works of some of the most talented young jewellery designers working in Greece today. Make sure you ask to see Katerina Psoma's gloriously ostentatious necklaces and bracelets adorned with antique trinkets and semi-precious stones, as well as Dimitris Dassios' lavish crinkled gold collars and cuffs studded with Swarovski crystals. While you are in the area, pop next door to the unusual Bebe Gallery, a children's art space with one-off paper dresses and christening baubles.

Elena Votsi

Xanthou 7, Kolonaki (210 360 0936/www.elena votsi.com). Metro Evangelismos. **Open** 10am-3pm Mon, Wed, Sat; 10am-8.30pm Tue, Thur, Fri. **Credit** AmEx, DC, MC, V. **Map** p252 H4.

This talented Greek designer worked for Gucci's accessories division before launching her own line, much to the delight of her many fans among A-list celebrities and jewellery aficionados. She made international headlines when she was chosen to redesign the 2004 Olympic medals. Votsi's impeccably finished creations that marry chunky semi-precious stones with 18-carat gold are the epitome of classic Greek elegance. If you're visiting the island of Hydra, pop into her white-painted store right on the seafront.

Folli Follie

Ermou 18, Historic Centre (210 323 0729). Metro Syntagma. **Open** 9am-3.30pm Mon, Wed, Sat; 9am-9pm Tue, Thur, Fri. **Credit** AmEx, DC, MC, V. **Map** p249/p251 F5.

There is nowhere better for reasonably priced, good-quality jewellery, watches, bags and scarves than this global accessories chain, which started here in Athens. The K Collection of heavy beaded necklaces with precious stones and antique elements is particularly impressive (prices start at around €120). **Other locations**: throughout the city.

Lalaounis

Panepistimiou 6 & Voukourestiou, Historic Centre (210 361 1371). Metro Syntagma. **Open** 9am-5pm Mon, Wed, Sat; 9am-9pm Tue, Thur, Fri. **Credit** AmEx, DC, MC, V. **Map** p252 G4.

For decades the shops of Ilias Lalaounis, one of the earliest masters to make a name for Greek jewellery on the international stage, have been attracting discerning customers for the jewellery designer's top-quality, Byzantine-inspired solid gold necklaces, bracelets and earrings. If you have time, it's well worth visiting the Ilias Lalaounis Jewellery Museum (*see p74*) near the Acropolis for an overview of the jeweller's oeuvre.

Maria Mastori

Alopekis 20, Kolonaki (210 729 5077). Metro Evangelismos. **Open** by appointment only. **Credit** AmEx, DC, MC, V. **Map** p252 H4.

Combining unusual materials such as wood, plastic, wire or rubber with gold, silver, mother-of-pearl or semi-precious stones, Mastori's sculptural necklaces and knuckleduster rings are bold and innovative. Her imaginative presentations during Athens Collections fashion week have grabbed international media attention, leading to collaborations with boutiques abroad as well as participation in fashion exhibitions such as Tranoi in Paris.

Lingerie & swimwear

Brazil by Brasil

Ermou 56 (in the arcade), Historic Centre (210 324 6955). Metro Monastiraki. **Open** 9.30am-6pm Mon, Wed, Sat; 9.30am-9.30pm Tue, Thur, Fri. **Credit** AmEx, DC, MC, V. **Map** p249 E5.

This showcase of Brazilian fashion lures Athenian shoppers with its itsy-bitsy printed bikinis, hot-hued slogan undies, Havaiana flip-flops and easy-to-wear beachdresses (among other delights). The swimwear selection is huge, with lots of brightly coloured floral, polka-dot or striped one-pieces and triangle bikinis with a choice of peekaboo half-cheek 'Brazilian-cut' bottoms or more modest, conventional 'European-style' briefs. Prices start from around €40 for swimsuits.
Other locations: Pindarou 38, Kolonaki (210 361 7540); Esperidon Square 3, Glyfada, Southern suburbs (210 894 7759).

Filidono

Tsakalof 11, Kolonaki (210 361 6780). Metro Syntagma. **Open** 10am-3.30pm Mon, Wed, Sat; 10am-8.30pm Tue, Thur, Fri. **Credit** AmEx, DC, MC, V. **Map** p252 G4/H4.

This abundantly stocked basement is where smart Athenian girls come to stock up on bikinis for the long, hot summer. Brands include La Perla, Miss Sixty, Soin, D&G, DKNY, Replay, Calvin Klein and Blu Bay. The men's range comprises boxers and briefs, but not, as yet, swimwear.

Vraki
Skoufa 50, Kolonaki (210 362 7420). Metro Panepistimio. **Open** 10am-6pm Mon, Wed, Sat; 10am-9pm Tue, Thur, Fri. **Credit** DC, MC, V. **Map** p252 G4.
A funky outlet selling affordably priced, Modus Vivendi underwear: mainly cheeky G-strings and brightly coloured boxers for guys, but there are also cute cotton briefs and vests for girls.

Luggage
Need a solid, kickproof suitcase in which to transport your precious cargo of olives and ouzo back home? **Attica** (*see p140*) stocks a wide range of hard-cover cases by TUMI, Delsey and Samsonite, as well as German brand Bree's practical holdalls and an exhaustive assortment of softer hand luggage. For durable overnight bags, why not look at the selection of handcrafted leather holdalls in the tourist areas of Plaka and Monastiraki? They are simple, stylish and will last for years.

Shoes
See also p155 **Pantelis Melissinos**.

All About Shoes
Ermou 65 & Eolou, Historic Centre (210 335 6442). Metro Monastiraki. **Open** 9am-6pm Mon, Wed, Sat; 9am-9pm Tue, Thur, Fri. **Credit** AmEx, DC, MC, V. **Map** p249 E5.
With its tempting displays, this shop gives no indication of being the bargain basement that it is. You'll find killer heels from Dolce & Gabbana and Ferragamo, suede loafers and squashy leather bags from Tod's and Hogan, glittering clutches from Yves Saint Laurent, kitten heels from Miu Miu and much more. The stock, which includes men's shoes, mostly dates back a couple of seasons, but who cares as long as it carries those all-important designer logos?

Left
Leventi 1, Kolonaki (210 723 8937). Metro Evangelismos or Syntagma. **Open** 10am-3.30pm Mon, Wed; 10am-9pm Tue, Thur, Fri; 10am-4.30pm Sat. **Credit** AmEx, DC, MC, V. **Map** p252 H4.
In summer, the crowd-pullers are the lovely beaded leather or suede sandals by Greek designer Ioannis. In spring and autumn, it's the soft ballet pumps by Repetto or Hookipa (another line by Ioannis), and winter sees an appealing window display of handsome Italian boots and tempting shoes with designer details such as clunky cone heels or studded straps.

Mesogeia: the traditional taste of Greece. *See p153.*

Get the Athens look

Over the years, Greece has given the fashion world such celebrated talents as Jean Desses and Sophia Kokosalaki, yet a homegrown industry is only just struggling to its feet. In a country where there are few incentives to create new design, a buying public addicted to Italian and French imports, and a government unwilling to give financial support to young talents, only a handful of couturiers managed, in the past decades, to scrape a living, chiefly through supplying made-to-order wedding gowns for celebrities and socialites.

But the advent of a Greek fashion week – Athens Collections, launched in March 2005 and since then taking place each March and October – is sparking new interest in a sector that has languished for far too long. Foreign press and buyers flown in to appraise the collections have cherry-picked the brightest stars and spread their work around the globe; government funding has become available to help Greeks participate in international exhibitions; and the media buzz has inspired local shoppers to pay up for Greek designs, rather than always opting for the 'safety' of multinational labels.

A quick tour of some of the most warmly praised designers' ateliers and shops will give you a good idea of what's happening in Greek fashion right now. As visionary and accomplished as they are modest, **Dimitris Alexakis** and **Grigoris Triantafyllou** of **Deux Hommes** (Kanari 18, Kolonaki, 210 361 4155, by appointment only) were picked out after their first Athens Collections showing to exhibit at the Paris Prêt à Porter fair; after their second catwalk display in Athens, they started a collaboration with luxury giant LVMH's guru Jean-Jacques Picard (advisor to John Galliano at Dior, among other luminaries), working towards a strong entry on the Paris Fashion Week calendar. Combining an instinct for future trends with an old-fashioned couture aesthetic, the talented duo produce coherent collections of structured clothes that follow the lines of the body. Perennial top-sellers are the elegant coats, exquisite evening gowns and crisp tailored trousers in luxury fabrics.

Another of Greece's most respected designers is softly spoken, self-effacing **Loukia** (Kanari 24, Kolonaki, 210 362 7334, by appointment only), who for the last two decades has been creating intricate, embroidered lace tops, lavish, swirling silk skirts and gossamer-fine wedding dresses for the Athenian elite. For Athens fashion week, Loukia, who cut her teeth in theatre costume design, launched a ready-to-wear collection of

neat white shirts paired with pinafore dresses, hourglass jackets and brogues, in addition to her signature embroidered and sequinned lace pieces. Received with great acclaim, Loukia was invited to show her prêt à porter collection at Tokyo's international fashion fair – the first Greek designer ever to exhibit in Japan.

Yiorgos Eleftheriades has a rather more casual approach. His vision of day-to-evening chic includes soft tailoring, 3D cuts and experimental use of fabrics (paper hats and bags, for example). At his **YEShop** (Agion Anargyron 13, Psyrri, 210 331 2622, *pictured*), you can expect the unexpected in his complementary collections for the modern urban male and female – *trompe l'oeil* shirt-jackets, high-waisted culottes and braces, slouchy suede boots with peep toes, glittering platform shoes and knitted mohair sleeveless cardigans. If you love his look but can't squeeze any more out of your credit card, don't miss Eleftheriades' more affordable line called Collage Social, sold at Shop (*see p144*).

After graduating from the Fashion Institute of Arnhem and working for a year at one of Rome's classic couture houses, young **Angelos Bratis** (Bousiou 24, Goudi, East Athens, 210 698 2536, by appointment only) returned to Athens to design one-off cocktail confections that are so beautiful they bring a tear to the eye. Simple and seamless, made by draping and pinning the most extravagant silk and tulle on a mannequin, these timelessly elegant dresses are nothing less than investment pieces. If you miss him in Athens, you can catch Bratis's designs on the catwalks of New York, Rome and Amsterdam, as well as in the windows at the Maria Luisa boutique in Paris and at the Space Downtown showroom in New York.

Another young designer who's turning heads is **Orsalia Parthenis** (Dimokritou 20 & Tsakalof, Kolonaki, 210 363 3158; also in Kifissia, Mykonos and Crete), who has taken over her father's high-street chain of shops selling cotton basics and sexed it up with draped jersey wrap dresses, body-hugging silk-jersey tunics, ribbed leggings and little chambrais shorts. The vivacious thirtysomething has also added collections of silk eveningwear, chunky heeled shoes, and huge satchel bags and metallic clutches, as well as keeping on a line of traditional Parthenis separates – T-shirts and ribbed vests, linen shift dresses and drawstring trousers, all in natural fabrics and subdued monochrome hues.

Eat, Drink, Shop

They sell stronger stuff, in addition to notable Greek vintages, at **Fine Wines**. *See p154.*

Lemisios

Lykavittou 6 & Alexandrou Soutsou, Kolonaki (210 361 1161). Metro Syntagma. **Open** 9am-3pm Mon, Wed, Sat; 9am-8pm Tue, Thur, Fri. **Credit** AmEx, DC, MC, V. **Map** p252 G4.

Platforms and kitten heels may come and go, but some shoes never go out of style. For decades Athenian women have been stepping on to the creaky floorboards of this family-run cobblers to buy durable, handcrafted ballet slippers, basic pumps and flat leather sandals that still look as elegant as they did when shoemaker Nicolas Georgiou (aka Lemisios) first rose to fame in the 1950s, fitting shoes for screen darling Aliki Vouyouklaki. The personal service at the store is impeccable: if a strap feels too tight, a heel too high or a sole too slippery, manager Costis Katsalis (Georgiou's great-grandson) will race the shoe over to the workshop for an instant revamp. The store also offers a made-to-order service.

Spiliopoulos

Ermou 63, Historic Centre (210 322 7590). Metro Monastiraki. **Open** 10am-5pm Mon, Wed, Sat; 10am-9pm Tue, Thur, Fri. **Credit** AmEx, DC, MC, V. **Map** p249/p251 E5.

A bargain-hunter's delight, this shop stocks seconds and last season's styles from such sought-after names as Alberta Ferretti, Kate Spade, Narciso Rodriguez, Calvin Klein, Donna Karan and many others at a fraction of their original prices. We should really have kept this one a secret…

Other locations: Adrianou 50, Monastiraki (210 321 0018).

Vassilis Zoulias Old Athens

Kanari 17, Kolonaki (210 361 4762). Metro Syntagma. **Open** 9.30am-3.30pm Mon, Wed; 9.30am-9pm Tue, Thur, Fri; 9.30am-4pm Sat. **Credit** AmEx, DC, MC, V. **Map** p252 G5.

Greek *Vogue* stylist Vassilis Zoulias takes inspiration from the elegant films and photographs of the 1950s and '60s for his beautiful collections of handmade pointy stilettos, ballet shoes and chunky platforms. Matching bags are also available, as well as luxuriously soft leather Gilda gloves. From autumn 2007 Zoulias also offers suitably retro shift dresses, chic suits and glorious swing coats. *Photo p143.*

Shoe repairs

Iliopoulos

Voulis 42, Historic Centre (210 324 5028). Metro Syntagma. **Open** 7am-6pm Mon-Fri; 7am-2pm Sat. **No credit cards**. **Map** p249/p251 F5.

In his tiny workshop, elderly Mr Iliopoulos does an impeccable job re-heeling, re-soling, dyeing or just tidying up your scruffy but beloved shoes and boots.

Takouni Express

Voulis 7 (in the arcade), Historic Centre (210 322 1545). Metro Syntagma. **Open** 9am-5pm Mon, Wed, Sat; 9am-9pm Tue, Thur, Fri. **Credit** DC, MC, V. **Map** p249 F5.

This shoe repair chain offers swift, efficient and reasonably priced service for basic operations such as replacing heels. Also sells a slippers and flip-flops.

Other locations: Skoufa & Pindarou, Kolonaki (210 363 7003); Filonos 35, Piraeus (210 412 2453).

Food & drink

For food markets, *see p141*; for Greek pastries, *see p138* **Beyond baklava**. To navigate local vintages, *see p128* **Greek wines**.

Greek specialities

Elixirion
Evripidou 41, Psyrri (210 321 5141). Metro Monastiraki. **Open** 7.30am-3.30pm Mon-Wed, Sat; 7.30am-5.30pm Thur, Fri. **Credit** AmEx, DC, MC, V. **Map** p249 E4.
On Athens' aromatic spice street, close to the meat market, Elixirion is well worth a visit for its interesting and tasteful interior as well as the spectacular array of mountain herbs, spices, teas, local honeys and traditional homeopathic remedies. Great bunches of oregano and camomile are suspended from the ceiling, baskets of dried rosebuds sit in the entrance, and the walls are lined with deep, glass-fronted drawers full of all manner of fragrant twigs and powders. *Photo p145.*

Gnision Esti
Christou Lada 2 & Anthimos Gazi 15, Historic Centre (210 324 4784). Metro Panepistimio. **Open** 9am-4pm Mon-Sat. **Credit** AmEx, DC, MC, V. **Map** p249 F4.
Barely more spacious than a larder, this shop is deservedly renowned for its traditional savouries and drinks, sourced from small producers all over the Greek countryside, who have perfected the art of making one delicious item: melt-in-the-mouth *koulourakia* (cookies), say, fiery *tsipouro* spirit, flavoursome honey, creamy scoops of feta cheese or green-hued virgin olive oil.

Mesogeia
Nikis 52 & Kydathinaion, Plaka (210 322 9146). Metro Syntagma. **Open** *June-Sept* 9am-5pm Mon, Wed, Sat; 9am-9pm Tue, Thur, Fri. *Oct-May* 9am-5pm Mon, Wed, Sat; 9am-8.30pm Tue, Thur, Fri; 10am-5pm Sun. **Credit** MC, V. **Map** p251 F6.
If you happen to be in Plaka, do your food shopping at this small store, which is packed to the gunnels with traditional (and often organic) goodies. The selection includes crusty *paximadia* (rusks), along with local olive oil, Greek wines and liqueurs, and cheeses and other edible specialities gathered from all over Greece. *Photo p149.*

To Pantopoleion tis Mesogeiakis Diatrofis
Sofokleous 1 & Aristidou, Historic Centre (210 323 4612). Metro Panepistimio. **Open** 9am-6pm Mon-Fri; 10am-5pm Sat. **Credit** MC, V. **Map** p249 E4.
This roomy delicatessen sells all the essential ingredients of the acclaimed Mediterranean diet. Come here for your extra virgin olive oil, hearty tomato sauces, glistening black olives from Kalamata, packets of pistachios and walnuts, wholewheat Cretan rusks, wheels of pungent goat's cheese and bottles

of local wine, as well as for syrupy *glyko tou koutaliou* (fruit spoon sweet), jars of tahini and digestion-aiding mastic liqueur.

Tsaknis
Panepistimiou 49, Historic Centre (210 322 0716). Metro Panepistimio. **Open** 9am-3pm Mon, Wed, Sat; 9am-8.30pm Tue, Thur, Fri. **No credit cards**. **Map** p249 F4.
Tucked away behind the façade of a handsomely restored neo-classical block, this cupboard of a shop has, for the past 70 years, been selling the finest, freshest sun-dried pistachio nuts from the isle of Aegina. It also has kegs of almonds, walnuts, peanuts and sesame seeds, as well as a selection of dried fruit and bottles of Metaxa brandy, whisky and gin to accompany the nuts.

Varsos
Kassaveti 5, Kifissia, Northern suburbs (210 801 2472/210 801 3743). Metro Kifissia. **Open** 7am-1am Mon-Fri; 7am-2am Sat; 7am-midnight Sun. **No credit cards**.
Varsos offers a taste of bygone Athens amid the many pop-pumping, latte-proffering modern cafés. It opened in 1892, was renovated in the '50s and has existed in a time warp ever since, with a complicated chit payment system, glass-fronted fridges of milky sweets, white-clad till staff and elderly waiters. Lately it has become cult again, and designer-clad youngsters sit at its rickety tables knocking back bitter cups of Greek coffee accompanied by creamy slices of *bougatsa* (filo pastry filled with crème pâtisserie) or honey-soaked rounds of nutty baklava.

Coffee

Loumidis
Eolou 106, Historic Centre (210 321 6965/210 321 4426). Metro Omonia. **Open** 8am-9pm Mon-Fri; 8am-6pm Sat. **No credit cards**. **Map** p249 E3.
The oldest *kafekopteio* (coffee grinders) in Athens, Loumidis offers a wide selection of beverages to suit all tastes, from bitter, thick Greek coffee to decaffeinated coffee to Colombian beans or fruity teas. You can also buy all the necessary accoutrements for preparing and serving coffee here, as well as the accompanying biscuits and chocolates.

Supermarkets

Champion Marinopoulos
Kanari 9, Kolonaki (210 362 4907). Metro Syntagma. **Open** 9am-9pm Mon-Fri; 8am-8pm Sat. **Credit** AmEx, DC, MC, V. **Map** p252 G5.
Marinopoulos is a small, run-of-the-mill city supermarket where you can pick up your basic staples: dairy produce, fruit and vegetables, alcohol and beverages, cosmetics, tinned and frozen goods and pet foods. The delicatessen section is pretty good, as is the limited range of warm, ready-cooked lunch

Eat, Drink, Shop

Discover the magical powers of mastica at the **Mastiha Shop**.

options. Make sure you arrive early if you want to sample the whole free-range chickens and freshly baked, floury loaves – they tend to sell out by noon.

Vassilopoulos Delicatessen
Stadiou 19, Historic Centre (210 322 2405). Metro Panepistimio. **Open** 8am-4pm Mon,Wed; 8am-8.30pm Tue, Thur, Fri; 8am-3.30pm Sat. **Credit** AmEx, DC, V. **Map** p249 F4.
Pricier than other supermarkets, this delicatessen stocks organic and gourmet treats like Green & Black chocolate and pre-packaged sushi, local specialities such as olive oil and feta, and some generic household staples.

Wine & spirits

Fine Wines
Lyssikratous 3, Plaka (210 323 0350). Metro Akropoli. **Open** 10am-8pm Mon-Sat. **Credit** AmEx, MC, V. **Map** p251 F6.
The crystal decanters in the window and dusky, bottle-lined interior are tempting enough, but add a comprehensive selection of fine vintages and a friendly owner with an encyclopaedic knowledge of Greek wines, and you've got a haven for oenophiles. Dimitris will help you pick out a light Assyrtiko for alfresco feasting or a bottle of bubbly rosé for a special occasion from the up-and-coming vineyards of Greece. (In the likely event that the shop is closed, Dimitris is probably delivering wine to a nearby taverna. Have a cold drink nearby and wait for him to come puttering back on his Vespa.) *Photo p152.*

Kylix
Karneadou 20, Kolonaki (210 724 5143/www. kylix.gr). Metro Evangelismos. **Open** 10am-10pm Mon-Fri; 10am-8pm Sat. **Credit** AmEx, DC, MC, V. **Map** p252 H5.
This store in chic Kolonaki is suitably sleek and streamlined; the stock is a well-chosen mix of wines from both Old and New World vineyards. From the local varities, try the Estate White (Assyrtiko and Malagouzia) from award-winning Ktima Gerovasiliou. **Other locations**: Oenocosmos, Orlof 5, Koukaki (210 921 2205).

Gifts & souvenirs

Benaki Museum Shop
Koumbari 1 & Leof Vas Sofias, Kolonaki (210 367 1045/www.benaki.gr). Metro Syntagma. **Open** 9am-5pm Mon, Wed, Fri, Sat; 9am-midnight Thur; 9am-3pm Sun. **Credit** AmEx, DC, MC, V. **Map** p252 G5.
The gift shop in the Benaki Museum *(see p87)* sells replicas of ancient artefacts, icons, jewellery and toys displayed in the museum, plus books on Hellenic and Byzantine history, modern Greek photography and art, postcards, silk scarves and local pottery. **Other locations**: Benaki Museum, Pireos Street Annexe, Pireos 138, Rouf (210 345 3111).

Centre of Hellenic Tradition
2nd floor, Mitropoleos 59 & Pandrossou 36, Plaka (210 321 3023). Metro Monastiraki. **Open** May-Sept 9am-8pm Mon-Fri; 9am-6pm Sat, Sun. Oct-Apr 9am-6pm daily. **Credit** AmEx, DC, MC, V. **Map** p249/p251 E5.

The arcade that leads to the Centre of Hellenic Tradition is filled with wonderful display cases of hand-painted pottery, icons and embroidery, giving a pretty good idea of what the extensive gallery upstairs specialises in. Here you will find traditional handicrafts – ceramics, tapestries, lace, carved wood and sculptures, paintings and rugs – from every corner of Greece.

K'alli thea

Mnisikleous 9 & Adrianou, Plaka (210 325 4283/ www.kali-thea.com). Metro Monastiraki. **Open** *May-Sept* 11am-9pm Tue-Sun. *Oct-Apr* 11am-7pm Tue-Sun.* **No credit cards.** **Map** p251 E5.

You could be forgiven for thinking that every souvenir shop in Plaka sells the same array of postcards – the insolent goats and inquisitive kittens, the gleaming marble statues and the grinning satyrs. For something more unusual, check out this backstreet store. Owner Spyros Kalambokas has collected a vast archive of photos and prints of everyday life in Greece from the late 19th and early 20th century, which he retouches on the computer and produces as postcards or wall-hangings. He also stocks countless reproductions of posters from the '50s and '60s, including iconic ads for Fix beer, Papastratos cigarettes and Malamatina ouzo, available as postcards or greeting cards.

Kombologadiko

Amerikis 9, Historic Centre (212 700 0500/ www.kombologadiko.gr). Metro Syntagma. **Open** 10am-4pm Mon, Wed, Sat; 10am-9pm Tue, Thur, Fri. **Credit** AmEx, DC, MC, V. **Map** p249 F4.

This is where traditional worry beads (*komboloi*) are transformed into works of art. Made from some of the rarest, finest quality materials from around the world, these elegant strings come in a huge range of prices. Some cost thousands of euros (for a version in precious red amber), but prices start at a mere €10. Choose between intricately worked Yusuri sets of black coral inlaid with turquoise and silver, Faturan Egyptian strings with amber beads, delicate mother-of-pearl rosaries or simple, affordable sets made from cat's eye or crystal.

Martinos

Pandrosou 50, Monastiraki (210 321 2414/www. martinosart.gr). Metro Syntagma. **Open** *Sept-mid June* 10am-3.30pm Mon, Wed, Sat; 10am-6.30pm Tue, Thur, Fri. *Mid June-July* 10am-3.30pm Mon, Wed; 10am-6.30pm Tue, Thur, Fri. Closed Aug. **Credit** AmEx, MC, V. **Map** p252 G4.

Located in what was once a glorious family home near the Ancient Agora, Martinos offers a tantalising whistlestop tour of some 5,000 years of Greek history. Many of the pieces on display – marble statuary, Byzantine icons and Cycladic urns – are ruled off the visitor's shopping list (antiquities cannot be purchased and taken from Greece without a special licence from the Archaeological Service), but there are also rather less valuable pieces of embroidery, jewelled daggers, necklaces and other baubles that make unique souvenirs. The Kolonaki branch of the store has a collection of international antiques, including African tribal masks and eighth-century Chinese ceramics.

Other locations: Pindarou 24, Kolonaki (210 360 9449).

Mastiha Shop

Panepistimiou 6 & Kriezotou, Historic Centre (210 363 2750/www.mastihashop.com). Metro Syntagma. **Open** 9am-9pm Mon-Fri; 9am-5pm Sat. **Credit** AmEx, MC, V. **Map** p249/p251 F5.

Here you can buy just about everything imaginable that could be made from the resin of the southern Chios mastic tree – that gum that is said to be a cure for all manner of ills, from stomach ulcers to cancer. Whether you're after mastic chewing gum, halva, bonbons, essential oils, candles, jars of mastic-infused savouries or vinegar, or just a book about the island of Chios, this is the place to find it. Don't miss the line of natural cosmetics made by Korres especially for the Mastiha Shop.

Mati

Athinas 17, Historic Centre (210 321 0285/210 324 7402). Metro Monastiraki. **Open** 10am-3pm Mon, Wed, Sat; 10am-9pm Tue, Thur, Fri. **Credit** AmEx, MC, V. **Map** p249 E4/E5.

For unique, decorative souvenirs, pop into this treasure trove hidden amid the tin tray and wellington boot shops of Athinas. For three generations, Rod Constantoglou's family has been creating evil eye-studded lucky charms, semi-precious necklaces, hefty worry beads and dainty *tamata* (silver figurines to hang in church for good health). Although the pieces are handmade, the prices are pleasantly affordable, with evil eye earrings starting from €5, key rings from €15 and *tamata* from €20.

Pantelis Melissinos

Agias Theklas 2, Monastiraki (210 321 9247). Metro Monastiraki. **Open** 10am-8pm Mon-Sat; 10am-6pm Sun. **No credit cards.** **Map** p249/p251 E5.

Plaka and Monastiraki are full of attractive leather shops, but generations of knowledgeable visitors from all over the world instead duck into this rather less flamboyant shop to stock up on Stavros Melissinos' long-lasting, handmade leather sandals. The smiling 'Poet Sandalmaker' (he is the author of several tracts) began making shoes in 1954, and has built on the original few styles to produce around 32 classically inspired designs. He has reputedly sold to the likes of John Lennon, Sophia Loren and Jackie Kennedy Onassis, so you'll be in illustrious company if you buy a pair.

Zoumboulakis

Kriezotou 7, Historic Centre (210 363 4454). Metro Syntagma. **Open** 10am-3pm Mon, Wed, Sat; 10am-8pm Tue, Thur, Fri. **Credit** AmEx, DC, MC, V. **Map** p252 G4/G5.

The giftshop of the celebrated contemporary Greek art gallery (situated nearby on Platia Kolonaki; *see p174*) offers numbered, signed silk screens or prints

by collectible local artists including Adamakis, Kottis, Bokoros and Fassianos. There is also a small collection of objets d'art such as glass candle-shields bearing the sketches of sculptor/painter Moralis, and colourful tin toy cars and ashtrays decorated with such motifs as 'I hate art' by Aidinis.

Health & beauty

For cosmetics, *see p158* **Nature's beauty**.

Hairdressers & barbers

For a classy (and costly) cut with one of Athens 'celebrity' hairdressers, book an appointment with **Giorgos Doudessis** (Voukourestiou 39, Kolonaki, 210 362 9960) or Stathis at **Bitsikas Hairlines** (Xanthippou 2, Kolonaki, 210 721 3573). Prefer to stick with a salon you know and trust? Go to **Toni & Guy** (Ermou 118, Monastiraki, 210 322 2120). Men who want a traditional Athens experience, on the other hand, should join the dapper old gentlemen having a shave and trim at the simply named **Koureion** (Barbershop) at Apollonos 12, Plaka (no phone)

Opticians

Optika Stavrou
Akadimias 60, Kolonaki (210 364 3012). Metro Syntagma. **Open** *9am-3.30pm Mon, Wed, Sat; 9am-9pm Tue, Thur, Fri.* **Credit** AmEx, DC, MC, V. **Map** p249 F3.

Whether you've lost a lens or just want a trendy pair of shades to attract the paparazzi flashes on Platia Kolonaki, this shop will solve your problem. It has everything from prescription lenses to the latest designer frames.

Pharmacies

For further information about duty pharmacies and prescriptions, *see p232*.

Litos
Stadiou 17, Historic Centre (210 322 2200). Metro Panepistimio. **Open** *May-Sept 8am-2.30pm Mon, Wed; 8am-2pm, 5.30-8.30pm Tue, Thur, Fri. Oct-Apr 8am-2.30pm Mon, Wed; 8am-2pm, 5-8pm Tue, Thur, Fri.* **Credit** AmEx, DC, MC, V. **Map** p249 F4.

One of the oldest pharmacies in central Athens, this shop has everything you could need, from sunscreen, shampoo and mosquito repellent to vitamin pills, aspirin and prescription medicines; most of the latter, interestingly, are available over the counter in Greek chemists.

Spas & salons

Ananea Spa
Life Gallery Hotel, 103 Thiseos Avenue, Ekali, Northern suburbs (210 626 0456). Bus 550 from Kallimarmaro or A7 from Kanigos Square, then bus 507, 508, 509, 536 from Kifissia. **Open** *11am-8.30pm (last appointment 7pm) Mon-Fri; 11am-7.30pm (last appointment 6.30pm) Sat, Sun.* **Credit** AmEx, DC, MC, V.

GB Spa Grande.

All marble and blue glass, this small spa in the sleek and stylish Life Gallery Hotel (*see p57*) is pure zen. Choose from a range of treatments from Morocco, Polynesia and Bali, then unwind in the candlelit meditation room. Feeling lethargic and lacking motivation? The Ayurvedic Ratna therapy uses crystals to rebalance your chakras, boosting energy levels (€120 for 90mins).

Cavalliert

1st Floor, Irodotou 18, Kolonaki (210 721 3546). Metro Evangelismos. **Open** 10am-1pm, 4-8pm Mon-Fri. **Credit** MC, V. **Map** p252 H5.

In their old-fashioned Kolonaki apartment, the Cavallieratos couple and their capable assistants cleanse, squeeze, knead, stroke and press away the various troubles and imperfections that plague tired, unhealthy, badly nourished city complexions. Pambitsa unblocks blackheads and purifies pores with her magic fingers; her husband Takis massages using creams made by hand to the Cavalliert recipe from flowers and plants grown on their organic estate in southern Attica.

Cocoon Urban Spa

9 Souliou & Erifylis, Agia Paraskevi, Eastern suburbs (210 656 1975). Metro Ethniki Amyna, then bus A5. **Open** 1-10pm Mon; 10am-10pm Tue-Thur; 10am-9pm Fri; 10am-6pm Sat. **Credit** AmEx, MC, V.

Owned by two glamorous Greek-American sisters, this minimalist three-storey spa is a haven of soothing sophistication. Besides facials, massages and waxing, and various treatments for men, there are drop-in Pilates, African dance and yoga classes, as well as a small swimming pool.

Divani Athens Spa & Thalasso Centre

10 Agiou Nikolaou & Iliou, Vouliagmeni, Southern suburbs (210 891 1900). Bus E22 from Sina & Panepistimiou. **Open** 10am-10pm Mon-Fri; 10am-8pm Sat; 11am-7pm Sun. **Credit** AmEx, DC, MC, V.

The largest and most luxurious thalassotherapy centre in Attica, this lavish beachside spa offers an endless selection of treatments inspired by the sea, and harnessing the therapeutic powers of marine algae, such as the bizarrely named by deeply detoxifying algotherapy. The hydromassage on giant water beds is said to be especially good for getting rid of cellulite.

GB Spa Grande

Hotel Grande Bretagne, Syntagma Square (210 333 0772). Metro Syntagma. **Open** 6am-10pm daily. *Treatments* 9am-8pm daily. **Credit** AmEx, DC, MC, V. **Map** p249 F5.

With its E'SPA products, herbal steam rooms, marble foot spas and an indoor pool lined with blue glass, the spa in the Hotel Grande Bretagne (*see p46*) is the ultimate pampering treat smack in the centre of town. The Nourishing Yoghurt, Honey and Sugar Treatment (€150 for 70mins) combines a foot ritual, an all-over scrub with olive oil, sugar and lemon, a yoghurt and honey body wrap and a soothing scalp massage.

Glow

Irodotou 10, Kolonaki (210 729 4396). Metro Evangelismos. **Open** 10am-7pm Wed; 10am-8pm Tue, Thur, Fri; 10am-5pm Sat. **Credit** MC, V. **Map** p252 H5.

Nature's beauty

Who needs costly, chancy chemical treatments such as Botox and microdermabrasion when you've got powerful antioxidants like grapes, pomegranates and olives growing right there in your back garden? Helen of Troy certainly didn't need petri-dish concoctions to tend to her peerless complexion. We can guess that olive oil, figs, yoghurt and honey were part of the beauty routine of the face that launched a thousand ships.

Today, cosmetics companies Korres, Apivita and Mastic Spa are helping modern women (and men) around the world to discover the effectiveness of traditional Mediterranean ingredients.

The first natural Greek cosmetics brand to step out into international markets, **Korres** now has sleek standalone stores in London's Chelsea and Barcelona, as well as prominent positions on the shelves of such prestigious department stores as Harvey Nichols and Henri Bendel. Here in Greece, the range of sunscreens, haircare, body creams, fragrant water sprays and make-up can be found on the shelves of your nearest chemist. Made to homeopathic formulas, and avoiding the use of mineral oils and silicone, these effective

and affordable lotions and potions claim to cure everything from dandruff to acne and sore throats (the first Korres product was a throat pastille made with honey and aniseed). Dehydrated, sun-stressed summer skins will love the rich, seductive Fig Body Butter. For the complete range of products, visit the original Korres pharmacy, east of the centre in Pangrati (Ivikou 8 & Eratosthenous, 210 722 2774), or the store-in-store at Attica (*see p140*).

Apivita has grown from an idea to create shampoo with propolis (the protective lining of a beehive) into a multimillion-euro company selling some 200 natural-based products in more than 800 shops around the world. Apivita sunscreens, shampoos and shower gels can be found in most chemists, but to see the full product line – propoline haircare, aromatherapy room sprays and facial creams, express make-up wipes and scrubs, and apitherapy products made with honey – visit the Apivita store in Kolonaki (Solonos 26, 210 364 0560), which also offers a made-to-order prescription skincare service and a small city spa where weary shoppers can book in for a relaxing massage or facial treatment.

Mastic Spa, meanwhile, harnesses the extraordinary power of the sticky resin produced by the mastic trees of southern Chios, in a series of products that includes toothpaste and mouthwash (recent studies have shown that mastic oil can reduce plaque and prevent mouth ulcers), sunscreen (it offers natural protection against the sun's rays), acne-healing potions (mastic is an extremely effective anti-bacterial agent), shampoos, soaps and bath foam. Discover the properties of this pharmaceutical marvel yourself at the Mastic Spa shop in Kolonaki (Irakleitou 1 & Solonos, 210 360 3413).

This funky little place is perfect for a quick beauty fix between shopping in Kolonaki and meeting friends for lunch or evening cocktails. The kind and friendly staff expertly pare off hard skin from your feet and hands, rub in delicious-smelling lotions and potions and paint your nails like shiny bon-bons as you lounge in a huge, soft, massage armchair. If your extremities need a bit of extra TLC, book the luxurious hot wax dip, which leaves skin as soft as a newborn's.

House & home

Antiques

Mandra
Iraklidon 75 & Pireos, Gazi (210 345 0003). Metro Keramikos. **Open** 9am-5pm Mon-Fri; 9am-3pm Sat, Sun. **Credit** AmEx, DC, MC, V. **Map** p248 B5.
In a former garage, shut off from busy Pireos by a coral-coloured gateway, this antiques warehouse is

packed with treasures picked up at fairs and sales throughout the country. Wander the dusty aisles under the tented roof (the name 'Mandra' means open-air market, but the antiques need protection from the elements) and you will find immense terracotta amphorae, carved marble basins from Turkish hammams, wooden butter churns and troughs, patterned ceramic tiles, bronze tea urns and candelabra. The best news for visitors is that Mandra will ship your purchases back home for you, wherever in the world you reside.

General

For department stores and malls, *see p140.*

ADC

Valaouritou 4, Historic Centre (210 361 0194). Metro Syntagma. **Open** 9am-3pm Mon, Wed, Sat; 9am-8pm Tue, Thur, Fri. **Credit** AmEx, DC, MC, V. **Map** p252 G4.

If you like outsized, conversation-piece crockery, you'll love Eleni Vernadaki's handpainted pieces in black and white stripes or geometric zigzags, with vivid splashes of crimson, lemon-yellow or cerulean. The vases are thigh-high, and some of the bowls are large enough to serve a big, fat Greek wedding party, but there are also more modest (in size as well as price) sets of soup plates, angular teapots with small, sturdy mugs, pot-bellied sugar shakers and fist-sized stone paperweights painted to resemble beetles.

Specialist

Mofu

Sarri 28, Psyrri (210 331 1922). Metro Thissio. **Open** 10am-3pm Mon-Wed; 10am-3pm, 5.30-9pm Tue, Thur, Fri; 10am-6pm Sat. **Credit** MC, V. **Map** p249 D4.

One of the best options around town if you're after truly unusual objects for the home. The shop's stock has been collected by the Cypriot-born owners themselves during their travels around the world, giving Mofu an identity all of its own. The groundbreaking design, the 1960s and '70s atmosphere, as well as the various pieces of designer furniture that are now a part of history, won't allow you to walk past here without wanting to take a good look inside.

Music

Metropolis

Panepistimiou 54, Historic Centre (210 380 8549). Metro Omonia. **Open** 9am-9pm Mon-Fri; 9am-8pm Sat. **Credit** AmEx, DC, MC, V. **Map** p249 F3.

Five storeys of international and Greek music catering to most mainstream tastes. Prices average €18-€20 for an imported CD, but sales racks often have relatively recent releases at bargain prices. **Other locations**: throughout the city.

Vinyl Microstore

Didotou 34, Exarchia (210 361 4544/www.vinyl microstore.gr). Metro Panepistimio. **Open** 10.30am-3.30pm Mon, Wed, Sat; 10.30am-8.30pm Tue, Thur, Fri. **Credit** MC, V. **Map** p252 G3.

Run by the owners of an independent record label called VM Recordings (as well as an internet music station called, unsurprisingly, VM Radio), this retro-looking store offers beautifully packaged LPs and CDs by Greek indie bands, as well as international imports. If you're after something specific, the owners will help you to track it down. Otherwise, lounge in the soft leather armchairs to listen to the records that have caught your eye before making your pick.

Sport & fitness

For basic sports clothes and trainers from brands such as Nike, Adidas, Reebok and New Balance, check out the selection at **Attica** (*see p140*). If you need more specialised equipment – tennis raquets, boxing gloves, skis, a set of weights or a pair of football boots, for example – head out to the **Intersport** superstore (Vouliagmenis 100, Glyfada, Southern suburbs, 210 963 6891).

Travellers' needs

For luggage, *see p149.*

Shipping

Need to get that shaggy *flokati* rug or marble replica of a Caryatid home? If the store you bought it from cannot arrange transport, get in touch with **DHL** (Filellinon 28, Plaka, 210 989 0000, www.dhl.com) or **UPS** (Kifissias 166, Marousi, Northern suburbs; or El Venizelou 43-45, Glyfada, Southern suburbs, 210 998 4000, www.ups.com). For more shippers, *see p228.*

Travel agencies

Travel Plan

Christou Lada 3, Historic Centre (210 333 3300). Metro Panepistimio. **Open** 9am-6pm Mon-Fri; 9am-2.30pm Sat. **Credit** AmEx, DC, MC, V. **Map** p249 F4.

Athens' largest travel agency can arrange holiday packages as well as book cruises and air tickets within Greece and abroad. For boat tickets to the islands visit its partner Triaena Travel (*see below*).

Triaena Travel

Harilaou Trikoupi 22 (in the arcade), Historic Centre (210 363 1928/210 363 1974). Metro Panepistimio. **Open** 9am-6pm Mon-Fri; 9am-2.30pm Sat. **Credit** AmEx, DC, MC, V. **Map** p249 F3.

This travel agency can book your hydrofoil, ferry and airline tickets.

Airline flights are one of the biggest producers of the global warming gas CO_2. But with **The CarbonNeutral Company** you can make your travel a little greener.

Go to **www.carbonneutral.com** to calculate your flight emissions then 'neutralise' them through international projects which save exactly the same amount of carbon dioxide.

Contact us at **shop@carbonneutral.com** or call into the office on **0870 199 99 88** for more details.

CarbonNeutral®flights

Arts &
Entertainment

Festivals & Events	162
Children	166
Film	168
Galleries	172
Gay & Lesbian	175
Music	179
Nightlife	187
Sport & Fitness	194
Theatre & Dance	199

Features

Rising to the occasion	164
'This is Sparta!'	171
The best Gay spots	175
Rembetika	181
Plug in to the local scene	185
Make it a double	188
Summer clubbing	190
A fighting chance for football	196
A dramatic start	202

Pallas Theatre. *See p200*.

Festivals & Events

Seasons' greetings.

Nearly half of Greece's population lives in Athens, so it's hardly surprising that most of the nation's annual festivals and arts and sports events take place in the capital. There's a particularly varied menu of cultural events during the summer months, when the city's frenetic pace slows, temperatures soar and Athenians start relaxing as they prepare for their holidays. And it's not only museums and galleries that host exhibitions and other events; newly pedestrianised avenues and long-neglected inner-city areas serve as the stages for innovative modern art exhibitions, book fairs and music festivals; and the city's splendid outdoor amphitheatres are the settings for concerts, plays and festivals.

Spring is dominated by Orthodox Easter, when celebrations light up the streets and churches. New Year celebrations at Syntagma may not be quite up to Scottish Hogmanay standards, but they get people out on to the streets. And up the road at Platia Kotzia you might catch a display of multicultural modern Athens – a circle of Indian, Albanian, Polish and Kenyan immigrants dancing a *hasaposerviko* with native Athenians, as Greek singers belt out popular songs on an outdoor stage outside the City Hall.

For more information, consult *Kathimerini*'s English edition (bundled with the *International Herald Tribune*, and also accessible at www.ekathimerini.com). Alternatively visit www.athensnews.gr (updated weekly). Also worth checking out is the City of Athens website (www.cityofathens.gr). You can also call the citizens' helpline on 195 (English speakers are available) or tune in to the English-language radio station AIR 104.4FM.

Spring

Megali Evdomada (Easter Week)
Various churches around Athens, including Athens Cathedral. Metro Monastiraki. **Date** Mar/Apr. **Map** p249/p251 E5/F5.
Equivalent in importance to Christmas in Britain and the US, *Pascha* (Easter) in Athens is a rewarding and colourful experience, drawing deep on Greece's rich Orthodox heritage. *See also p164 Rising to the occasion.*

Labour Day
Date 1 May.

Labour Day is generally celebrated with a mass exodus to the countryside for picnics. For those who stay in town there are marches organised by left-wing groups and workers' unions.

Summer

Athens Festival
210 928 2900/www.greekfestival.gr.
Date May/June-Sept/Oct.
Lycabettus Theatre *Lycabettus Hill, Kolonaki. Metro Evangelismos.* **Map** p252 J3.
Odeon of Herodes Atticus *Acropolis. Metro Akropoli.* **Map** p251 D6.
The Athens Festival is the urban incarnation of the Hellenic Festival. Since its inception in 1945 it has been a major highlight of the city's summer cultural activities (a time when indoor venues tend to suspend activities). Music concerts ranging from jazz to classical, along with drama and dance productions, take place at the Odeon of Herodes Atticus and the Lycabettus Theatre. One couldn't ask for better settings: the latter boasts the best views of the city from the top of the hill, while the former offers the classical splendour of the Parthenon as a backdrop for performances. High heels are frowned upon at the Herodeion (for fear of damage to the marble), though Athenian socialites usually tend to ignore the rules. Stilettos are not an issue at the Lycabettus, and a small bus shuttling to the theatre from the foot of the hill means you can give your Manolos a good outing. Headliners in 2007 included singers Laurie Anderson, Norah Jones, Elvis Costello and Allen Toussaint, and the National Ballet of China; tributes to opera diva Maria Callas were also scheduled. For big-name events, book well in advance – tickets tend to sell out quickly. *See also p199.*

Acropolis Rally
Various locations throughout the city (www.acropolisrally.gr). **Date** mid June.
Launched half a century ago, the Acropolis Rally has developed a huge following. The route starts at the foot of the Acropolis and takes drivers through rugged terrain on the Greek mainland for three days before leading them to the finish line at the Panathenaic Stadium. Join the rest of Athens by standing at the side of the road and watching the drivers whiz past.

Vyronas Festival
Melina Mercouri Vrachon Theatre, Vyronas, Eastern suburbs (210 765 5748). Bus 214/trolleybus 11.
Date 6wks June-Sept.

Acropolis Rally.

The municipality of Vyronas has done a pretty good job of attracting well-known Greek and foreign acts to an otherwise drab area. Nearly two decades since its inception, the festival (dubbed the People's Festival) offers jazz, rock, ethnic and contemporary Greek music at good prices under the shadow of a huge rocky outcrop.

Rockwave Festival

Various venues around Athens (210 882 0426/ www.didimusic.gr). **Date** 3 days late June/early July.
Since 1996 Rockwave has been taking its ear-splitting show to venues in and around Athens, to the delight of hairy headbangers and pale Goth rockers. In 2007 the venue was the Malakassa junction, 37km (23 miles) north of Athens on the Athens–Lamia highway, with Led Zeppelin god Robert Plant, ex-Soundgarden grunge king Chris Cornell and growly old-timers Metallica headlining.

Anti-Racism Festival

May 1st Square (Proti Maiou), Evelpidon, Pedion Areos (210 381 3928). **Date** early July.
This three-day event is organised by the Network for Social Support for Refugees and Immigrants. Since its debut in 1996, the festival hasn't looked back. Involving some 40 migrant communities and

more than 100 human-rights and anti-racism groups, the event includes live music and dance by immigrant groups or acts from abroad (in 2007 performers hailed from countries such as Albania, Ukraine, Bulgaria, Tanzania, Pakistan and the Philippines), as well as top-line native Greek musicians (singer-songwriter Socrates Malamas was on the schedule for 2007). There are also activities for children and exotic refreshment stalls.

International Aegean Sailing Rally

Along the Saronic coast. Hellenic Offshore Racing Club, Akti Dilaveri 3, Mikrolimano, Piraeus (210 412 3357/210 411 3201/www.aegeanrally.gr/ www.horc.gr). **Date** early-mid July.
Sailing fans have been heading down to the coast for one of Greece's biggest sailing events ever since 1964. Organised by the Hellenic Offshore Racing Club, the regatta gathers contestants from all over the world and lasts for a week. You can watch the aquatic action from any of the seaside suburbs.

Autumn

Athens International Film Festival

Various venues around Athens (210 606 1363/ www.aiff.gr). **Date** 10 days mid-late September.

Rising to the occasion

Syntagma Square is a good vantage point to see several processions, as many of them cross on Filellinon. And the procession that climbs Lycabettus Hill to the chapel of **Agios Georgios** is a dramatic one to follow: the view from the hill is awesome.

On Saturday, at around 11pm, people gather once again in churches, this time holding unlit candles as they wait for Christ's symbolic resurrection, *Anastasi*, at midnight. It's a dramatic ceremony: as the hour strikes, the church is plunged into darkness. Then a priest emerges from behind the curtains concealing the altar with a lit candle and proclaims, '*Christos anesti!*' ('Christ is risen!'). He passes the flame to the congregation, who light their own candles and greet each other with cries of '*Christos anesti*', or the response '*Alithos anesti*' ('Indeed he is risen'). Firecrackers go off all around the city and church bells peal. Then familes head home to mark the end of Lent with a feast of *mageiritsa* (a soup made of lamb innards), *tsourekia* (a sweet Easter bread) and, of course, Easter eggs. But in Greece, they're not made of chocolate; instead, the Greeks crack boiled eggs painted red to symbolise the blood of Christ in a tradition that links pre-Christian rites of spring with Byzantine Christian culture. The egg, an ancient and universal symbol of rebirth, is used here to represent the crucifixion and resurrection.

Celebrations culminate on Easter Sunday (*Kyriaki tou Pascha*), when lambs are roasted on spits and most Athenians spend the rest of the day eating and drinking. Everywhere is closed, so you may as well join them: this is a good day to have lamb in tavernas in Plaka.

When you're planning your Easter in Athens, bear in mind that the Eastern Orthodox churches use the Julian rather than the Gregorian calendar, so Easter dates do not usually coincide.

Easter Sunday 2008 27 April.
Easter Sunday 2009 19 April.

If you visit Athens during *Megali Evdomada* (Orthodox Easter Week), set aside the evening of Good Friday for a wander around town. *Pascha* (Easter) is the most important event of the Greek religious calendar (on a par with Christmas in Britain and the US), and on this night you'll find Athens a city transformed. In the darkness, hymns and chants emanate from churches, bells toll, and candlelit processions – accompanied by chanting and wreathed in clouds of incense – pass through the streets. In each procession an *epitaphios* (bier) is carried, representing Christ's funeral. The experience is especially intense in Plaka, and Good Friday evening is best enjoyed strolling from church to church here, taking in the Byzantine chants, the flickering candles, the people clad in the dark colours of mourning, and the incense-infused air.

Churches in Plaka particularly worth checking out include **Agia Ekaterini** (Church of St Catherine; *see p71*), **Metamorphosi Sotiros** (on Kydathinaion) and **Agia Sophia** (on Dionysiou Aeropagitou). It's also interesting to visit the Russian church of the **Agia Triada** (Church of the Holy Trinity; *see p71*) on Filellinon at midnight on Saturday. Many Greeks attend to listen to the awe-inspiring Russian Orthodox hymns, and to watch the priests bless baskets of food (including bread and eggs) laid out by the faithful in the churchyard.

The most important Good Friday procession begins at **Athens Cathedral** (Mitropolis; *see p69*) and winds through Central Athens.

Not to be confused with the better-known and longer-running Thessaloniki Film Festival, the AIFF is gaining steam as an event spotlighting the best in emerging and international cinema. Movie buffs can enjoy 100-plus features and short films from more than two dozen countries.

International Month of Photography

Hellenic Centre of Photography, Hatzichristou 3, Makrygianni (210 921 0545/www.hcp.gr). Metro Akropoli. **Date** mid Sept-mid Nov. **Map** p251 E7.
Always expanding its subject matter, this two-month event brings together photographers – from young Greek artists to established international names – in a range of venues across the city.

Athens Book Fair

Information 210 330 3942. **Date** late Sept.
Now in its third decade, this highly popular 16-day fair exhibits books from a wide range of Greek publishers. Dozens of stands and over 300 booksellers set up along the Dionysiou Areopagitou pedestrianised walkway that passes under the Acropolis, while buskers and food stalls complete the picture. The books are in Greek, of course.

Ohi Day

Date 28 Oct.
This national holiday commemorates Greece's resounding rejection – '*ohi*' ('no') – of an ultimatum from Benito Mussolini demanding that Italian troops be allowed to pass through Greece during World War II. School parades take place in the heart of the city (along Leof Vas Amalias, in front of the Greek Parliament).

Winter

Athens Marathon

www.athensmarathon.com. **Date** Sun in early Nov.
Runners from Greece and abroad follow the original 42km (26.2-mile) route of Pheidippides, the messenger who ran to Athens from Marathon in 490 BC to report that the invading Persian army had been defeated, then dropped dead from exhaustion. The race begins at the modern village of Marathon and ends at the Panathenaic Stadium (site of the first modern Olympic Games in 1896).

17 November

Begins at Athens Polytechnic, Patission & Stournari, & ends at the US Embassy, Leof Vas Sofias. Metro Omonia & Syntagma. **Date** 17 Nov.
Although to outsiders 17 November is inextricably linked to the urban guerrilla group of that name, it's also the day that marks an important event in Greece's modern history. Every year, Athenians march to commemorate the night of 17 November 1973, when the military dictatorship brutally used tanks to storm a student protest at the Athens Polytechnic, killing 34 demonstrators. The uprising's tragic end was a factor in the down-

fall of the Junta the following year. Organised by left-wing groups and workers' unions, the march has broad appeal and cuts across generations. The US Embassy is often pelted with eggs and other objects, and graffiti is sprayed on neighbouring buildings – in protest at Washington's widely acknowledged support for the colonels. Depending on the political climate of the time, there is sometimes a stop at the British Embassy. Although more sedate in recent years, in the past the march would routinely deteriorate into street clashes between self-styled anarchists and riot police. (*See also p80* **Demo-crazy**.)

Christmas & New Year

Date 24, 31 Dec & 5 Jan.
Not as important as in Western Europe, but still a major event on the Greek calendar. Children sing carols *(kalanta)* door to door while charity groups do their rounds. After midnight on New Year's Eve, a fragrant cake *(vassilopita)* containing a coin is sliced. The person who gets the coin is blessed with good fortune for the year to come.

Epiphany

Along the Piraeus coast. **Date** 6 Jan.
The traditional Blessing of the Water that takes place every Epiphany is steeped in Orthodox tradition, with roots stretching perhaps as far back as pagan antiquity. The faithful congregate by the sea to watch the spectacle of young men diving into the chilly waters to retrieve a cross hurled by the presiding priest. The diver who retrieves the crucifix is blessed with good luck for the year.

Apokries (Carnival season)

Various locations. **Date** last wk Feb/beginning of Lent.
Municipal orchestras and choirs, jugglers, mime artists, singers and float parades take to the streets during Carnival season, when fancy-dress parties and lots of booze are the norm. A pervasive 'anything goes' atmosphere grips the city, particularly in Plaka, where groups of young males roam around bashing just about anybody they can find with plastic clubs. Celebrations include *Tsiknopempti* ('Smoke Thursday'), the week before Lent begins, when Greeks spend the evening gorging on grilled meat and drinking; and the traditional party *(koulouma)* on *Kathari Deftera* (Clean Monday), with kite-flying and picnics on Philopappus Hill. Clean Monday also marks the beginning of *Megali Sarakosti* (Lent), leading up to Easter.

Independence Day Parade

Leof Vas Amalias, in front of Parliament.
Date 25 Mar. **Map** p251/p252 G5.
Military fighter jets whiz by overhead as the city's residents turn out in droves to watch the military and school parades pass by and celebrate the proclamation of the Greek revolution in 1821 against the Ottoman Empire. The feast of the Annunciation is celebrated on the same day.

Arts & Entertainment

Children

Fun for the young.

Before you decide that Athens and children definitely don't mix – what with the heat, pollution and lack of baby-changing facilities – take a moment to consider that this paradoxical society adores children and welcomes them into most public places. In the summer months, you might even find some kids going out with their parents to the open-air bar/cafés, until around midnight or just after. And all tavernas are child-friendly zones.

After your children have got their education on ancient Greek culture from the central museums and ancient sites – or even some of the children's music or theatre events organised by the **Athens Festival** (*see p162*) during the summer – they'll want to have some fun. Apart from the **National Gardens** (*see p83*), children's parks and outdoor playgrounds are mostly situated in more suburban areas, which means hopping on the tram or on a bus.

Some adventure-type attractions have what seem like bizarre hours, opening their doors at five or six in the afternoon and staying open late into the night. The reason is the Athens summer heat: the metal on the equipment used for the activities becomes too hot to touch.

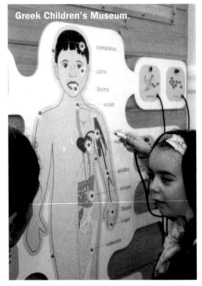

Greek Children's Museum.

Sightseeing

Avoid the noon heat by starting early with a visit to the **Parliament Building** (*see p81*) in Syntagma, where you can watch the slow-motion goose-stepping Evzones (guards). Then take a stroll down to **Plaka** (*see p69*) for a tour of the capital's oldest neighbourhood on the open 'train' that departs from the corner of Eolou and Adrianou (35 minutes, €5, €3 under-12s). Older kids will get more out of a visit to the **Acropolis** (*see p64*) if you employ the services of a guide (book on 210 322 0090, 9.30am-3pm Mon-Fri).

In summer, with temperatures soaring past 35°C (95°F) on some days, it's best to avoid the city centre. Instead, take the metro and head north to leafy **Kifissia** (*see p98*), where kids love the 'grand tour' by horse-drawn carriage (Platia Kefalari, €15 for a 15-minute ride).

Along the coastal road running south-east from Faliro to Glyfada, there are various beaches and playgrounds (with entrancing sea views along the way). All are accessible by tram – you'll spot the main ones between the stops of Flisvos and Loutra Alimou. In addition to a number of playgrounds in **Faliro**, the **Village Centre** (210 948 5200, 210 810 8080, tram Ag Alexandros) is an entertainment complex with a nine-screen cinema and a trendy bowling centre with 15 bowling lanes and plenty of pop music, billiards and electronic games, plus shops, cafés and restaurants.

Further along, in **Alimos**, you can relax at the **Ostria** café (Leof Posidonos 10, 210 985 0118) while your kids tear around the large playground next door. In **Agios Kosmas** (*see p104*) the pace at nearby **Eurobaby** (Leof Posidonos and Moraitini 3, 210 982 9655, open 6-11pm daily, accessible by tram and buses A1, A2, first Ellinikon stop) will suit younger children, with giant inflated slides and castles.

Glyfada's municipal park is one of a few in Athens where kids can skateboard (9am-9pm daily); there's also a funfair (6pm-1am, rides €2-€5) by the sea here. Beyond Glyfada, near the beaches of **Voula** (*see p105*), you'll find **Notos Café** (210 899 3702, 8am-2am, bus A1, A2 to Voula, next stop after the Asklipion), which does great milkshakes and frozen chocolate drinks, and sandwiches, and recently opened a restaurant section overlooking the sea.

Adjoining it is a big playground and mini funfair, which means you can have your cake, and eat it while watching the kids play.

A visit to one of Attica's many beautiful and sandy **beaches** is not only fun in its own right but a good way to integrate. For suggestions, *see pp103-106*. The water is clean and free of dangerous currents or drops, but note that lifeguards can be absent. Visiting a public pool is a bureaucratic nightmare because you need a certificate from a paediatrician, so it's much easier to use hotel pools or beaches.

Museums

At the **Foundation of the Hellenic World** (*see p94*), children can go on a virtual reality tour around ancient Miletus, or enter the 'Tholos', the dome-shaped theatre that offers visitors some time travel to the Ancient Agora. The **Greek Children's Museum** in Plaka features interacive educational exhibits offering an insight into a variety of subjects, including the human eye, the deep and nutrition. Greeks are proud of their traditional shadow-puppet theatre (*karaghiozis*), so a visit to the **Spathario Museum of Shadow Puppets** is worthwhile. Future pilots can jump into the cockpit of a World War I plane at the **National War Museum** (*see p83*), while displays at the Museum of Greek Musical Instruments (*see p71*) offer a fun introduction to Greek music.

Greek Children's Museum

Kydathinaion 14, Plaka (210 331 2995). Metro Akropoli or Syntagma. **Open** 10am-2pm Tue-Fri; 10am-3pm Sat, Sun. **Admission** free. **Map** p252 F6.

Spathario Museum of Shadow Puppets

Platia Kastalias, Vas Sofias & Ralli D, Marousi, Northern suburbs (210 612 7245/www.karagiozis museum.gr). Metro Marousi. **Open** 9am-2pm Mon-Fri; also 6-8pm Wed. **Admission** free.

Animal encounters

Attica Zoological Park

Yalou, Spata (210 663 4724). Bus 319 to end of route; change to bus 304, 305 (Zoological Park stop). **Open** *May-Sept* 9am-8pm daily. *Oct-Apr* 9am-5pm daily. **Admission** €12; €9.50 under-12s. **Credit** V. It's worth the trek out near the airport to visit this massive zoo. Visitors can enjoy a pleasant stroll around well-kept enclosures housing bears, giraffes and lions, among other animals. There's also the World of Reptiles, a petting zoo, a monkey forest and walk-in aviaries – home to one of the largest bird collections in the world (1,500 birds from 300 different species). Useful information is supplied in Greek and English. Don't forget sunhats and suncream in summer.

Theme parks

Adventure Park

Athens–Lamia Highway, Markopoulos exit (210 339 0985/229 509 8335/www.adventure-park.gr). KTEL bus from Pedion Areos to Oropos via Malakassa (bus stop at park entrance). **Open** 10.30am-dusk Wed-Sun & public hols. **Admission** free. **Activities** €6-€16. Let the kids swing (or 'fly', suspended by ropes) from tree to tree (special gear and equipment all available on site) or try the bungee-trampoline, or maybe archery or paintball. Although the Adventure Park is a trek well north of Athens, the reward is hours of fun for both children and adults. Activities have different levels of difficulty, and there's also a 'minikid' section for children aged two to seven.

Allou! Fun Park

Kifissou & Petrou Ralli, Rendi, Western suburbs (210 425 6999). Bus B18, G18/trolleybus 21 to Kan Kan/ Fix stop. **Open** 5pm-2am Mon-Fri; 11am-2am Sat, Sun. **Admission** free. *Rides* €2-€10. **No credit cards.** The closest you'll get to Disneyland in Greece. Attractions like the Carousel and Bongo should get younger children going, while adults will enjoy La Isla, where you can try rafting, and the adrenalin-inducing Shock Tower. A go-kart area has recently been added, while the 'Kidom' section makes sure that the younger ones (up to 13 years old) also have some fun. There are all sorts of refreshments available on site and, if you're driving, there's the added benefit of free parking.

Oropos Water Park

Chalkoutsiou, Skala Oropou, Attica (229 503 7570/1). KTEL bus from Mavromateon (near Pedion Areos) to Oropos, bus stop Skala. **Open** 10am-7pm Mon-Fri; 10.30am-7.30pm Sat, Sun. Closed Oct-May. **Admission** €7 5-11s; free under-4s. **No credit cards.** It's a good hour's drive from Athens to this well-organised, safe water park, but it's kids' heaven when you get there, with water games, waterslides (for under-12s) and beach volleyball. There's also a restaurant and snack bar.

Cinemas

There are multiplexes dotted around the city, but children are likely to find a trip to an outdoor cinema more exciting, though all screenings are in the evenings (and in summer only). Most films tend to be shown in their original language, but animated films and other movies aimed at youngsters are often dubbed; listings in the press should indicate this. For cinemas, *see pp168-171*.

Young visitors should also be impressed with a visit to the **Evgenidio Planetarium** (*see p99*). The state-of-the-art domed projection screen is the size of two-and-a-half basketball courts, and offerings include short films on topics ranging from space to the natural environment.

Arts & Entertainment

Film

Athens undubbed.

Aigli.

Arts & Entertainment

Non-Greek speakers can breathe a sigh of relief. Almost all foreign films shown in Greece are in the original language, with the exception of films aimed at young children, which are usually dubbed into Greek. North Europeans or Americans, used to silence in the cinema, may be less happy about the Greek habit of whispering during performances, and even serious events like the Thessaloniki film festival have a background noise level that surprises cinephiles from northern Europe. The odd complaint may lower the volume a bit, but it's better to give in and see a visit to the cinema here as a cultural experience, the prologue to a post-film discussion in a nearby bar or taverna.

MORE THAN SWORDS AND SANDALS

The biggest multiplex chain, Village Cinemas, has branched out into production, financing a handful of mainstream and – by Greek standards – big-budget films, such as *Alter Ego* (2007), a vehicle for Eurovision popster Sakis Rouvas. As a mainstream Greek film set in contemporary Athens, *Alter Ego* is rather unusual: a slew of recent hits have all tackled stories drawn from Greece's recent past (*see p171* **'This is Sparta!'**).

Another Village production, Tasos Boulmetis' *Politiki Kouzina* (*A Touch of Spice*, 2003), deals with the story of a family caught between Constantinople and Athens – with some sensitivity and the odd dollop of sugary sentimentality. Together with Pantelis Vourgari's Martin Scorsese-produced *Nyfes* (*Brides*, 2004) – set in 1922, about a mail-order bride destined for the US – these period films stormed the local box office to build on a recent mini revival of Greek cinema.

More recently, *Sirines tou Egeou* (*Sirens of the Aegean*, 2005), a comedy sequel to director Nikos Perakis' 1984 Junta and army satire *Loufa kai Paralagi*, took more than €5 million at the box office even though (or perhaps because) it lacked the considerable political edge of the original by the same director.

Younger filmmakers tackling less mainstream themes include Constantinos Giannaris and Yiannis Ekonomidis. Giannaris is known for his portrayal of people living on the margins of Greek society in films like *Dekapentaugousto* (*One day in August*, 2001) and *Omiros* (*Hostage*, 2005); Ekonomidis for his raw and claustrophobic studies of modern life in *Spirtokouto* (*Match Box*, 2003) and *Me Psychi sto Stoma* (*Soul Kicking*, 2006), which have earned him a small but nevertheless dedicated following.

The current film revival is significant, but it doesn't compare to the golden age of Greek cinema of the 1950s and '60s, when over 60 films a year were produced here (today the figure is around 30). Back then, Greeks flocked to cinemas to enjoy tear-jerking melodramas and light-hearted comedies featuring local stars revered by an adoring public. Famous names include blonde legend Aliki Vougiouklaki, her dark-haired nemesis Jenny Karezi, and many others still familiar to the public. Domestic film production won international renown through the likes of Michael Cacoyannis, the director of *Alexis Zorbas* (*Zorba the Greek*, 1964), actresses Melina Mercouri and Irene Papas, and composers Mikis Theodorakis (*Zorba the Greek*) and Manos Hadjidakis, who won an Oscar for *Pote tin Kyriaki* (*Never on Sunday*, 1960). By the early '70s the golden age was clearly over, despite the emergence of the internationally acclaimed New Greek Cinema, which worked through the difficult political climate of the Junta (Alexis Damianos' *Evdokia*, 1971 is a prime example).

Internationally, Greek cinema is synonymous with director Theo Angelopoulos, one of Europe's great filmmakers. The 1998 winner of Cannes's Palme d'Or with *Mia Aioniotita kai Mia Mera* (*Eternity and a Day*), Angelopoulos is now celebrating more than 40 years in the industry. Other diaspora directors to look out for are Paris-based political auteur Costa-Gavras (*Missing*, 1982; *Z*, 1969) and Alexander Payne (*Sideways*, 2004) who, despite his current name, was actually born a Papadopoulos.

SUMMER NIGHT CINEMA

There are over 180 screens in the city, from family-run, old-school affairs from cinema's golden age to brand new multiplexes. But for most visitors, and Athenians too, the most memorable evenings are those spent under the stars at the open-air summer cinemas. As soon as the spring rains seem to have abated (usually around mid May) until well into autumn, they provide a unique cinema-going experience. The venues themselves range from the quirkily urban, such as the **Athinaia**, where it's not unusual to see slipper-clad neighbours sneaking a view from their balconies, to slicker locations such as **Aigli**, which hosts the summer's glitzy premières, to the downright eccentric art-house theatres like **Zefeiros** and **Riviera**. Wherever you choose, there is nothing like sitting outside after a hot day to watch a good film with an iced drink in the cool of the evening. So popular is this tradition that even the big multiplexes

have got in on the act, offering one or two summer screens for customers who prefer natural air-conditioning.

TICKETS AND INFORMATION

Adult ticket prices tend to hover around the €5.50-€8 mark. English-language listings can be found in the weekly *Athens News* and *Kathimerini* (online at www.ekathimerini.gr). Screening times at indoor and outdoor cinemas are normally around 9pm and 11pm. During the lighter summer months, it's wise to catch the late screening (11pm), since Mother Nature doesn't switch the lights off until about half an hour into the earlier show.

Some Athenian cinemas carry the name of their sponsors. Since these may change with time, we have used the original name of the venue; be ready for variations in local listings.

Summer cinemas

The cinemas listed below usually operate between May and September. The **Alfaville** (*see p170*) also goes open-air in summer.

Aigli

Zappeion, National Gardens (210 336 9369/210 336 6970). Metro Syntagma. **Tickets** €7.50. **No credit cards. Map** p252 G6.
A classic outdoor cinema built in the early 20th century and located within the leafy National Gardens. It shows mainly American blockbusters.

Athinaia

Haritos 50, Kolonaki (210 721 5717). Metro Evangelismos. **Tickets** €7; €5 concessions. **No credit cards. Map** p252 H4.
Tell anyone you went to the Athinaia last night, and the first question will be: 'How was the cheese pie?' And then maybe they'll ask what film you saw. Famous home-made *tiropitas* aside, this is a good modern summer cinema with a half-decent sound system. However, that's almost irrelevant on Friday and Saturday nights, when the loud buzz from the busy bars outside the cinema will make it nearly impossible to hear a single line of dialogue.

Cine Paris

Kydathinaion 22, Plaka (210 324 8057/210 322 2071). Metro Akropoli or Syntagma. **Tickets** €7. **No credit cards. Map** p249 F6.
One of the largest, most picturesque cinemas in the city and the only one in Plaka, Cine Paris is perched on a rooftop, right in the heart of the action. If you sit up high enough, you can alternate your gaze between a 21st-century blockbuster and the fifth-century BC Acropolis.

Ciné Psirri 5

Sarri 40, Psyrri (210 324 7234/210 321 2476). Metro Thissio. **Tickets** €7; €5 concessions. **No credit cards. Map** p249 D4.

In the heart of urban Psyrri, this cinema has a good bar in the back of the yard, its own restaurant and a repertoire of modern (and not-so-modern) classics (think Coen Brothers, Bergman and Hitchcock) mixed with re-runs of last year's blockbusters.

Dexameni-Frame

Platia Dexamenis, Kolonaki (210 362 3942/210 360 2363). Metro Evangelismos or Syntagma. **Tickets** €7; €5 concessions. **No credit cards. Map** p252 H4. Situated next to an *ouzerie* on a quiet little square in the heart of Kolonaki, this cinema is surrounded by trees and greenery and has late-night Friday and Saturday screenings of various art/cult films.

Riviera

Valtetsiou 46, Exarchia (210 383 7716/210 384 4827). Metro Panepistimio. **Tickets** €7; €5 concessions. **No credit cards. Map** p249 G2. Your average desktop speakers are probably more efficient than the Riviera's sound system. And then you have to contend with the insects, falling leaves and vegetation covering a good portion of the screen. But don't let that put you off – they show some very good films here, and some of Athens' friendliest bars and restaurants are just around the corner for that post-movie post-mortem.

Thisseion

Apostolou Pavlou 7, Thissio (210 347 0980/210 342 0864). Metro Thissio. **Tickets** €7; €5 concessions. **No credit cards. Map** p248/p250 C5. The Unification of Archaeological Sites walkway has benefited many of Athens' ancient sights, and it has helped the Thisseion too. While it used to suffer heavily from the traffic outside, it is now one of the quietest cinemas in town. Add to that the view of the Acropolis and the countless cafés and bars in Thissio, and you have a serious contender for best open-air cinema in Athens.

Zefeiros

Troon 36, Thissio/Ano Petralona (210 346 2677). Metro Petralona. **Tickets** €7. **No credit cards.** Character is the key to this unique repertory cinema: the film stock is generally as old as the films themselves and the sound system is basic. On the other hand, where else can you watch anything from Eisenstein to Italian New Wave to Monty Python with some of Athens' best tavernas on the doorstep?

Arthouse & rep

Alfaville

Mavromichali 168, Exarchia (210 646 0521). Metro Panepistimio, then 15min walk. **Tickets** €7. **No credit cards.** In Exarchia, Athens' alternative quarter, the Alfaville rules. This slightly run-down cult cinema in a theatre-dense area is a true art house, offering retrospectives of '60s Japanese film, French New Wave and so on. In summer, the roof opens and the cinema becomes an open-air venue.

Attikon

Stadiou 19, Historic Centre (210 322 8821/210 325 2817/phone bookings 801 11 300 400/www. cinemax.gr). Metro Panepistimio. **Closed** June-Sept. **Tickets** €8; €6 concessions. **Credit** (phone bookings only) MC, V. **Map** p249 F4. Built in 1914, the Attikon offers both European and American features. Along with the Apollon (210 323 6811) and Danaos (*see below*), the Attikon is one of the home cinemas of the Athens International Film Festival (*see p163*).

Danaos

Leof Kifisias 109, Ambelokipi (210 692 2655). Metro Panormou. **Closed** July, Aug. **Tickets** €7.50. **Credit** (phone bookings only) MC, V. For Athenians, the name Danaos is synonymous with non-Hollywood, quality films and the Athens International Film Festival (*see p163*). The duplex cinema also entices with a nice bar, sophisticated crowds and film books for sale in the foyer.

Mikrokosmos

Syngrou 106, Makrygianni (210 921 5305). Metro Syngrou-Fix. **Tickets** €7; €5.50 concessions. **No credit cards. Map** p251 D8. With cutting-edge minimalist design, this brand new player on the cinema circuit is more Hoxton or SoHo than Syngrou. The design makes the most of the limited space in the foyer, and the likeable owners will greet you with a smile. Art house and avant-garde are the main staples here.

Multiplexes

One of the main attractions of mutiplexes is their air-conditioning, making them a natural place to escape from the summer heat.

Odeon StarCity

Syngrou 111 & Leontiou, Neos Kosmos, South Athens (210 678 6000/801 116 0000). Metro Syngrou-Fix/tram Kasomouli. **Tickets** €7.50-€8; €6.50-€7 children. **Credit** (phone bookings only) AmEx, MC, V. **Map** p250 C9. Opened in 2006, this ten-screen multiplex has a café-restaurant on the ground floor. Some of the screens include interactive chairs and disco lights for special kids' shows (usually in Greek but you can book English screenings for groups).

Village 15 Cinemas @ The Mall

Andrea Papandreou, Psalida, Marousi, Northern suburbs (210 610 4100/801 100 9191/ticket reservations 210 810 8080/www.villagecinemas.gr). Metro Neratziotissa/bus X40 from Syntagma. **Tickets** €8; €6 before 6pm. **Credit** MC, V. Fourteen screens, including a giant VMax and three luxury screening rooms, in the biggest shopping and entertainment complex in Athens. The distance from the centre is made up for by its proximity to the metro and on-site amenities such as the well-stocked FNAC, with a great selection of DVDs. Film, meal and drink deals are available for €20 on selected films.

Arts & Entertainment

'This is Sparta!'

There was a real feeling of expectation back in 2004, when along with the publicity generated by the Olympic Games and on the back of Wolfgang Peterson's *Troy*, not one, but two Alexander the Great movies were in the pipeline. Only Oliver Stone's *Alexander* eventually made it to the screen, but after years of straight-to-video B-movies and camp TV serials, it finally seemed that Hollywood was taking Ancient Greece seriously again. Debates about the historical accuracy of the films, their fidelity to sources, the political context of their release and even the sexuality of the protagonists all made the rounds of Athens' cafeterias and editorial pages.

'Sword and sandals' films were hugely popular in the late 1950s and early '60s, as major studios competed with each other to produce the biggest, most action-packed epic. Making the most of new widescreen formats and enormous sets, the films' escapist settings and clear moral battles were a winning formula. Big names and big budgets fought heroic struggles in the name of freedom, fate and the gods. Richard Burton donned a toga and starred in the 1956 *Alexander the Great* – 'Now the Colossus of Motion Pictures' – in which a troubled Alexander ends up dying to save humanity from the tyranny he rather belatedly realised he was creating. Even Sergio Leone, now best known for his Westerns, cut his directorial teeth making the 1951 *Colossus of Rhodes*, a spectacular two and a half hour epic with the tagline 'A Monster Statue Of Bronze And Stone Twenty Stories Tall Guarded Their Secret!'

But as with many clichés, others had got there first. The 1941 Bollywood classic *Sikandar* (Alexander) rearranged the story from an Indian perspective: the battles were downplayed and the romance between Persian Rukhsana and Macedonian Alexander emphasised. But it was the film's patriotic dialogue and political subtext that upset the British colonial authorities in India enough to ban it in some towns.

The latest addition to the genre is director Zak Snyder's *300* (*pictured*), a faithful interpretation of Frank Miller's graphic novel that was filmed entirely in a special effects studio, with awesome results. The heroes are heroic and beautiful, the Persians decadent and deformed, the traitor Ephialtes a hideous hunchback: rarely has a major film taken such dubious clichés to such extremes. Comparing it to Rudolph Mate's 1962 *300 Spartans* (a film with the rare distinction of actually being filmed in Greece, and which has a soundtrack by the celebrated Greek composer Manos Hadzidakis), the older film looks rather quaint. It pales before Zak Snyder's romp in terms of action and pace: the older film's battles are less shock and awe and more gentlemanly skirmishes in olive groves.

Ultimately, however, and despite widespread derision of its historical accuracy, *300* gained the seal of modern Greek approval: soon after its release, students from the University of Patras, demonstrating against educational reforms and inspired by the film's gung-ho dialogue, started chanting 'This is Patra!' and 'Aoog!' at the bemused riot police.

Galleries

The Athens art scene goes global.

Contemporary art in Athens is burgeoning. The emergence of dozens of new artists – many of them foreign-trained – on the scene each year is reflected in the galleries and institutions, which now regularly include international artists in their programmes and host independently curated group shows. The permanent home of the National Museum of Contemporary Art (EMST, www.emst.gr) is still under construction, but this hasn't prevented it staging a series of successful shows in other venues.

The central area of Psyrri, traditionally the domain of craftsmen and small-scale industry, is now one of Athens' main culture zones. Meanwhile, the former industrial wasteland of Pireos Street is fast gaining ground as an art hub. The stunning **Benaki Museum – Pireos Street Annexe** (*see p94*) stages exhibitions of contemporary art and design. The huge, multi-purpose **Technopolis** (*see p94*) includes art exhibitions among its cultural activities and was the venue for the first Athens Biennial, entitled 'Destroy Athens', opening in September 2007 (www.athensbiennial.org). The **School of Fine Arts** (Pireos 256, 210 480 1315) is known for the shows of its graduates as well as retrospectives and exhibitions of top contemporary artists.

Another key player in the contemporary art arena, the **Hellenic American Union** (Massalias 22, Kolonaki, www.hau.gr), hosts an active exhibition programme in its two ground-floor galleries. It kicked off its 50th anniversary celebrations in 2007 with a neon installation by Stephen Antonakos, part of which remains on permanent display, followed by 'Made in USA', a survey of 20th-century American design.

Several private collectors have opened their collections to the public through various foundations and exhibition spaces: the **Emfietzoglou Collection** (Terma Finikon, Anavrita-Marousi, 210 802 7026) of modern and contemporary Greek art; the **Portalakis Collection** (Pesmazoglou 8, Historic Centre, 210 331 8933, www.portalakiscollection.gr) of mainly modern Greek art; the **Frissiras Museum** (Monis Asteriou 3-7, Plaka, 210 323 4678, www.frissirasmuseum.com), whose permanent collection focuses on paintings of the human form; and the huge **Deste Foundation Centre for Contemporary Art** in the northern district of Nea Ionia (Filellinon 11 & Em Pappa, 210 275 8490, www.deste.gr). Deste has put Athens on the global art map by showcasing world-class and cutting-edge contemporary artists (Jeff Koons, Noble & Webster, Matthew Barney and Barry McGee to name just a few). The foundation produces innovative curatorial and artist-generated

Ileana Tounta Contemporary Art Center. *See p174.*

projects, and has an art library open to the public. It also awards the Deste Prize, a biennial award given to a Greek artist.

Most galleries close between July and September, so it's a good idea to phone ahead or pick up a copy of the free bilingual brochure *Athens Contemporary Art Map* (available at most galleries and online, in English, at www.athensartmap.net) to find out what's on.

a.antonopoulou.art

Fourth Floor, Aristofanous 20, Psyrri (210 321 4994). Metro Monastiraki. **Open** 4-9pm Tue-Fri; noon-4pm Sat. **Map** p249 D4.

This well-designed space, with its balcony overlooking the city, concentrates on Greek contemporary work. Artists in its stable include Alexandros Psychoulis, Despina Christou and Mark Hadjipateras.

AD gallery

Pallados 3, Psyrri (210 322 8785/www.adgallery.gr). Metro Monastiraki. **Open** noon-9pm Tue-Fri; noon-4pm Sat. **Map** p249 E4.

In operation for some 20 years, AD gallery focuses primarily on modern and conceptual Greek art. Its repertoire includes such international artists as Jan Fabre, plus emerging and mid-career Greek artists such as Stefanos Tsivopoulos and Steve Giannakos.

Apartment

Fifth Floor, Voulis 21, Syntagma (210 321 5469/ www.theapartment.gr). Metro Syntagma. **Open** 11am-7pm Thur-Sat. **Map** p249/p251 F5.

The mission here is to exhibit and promote the work of emerging international and Greek artists, and it encourages artists to work on a project basis. Artists represented include Nina Bovasso, Maria Finn, Caroline May, Daniel Sturgis and Vassili Balatsos.

Batagianni Gallery

Agion Anargyron 20-22, Psyrri (210 322 1675/ www.batagiannigallery.gr). Metro Monastiraki. **Open** 4-9pm Tue-Fri; noon-4pm Sat. **Map** p249 D4.

Owner Vasso Batagianni's ties to the Berlin scene are reflected in her programme, which features contemporary Greek artists, like Andreas Lyberatos and Deste Prize winner Panayota Tzamourani, but also includes Berliners, such as Dimitris Tzamouranis, and expat American Indian Jimmie Durham.

Bernier/Eliades

Eptahalkou 11, Thissio (210 341 3935/www.berniereliades.gr). Metro Thissio. **Open** 10.30am-8pm Tue-Fri; noon-4pm Sat. **Map** p248/p250 C5.

One of the oldest and most respected galleries in Athens, founded in 1977 by Jean Bernier and Marina Eliades, Bernier/Eliades has shown a wealth of big names over the years: Sue Williams, Tony Oursler and Thomas Schutte, to name but a few.

Breeder

Evmorfopoulou 6, Psyrri (210 331 7527/www.the breedersystem.com). Metro Monastiraki or Thissio. **Open** noon-4pm Tue; 1-8pm Wed-Fri; noon-8pm Sat. Closed July, Aug. **Map** p249 D4.

Highly active on the international scene, the Breeder showcases some of the most interesting up-and-coming artists, such as Iris van Dongen, Marc Bijl, Vangelis Vlahos, Ilias Papailiakis, Matt Connors and Mindy Shapero. Exhibitions here frequently entail ambitious installations, as well as painting and video.

Cheapart

Themistokleous & A Metaxa 25, Exarchia (210 381 7517/www.cheapart.gr). Metro Omonia. **Open** 2-9pm Mon-Sat. **Map** p249 F2.

Cheapart began in 1995, when artist brothers George and Dimitris Georgakopoulos turned their studio over

Bernier/Eliades.

to dozens of artists to display and sell small artworks for €70 each. Now a non-profit institution, the gallery provides a forum for experimental and less-than-commercial projects by artists and curators. Cheapart has made a name for itself internationally, at the 2004 Bienal de Sao Paolo with Harris Kondosphyris, and in Vienna with 'ArtmArt', a mega-international version of its original concept. This popular Christmas tradition continues today, in conjunction with a.antonopoulou.art (see p172).

Eleni Koroneou Gallery

Mitsaion 5-7, Makrygianni (210 924 4271/www. koroneougallery.gr). Metro Akropoli. **Open** 11am-3pm, 5-8pm Tue-Fri; 11am-4pm Sat. By appointment July, Aug. **Map** p251 E7.

Opened back in 1988 with a programme centred on painting and photography, this gallery has featured Chen Yuzheng, Christopher Wool, Michael Schmidt, and the renowned Swiss artist Dieter Roth.

E31 Gallery

Evripidou 31-33, Psyrri (210 321 0881/www.e31 gallery.com). Metro Monastiraki. **Open** 4-8.30pm Tue-Fri; noon-4pm Sat. Mornings by appointment. **Map** p249 E4.

Founded in 2005 by Nancy Kougioufa, E31 Gallery takes a fresh, experimental approach via artist-generated group shows as well as innovative installations and video projects by mostly emerging Greek and foreign artists. Those recently exhibited include Jack Early, Clement Page and Katerina Kanna.

Gallery 7

Zalokosta 7, Kolonaki (210 361 2050). Metro Syntagma. **Open** 11am-2pm, 6-9pm Tue-Fri; 11am-2pm Sat. Closed July, Aug. **Map** p252 G5.

Gallery 7 has recently begun to place emphasis on a younger generation of emerging artists, many of them graduates of the Athens School of Fine Arts.

Gazon Rouge

Victoros Ougo 15, Metaxourgio (210 524 8077/ www.gazonrouge.com). Metro Metaxourgio. **Open** noon-8pm Tue-Fri; noon-4pm Sat. **Map** p249 E4.

This lively space focuses mostly on the younger generation of Greek artists (such as Deste Prize nominee Eleni Kamma), but its programme also includes prominent mid-career artists, like Totsikas and Rena Papaspyrou. The gallery is located on the first floor of a refurbished neo-classical building, above a coffee shop and art bookstore.

Ileana Tounta Contemporary Art Center

Armatolon 48 & Klefton, Lycabettus, Neapoli (210 643 9466/www.art-tounta.gr). Metro Ambelokipi. **Open** *Sept-June* 11am-8pm Tue-Fri; noon-4pm Sat. *July* 11am-8pm Tue-Fri. Closed Aug.

The Ileana Tounta Center includes two exhibition-spaces, a bookstore and the stylish 48 The Restaurant (see p118). The gallery shows contemporary Greek and foreign artists such as Pedro Cabrita Reis, Maro

Michalakakos and Costas Varotsos. It also supports independent group shows like the recent Dark Victory, featuring New York artists and curated by Dimitrios Antonitsis. *Photo p172.*

Nees Morfes

Valaoritou 9A, Kolonaki (210 361 6165/www.nees morfesgallery.gr). Metro Syntagma. **Open** 10am-2pm, 6-9pm Tue-Fri; 10am-3pm Sat. Closed July, Aug. **Map** p252 G4.

The oldest contemporary art gallery in Athens, Nees Morfes was established by Julia Dimakopoulou in 1959. The gallery's focus over the years has been painting, particularly abstraction, holding solo presentations of established Greek painters. It recently introduced younger artists as well.

Qbox

1st Floor, Armodiou 10, Platia Varvakeios, Central Market, Historic Centre (211 119 9991/www. qbox.gr). Metro Monastiraki. **Open** 3-9pm Tue-Fri; noon-5pm Sat. Or by appointment. **Map** p249 E4.

Another of the several recent additions to the Psyrri art scene, Qbox was founded in 2005 by Myrtia Nikolakopoulou. In 2006 it moved to its current location, where it presents emerging Greek and international talent. Its artists include Nina Pappa, Dimitris Merantzas and Alexis Avlamis.

Vamiali's

Samou 1, Platia Karaiskaki, Metaxourgio (210 522 8968/www.vamiali.net). Metro Metaxourgio. **Open** 2-8pm Wed-Fri; 1-5pm Sat. Or by appointment. **Map** p248 D2.

Run by curator Sofia Vamiali and her artist sister Dimitra, this architecturally idiosyncratic space provides a unique backdrop for the innovative, mostly international and primarily British artists it features. Sam Herbert, Janice Kerbel, Liam Gillick and Phillippe Parreno have recently shown here.

Xippas

Sofokleous 53D, Historic Centre (210 331 9333/ 210 331 9341/www.xippas.com). Metro Omonia. **Open** noon-8pm Tue-Fri; noon-4pm Sat. Closed Aug. **Map** p249 D1.

The Athens outpost of the established Greek-owned Paris gallery, Xippas is one of the largest and best-designed commercial spaces in the Greek capital. Among the renowned artists recently exhibited are Vic Muniz, Rineke Dijkstra, Peter Halley, Thomas Struth and Apostolos Georgiou.

Zoumboulaki

Platia Kolonaki 20, Kolonaki (210 360 8278/ www.zoumboulakis.gr). Metro Syntagma or Evangelismos. **Open** 11am-2pm, 6-9pm Tue-Fri; 11am-3pm Sat. **Map** p249 G5.

One of the best-known, most commercially successful gallery names in Athens, Zoubboulaki collaborates with established figures in Greek painting such as Yiannis Psychopaidis, Giorgos Avgeros and Yiannis Moralis. A nearby branch at Kriezotou 7 (see p155) deals in prints, multiples and small original pieces.

Gay & Lesbian

Where the boys (and girls) are.

The cradle of homosexuality 2,500 years ago, Athens still has a thing or two to offer in the way of gay life. The Athenian gay scene is an exciting fusion of a Middle-Eastern party atmosphere and Western-style aesthetics. And, as more and more Greeks are finally stepping out of the closet, gay venues are following suit. A gentle breeze of change is blowing across the city, with a nascent gay village in the Gazi area, the first **Gay and Lesbian Film Festival** in 2007, and a small but dynamic gay pride festival. Less a party and more of a political statement, the **Athens Pride** parade (www.athenspride.eu) started modestly in 2005 with a mere 500 marchers, doubling the following year and again in 2007 (in spite of a 42°C/108°F heatwave). It's a genuine grassroots event, with little of the jadedness one sometimes witnesses at the larger, more established pride parties around the world.

The biggest problem about being gay here is not so much a lack of acceptance by society at large as by gay men and women themselves. Despite palpable changes, being male, gay and Greek remains a complicated business for many. It's common for men to be hung up about their sexuality, which can make flirting difficult. Most tend to be friendlier to foreigners than to fellow gay Greeks. The age of consent is 17.

STEPPING OUT

There are none of the huge gay dance clubs or sex clubs you may be used to in northern Europe or the US, but then again you will get a feel for the Mediterranean way of painting the town red. Be advised that nightlife starts late in Greece; hardly anyone hits the bars before 11pm or midnight, and the clubs are practically empty until 1am.

Gay Greeks tend to congregate in two hotspots in the city: around the crossroads of Iera Odos and Konstantinoupoleos (the blossoming village at Gazi), and around the beginning of Syngrou, near the Temple of Zeus. There are no lesbian-only bars, but women are welcome at (and frequent) all but the most hardcore gay bars. **Myrovolos**, **Sappho** and especially **Noiz** are the hottest lesbian haunts.

INFORMATION AND MEDIA

The most useful website for foreign visitors is **www.gaygreece.gr**, as it contains a lot of information in English about cruising and gay places across the country. The online edition of **10%** (www.10percent.gr) is quite impressive, but the majority of it is in Greek. However, there's a useful section in English (www.10percent.gr/issues/200408en), with information about gay life, cruising, going out, health, and so on. Other useful sites (but only if you speak Greek) are the online edition of *Antivirus* magazine (www.avmag.gr) and that of the **Lesbian Group of Athens** (http://clubs.pathfinder.gr/lesviakiomada athinas). For information about other gay and lesbian organisations, *see p230*.

Cafés

Blue Train

Konstantinoupoleos 84, Gazi (210 346 0677/ www.bluetrain.gr). Metro Keramikos. **Open** 8pm-4am daily. **No credit cards. Map** p248 B4.
A gay café that plays the latest hits and spills out on to the pavement, with tables right by the railway tracks where you can watch the trains – and the boys – go by. It transforms into a bar as the

The best | Gay spots

For waking up slowly
Start your day with coffee or weekend lunch in the piazza outside **Myrovolos** (*see p176*).

For early drinks
Head to **Blue Train** (*see above*) or **S-cape Summer** (*see p176*) in Gazi.

For lazy Sundays
Happy hour at **Aleco's Island** (*see p177*).

For dinner
Try Lesbian dishes at **Sappho** (*see p176*).

For clubbing
Fou Club (*see p177*), **S-cape Army Academy** (*see p178*) and **Sodade** (*see p178*) are three good party spots – but only after midnight.

For late-night chilling out
Enjoy the summer breeze on the rooftop lounges of **Kazarma Summer** (*see p178*) or **Mayo** (*see p178*).

Blue Train. *See p175.*

evening progresses and is perfect for an early drink or two before you hit the clubs in the area.

Enidrio Internet Café
Syngrou 13 & Lembesi, Makrygianni (210 921 2050/ www.enydrio.gr). Metro Akropoli. **Open** 8pm-1am Mon-Thur; 24hrs Fri, Sat; 5.30pm-1am Sun. **No credit cards. Map** p251 E7.
A perfect spot at which to check your email or arrange a hot date while having a light snack, lunch, dinner, ice-cream or drink. It's very close to Lamda (*see p177*) and Granazi (*see below*).

S-cape Summer
Konstantinoupoleos 84, Gazi (210 341 1003). Metro Keramikos. **Open** 7pm-late daily; 4pm-late Sun in summer. **No credit cards. Map** p248 B4.
Next door to Blue Train, this is a flamboyant café-bar with ab-fab red leatherette sofas indoors, as well as seating by the railway on the gayest street of Athens. There's finger food for the peckish.

Restaurants

For restaurant price codes, *see p108*.

Cookou Food
Themistokleous 66, Exarchia (210 383 1955). Metro Omonia, then 10min walk. **Open** 1pm-1am Mon-Sat. Closed Aug-mid Sept. **Average** €. **No credit cards. Map** p249 F2.
Imaginatively decorated, Cookou Food is a central, gay-friendly restaurant in the bustling Exarchia area, offering superb and inexpensive Modern Greek cuisine with a twist. Great for lunch downtown before heading off to the nearby Archaeological Museum.

Myrovolos
Giatrakou 12, Metaxourgio (210 522 8806). Metro Metaxourgio. **Open** 11am-2am daily. *Kitchen* 4pm-1.30am Mon-Fri; 1pm-1.30am Sat, Sun. **Average** €€. **No credit cards. Map** p248 D3.
Making the most of Athens means hanging out in this gorgeous piazza on a sultry summer evening, enjoying a drink or one of the small choice of interesting dishes that Myrovolos offers. A favourite haunt for girls who love girls, it's also frequented by the lads. It's one of the few gay spots in the city where you can sit down for a midday coffee or, at weekends, an early lunch.

Petalo
Xanthis 10 & L Karayanni, Kypseli, North Athens (210 862 2000). Metro Victoria, then 15min walk. **Open** 8.30pm-late Tue-Sun. Closed June-Aug. **Average** €. **No credit cards.**
The best gay-friendly traditional Greek taverna in town, tucked away in a tiny street off the Fokionos Negri pedestrian zone in Kypseli. You'll love its wide variety of delicious traditional dishes and low prices (around €13 per person). The pies with homemade filo pastry are fabulous. For dessert, try the chocolate pie, or the quince, wild cherry and grape preserves.

Prosopa
Konstantinoupoleos 84, Gazi (210 341 3433). Metro Keramikos. **Open** 8pm-2am daily. **Average** €€. **No credit cards. Map** p248 B4.
A cool ambience and reasonably priced, innovative food with a Mediterranean flair are the hallmarks of this gay-friendly restaurant. It's a perfect spot for a romantic dinner or a meal with your mates before you hit the area's bars and clubs. There is also seating outdoors right by the railway.

Sappho
Megalou Alexandrou 35, Metaxourgio (210 523 6447). Metro Metaxourgio. **Open** noon-late daily. **Average** €. **No credit cards. Map** p248 D3.
Not only are the owners Maria and Thalia lesbian, they are also from Lesbos island, where they had the famous Canteen in Eressos for many years. The newest gay and lesbian restaurant in Athens has delightful traditional Lesbian recipes, fresh fish and really good prices. Within walking distance of the gay bars, it's very popular with the girls.

Bars & clubs

Acropolis & around

Granazi
Lembesi 20 & Kallirois, Makrygianni (210 924 4185). Metro Akropoli. **Open** 6pm-4am daily. **No credit cards. Map** p251 E7.
Be sure to make a pilgrimage to Granazi, which has the distinction of being the oldest gay bar in the capital. Close to the Acropolis, it's very laid-back and friendly, with predominantly Greek music for men mostly over 30, and shows at the weekend.

Myrovolos.

Koukles

Zan Moreas 3, Koukaki (no phone). Metro Syngrou-Fix. **Open** 11pm-5am Wed-Sun. **No credit cards.** **Map** p251 D8.

Koukles is home to the best drag shows in town, at weekends. When they go out, most of Athens' transvestites and their admirers hang out here.

Lamda

Lembesi 15 & Syngrou 9, Makrygianni (210 922 4202/www.lamdaclub.gr). Metro Akropoli. **Open** 11pm-4am daily. **No credit cards.** **Map** p251 E7.

This Athens classic is not to be missed, particularly at weekends when it gets packed to the rafters. There's a dancefloor upstairs playing the latest hits, and a more cruisey area downstairs that sports a backroom – the only one in town. Bring your own lube and condoms.

North of the Acropolis

Aleco's Island

Sarri 41, Psyrri (no phone). Metro Thissio. **Open** 9.30pm-3am daily. **No credit cards.** **Map** p249 D4.

The historic Aleco's Island, where scores of young men have taken their first steps out of the closet, is still going strong in its new location in Psyrri. This place is ideal for an early drink, as it's one of the few bars to get going before midnight. Don't miss the Happy Sundays Party starting at 6pm, when for just €10 you can get two drinks or three beers and sample the buffet.

Big Bar

Falesias 12 & Iera Odos 67, Gazi (210 347 4781/ www.bigbarathens.gr). Metro Keramikos. **Open** 8.30pm-2am Tue-Sun. **No credit cards.** **Map** p248 C4.

The first Athenian bar-club to cater to bears, cubs and their fans, it's famous for its friendly atmosphere and cheap drinks. The local gay community holds weekly ballroom dance classes here in winter. Leather party on the first Wednesday of the month.

Fou Club

Iera Odos & Keleou 8, Gazi (210 346 6800). Metro Keramikos. **Open** 11.30pm-5am daily. **No credit cards.** **Map** p249 D4.

This is the only gay club in Athens to proudly fly the rainbow flag. The music selection leans toward the mainstream, with Greek and foreign hits, and the clientele is easy-going. Don't miss the hot 'wet' shows on Saturdays, drag shows on Fridays at 2am, and karaoke nights on Tuesdays.

Group Therapy Bar

Lepeniotou 11, Psyrri (210 323 4977). Metro Thissio or Monastiraki. **Open** 7pm-late Mon-Fri; noon-late Sat, Sun. Gay- and straight-friendly bar in the heart of Psyrri. It's pretty relaxed early in the evening, but the mood heats up as the night progresses.

Kazarma

1st floor, Konstantinoupoleos 84, Gazi (210 346 0667). Metro Keramikos. **Open** *Summer* midnight-5am daily. *Winter* midnight-5am Wed-Sun. **No credit cards.** **Map** p248 B4.

Upstairs from Blue Train (*see p175*), this is the club in which to dance among sweet young things swaying to mix 'n' match music. Popular with all ages.

Kazarma Summer
2nd floor, Konstantinoupoleos 84, Gazi (210 346 0667). Metro Keramikos. **Open** 10.30pm-late daily. **No credit cards. Map** p248 B4.
Too much dancing or necking in Kazarma? Head upstairs to the lounge terrace of Kazarma Summer to cool off and relax to feelgood tunes under the stars.

Mayo
Persefonis 33, Gazi (210 342 3066). Metro Keramikos. **Open** 8pm-5am daily. **No credit cards. Map** p248 B4.
Gay- and straight-friendly bar, with minimalist decor and just about the greatest rooftop in Athens, with a captivating view of the Acropolis.

Micraasia Lounge
Konstantinoupoleos 70, Gazi (210 346 4851). Metro Keramikos. **Open** 8pm-5am daily. **No credit cards. Map** p248 B4.
Lounge on a sofa surrounded by Middle Eastern decor on the rooftop of this ethnic bar, which has the feel of a very hospitable private home.

Moe
Keleou 1-5, Gazi (no phone). Metro Keramikos. **Open** midnight-6am daily. **No credit cards. Map** p248 B4.
Across from Fou (*see p177*), this is an after bar with Greek music. The action doesn't start before 1am and gets seriously busy around 4am. It's small, but that can make it all the more interesting.

Noiz
Konstantinoupoleos 70, Gazi (210 342 4771). Metro Keramikos. **Open** 11pm-late daily. **No credit cards. Map** p248 B4.
The best place in town for girl-on-girl action, Noiz plays the latest hits (as opposed to heavy Greek torch songs) and is favoured by a younger crowd, ranging from femme to butch. Men are also welcome.

S-cape Army Academy
Megalou Alexandrou 139, Gazi (210 345 2751). Metro Keramikos. **Open** 11pm-late daily. **No credit cards. Map** p248 B4.
Camouflage decor, army bunks and military-clad waiters – you get the works at the largest gay club in Athens, not to mention that it gets packed with hunky Greeks. Monday is karaoke night, while on Thursday you'll be treated to mastika liqueur shots for the Greek music night.

Sodade
Triptolemou 10, Gazi (210 346 8657). Metro Keramikos. **Open** 11pm-6am daily. **No credit cards. Map** p248 B4.
You're bound to be swept off your feet by the best dance music in town in one of Sodade's two rooms, which are connected by a corridor where girls and boys are only too happy to rub past you.

Bookshops

Colourful Planet
Antoniadou 6, Platia Victoria, North Athens (210 882 6600/www.colourfulplanet.com). Metro Victoria. **Open** 9am-8.30pm Mon-Fri; 9am-5pm Sat. **Credit** MC, V.
The first and only gay bookshop in Greece. You'll find the largest collection of Greek gay literature, fiction and non-fiction, as well as calendars, gay foreign press and knick-knacks. The staff are very friendly.

Saunas

Alexander
Megalou Alexandrou 134 & Iera Odos, Gazi (no phone/www.alexandersauna.gr). Metro Keramikos. **Open** *Summer* 7pm-3am Mon-Thur; nonstop from 7pm Fri to 3am Mon. *Winter* 5pm-1am Mon-Thur; nonstop from 5pm Fri to 1am Mon. **Admission** €15. **No credit cards. Map** p248 B4.
The newest sauna in Athens (opened February 2007), with a spacious steam room and sauna, a large jacuzzi, the city's best standards in hygiene and cleanliness, and opening hours that make sense: it stays open throughout the weekend. Check the website for regular special events and price deals (such as two visits within 12 hours for €20).

Flex
Polyklitou 6, Historic Centre (210 321 0539). Metro Monastiraki. **Open** 5pm-2am Thur-Sun. **Admission** €15. **No credit cards. Map** p249 E4.
New, very central and easily accessible by metro, this outfit is small but spotlessly clean. Amenities include spacious lockers, a sauna and gym facilities.

Beaches

Limanakia is a gay-frequented coastal area comprising three consecutive coves between the southern suburbs of Vouliagmeni and Varkiza (for these and other beaches, *see pp103-106*).

Pack your towel, suntan lotion, swimming trunks (optional) and mosquito repellent (essential), and take the express bus E22 from Akadimias. Alternatively, catch the tram to Glyfada and then hop on the E22 bus there. Get off at Limanakia (the third stop) – ask the driver or another passenger to tell you when.

From the two parking lots opposite the one and only roadside canteen (this is your last chance to stock up on snacks and water), follow the trails down the slope to the sea. There is not a single inch of sand or a tree in sight (you jump directly into the clear blue water), but the view more than compensates: bronzed men in various states of undress are sprawled over the rocks sunbathing. Limanakia gets especially cruisey around sunset, and it's not unusual to see some open-air action around dusk.

Music

The Athens scene hits all the right notes.

In ancient Greece, music was considered the highest form of art. It is believed to have accompanied everything from religious rites to labour. Recently, there have been many efforts to recreate the sounds of the classical era, but it's hard to say how close to the source the results are, and how much ancient music has influenced later Greek music. What is certain is that in 21st-century Athens, music remains omnipresent. And when it comes to the music scene, it's the outdoor venues that separate this city (and its environs) from the rest. No matter what you like – a symphony orchestra at the ancient Odeon of Herodes Atticus, at the foot of the Acropolis; a rock band at the top of Lycabettus Hill with the lights of Athens flickering far below, or a singer-songwriter festival with the massive rock at the Theatre Vrachon as a backdrop – your summer musical experience is guaranteed to be special. In the warmer months, the venues themselves become part of the performance.

TICKETS AND INFORMATION

Tickets can be bought from the relevant venues, online at www.ticketnet.gr, and from record stores and ticket agencies. Their websites have listings, as do the weekly English-language *Athens News* and daily *Kathimerini English Edition*, which is sold as a supplement to the *International Herald Tribune* (*see also p233*).

Ticket Hellas

1st floor, Aithrio Department Store, Agiou Konstantinou 40, Marousi (210 618 9300/www.ticket-hellas.gr). Metro Marousi. **Open** 9.30am-6pm Mon-Fri; 10am-3.30pm Sat. **Credit** MC, V.

Ticket House

Panepistimiou 42, Historic Centre (210 360 8366/www.tickethouse.gr). Metro Panepistimio. **Open** 10.30am-6.30pm Mon-Fri; 10.30am-4pm Sat. **No credit cards**. Map p249 F4.

Sacred Music, Classical & Opera

Western classical music is a relatively new phenomenon in Greece. In 1828, when the Turks left the country and the first generation of Greek composers, including Nikolaos Mantzaros and Manolis Kalomiris, started out,

Megaron Mousikis. *See p180.*

Beethoven was already dead and the rest of the world was well into the Romantic era. But the fact that Greece 'missed' the first centuries of Western classical music is compensated for by its alternative musical history.

Byzantine chant

The greatest contribution to the Greek music world was made without doubt by the unique Byzantine chant, a musical system dating back to the first centuries of Christianity and the scholarly music of the vast Byzantine Empire. Created before Gregorian chant, with its own principles and sophisticated use of notation, Byzantine chant is still alive and well, although after the fall of the empire in 1453, the Greek Orthodox Church pursued its own course of artistic expression.

Byzantine music has remained essentially vocal. It is monophonic and has inherited microtonal intervals, probably from the music of ancient Greece. Without the use of harmony or counterpoint, it has created a world of rich

Greek National Opera. *See p182.*

melodies and complex musical forms. Byzantine chant formed a solid base from which, much later, Greek secular music sprung.

The best place to hear Byzantine chant is at Sunday mass. Chants start at 7am and go on until 11am. **Agias Irini** on Eolou is the home of the renowned Greek Byzantine Choir (210 862 4444), performing the classic monophonic chants on Saturdays (winter only) and Sundays. At **Agios Dionysos** on Skoufa you can hear the rival (and less common) school of polyphonic chant.

Classical music

Although Vienna need not fear the competition, there is no shortage of big-name classical performers in the city. But the music scene is very centralised, with almost all of the action taking place at the Athens Concert Hall, the **Megaron Mousikis**, inaugurated in 1991, with major extensions in 2004. The Megaron is a state-of-the-art performing arts centre, impressive by any standards and renowned for its good acoustics. But for Athens, it is more than just a music venue. The long-awaited building also embodies the modern cultural aspirations of the city and its desire to be on a

par with other EU capitals. There is not a great deal of classical music to be heard beyond the Megaron, however. A major difference in the musical life of Athens, compared to most other European cities, is the lack of church concerts.

Other venues where you can hear concerts are the *odeia* (music schools), and the foreign institutes, such as the **Goethe Institut** (Omirou 14-16, Historic Centre, 210 366 1000, www.goethe.de/athen), the **French Institute** (Sina 31, Kolonaki, 210 339 8600,www.ifa.gr) and the **Hellenic-American Union** (HAU; Massalias 22, Kolonaki, 210 368 0900, www. hau.gr). As the weather gets warmer, the action moves outdoors. The main organiser for summer music is the **Athens Festival** (*see p162*), from May to September; the major events, including concerts and operas by the major Greek orchestras and big international names, take place at the **Odeon of Herodes Atticus** (*see p66*) and the **Lycabettus Theatre** (*see p183*).

Considering the limited venues available, the number of Athens-based classical groups is quite impressive, with two symphonic ensembles, two major chamber orchestras and the opera orchestra. Apart from the **Camerata Friends of Music**, none can compete with the top ensembles in Europe, but they are still able to surprise under the leadership of an inspired conductor.

Venues

Megaron Mousikis (Athens Concert Hall)
Leof Vas Sofias & Kokkali, Kolonaki (box office 210 728 2333/information 210 728 2000/www. megaron.gr). Metro Megaro Mousikis. **Box office** 10am-6pm Mon-Fri; 10am-2pm Sat. **Tickets** €15-€90. **Credit** AmEx, DC, MC, V.
The completion of the extension of the Megaron in 2004 has made it one of the major cultural centres in the city, housing conference halls, exhibition areas, a music library, shops and restaurants. The Megaron mainly hosts operas and symphonic and chamber music, from Greek and international names; it is also the home of the Camerata Friends of Music. The main Hall of the Friends of Music, renowned for its flawless acoustics, seats around 1,960; the smaller Dimitri Mitropoulos Hall holds around 450. The new Alexandra Trianti Hall (opened in 2004), intended mainly for opera and other staged productions, seats 1,750. The season runs from October to June. *Photo p179.*

Benaki Museum – Pireos Street Annexe
Pireos 138 & Andronikou, Rouf (210 345 3111/ www.benaki.gr). Metro Keramikos/bus O49

from Omonia. **Open** *Museum* 9am-5pm Wed, Thur, Sun; 10am-10pm Fri, Sat. **Tickets** vary. **Map** p248/p250 A5.
Since opening in 2004, the Benaki Museum annexe on Pireos has become one of the most interesting cultural sites in Athens. It now showcases classical music, and hosts a chamber music concert series promoted by the music website www.classicalmusic.gr.

Parnassos Literary Society
Platia Agia Georgiou, Karytsi 8, Historic Centre (210 322 1917/210 322 5310/www.lsparnas.gr). Metro Syntagma. **Open** 9am-3pm daily. Closed July-Sept. **Map** p249 F4.
An organisation with a lengthy tradition (it was founded in 1865), the literary society recommenced its chamber music programme in 2007.

Rembetika

Arguably the only genuine Athenian music, *rembetika* can be described as songs from the urban underworld (or the blues of the Balkans). The roots of the genre can be traced to the 1920s Piraeus hash dens, populated by the immigrants from the big population handover between Greece and Turkey. Drawing inspiration from Turkish café music, or *aman*, *rembetika* adopted a simple style and instrumentation, and became the voice of the dispossessed and miserable immigrant workers in Piraeus. Originally, the main instruments were the bouzouki and the smaller *baglamas*; the rhythm was tapped with feet, with spoons on glasses or anything else to hand. The lyrics, often improvised, focused mainly on prostitutes, drugs and how to humiliate the police. *Rembetika* became popular during the '30s, turning some of the poor *rembetes* into stars who drove Rolls-Royces, before falling into oblivion until a new generation, oppressed by the Junta, rediscovered the old songs and their rebellious lyrics, and turned them into their national songs of freedom.

The legendary names are the members of the Piraeus Quartet: Markos Vamvakaris, Stratos Payoumdzi and Giorgos Batis. But for the fourth member, Anestos 'Artemis' Delias, fortune was short-lived: addicted to hard drugs, he died in the streets at the age of 29. But if *rembetika* had a superstar it was bouzouki wizard Yiannis Tsitsanis, who was connected with the westernisation of *rembetika*.

Today, *rembetika* is synonymous with Greek music and seen as fundamental in much of today's scene. Pure *rembetika* no longer exists, living on only in old recordings. But various venues strive to keep the form alive. The quality of the singers varies, but there are still a couple of performers out there with that old *rembetes* feel in their veins. And *rembetika* certainly exists in the hearts of Greeks. It's truly amazing listening to generations of Greeks at family gatherings, singing along to the old *rembetes* praising hookers and dope.

Mantala – rembetiko steki
Ydras 14 & Kipselis, Kipseli, Northern suburbs (210 823 4511). Bus 022 from Platia Kolanaki. **Open** 11pm-4am Fri, Sat. Closed June-Sept. **Admission** free. **No credit cards.**
This is a classic neighbourhood *rembetika* joint in densely populated Kipseli. Try to catch a night with Babis Goles, one of the best singers and bouzouki players around.

Perivoli t'Ouranou
Lisikratous 19 & Leof Vas Amalias, Plaka (210 322 2048). Metro Akropoli. **Open** 10pm-4am Wed-Sat. Closed June-Sept. **Admission** free. **Credit** AmEx, MC, V. **Map** p251 F6.
Located right by the Acropolis, this tasteful venue has remained in business for over three decades thanks to its fine entertainment and food. Home to respectable old-school *laiko* and *rembetika* acts, Perivoli t'Ouranou has maintained a delightful traditional character, giving an insight into Athenian nightlife as it was back in the 1960s.

Stoa Athanaton
Sofokleous 19, Historic Centre (210 321 4362). Metro Omonia. **Open** 3-7.30pm, 10pm-4am Mon-Sat. Closed June-Sept. **Admission** free. **No credit cards**. **Map** p249 E4.
Athens' premiere *rembetatiko*. Old-timers with suits and cigars shower musicians with flowers and, when the mood strikes, dance passionately to songs of heartbreak and destitution. Reservations are essential on Fridays and Saturdays.

Taximi
Harilaou Trikoupi & Isavron 29, Exarchia (210 363 9919). Metro Omonia, then 15min walk. **Open** 10pm-2am Thur-Sun. Closed June-Aug. **Admission** free. **No credit cards**.
Most of Greece's *rembetika* stars have played here at some point, and the atmosphere remains deliciously old-time, illuminated by red candles and burning cigarettes. The smoke-stained walls are adorned with black and white photos of the greats.

Ensembles

Athens State Orchestra

210 725 7601/www.megaron.gr/
www.athensfestival.gr.
'The main symphony orchestra in the history of Greek music' (as it describes itself) was formed more than a century ago, though the current name goes back only to 1942, when the ensemble was assured the state funding it still enjoys. The current chief conductor, Vyron Fithedjis, is committed to performing new (and rediscovering old) Greek music.

Camerata Friends of Music

210 724 0098/www.megaron.gr.
Formed in 1991 as the Megaron house band, in just over a decade this chamber orchestra has, under the continuing, devoted leadership of Alexandros Myrat, achieved international renown. Respected Academy of St Martin in the Fields maestro Sir Neville Marriner was appointed honorary chairman in 2001.

Hellenic Group of Contemporary Music

Information: Megaron Mousikis box office (see p180).
The leading contemporary music ensemble in Greece was formed by the composer and conductor Theodore Antoniou, president of the National Greek Composers Organisation and the director of the Experimental Stage at the Greek National Opera. The ensemble has no permanent venue, but the Megaron is where you'll most likely catch them.

Orchestra of Colours

210 362 8589/www.orchestraofcolours.gr.
Much-loved composer/conductor Manos Hadjidakis formed this ensemble in 1989 with the intention of performing works not usually included in conventional repertoires. The maestro succeeded in this heroic task by investing in extensive rehearsals and financing his vision with his own money. Since Hadjidakis's death in 1994, the orchestra has been under shaky state patronage. The current chief conductor is Miltos Logiadis. The ensemble regularly performs at the Megaron and the Melina Mercouri Cultural Centre (*see p76*), and also organises the annual Dimitris Mitropoulos competition.

Opera

One would expect the country that gave the world Maria Callas to honour the opera company where she started her career. But the **Lyriki Skini**, the Greek National Opera, founded in 1939, has never had a permanent home and is still in its 'permanently temporary' accommodation at the Olympia Theatre on Akadimias, though this situation will hopefully change within the next decade with the decision to build it a permanent home. Despite this state of affairs, the audience is loyal, enthusiastic and growing. The GNO recently opened the new **Experimental Stage** in Rouf, which has a capacity of just 200 and is overseen by composer Theodore Antoniou. It brings 'classical' music out from the centre of town and into the nascent art district of Athens around Gazi and Rouf.

Ethniki Lyriki Skini (Greek National Opera)

Olympia Theatre, Akadimias 59-61, Historic Centre (210 361 2461/www.nationalopera.gr).
Metro Panepistimio. **Box office** 9am-9pm daily. **Tickets** €20-€52. **Credit** MC, V. **Map** p249 F3.
The Greek National Opera is a competent company that hasn't had the means to develop fully, in part thanks to the limitations of its temporary home: the Olympia Theatre seats only 800. Artistic director Loukas Karytinos runs the activities in the problematic venue, and it seems that his fight for a permanent home has now been won (*see p34* **Designs on tomorrow**). The indoor opera season runs from November to May. In the summer the company plays at the Odeon of Herodes Atticus and occasionally tours other parts of Greece and abroad. The nearby Acropol Theatre (Ippokratous 9-11) stages operettas and children's shows, while the new Experimental Stage in Rouf (Pireos 199 & Alkminis) puts on Greek operas commissioned by the GNO, as well as presenting Greek premières of 20th-century works such as Bernstein's *Trouble in Tahiti. Photo p180.*

Rock, Pop & Jazz

People are still talking about the Franz Ferdinand gig at the Rodon in November 2004. One reason is that it was one of the last gigs at the legendary venue, which has now been turned into a garage. Sadly, another reason is that it seems like it was one of the few times that a 'fresh' foreign band had visited the city – though to be fair, there have been others, such as the Kaiser Chiefs in July 2007, and events such as the **Rockwave Festival** (*see p163*) hold much promise. Most of the time, though, Athenian music lovers have to pay €30 for the new solo project of the guy 'who used to play drums in that solo project by the bass player from Def Leppard'. Or something along those lines. Yet despite the 'has been' characteristic of the international bands that typically come to Athens, the local scene is exploding.

If myspace has changed the global music scene, it has revolutionised Greek music. In years gone by, there was one band people were talking about, such as Last Drive in the '80s, Closer in the '90s or, in recent years, Raining Pleasure. Now there is an entire indie scene with bands such as Film, the Ducky Boyz, Dread Astaire, My Wet Calvin, the Callas, Mary and the Boy, Marscheaux, Fuse for Pekar, Menta

An Club.

and the singer-songwriter sensation Monika – to mention just a few. None of them sells many records, and most don't even have a record deal, but they have a great new-found confidence. Proof of this could be found at the ATH-LDN festival in London in April 2007, which showcased many of the above-mentioned bands along with electronica veterans K.BHTA (Konstantinos Vita) and Coti K.

The heart of the Greek indie scene has for many years been the little record store **Vinyl Microstore** (*see p184*). Every year, in November, the tiny space hosts the **Festival Yuria**, showcasing Athens' most interesting indie bands. During the rest of the year, their own indie radio station, VM Radio, broadcasts from the mezzanine, playing international indie as well as recordings from house label Pop Art.

Greek bands of international fame are harder to come by. Dig really deep and you come up with progressive rockers Aphrodite's Child, big in France in the 1960s, and Leuki Symphonia, who are said to have been seen on MTV in 1989. The one band with a substantial following outside Greece is the gloomy men with the fairly unorthodox name of Rotting Christ, often described as pioneers on the black metal scene. The band released their tenth album, *Theogonia*, in 2007, featuring a large choir singing in ancient Greek throughout the album.

Venues

An Club

Solomou 13-15, Exarchia (210 330 5056). Metro Omonia. **Open** usually from 8pm Mon, Thur-Sun. Closed June-Sept. **Tickets** prices vary. **No credit cards. Map** p249 E2.
One of Athens' smallest but best-loved rock clubs is set right in the heart of rocker- and anarchist-packed Exarchia. This is a great place to catch local acts as they play their first riffs on their way towards stardom, but also once in a while the odd international act, such as Sparklehorse or Backyard Babies.

Bios

Pireos 84, Keramikos (210 342 5335/www.bios.gr/ www.myspace.com/biosathens). Metro Keramikos or Thissio. **Open** 11am-4am daily. **Admission** free. **No credit cards. Map** p248 C2.
Bios is a truly multi-purpose venue for music, electronic and digital arts, drawing crowds with an incredibly ambitious programme of screenings, concerts and lectures. Whether it's video dance, Austrian laptop improvisation, Mexican electronica acts or photo exhibitions, the place is rammed. The venue is adjacent to the bar (*see p192*) and you can go to and fro as you please. Entrance is often free; if not, it'll cost less than show tickets elsewhere. *See also p94.*

Gagarin 205 Live Music Space

Liossion 203-205, Thymarakia, North Athens (210 854 7600/www.gagarin205.gr). Metro Attiki. **Open** usually 9pm-3am Mon, Thur-Sun. Closed Mid July-Sept. **Tickets** €20-€30. **Credit** MC, V.
Since the Rodon closed down, the Gagarin remains the only mid-sized (1,200-capacity) proper rock venue in town. Featuring the likes of the Kaiser Chiefs, Calexico and a fair dose of industrial, it has recently hosted successful mini festivals that turned the spotlight on to new Greek indie bands. The venue also converts into a cinema from time to time, showing retro musicals and cult movies.

Lycabettus Theatre

On top of Lycabettus Hill, Kolonaki (210 722 7209). Metro Evangelismos or Megaro Mousikis, then 15min walk/funicular (every half hour 8am-3am daily from corner of Aristippou & Ploutarchou). **Box office** from 2hrs before performances. **Tickets** vary. **Credit** AmEx, MC, V. **Map** p252 J3.
This modern amphitheatre, which hosts major acts from June to September, was created by one of the country's most important architects, Takis Zenetos. In the last few years artists such as Placebo, Massive Attack and Jane Birkin have made an appearance here, above the calm carpet of city lights far below. Tickets can be pricey, but you can listen for free by climbing the surrounding rocks (agility is required). You don't even need to bring booze: freelance entrepreneurs climb around selling ice-cold drinks.

Arts & Entertainment

Lycabettus Theatre. *See p183.*

Melina Mercouri Vrachon Theatre

*Vyronas (210 764 8675/210 766 2066). Bus 214/
trolleybus 11.* **Box office** from 6pm on performance
days. **Tickets** prices vary. **Credit** MC, V.
Map p251 E5.

This outdoor theatre, impressively located in front
of a cliff face, hosts concerts by top Greek musicians,
with a liberal sprinkling of international acts – past
performers range from the Buena Vista Social Club
to Antony and the Johnsons and Iggy Pop – during
the June to September season.

Mikromousiko Theatro
(Small Music Theatre)

*Veikou 33, Koukaki (210 924 5644/www.small
musictheatre.gr). Metro Akropoli.* **Open** 9pm-3am
daily. Closed June-Sept. **Tickets** €5-€15. **No credit
cards. Map** p251 E7.

A tiny venue with grand programming. It started
in 2000 with a focus on experimental, free improvised and electronic music. But it also features
avant-garde rock, jazz, folk and chamber music,
local rock bands and, once in a while, the odd international act. Not content with that, it hosts the 2:13
Experimental music club, with monthly live dates,
and the yearly three-day 2:13 December Festival
with Greek and global artists.

Vinyl Microstore

*Didotou 34, Exarchia (210 361 4544/www.
vmradio.gr). Metro Omonia.* **Open** 10am-3pm Mon,
Wed, Sat; 10am-8pm Tue, Thur, Fri. **Credit** MC, V.
Map p252 G3.

For many years, Athens' indie crowd has climbed
over the dog Yuri (who always sleeps on the pavement outside the shop) to get the latest import CDs,
attend an unplugged gig in this tiny space or just
have a chat with owner Nektarios. The shop also
arranges the indie festival Yuria, recordings of
which are sold in the shop.

Jazz & folk

To Baraki tou Vasili

*Didotou 3, Kolonaki (210 362 3625). Metro
Panepistimio or Syntagma.* **Open** usually 10.30pm-
3am daily. Closed June-Sept. **Tickets** €13 (incl 1
drink). **No credit cards. Map** p252 G3.

A small, cosy venue in a quiet street, run by a music
freak who unfailingly introduces performers to
audiences. It stages up-and-coming local acts, both
traditional and contemporary, and, less frequently,
established artists too.

Half Note Jazz Club

*Trivonianou 17, Mets, East Athens (210 921 3310/
www.halfnote.gr). Metro Syngrou-Fix, then 10min
walk/tram Leof Vouliagmenis.* **Open** from 10.30pm
Thur-Sat; from 8.30pm Sun. Closed June-Sept.
Tickets €30 (incl 1 drink); €20 concessions.
Credit MC, V. **Map** p251 F8.

The Athens jazz scene circles more or less entirely
around this legendary venue next to the First Athens
Cemetery. A great club with the right atmosphere,
attracting international and Greek names in both
jazz and world music.

Greek Popular Music

Greek popular music, or **laiko** (literally 'music of the people'), descends from the gritty strains of *rembetika* (*see p181* **Rembetika**) but has morphed, via 1950s lounge singers, plate-smashing nightclubs and an affinity for love songs and glitter, into a one-of-a-kind music (and entertainment) experience that blends the centuries-old bouzouki with the showmanship of Western pop. There are different strains of *laiko*, but in the same way that most Western pop can trace its origins to gospel, jazz and blues, so the roots of Greek popular music can be found in the earthy, almost Middle Eastern sounds of *rembetika*. This new music, and the clubs that play it, are called **bouzoukia**, after the primary instrument involved.

In modern Athens, *bouzoukia* fall into a couple of different categories. Though all favour fancy stage shows, vast consumption of alcohol, liberal spending and thoroughly decked-out performers and clientele, some play a high quality of more traditional Greek music, with old-school singers such as Costas Makedonas, Dimitris Bassis, Eleni Tsaligopoulou, Gerasimos Andreatos and Yiannis Kotsiras.

Another branch of *bouzoukia* is heavily mixed with Western, commercial pop – these performances tend to favour laser-light spectacles and catchy tunes that are often made into videos. The kings and queens of this scene are just as likely to perform in tight leather pants and bustiers as in sparkling evening gowns. The ruling divas here are Anna Vissi, Kaiti Garbi and Despina Vandi.

The lowest form of *bouzoukia* is called *skiladiko*, literally 'dog clubs'. These are places where the level of tackiness and ostentation is so high, and the quality of music (and level of décolletage) so low that they attract the lowest class of customer. If you want to see this scene, it's best to book a table at one of the clubs (for which you'll also pay for an obligatory meal). Expect the cost of ticket, meal and drinks for a couple to run to around €200 – more if you buy flowers to throw at the singer.

But there's also a much less commercial and more sophisticated take on modern Greek music. In the 1960s, when nightclub singers were co-opting *rembetika* and marketing their pop version to the masses, Greece's most celebrated classical composers, Mikis Theodorakis and Manos Hadjidakis, combined traditional Greek music with Western-style symphonies, and accompanied them with lyrics by major poets, including Nobel Prize winners Odysseus Elytis and George Seferis.

These innovative and beautiful pieces are still performed at Greece's most prestigious venues, and laid the groundwork for a new type of *laiko* called **entechno**, meaning 'art music'. *Entechno* is defined by a higher level

Plug in to the local scene

Greek-language hip hop, indie pop, beat-based electronica, nostalgic instrumental music, art song (*entechno*), vibrant folk music and the tacky but always entertaining pop-*laiko*: these are just some of the many sounds you can hear around Athens.

Tops of the pop crop are Cypriot-born crooner Michalis Hadjiyannis, who combines boy-next-door charm with a velvety voice; Greek-Swede Eurovision sex kitten Elena Paparizou, with her upbeat blend of europop and techno dance; all-dancing heart-throb Sakis Rouvas; and the greatest of them all, the Madonna of Greece, Anna Vissi.

Away from the europop and pop-*laiko* axis, look out for the solo efforts of the two former members of Greek electronica pioneers Stereonova – the jazzy house of Mikael Delta, and the clever electronica of K.BHTA (Konstantinos Vita), whose soundtrack to the dance performance *2* sold gold against all

odds. Fusion outfit Mode Plagal lets its funky improvisations of traditional Greek *demotika* (folk) do the talking. Indie outfit Raining Pleasure was the second English-language band ever to get signed to a major local label, making their indie fans proud to have a Greek band that sounds so 'un-Greek'.

The crystal-clear, resonant voice of Alkistis Protopsalti aims straight for the heart with songs that are integrally Greek, yet globally influenced, while world-music star Eleftheria Arvanitaki's spine-chilling vocal acrobatics have enchanted fans. Also look out for Savina Yannatou, an artist of exceptional talent; her vocal mannerisms – raw and primitive one minute, lyrical and sublime the next – strike an openly religious note. Armed with a sensuously gruff voice, a style with its roots in *rembetika* and a gripping stage presence, Haris Alexiou (known lovingly as Haroula) embodies the Greek spirit.

Centrally located **Rex** is a classic *bouzoukia* that's popular with tourists and locals.

of song-writing, but more so, a strong focus on the lyrics. It still sounds very Greek but is definitely open to various influences, generally more folky and international rather than Western and commercial. *Entechno* artists such as Socrates Malamas, Orpheas Peridis and Thanassis Papaconstantinou tend to be deep-digging songwriters rather than straight-out entertainers. But, even so, they can provide a heady night on the strength of their material and rapport with fans. Shows are usually limited to short runs at clubs with 400 to 500 capacities, because the acts aim to 'keep it real'.

None of these should be confused with folk music, which in Greece differs widely from region to region and is a major chapter in itself, with influences from ancient Greece, Byzantium and the later occupying powers. A good place to hear the real stuff is at the **Dora Stratou Garden Theatre** (*see p201*) where it comes complete with authentic costumes. Don't be put off, though – this is not a touristy 'real Greek music' show, but a serious institution based on extensive ethnographic research under the direction of Professor Alkis Raftis.

Venues

Bouzoukia

Athinon Arena
Pireos 166, Tavros (210 347 1111). Metro Keramikos/bus O49 from Omonia. **Open** 11pm-4am Thur-Sat. Closed Apr-Oct. **Tickets** €15 (incl 1 drink) standing room; €170 (incl alcohol) table for 4. **Credit** AmEx, DC, V.
This new arena, unprecedented in everything from cost to size to technology, is the Las Vegas of Greek music. The venue, which can hold up to 7,000 people, opened in December 2004 with pop-sters Yorgos Dalaras and Antonis Remos in an excellent double show.

Rex
Panepistimiou 48, Omonia (210 381 4591). Metro Omonia. **Open** *Dec-mid Apr* 11pm-4am Thur-Sun. Closed mid Apr-Nov. **Tickets** €20 (incl 1 drink) standing room; €190 (incl alcohol) table for 4. **Credit** AmEx, DC, V. **Map** p249 F3.
One of the few big bouzouki clubs in central Athens, Rex recently featured a true diva, Despina Vandi, together with *Fame Factory* products Kalomira and Thanos Petrelis.

Romeo Plus
Kallirois 4, Syngrou (210 923 2648). Metro Syngrou-Fix. **Open** *Nov-Apr* 11pm-4am Wed-Sat. Closed May-Oct. **Tickets** €10-€15 (incl 1 drink) standing room; €130 (incl alcohol) table for 4. **Credit** AmEx, DC, V. **Map** p251 F7.
One of the hottest places in town for pop-*laiko*. In the summer, the club moves out to the coastal area, at Ellenikou 1, Glyfada (210 894 5345).

Thalassa
Leof Posidonos 58, Glyfada, Southern suburbs (210 898 2979). Tram Glyfada. **Open** 11pm-4am Wed-Sat. Closed Sept-Apr. **Tickets** €15 (incl 1 drink) standing room; €80-€170 (incl alcohol) table for 4.
This is the hottest 'beach' club (as the summer clubs are called) but don't expect a chilled show in the sand. Thalassa is a big venue with the atmosphere to match: girls dressed to their teeth dancing and shaking away on the tables while their men, in a uniform of jeans, pointy shoes and jacket throw seriously overpriced flowers at them.

Entechno

Zygos
Kydathinaion 22, Plaka (210 324 1610). Metro Syntagma. **Open** *Nov-Apr* 11pm-3am Thur-Sat; 9pm-1am Sun. Closed May-Oct. **Tickets** €15 (incl 1 drink) standing room; €160 (incl alcohol) table for 4. **No credit cards. Map** p251 F6.
This historic venue in the city centre is the hub of authentic Athenian *entechno*.

Nightlife

City-centre hot spots and cool coastal clubs.

If you can't take the beats, chill out at **Inoteka**'s pavement tables. *See p188.*

See p188.

The Greeks have a word for it, and that word is *kefi*, which means not simply having a good time but truly relishing it. Whatever your *kefi*, the bar, club and dance scene of Athens will surely quench your thirst, whether your idea of fun is a high-end hotel restaurant-lounge with a panoramic view of the Acropolis, summer beachside clubbing, or a working man's hangout with barrels of ouzo and cognac on the walls.

If you've stopped for a frappé at a little café after a day of sightseeing, it's more than likely that at sundown staff will dim the lights, turn the music up and the place will transform itself from café to bar. True nightspots don't open their doors until after 10pm, though, and the style-conscious wouldn't think of leaving home until after midnight. There's no need to worry about last orders: most places stay open as long as there are customers to serve and, especially at weekends, the sun may come up before the bar shuts down.

The traditional nightlife districts are the downtown areas of Psyrri and Exarchia, and upmarket Kolonaki, between Syntagma and Evangelismos metro stations. The metro's recent extension to Gazi (Keramikos station), has helped boost that area's fashionable and already burgeoning nightlife.

The capital's nightlife is seasonal, with most established clubs closing their downtown venues and shifting to the coast in the hotter weather. During summer, large dinner and dance clubs open all along coastal Leof Posidonos (*see p190* **Summer clubbing**). The wooded northern suburb of Kifissia is an alternative respite from the city heat, popular with moneyed, somewhat older people.

BEWARE OF DODGY DRINKS
Just like every other large city, Athens has its fair share of seedy joints that charge an arm and a leg for, at best, a mediocre experience. And the gleaming bottles of branded whisky and vodka – or any other spirit for that matter – lined up behind the bar may not be all they seem. Some venues cut on costs by diluting their spirits with illegally imported rough – and potent – alcohol. These adulterated spirits are referred to as *bombes* by Athenians, and

see p190

Arts & Entertainment

Make it a double

The rule about Athens nightlife is to pace yourself, as joints don't really start jumping until the early hours. So if you find somewhere quiet at 9pm, that's because it's still dinner time; drinks and dancing don't begin until long after the meal has settled and everyone else has also come out to play.

At any of the most popular hotspots, customers settle themselves at an outdoor table (in summer and winter) and have a nip and a bite while checking out passers-by before moving on to more lively environs and a bigger dance space. Here are a couple of nights out according to area and how things hot up. If you've got the energy for a third night (or are looking for something a bit more refined), admire the Acropolis from the Hilton's **Galaxy** lounge (*see p191*) and follow the crowds from there around Kolonaki's trendy bars.

Monastiraki-Plaka-Thissio

Begin with a fruity cocktail at the comfy inner courtyard at **Stavlos** or wine-bar **Inoteka** (for both, *see right*) in the middle of the flea market, before moving on to watch things get jumping from the sanctuary of **Liosporos** (*see p192*) or **Brettos** (*see right*). Just a short walk away, there's lots to put one in the mood for more at fun and friendly **Thirio** (*see p192*) or **Booze Cooperative** (*see p189*), before heading on to dance the night away at **Soul Garden** (*see p192*) or **Bar Guru Bar** (*see p189*).

Gazi

Cultural events – anything from jazz concerts to comedy – overflow into the streets from the former gas works turned arts complex that gives the district its name. The area's new-found popularity has been boosted further by the opening of a new metro station at Keramikos. Start with a bite at **Mamacas** (*see p192*), the most established spot on the block, before moving either to its own adjacent dance club or any of these: arty **Hoxton**, across the quad; **Tapas** (*see p192*), around the corner; or pretty **Dirty Ginger**, next to that. Bohemian **Gazaki** (*see p192*) rules the roost as the late-night party spot, or you could try gay venue **Sodade** (*see p178*), which has great music.

large doses are potentially lethal. Your taste buds will hardly notice, but your head and your liver definitely will, so it's worth being careful. The best way to tell if drinks are spiked somewhere is to see what everyone else is drinking – and if they're all on the bottled beer, there's usually a good reason.

THE LISTINGS

In the following listings you'll notice that many of the bars and clubs operate as restaurants as well. The listed opening hours refer to the bar sections and, in general, are flexible. Places may stay open way past the listed closing time if they're busy, or close early if they're not.

Clubs along the coast (*see p190* **Summer clubbing**) are open in summer only. They often pride themselves on redecorating every season, so themes can change. Also bear in mind that venues come and go; this is especially true of Athens' summer clubs.

Acropolis & around

Brettos
Kydathinaion 41, Plaka (210 323 2110/www.brettos plaka.com). Metro Acropolis. **Open** noon-2am daily. **Admission** free. **No credit cards. Map** p251 F5.
A quirky hole in the wall, lined top to floor with bottles filled with an assortment of brightly coloured traditional liqueurs, which are also for sale.

Gallery Café
Adrianou 33, Monastiraki (210 324 9080). Metro Monastiraki. **Open** 10am-2am Mon-Sat; 9am-2am Sun. **Admission** free. **No credit cards. Map** p249/p251 E5.
This quaint café on bustling Adrianou has the Acropolis in full view. Come nightfall, it turns into an inviting little bar where you can enjoy cool lounge grooves surrounded by stone and wood decor. Keep an eye out for various exhibitions and live events.

Inoteka
Platia Avyssinias 3, Monastiraki (210 324 6446/ www.intoteka.com). Metro Monastiraki. **Open** 4pm-5am Mon-Sat; 2pm-5am Sun. **No credit cards. Map** p249/301 D5.
Set in the middle of the old Athens flea market, this shadowy, minimalist beacon offers DJ-spun electro-pop, scuzzy leftfield beats and dirty house to a trendy crowd. The outdoor tables make a good alternative for a traditional quiet drink. *Photo p187.*

Stavlos
Iraklidon 10, Thissio (210 346 7206/www.stavlos.gr). Metro Thissio. **Open** 10am-3.30am daily. **Admission** free. **Credit** AmEx, MC, V. **Map** p248 C5.
An all-time classic choice in the heart of Thissio. Laze the afternoon away in the tree-lined courtyard to chilled-out funk, soul and jazz. In the evening the mood gets livelier as DJs spinning anything from house and electro-pop to retro classics.

Historic Centre

Bar Guru Bar
Platia Theatrou 10 (210 324 6530). Metro Omonia.
Open 10pm-3.30am daily. Closed 25 July-25 Aug.
Admission free. **Credit** AmEx, MC, V. **Map** p249 D4.
A lively and endearing bar-club run with an infectious passion, Bar Guru Bar's crowd includes young, funky twentysomethings on the town and older couples who come for the Thai finger food of the restaurant. Weekly live jazz events in the upstairs bar are sure to keep musos happy; downstairs, the crowds get down to 1970s soul, grizzled house and R&B.

Booze Cooperative
Kolokotronis 57, Syntagma (no phone). Metro Syntagma or Monastiraki. **Open** 10pm-4am daily.
Admission free. **No credit cards**. **Map** p249 E4.
A well-kept secret among artistic types, this three-storey neo-classical building hosts exhibitions and plays on the upper floors. Downstairs, sounds are alternative or world music. A 6m (20ft) picnic table is the focal point, and mismatched couches near the back are handy for a break from the dancefloor.

Kolonaki & around

Baila
Haritos 43, Kolonaki (210 723 3019). Metro Evangelismos. **Open** 8.30pm-3am daily. **Admission** free. **Credit** MC, V. **Map** p252 H4.
A great meeting point for socialising on pedestrianised Haritos. The decor is sleek, stylish and red all over, and the stream of radio-friendly hits are kept at an amiably conversation-encouraging level.

Balthazar
Vournazou & Tsocha 27, Ambelokipi (210 641 2300). Metro Ambelokipi. **Open** 9pm-4am daily.
Admission free. **Credit** AmEx, MC, V.
For the past 30 years, Balthazar has been making its presence felt on the Athens nightlife circuit.

Housed in a neo-classical mansion, it is one of the most refreshing venues in the city centre. Local celebrities and out-of-towners flock to the island-esque courtyard bar, where there's also a garden restaurant serving Mediterranean cuisine.

Briki
Dorilaiou 6, Platia Mavili, Kolonaki (210 645 2380). Metro Megaro Moussikis. **Open** 8.30am-3.30am Mon-Thur, Sun; 8.30am-5.30am Fri, Sat. **Admission** free. **No credit cards**.
This small but lively watering hole holds a special place in the hearts of all those who have visited it throughout the years. Located in the conveniently central Mavili Square, it's a great place to start or end your night. The eclectic mix of funk, acid jazz and rock is guaranteed to raise the spirit, and the killer air-con system makes sure you stay cool in the hot and sticky summer evenings.

Caffeina
Kiafas 6 & Zoodochou Pigis, Exarchia (210 384 1282). Metro Panepistimio. **Open** 10.30am-3am Mon-Sat; 2pm-3am Sun. **Admission** free. **No credit cards**. **Map** p249 F3.
Come early if you want to grab one of the few comfy sofas at this tiny but cute café-bar in the heart of the city. This is where stylish groups of twentysomethings gather for a good chat and get down to a fair bit of electronica.

En Delphis
Delfon 5, Kolonaki (210 360 8269). Metro Panepistimio. **Open** 8am-3am Mon-Sat; 9am-3am Sun. **Admission** free. **No credit cards**. **Map** p252 G3.
The king of the bars on Delfon for a number of years now, En Delphis is a spacious, sophisticated hangout. The soundtrack is chart pop with a few house beats thrown in for good measure. If you fancy a spot of lounging, head for the upstairs room, where you can sprawl out on soft orange seats and window benches.

Booze Cooperative.

Summer clubbing

From May until the end of September, when the summer sun beats down on Athens, clubbing goes coastal: the strip that runs along Leof Posidonos for 25 kilometres (16 miles) from Faliro through the municipalities of Helliniko, Glyfada, Voula, Vouliagmeni and Varkiza (map p105) is seething with music joints, seafood restaurants and seaside nightclubs.

It's a glamorous mass exodus. The only drawbacks are the sometimes stiff entrance fees, expensive drinks and the time – and taxi fare – it takes to get there. Summer clubs draw heavy crowds and you may end up sitting in Athens' infamous traffic for more than an hour with everyone else who's had the same idea. The tram might be a better idea: the line goes as far as Glyfada and on weekends runs all night, though infrequently. Also bear in mind that the more prestigious of these clubs operate a strict dress code – so don't turn up in shorts and sandals.

Luxurious **Island** and **Akrotiri** are the aristocrats of Athens summer club scene, with celebs and their out-of-town guests often commanding the best tables and views. Try **Mao** where an up-for-it twenty- to thirty-something crowd look to relieve stress on the dancefloor and make some friends. **Galea** is fun and often has the longest queue, but the action here is a bit more restrained when it comes to mixing. **Babae** attracts a more approachable international crowd, while **Envy** caters for younger clubbers, with chart music and plenty of room to dance. **Bo** is the place to actually get your toes in the sand with a drink in hand.

Akrotiri Club Restaurant

Leof Vas Georgiou B5, Agios Kosmas (210 985 9147-9). Bus A2 from Akadimias/tram 2nd Agia Kosma, then 10min walk. **Open** 10.30pm-5am daily. **Admission** (incl 1 drink) €10 Mon-Thur, Sun; €15 Fri, Sat. **Credit** AmEx, DC, MC, V.
A massive open-air club with a capacity of around 3,000, Akrotiri attracts a mixed crowd of twenty- to thirtysomethings who come to pose with a drink in hand while gazing at amazing sea views. The decor doesn't hold back: it's black and gold, and features two giant gold rhinoceroses. Mainstream club sounds and lounge (with a later mix of Greek pop) are the playlist staples. The Wednesday R&B night is especially popular.

Babae

Posidonos 88, Glyfada (210 894 1620). Bus A2 from Akadimias/tram Kolimvitirio. **Open** 11pm-5am Wed-Sun. **Admission** (incl 1 drink) €12 Wed, Thur, Sun; €15 Fri, Sat. **Credit** AmEx, MC, V.
The former Balux has changed its name and style, though kept its swimming pool. The impressively large and airy club, right on the sand, draws a trendy crowd who let their hair down to mainstream and occasionally more progressive sounds from two resident DJs; there are Greek sounds on Wednesdays and band Dream performs on Sundays.

Bo

Karamanli 14, Voula (210 895 9645). Bus E2, A2 from Akadimias to the bus terminal. **Open** 11am-5am daily. **Admission** free. **Credit** MC, V.
Boasting one of the best sea views of all the seaside venues, Bo is equipped with a gorgeous beachside cocktail bar, along with exotic plants and plush sofas, bamboo umbrellas and tables right next to the surf. DJs play a steady stream of mainstream and Greek hits.

Envy Mediterraneo

Platia Agia Kosma, Helliniko (210 985 2994/mobile 6937 033303). Bus A2 from Akadimias/tram 2nd Agia Kosma. **Open** 11.30pm-5am Mon-Sat; 9pm-4am Sun. **Admission** (incl 1 drink) €10 Mon-Fri; €15 Sat, Sun. **No credit cards**.
Young Greeks love this mainstream open-air club with canary-yellow sofas on a dais that overlooks the throng mingling it up below . Wednesday is Greek Hits Night. If that's not for you, opt for the Sunday Sunset Parties instead. Things get going at 9pm, and feature anything and everything from '80s and chart pop to R&B and house.

Galea

Karamanli 4, Voula (210 894 4990). Bus A2 from Akadimias. **Open** 10pm-4am daily. **Admission** free. **Credit** AmEx, MC, V.
Galea is a massive yet inviting space where the beautiful people get down to house, R&B and Greek pop. The decor aims for an aristocratic look, with lit-up marble stands and an attractive veranda. The party-goers are a mixed bunch, including a fair number of VIPs and wannabes.

Island

*Limanakia Vouliagmenis (210 965 3563).
Metro Dafni, then bus 171 or A2 to the
bus terminal, then bus 114 to Limanakia.*
Open 9.30pm-4am Mon-Fri; 9.30pm-
5am Sat, Sun. **Admission** free. **Credit**
AmEx, MC, V.

It may be a long trek to get to trendy
Island, but it's worth it: an enchanting
location and amazing sea view will make
you feel as though you are way out in the
Aegean. Snappily dressed customers dine
at the finger food bar and dance under
the stars – it's a good place for a romantic
night out. Tunes range from loungey
ethnic beats and chilled-out house to
disco; it regularly issues CD compilations
of its summer anthems.

Mao

*Diadoxou Pavlou, Glyfada (210 894 4048).
Bus A2, B3 from Akadimias/tram Paralia
Glyfadas.* **Open** 10pm-3am Mon-Thur, Sun;
10pm-5am Fri, Sat. **Admission** (incl 1
drink) €10 Mon-Thur, Sun; €15 Fri, Sat.
Credit MC, V.

One of the most popular mainstream
clubs in Psyrri moves to a massive 5,000-
capacity venue in the southern suburbs
for the summer. Inside it's minimalist grey
and white with shades of lavender print.
The predominantly twentysomething
crowd gathers round a swimming pool,
also open during the day, surrounded
by sofas and recliners, and parties to
mainstream club sounds.

Vinilio

*Next to Riba's, km30 Athens-Sounion
coastal road, Varkiza (210 965 5555/
210 968 1056). Bus E22 from Akadimias.*
Open 11.30pm-5am Fri, Sat. **Admission**
(incl 1 drink) €15. **Credit** MC, V.

This newest open-air club hypes itself as
Athens' only authentic disco: the pulsating
neon blue and pink outdoor dancefloor and
disco glitter prove they mean what they
say. Vinilio has a fanatic following of all
ages, who strut their stuff to DJs mixing
and remixing the best hits of the '70s
and '80s. It's a long way out along the
Athens-Sounion road, but the deserted
location is beautiful. And don't forget
your sunglasses – the music doesn't
stop here until well after sunrise.

Frame Bohemian Bar

*St George Lycabettus, Platia Dexamenis, Kolonaki
(210 721 4368). Metro Evangelismos.* **Open** 11am-
3am daily. **Admission** free. **Credit** AmEx, DC, MC,
V. **Map** p252 H4.

Located on the ground floor of the St George
Lycabettus hotel (*see p50*), this lounge-restaurant-
bar attracts a generally well-heeled clientele, but the
retro-style decor creates a welcoming atmosphere
for everyone. In the summer, the action moves
across the street to the garden area of Dexamenis
Square, where you can sit back on comfy sofas and
enjoy lounge and chill-out music.

Galaxy

*Athens Hilton, Leof Vas Sofias 46, Kolonaki (210
728 1000). Metro Evangelismos.* **Open** 6pm-3am
Mon-Thur, Sun; 6pm-4am Fri, Sat. **Admission** free.
Credit AmEx, DC, MC, V. **Map** p252 J5.

An impossibly chic lounge bar located on the top
floor of the Hilton (*see p49*), Galaxy is a great place
at which to enjoy a relaxed drink with a fantastic
view of the city skyline and the Acropolis.
The vistas come at a price – drinks are on the expensive side – but you get what you pay for. *Photo p193.*

Mike's Irish Bar

*Sinopis 6, Ambelokipi (210 777 6797/www.mikes
irishbar.gr). Metro Panormou.* **Open** 8pm-4am daily.
Closed Aug. **Admission** usually free; €6-€8 live
music. **No credit cards**.

Every Monday and Tuesday, this fun basement pub
gets jam-packed as the mic comes out for karaoke.
Irish flags and football shirts, darts Murphy's by the
pint will make homesick pub-lovers feel right at
home. Large screens regularly show sports events;
on other nights bands play pop and rock standards.

Mommy

*Delfon 4, Kolonaki (210 361 9682). Metro
Panepistimio.* **Open** 11am-3am daily. Closed Aug.
Admission free. **Credit** AmEx, MC, V. **Map** p252 G3.

A hugely popular meeting place for trendy young
Athenians, this cool yet boisterous bar-restaurant has
impressive decor. The interior is set out like a house
and decorated with kitschy accessories and low sofas;
keep an eye out for mini exhibitions of paintings. In
summer, head for the outdoor area, where the mainstream dance music kicks off the night and later turns
to joyous, pumping house.

Palenque Club

*Farandaton 41, Platia Agiou Thoma, Ambelokipi
(210 775 2360/www.palenque.gr). Metro Ambelokipi.*
Open 9.30pm-4.30am Mon-Thur; 10pm-6am Fri,
Sat; 9pm-4am Sun. **Admission** (incl 1 drink) €10.
No credit cards.

The city's premier Latin club has built up a sturdy
reputation over the years. If you feel you need to
work on your tango, experienced teachers are on
hand most days of the week to offer early evening
(9-11pm) dance lessons. Palenque also regularly
plays host to various events and live performances
by Latin American and European bands.

Tribeca

Skoufa 46, Kolonaki (210 362 3541). Metro Panepistimio. **Open** 10am-3am Mon-Thur, Sun; 10pm-4am Fri, Sat. **Admission** free. **No credit cards. Map** p252 G4.

There's a distinctly Manhattan feel to this hip bar, which is something like a minimalist living room in appearance. Young, go-for-it crowds pile into the small indoor space to jiggle along to a rainbow of alternative pop tunes. The pavement tables are quieter, but crackle with the same swish atmosphere.

North of the Acropolis

Banana Moon

Iera Odos & Megalou Alexandrou 139, Gazi (210 341 1003/210 341 1513). Metro Keramikos/bus A17, B17 from Omonia. **Open** 8pm-3.30am Mon-Thur, Sun; 8pm-4.30am Fri, Sat. **Admission** free. **Credit** AmEx, MC, V. **Map** p248 B4.

Banana Moon has summer written all over it: the mainly wooden interior is enhanced by banana trees all around, and banana-shaped half-moon lanterns hang from any available space. The music policy embraces old-school dance hits and throws in a few new ones for good measure.

Bios

Pireos 84, Keramikos (210 342 5335). Metro Keramikos or Thissio. **Open** noon-2.30am daily. **Admission** free. **No credit cards. Map** p248 C2.

This cutting-edge bar in a modern art and events space is frequented by the hippest crowd in Athens. There are regular exhibitions (*see p94*), and short films are projected on to the no-nonsense concrete walls. You'll hear anything from house, dance and electro to avant-garde noise and trippy chill-out tunes at varying sound levels, depending on the DJ's mood.

Gazaki

Triptolemou 31, Gazi (210 346 0901). Metro Keramikos. **Open** 9pm-3.30am Mon-Thur, Sun; 8pm-5am Fri, Sat. **Admission** free. **No credit cards. Map** p248 B4.

The oldest watering hole in Gazi, Gazaki is a regular hangout for the ever-sociable Greek theatre crowd: the friendly atmosphere in this bustling bar makes everyone feel welcome. Rustic wood and dark blue decor lends a bohemian feel, and the sounds here are eclectic to say the least (anything from old-school rock to '60s movie tunes). The outside pavement tables are ideal for a summer evening drinks.

Liosporos

Miaouli 24 & Platia Iroon (210 331 1841). Metro Monastiraki. **Open** 8pm-2am daily. **Admission** free. **No credit cards. Map** p249 E4.

There's not much room for more than a set of decks, a six-stool bar and a couple of tables on the sidewalk at this happy, homey little oasis in the midst of Psyrri. A great spot to meet at before heading elsewhere, Liosporos favours retro hits, dug-in soul and some old-time psychedelic to set the pace.

Mamacas

Persefonis 41, Gazi (210 346 4984). Metro Keramikos. **Open** 9.30pm-4am daily. **Admission** free. **Credit** AmEx, MC, V. **Map** p248 B4.

A major meeting point in Gazi (and a top restaurant by day; *see p125*), this atmospheric all-white island-themed bar attracts a flirty and stylish young crowd with a fondness for mingling and cocktails. After 1am, once the DJ gets into gear with a selection of deep and jazzy house, the roof opens to reveal the Athenian sky – a true summer experience.

Nipiagogio

Elasidon & Kleanthous 8, Gazi (210 345 8534). Metro Keramikos. **Open** 9pm-3.30am Mon-Thur, Sun; 9pm-6am Fri, Sat. **Admission** free. **No credit cards. Map** p248 B5.

Set in an old nursery school, Nipiagogio ('kindergarten') retains the kind of fun, carefree vibe synonymous with finger painting. Silhouetted kiddie designs line the walls and stained-glass flowers decorate the place. The small dancefloor gets packed with a friendly bunch of twenty- to thirty-somethings getting down to lounge and electronica. A dreamy walled garden, lit with fairy lights, acts as a second chill-out room.

Soul

Evripidou 65, Psyrri (210 331 0907). Metro Monastiraki. **Open** 9.30pm-3.30am Mon-Thur, Sun; 9.30pm-6am Fri, Sat. **Admission** free. **Credit** DC, MC, V. **Map** p249 E4.

One of the most popular bar-restaurants in the Psyrri area, Soul has a club on the top floor that opens only on Fridays and Saturdays. Its summer pulling power lies in its gorgeous garden decked out in a profusion of plants, comfy sofas and big bar that serves a range of refreshing cocktails, including one of the best mojitos in town. The music is a breezy blend of carefully selected chart pop, hip hop, R&B, house and electronica.

Tapas Bar

Triptolemou 44, Gazi (210 347 1844). Metro Keramikos. **Open** 8pm-3am Mon-Thur, Sun; 9pm-4am Fri, Sat. **Admission** free. **Credit** AmEx, MC, V. **Map** p248 B4.

The small but always upbeat Tapas Bar plays more down-tempo jazz and funk on weekdays, when crowds turn up for a meal or a quiet drink, and spicy upbeat Latin sounds at the weekend. The drinks selection is excellent, notably the refreshing cocktails.

Thirio (Beast)

Lepeniotou 1, Psyrri (210 521 7836). Metro Monastiraki. **Open** 9pm-4am daily. Closed June-mid Sept. **No credit cards. Map** p249 D4.

Although this happens to be one of Psyrri's most popular late-night bars, you'll have to look hard to find the door – a doorman and a booming beat may be your only clues. Inside is a New Age grotto. If it's packed downstairs try to take over one of the little alcoves upstairs. Sounds range from world music to alternative rock.

Galaxy. See p191.

for the small, verdant garden and get busy to a cool selection of reggae, Latin and soul sounds.

Wabi
Eleftherotrias 25, Politeia (210 801 7673). Metro Kifissia, then bus 524. **Open** 10am-3am daily. **Admission** free. **Credit** DC, MC, V.
The minimalist decor of this Zen-inspired bar in the shady northern suburb of Politeia attracts a stylish crowd. Mainstream house and lounge sounds are the order of the day.

Western suburbs

Enzzo de Cuba
Agias Paraskevis 70, Bournazi. Peristeri (210 578 2610). Metro Aghios Antonios. **Open** 9am-4am Mon-Fri, Sun; 10am-7am Sat. **Admission** free. **Credit** V.
This popular bar-restaurant sways to Latin rhythms every night. Take in a live tango show or lounge on white sofas for a great view of the square. The mostly young crowd comes from the surrounding suburbs with drinking and flirting in mind.

Southern suburbs

The scene along the coast south of Athens explodes when the weather hots up. *See p190* **Summer clubbing** for the best beach clubs.

Fuego
Omirou 69, Nea Smyrni (210 931 9075). Metro Tavros, then bus 219/tram Agias Fotinis (Platia). **Open** 10.30pm-3.30am Wed-Fri, Sun; 11pm-4am Sat. Closed mid June-Sept. **Admission** (inc 1 drink) €10. **No credit cards**.
Vibrant Latin American decor and live music make for a real energy here. Tuesday is Brazilian night; on Thursdays Cuban bands take the stage. There are dance lessons every Wednesday and Sunday.

Molly Malone's
Giannitsopoulou 8, Glyfada (210 894 4247). Bus B3 from Akadimias/tram Platia Esperidon. **Open** noon-4am daily. **Admission** free. **Credit** AmEx, DC, MC, V.
Anyone homesick for their local back home should make the trip to Molly Malone's. where you'll find a good selection of beers (Murphy's, Kilkenny) as well as a range of Irish malts. There's also agreeable pub food, including (what else?) fish and chips.

Piraeus

Lemon
Akti Themistokleous 154, Piraiki (210 428 1164). Metro Piraeus, then bus 904. **Open** 10am-1am Mon-Thur, Sun; 10am-2am Fri, Sat. **Admission** free. **No credit cards**.
Amazing sea views make this a great place in which to chill out. Pop art decoration creates a playful atmosphere, and the adventurous electronica beats will grab your attention.

East Athens

Exo-Vitrine
Ardittou & M Mousourou 1, Mets (210 924 2444/ www.vitrine.gr). Metro Syntagma, then 10min walk/ tram Zappeio. **Open** 10pm-2am Mon-Thur; 10pm-5am Fri, Sat. Closed Feb-Apr. **Admission** free. **No credit cards. Map** p252 G7.
Just up the slope from On the Road (*see below*), Exo-Vitrine is snuggled up next to the forest on Ardittou Hill. From the extensive balcony there are direct views of the Acropolis, Temple of Zeus, National Gardens and Lycabettus Hill. The crowd is made up of the young and hip, and the music is a mix of mainstream sounds with some retro '80s and '90s.

On the Road
Ardittou 1, Mets (210 347 8716/210 345 2502). Metro Syntagma, then 10min walk/tram Zappeio. **Open** 10.30pm-5am daily. **Admission** free. **No credit cards. Map** p252 G7.
This aptly named open-air bar-club gets high marks for being an unusual venue: it's in the middle of busy Ardittou, shielded by lots of greenery. The playlist is broad-ranging and The theme nights include golden oldies, R&B and oriental.

Northern suburbs

Local
Christou Lada & Olympou 21, Kifisia (210 801 8236). Bus 550. **Open** 9pm-1.30am Mon-Sat. **Admission** free. **Credit** AmEx, MC, V.
Perhaps the hippest bar in the northern suburbs, Local attracts an affluent local crowd. Make a beeline

Arts & Entertainment

Sport & Fitness

There's a time and place for everything, including exercise.

Athens Hilton. *See p198.*

The ancient Hellenes believed a good workout was as essential as a solid education. Sadly, their modern counterparts have largely abandoned this ideal. Most modern Greeks are happy to leave physical exertion to the professionals, while they bask in outdoor cafés, cigarette and trusty mobile phone in hand.

It's not that the city lacks gyms – there's more than one in every neighbourhood. But there is also a time and a place for everything, the Greeks will tell you, and so it is with exercise. Ideally, the workout starts just ahead of summer.

For the ladies, shedding those extra pounds may not even entail doing a single push-up, as proved by the dozens of spas and slimming salons around town (*see p157*). For the men, a recent addition to the city's numerous pools, sailing marinas and multi-sports grounds are five-a-side mini-soccer pitches, wildly popular with work-harried execs looking to burn off stress and banter with friends (*see p197*).

FAN BASES

Football and basketball dominate fan interest in Greece, with the former skyrocketing after the Greek national team's shock capture of the European championship in July 2004. Volleyball and water polo bring up the rear, along with any other sport where Greek athletes happen to be excelling at the time. In the past, this list has included weightlifting, diving and athletics – though in the Athens 2004 Games, the home crowd's early hopes of sprint glory were dashed when their best runners, Costas Kenteris and Katerina Thanou, were ejected for missing a doping test, a story that rankles Greeks to this day.

The construction of some two dozen new facilities for the Athens 2004 Olympics was supposed to boost the capital's sports potential even further. But although several of these stadiums have now been leased to private developers, the majority remain under lock and key to minimise state maintenance costs.

Spectator sports

Basketball

Greece's favourite sport in the late 1980s and '90s, basketball owed its popularity to the national team's unexpected capture of the European championship in 1987. It now lags behind football, even though Greeks still do better at basketball abroad. A second European crown was added in 2005, and Greece's hoopsters topped that in 2006 by beating a lineup of American players from the NBA in the World Championships – the equivalent of beating Brazil in the football World Cup – for a top-two finish.

AEK Athens
210 681 3200/www.aekbc.gr.
AEK were the pioneers of Greek basketball glory in Europe, winning the 1968 European Cup in front of 80,000 home fans at the all-marble stadium built for the 1896 Olympics. The club plays at the Indoor Hall of the Athens Olympic Sports Complex in Marousi (*see p98*), sharing the arena with cross-town rivals Panathinaikos.

Olympiacos Piraeus
210 414 3000/www.olympiacos.gr.
The first Greek club to win a 'triple crown' of titles – the European championship, domestic championship and cup in 1997 – Olympiacos enjoyed unparalleled home success during the '90s, with five straight league titles between 1993 and 1997. The team plays at the renovated Peace and Friendship Stadium (Leof Posidonos, metro Faliro).

Panathinaikos
210 610 7160-1/www.paobc.gr.
With 27 domestic championships under their belt, Panathinaikos recently added a fourth European championship to their trophy case to cement their

reputation as the country's best basketball club by a mile. The first Greek team to win a European championship, in 1996, the Greens have since built a reputation for no-nonsense efficiency, snapping up the best players and staying hungry for success. The club play at the Indoor Hall of the Athens Olympic Sports Complex in Marousi (*see p98*).

Football

Athens alone boasts a dozen sports dailies, not counting an equivalent number of metro handouts, betting papers and fanzines. The papers' allegiance is essentially distributed among the capital's football powerhouses – AEK, Olympiacos and Panathinaikos – and widely differing accounts of the same Sunday match are the norm.

AEK Athens
210 612 1371/www.aekfc.gr.
A club formed by refugees from Asia Minor who fled to Athens following the 1922 ethnic purge of Greeks in Turkey, AEK traditionally carry the old Byzantine Empire symbol – a double-headed eagle – on their shirts. Officially homeless after their derelict ground in Nea Philadelphia was demolished in 2003, AEK get to play on Greece's grandest stage, the Olympic Stadium (at the Athens Olympic Sports Complex; *see p98*) while plans for a new venue inch forward.

Olympiacos Piraeus
210 414 3000/www.olympiacos.gr.
Historically the club of sailors and dock workers – hence the nickname 'anchovies' – Olympiacos are the ranking leader in Greek football titles. Their home ground, the Karaiskaki Stadium (Leof Posidonos, metro Faliro), was torn down and rebuilt for the 2004 Olympics; it is now immeasurably more comfortable for fans and visiting opponents alike, with a lounge bar/restaurant, shops and VIP boxes.

Panathinaikos
210 809 3630/www.pao.gr.
The club traditionally linked to the wealthier end of Athenian society, and eternal rivals of Olympiacos, Panathinaikos are in talks to construct their answer to Karaiskaki Stadium in Votanikos, a run-down industrial area west of the centre. Until that dream comes true – in 2009 at the earliest – the Greens will be playing at their traditional home ground, Leoforos Stadium (Leof Alexandras, metro Ambelokipi).

Panionios
210 931 1189/www.pgss.gr.
Another team of Asia Minor origin, founded in 1890, Panionios are among Greece's oldest sports clubs and are regularly raided by bigger clubs for young talent. Sadly, the team's Nea Smyrni stadium (Chrysostomou 1, tram Megalou Alexandrou) missed out on the Olympic bonanza. Built in 1939, it feels nearly as venerable as the historic club itself.

Bungee Jumping

Zulu Bungy

Corinth Canal, Corinth (210 514 7051/mobile 6946 301462/mobile 6932 702535/www.zulubungy.com). Shuttle bus from Corinth rail station, phone for information. **Open** *Apr* 10am-6pm Sun. *May-mid June* 10am-6pm Sat, Sun. *Mid June-mid Sept* 10am-6pm Wed-Sun. **Rates** €60/jump.

The Corinth Canal (*see p214* **Corinth Canal**) cuts mainland Greece off from the Peloponnese. Jumping from its sheer, steep banks into the depths below can be a very dramatic experience. An additional €15 gets you a T-shirt and a DVD of your plunge.

Gyms

Athens Hilton – Sport Academy

Leof Vas Sofias 46, Kolonaki (210 725 7072). Metro Evangelismos. **Open** 6am-11pm Mon-Fri; 9am-9pm Sat, Sun. **Rates** €50/day. **Credit** AmEx, DC, MC, V. **Map** p252 H5.

The Hilton Sport Academy opened its doors in 2004. The price tag may seem steep, but included in the price is a fully equipped gym with personal trainers on site, an indoor pool with aquatherapy available,

A fighting chance for football

In Greek football, everything these days is measured in terms of what happened 'before Portugal' and 'after Portugal'. It was in Lisbon, in July 2004, that the Greek national team stunned punters across the continent – not to mention themselves – by overcoming 100-to-1 odds to win the European Championship in one of the biggest upsets in European sporting history.

In the wake of that shock triumph – unimaginable on the basis of what Greek players had achieved before or since – an entire nation dared to hope that the mediocrity and violence plaguing Greek football for decades would somehow be swept away. Reality, though, asserted itself two months later, when Greece lost to Albania in a World Cup qualifying match, and an Albanian fan was stabbed to death on the island of Zakynthos for daring to celebrate his team's victory over the European champs.

The Greek authorities insist they're serious about tackling endemic fan violence. Though they have made statements to that effect every couple of years for some time, there is evidence that things are changing for the better. As the main Greek clubs took on a new league format for the 2007 season, they promised – in a rare show of solidarity – to pump money into the sport, curb violence and restore the reputation of a championship long tarnished by claims of match-fixing.

Laws on hooliganism have been toughened, and errant fans have been sent to prison. To cap it all, from 2008, fans will not only have CCTV cameras trained on them at more than 20 stadiums around the country, but personalised match ticketing will also be introduced to improve the chances of identifying offenders.

But despite signs of progress (family crowds are starting to return to games, for example), bad habits are slow to change. When Greece took on regional rivals Turkey in a high-risk 2008 European Championship qualifier in March 2007, the organisers made a point of not inviting Turkish fans as a precaution. Not to be deterred, Greek fans in one of the stands promptly started a brawl amongst themselves.

It is also true that watching Greek football can be far from inspiring. Part of the problem lies with the sorry state of many pitches, not to mention the stadiums themselves. With the exception of half a dozen grounds upgraded for the 2004 Olympics, most could pass for training pitches, and offer the bare minimum in services. Forget about bringing your car, for a start, as few stadiums have organised parking, and consider yourself lucky if you manage to find a clean place to sit. Greek fans like to jump on their seats for emphasis, and to pelt the opposing side with water bottles and coffee cups.

With such a fiery atmosphere, it's no surprise that most Greeks prefer to watch football on cable TV in bars, or from the comfort of their sofa, making a night of it with friends. But for those eager to try the Greek stadium experience, avoid the (usually cheaper) seats behind the goals to enjoy a trouble-free game. Once inside the ground, don't fret if you can't understand what the fans are chanting. In most cases, they will be about various forms of sexual activity involving the opposing club, players, the referee and/or their female relatives. For the most part, the word you'll want to catch – goal – is the same in Greek as in English, as are 'foul', 'offside' and 'penalty'.

Jogging around the **Panathenaic Stadium**.

a sauna and steam room. Aerobics, yoga, tae-bo and pilates are also available. Not bad value for lounging around with the rich and famous.

Ergofit

Despos Sechou 19, Kinossargous, East Athens (210 924 6881/www.ergofit.gr). Metro Syngrou-Fix. **Open** 9am-11pm Mon-Fri; 11am-8pm Sat; 11am-3pm Sun. **Rates** €10/day. **No credit cards.** **Map** p251 E8.
As well as conventional programmes such as aerobics, tae-bo, power pilates and normal pilates, this centrally located gym also offers physiotherapy services. It's run by a clinical exercise physiologist who knows her bones and ligaments.

Joe Weider Fitness Gyms

Stadiou & Korai 4, Historic Centre (210 324 1441/ www.joeweider.gr). Metro Panepistimio. **Open** 7am-11pm Mon-Fri; noon-8pm Sat, Sun. **Rates** €15/day. **Credit** MC, V. **Map** p249 F4.
Joe Weider has gyms and spas throughout Greece. The gyms are clean and airy, with a good range of up-to-date equipment, aerobics classes and a sauna. All welcome day guests.

Mini-soccer

Mini-soccer fields have been sprouting up all around Athens recently, attracting mostly men and a few women, who proudly don the kit of their favourite teams and head on to the synthetic pitches in teams of between five and eight. Pitches can be booked at a cost of around €60-€80 per hour. Should you and your friends fancy a kickabout, call one of the numbers listed below and book yourselves a game. The people in charge should be able to organise some opposition.

Paradise Mini Football

Metamorfoseos 100, Agia Sotira, Acharnes, Northern suburbs (210 246 6466/www.mini footballparadise.gr). Bus A9, 116. **Open** 9am-1am daily. **Rates** €70/75mins. **No credit cards.**
The club also houses a spa (use of which is not included in the price).

Protasof Club

Kapodistriou 2, Cheroma, Vari, Southern suburbs (210 965 3400). Metro Dafni, then bus 171. **Open** 4pm-midnight Mon-Fri; 5-10pm Sat, Sun. **Rates** €60/hr. **No credit cards.**

Running

The old **Panathenaic Stadium** (*see p96*) is popular with joggers, who either use the track on the surrounding hill or run up and down the marble stadium's steps. The **National Gardens** are a reasonable central option, though they can often be people- and pushchair-choked.
The daring who wish to follow the footsteps of Pheidippidis can run the **Athens Classic Marathon** (www.segas.gr), organised every year on the first Sunday of November. The 42-kilometre (26-mile) uphill slog from the rural town that gave long-distance races their name attracts thousands of participants every year.
If you prefer a more sociable jogging experience, try going out on a run with the Athens branch of the **Hash House Harriers** (www.athenshash.com, phone Sam Briggs on 229 404 7094 or check *Athens News* listings for details of forthcoming runs). Entirely non-competitive and requiring no level of fitness, the ad hoc group meets weekly at 7pm on Mondays during summer and 11am on Sundays in winter. An hour's run or walk around town or into the surrounding hills is followed by a taverna meal and drinks: it's as much about socialising as exercising. Visitors are welcome; you can often cadge a lift from a metro station.

Scuba diving

Divers Club – Marathon Bay

Leof Marathonas 417, Marathon, Attica (229 406 9196/mobile 6944 418423/www.diversclub.gr). KTEL bus from Pedion Areos. **Open** 9am-9pm daily. Closed Nov-Apr. **Rates** €50-€80/dive, all equipment included. **Credit** AmEx, MC, V.
Specialising in shipwreck diving, the Divers Club organises excursions in Attica and South Evia Bay.

Courses are available for beginners and experienced divers alike. The club also has a private beach at Zouberi in Nea Makri, where other sports are available too.

Vythos
Leof Eleftheriou Venizelou 56, Nea Smyrni, Southern suburbs (210 933 3260/www.vithos-diveshop.gr). Tram Megalou Alexandrou. **Open** 8am-3pm Mon, Wed, Sat; 8am-9pm Tue, Thur, Fri. **Rates** 2wk courses from €260. **Credit** AmEx, DC, MC, V.
As well as organising classes for beginners, Vythos operates experienced divers' excursions around the coast of Attica. The cost varies for short dives, depending on the equipment needed.

Swimming

Summertime in central Athens can be sweltering, so it's nice to know that there are plenty of pools where you can cool off. Though hotel pools are rather pricey, you may find them preferable to their municipal counterparts owing to the excessive admission bureaucracy of the latter. For information about beaches, *see pp103-106* and *p206* **Drive-by beaches**.

Athens Hilton
Leof Vas Sofias 46, Kolonaki (210 728 1000). Metro Evangelismos. **Open** *Outdoor pool* 10am-8pm daily. Closed Oct-Apr. *Indoor pool* 10am-6pm daily. **Rates** €15 Non-Fri; €45 Sat, Sun. **Credit** AmEx, DC, MC, V. **Map** p252 J5.
The Hilton's impressive outdoor swimming pool – the largest in central Athens – was an integral part of the hotel's €96 million refurbishment, and reopened in August 2003 with a swanky party. If you want to lounge around the pool with the in crowd, this is the place to go to. And at €15 per day during the week, it isn't bad value for the luxury. *Photo p194.*

Athens Municipal Swimming Pool
Leandrou & Iphigenias, Kolokynthous, Northern suburbs (210 515 3726). Metro Sepolia/trolleybus 12. **Open** 8am-7pm Mon-Fri; 9am-5pm Sat, 9am-2pm Sun. Closed mid July-Aug. **Rates** €24/mth (valid for 15 swims/mth). Members only. **No credit cards.**
To swim here you'll need a health certificate from a pathologist or a cardiologist, another one from a dermatologist, two passport-sized photos and a photocopy of your passport. So, if you're only in Athens for a short stay, you're better off heading to one of the hotel pools.

Holiday Inn
Michalakoupolou 50, Kolonaki (210 727 8000). Metro Megaro Moussikis. **Open** 11am-7pm daily. Closed Nov-Apr. **Rates** €25 (towels included). **Credit** AmEx, DC, MC, V.
The Holiday Inn's pool isn't exactly big, but with superb views of Lycabettus Hill, its smart rooftop setting (complete with a bar and restaurant) is a great place in which to cool down and unwind while Athens life continues apace beneath you.

Tennis

Pete Sampras may be the son of Greek immigrants, but Eleni Daniilidou is the nearest Greece has to its own tennis star. There are plenty of courts in Athens for budding Serenas and Leytons to practise on. As well as the tennis courts at the public beaches of Voula A (*see p105*) and Attica Vouliagmeni (*see p106*), the following courts are worth a try.

Athens Lawn Tennis Club
Leof Vas Olgas 2, Historic Centre (210 923 2872/ www.oaa.gr). Metro Syntagma or Akropoli. **Open** *Non-members* 7am-10.30pm Mon-Sun. **Rates** *Non-members* €20 per person per hr. **Credit** MC, V. **Map** p251 F7.
This centrally located upmarket club has ten outdoor courts (six clay, four artificial grass, all floodlit). There are also three squash courts and a gym. Members have priority on courts.

Ilioupolis Municipal Court
Angelou Evert 1 & Keffalinias, Ilioupoli, Southern suburbs (210 993 0452). Bus 237. **Open** 3.30-11pm Mon-Fri; 9am-1pm, 5-10pm Sat, Sun. **Rates** free.
These five clay and four hard courts are free to use and therefore very busy.

Ten-pin bowling

Athens Bowling Centre
Patision 177, Patissia, Northern suburbs (210 865 6930/210 866 5573). Metro Ano Patissia. **Open** 10am-2am daily. **Rates** €2.50/game 10am-5pm Mon-Fri; €3/game 5pm-2am Mon-Fri; €5/game 10am-2pm Sat, Sun; €1.50-€3 concessions. **No credit cards.**
An eight-lane alley that, while perhaps not Athens' best, is certainly the most central.

Super Bowl
Kanapitseri 10, Rendi, Western suburbs (210 561 3447/210 561 3678). Bus B18. **Open** 10am-2am daily. **Rates** €5/game 1pm-2am Mon-Thur, 10am-2am Fri-Sun; €3.50/game 10am-1pm Mon-Thur; €3 concessions. **Credit** AmEx, MC, V.
This 30-lane, well-equipped modern bowling centre is worth the short trip out of town.

Trekking

Trekking Hellas
Filellinon 7, Plaka (210 331 0323/www.trekking.gr). Metro Syntagma. **Open** 9am-5pm Mon-Fri. **Rates** €27-€40. **Credit** AmEx, MC, V. **Map** p251 F5.
Attica's countryside will come as a pleasant surprise to those who thought Greece was nothing but sun, sea and sand. Trekking Hellas' simple yet interesting four-hour trek close to Athens is highly recommended. Starting in the foothills of Mount Parnitha at the Church of St Triada, it takes you through Skipiza spring and ends up at the Bafi lodge. The cost includes a picnic lunch.

Theatre & Dance

Greek drama has been keeping bums on seats for two and a half millennia.

Athens Festival at the Herodeion.

Theatre

The formerly stagnant waters of Athenian theatre have given way to a flourishing, progressive scene in this cradle of ancient drama. Not only do the 180 venues host a bounty of different productions, but a slew of contemporary theatre festivals – the capital's new trend – are reflecting this optimistic image.

If you seek the so-called 'underground' scene, try those venues located in the areas north of the Acropolis (Psyrri, Gazi, Metaxourgio). Expect urban or minimalist design, not-so-comfortable seats – in some cases no seats at all – and, often, the most up-to-date technological equipment. In the Historic Centre, around Syntagma and Panepistimiou, and in nearby Kolonaki, you will find theatre at its most luxurious: renovated neo-classical buildings, auditoriums with thick red carpets and velvet seats, and elaborate sets. Imported shows and musicals are also staged at some of the venues

originally built to host the 2004 Olympics, such as the **Badminton Theatre** in Goudi.

SEASONS AND FESTIVALS

The theatre season runs from mid October to the end of April, after which many companies leave town to tour the provinces. In summer, focus shifts to the open-air theatres (the **Park**, **Alsos** and **Athineon**) in the triangle made by Leof Alexandras, Patision and Prigiponison. They usually host light comedies or *epitheorises*, a theatrical descendant of Aristophanian comedy with sharp political and social commentary punctuated by musical numbers.

The quintessential Greek experience is, of course, seeing ancient drama in its birthplace, preferably in an amphitheatre where it would have been performed in classical times. The **Athens Festival** (*see p162*), part of the nationwide **Hellenic Festival**, provides a unique opportunity to do exactly that. It's best to make a summer trip to the **Ancient Theatre of Epidaurus** (*see p218*), a couple of hours away in the Peloponnese. But there are frequent performances in Athens as well, at the **Odeon of Herodes Atticus** (popularly known as the Herodeion; *see p66*), where you can occasionally see the classics in English too.

TICKETS AND TIMES

Many theatres are closed on Mondays and Tuesdays. Performances start late, at around 8.30-9.30pm, and at weekends there are matinées. Shows popular with younger audiences usually have an after-midnight performance on Fridays or Saturdays. Ticket prices are around €10 to €25 (cheaper for matinées). You can buy tickets directly from theatre box offices or in advance by credit card at an agency (for an additional 16.5 per cent charge). For most of the shows at the Megaron Mousikis, Olympia Theatre, Herodeion and Lycabettus, book as far as a month in advance.

Hellenic Festival Box Office

Panepistimiou 39, Historic Centre (210 928 2900/ www.greekfestival.gr). Metro Panepistimio. **Open** 8.30am-4pm Mon-Fri; 9am-2.30pm Sat. **Credit** MC, V. **Map** p249/p251 F5.
Tickets for events, including the Epidaurus Festival, are available here and at the Herodeion box office, as well as at Epidaurus's two box offices, which open two hours before the performance. Credit card bookings are accepted on the above number until 4pm on the day of the performance.

Ticket House

Panepistimiou 42 (210 360 8366/www.ticket house.gr). Metro Panepistimio. **Open** 10am-6pm Mon, Wed; 10am-10pm Tue, Thur, Fri; 10.30am-4pm Sat. **No credit cards. Map** p249 F4.
This is a useful, central walk-in office, but payment is cash only.

Major venues

Amore (Theatro Tou Notou)

Prigiponison 10, Pedion Areos (210 646 8009/ www.amorenotos.com). Metro Victoria. **Box office** 10am-10pm daily. Closed July, Aug. **Tickets** €20; €14 concessions. **No credit cards.**
Founded in 1991 by Yannis Houvardas, the Notos Theatre Company – housed in Amore – remains one of the leading companies in Greece, thanks to its producers' ability to bring to the stage a wide range of plays from the international modern and classical repertoires. You'll not only find the most promising Greek actors and playwrights, but also works by the likes of Shakespeare, Strindberg and Calderon.

Badminton Theatre

Military Park, Goudi, Eastern suburbs (210 884 0600/reservations 211 108 6084/www.ticketnet.gr). **Box office** (Kifissias 45, Ambelokipi) 9am-8pm Mon-Fri; 9am-2pm Sat. Closed July, Aug. **Tickets** prices vary. **Credit** MC, V.

Completely altered from its Olympic venue origins, the newest theatre in town has staged international touring productions such as Matthew Bourne's *Swan Lake* and Andrew Lloyd Webber's *Jesus Christ Superstar*. The 2,500-seat auditorium – equipped with a 30m (100ft) by 18m (60ft) performance area, an orchestra pit and all the latest audiovisual technology – has been a big hit with audiences.

Coronet

Frynis 11, Pangrati, East Athens (210 701 2123/ www.coronet.gr). Metro Evangelismos, then 20min walk. **Box office** 9am-9pm daily. Closed May-Sept. **Tickets** prices vary. **Credit** MC, V. **Map** p252 J7.
This former cinema has been transformed into a luxurious theatre hosting a variety of companies. One of its most frequent visitors is the Black-Light Theatre of Prague, whose unique, dream-like technique, famous among theatre fans around the world, has its roots in the 17th century.

Ethniko Theatro (National Theatre)

Aghiou Konstantinou 22-24, Omonia (210 522 3242/www.n-t.gr). Metro Omonia. **Box office** 10am-1pm, 5-10pm Tue-Sun. Closed June-Oct. **Tickets** €15-€20; €10 concessions. **No credit cards. Map** p249 E3.
Housed in a beautiful neo-classical building, the National Theatre hosts a variety of shows – classic and modern theatre, as well as musicals. It has several other locations scattered around Omonia, such as the Experimental Theatre and the New Theatre, where productions often get rave reviews. For the 2007-08 season new director Yannis Houvardas has announced 18 house premières, including Aeschylus' *Prometheus Bound* and Dostoevsky's *The Idiot*.

Ilissia Denisi

Leof Vas Sofias 54, Kolonaki (210 721 0045). Metro Megaro Mousikis. **Box office** 10am-1pm, 5-9pm Tue-Sun. Closed May-Oct. **Tickets** €21-€23; €18-€21 concessions. **Credit** V.
Named after the Greek star Mimi Denisi, this is a wonderfully extravagant venue – luxurious interior facilities and a huge stage – that programmes some of the most lavish shows in town. A short walk south of Ilissia Denisi, at Papadiamantopoulou 4, is an intimate studio-like venue, Ilissia Volanaki, which generally presents contemporary plays that feature promising young Greek actors.

Pallas

CityLink, Voukourestiou 5, Syntagma (210 321 3100/www.ticketshop.gr). Metro Syntagma. **Box office** 10am-2pm, 5-9pm Tue-Sun. **Tickets** €40-€150. **Credit** MC, V. **Map** p249/p252 G4.
The reopening of the Pallas in 2006 was marked by a great success when the innovative production *2* by Dimitris Papaioannou – the choreographer of the opening and closing ceremonies at the Olympics – shattered all previous box office records, bringing the completely refurbished venue back to its former glory. Two smaller theatres – the Aliki and Mikro Pallas – have raised curtains in the same complex.

The curtain rises again at the gloriously refurbished **Pallas** theatre.

Theatro Tou Neou Kosmou

Antisthenous 7 & Tharypou, Kinossargous, South Athens (210 921 2900). Metro Syngrou-Fix. **Box office** 11am-2pm, 5-10pm daily. Closed May-Sept. **Tickets** €15. **No credit cards. Map** p251 E8.
This venue consists of three different stages, and has a constantly changing repertoire. Two recent productions are *Kata sinthiki pseudi*, based on characters by Jean Cocteau and August Strindberg, and *Katsarida (The Cockroach)*, by aspiring Greek playwright Vassilis Mavrogeorgiou.

To Treno Sto Rouf

Leof Konstantinoupoleos & Petrou Ralli, Rouf (210 529 8922/mobile 6937 604988). Metro Keramikos. **Box office** 10am-2pm, 6-9pm Tue-Sun. **Tickets** €20; €14 concessions. **No credit cards. Map** p248/p250 A5.
A carriage of a train has been transformed into this unique venue. Shows are followed by a candlelit dinner in an *Orient Express* atmosphere.

Dance

The growing interest of Athenians in modern dance has led more and more venues and companies to regularly organise or host dance acts and festivals. One of the most important is the **Athens Dance Festival**, organised by the Greek Choreographers' Association, which brings 20 or so of the best local groups to five downtown venues in May and June. Mini open-air festivals also take place all over town, especially during the summer. Traditional dances are presented at the romantic **Dora Stratou Garden Theatre**, whereas foreign dance acts are often hosted at the acclaimed **Kalamata International Dance Festival**.

Classical ballet always remains the city's missing link, though, and there is little local ballet activity. **Megaron Mousikis** and the **Olympia Theatre** usually host foreign guest ballet companies during the winter.

THE COMPANIES

Dance groups to look out for include Dimitris Papaioannou's well-established **Omada Edafous**; Kiki Baka's **Sinequanon**; Ioanna Portolou's **Griffon**; Fotis Nikolaou's **X-it**; and Mariella Nestora's **Yelp**.

Venues & festivals

Dora Stratou Garden Theatre

Philopappus Hill, Acropolis (box office 210 921 4650/www.grdance.org). Metro Akropoli, then 15min walk. **Box office** (Skoliou 8, off Adrianou 122, Plaka) 8-10.30pm Tue-Fri. Closed Oct-May. **Performances** 9.30pm Tue-Sat; 8.30pm Sun. **Tickets** €15. **Credit** MC, V. **Map** p250 C7.
Founded by Dora Stratou, a cornerstone of the movement to keep traditional Greek dance alive, this venue is known as 'the living museum of Greek dance'. The 900-seat garden theatre stands in the beautiful setting of Philopappus Hill. Dances, songs and music

Arts & Entertainment

A dramatic start

Aeschylus, Sophocles, Euripides and Aristophanes: sounds Greek to you? Well, it shouldn't. The three most renowned tragic poets of antiquity and the 'father of comedy' not only paved the way for modern theatre, but also inspired artists such as Shakespeare, Ibsen and even Woody Allen.

A great philosopher and theologian, as well as a war hero, **Aeschylus** was the earliest of the three great dramatists. His experience of fighting at the battles of Marathon and Salamis against the Persian army inspired his writing, which is acclaimed for its magnificent imagery. Of the 70 tragedies attributed to him, only seven survive.

Following in the footsteps of Aeschylus, **Sophocles** is considered to be a great innovator of the Greek dramatic form. Not only did he write independent plays rather than the traditional tetralogies (series of four dramas), but he also increased the numbers of the chorus from 12 to 15. *Antigone* and *Oedipus Rex* are his most important plays.

After seeking sanctuary in a cave on the island of Salamis, **Euripides** wrote some magnificent plays that reformed and redefined Greek drama. Although he was often accused of not respecting the religious tradition of theatre, he managed to win a great number of prizes in dramatic contests. Nineteen of his plays are extant in complete form.

Aristophanes is the giant of ancient Greek comedy. Since the works of his contemporaries Cratinus, Eupolis and Chionides are lost, Aristophanes' hilarious stories are unique samples of ancient comedy, combining real facts with mythological elements in order to ridicule – or satirise – the politicians and other public figures of his day.

Veteran theatre-goers will know that classical theatre is usually far from dull. But it is, of course, in Greek – so take a translated text with you, or read the plot summary in the programme before the lights go down, then sit back and enjoy.

are presented in the form that they were (or are still) performed in at the villages where they originated, thanks to Stratou's meticulous research. Even the costumes are museum pieces, handmade in different parts of the country a century ago. Dora Stratou also offers workshops in Greek folk dance and culture, with English-speaking instructors. The daily programme includes dance classes, visits to the theatre's extensive wardrobe of over 2,500 village-made costumes and entrance to the evening's performance.

Kalamata International Dance Festival

Pan Kessari 6, Kalamata, Peloponnese (272 108 3086/www.kalamatadancefestival.gr). **Tickets** €20; €15 concessions. **Credit** MC, V.

Trisha Brown, Jerome Bell and Jan Fabre are just some of the artists to have participated in Greece's most important dance event. The festival is held in Kalamata, in the Peloponnese (three hours away), in July. Audiences appreciate the opportunity to see the best-known Greek dance groups, along with the crème de la crème of the international dance scene.

Leda Shantala 'Shantom'

Tripoleos 35A & Evoias, Halandri, Northern suburbs (210 671 7529/www.shantala.gr). Metro Halandri. **Box office** 10am-8pm Mon-Fri. **Tickets** prices vary. **Credit** MC, V.

After spending years studying Indian culture, choreographer and dancer Leda Shantala created this small venue in order to host her own oriental dance acts and yoga seminars.

Megaron Mousikis (Athens Concert Hall)

Leof Vas Sofias & Kokali 1, Kolonaki (210 728 2000/www.megaron.gr). Metro Megaro Mousikis. **Box office** *Performance days* 10am-8.30pm Mon-Fri; 10am-2pm, 6-8pm Sat, Sun. Closes 2hrs before performances. *Other days* 10am-6pm Mon-Fri; 10am-2pm Sat. Closed July-mid Sept. **Tickets** prices vary. **Credit** AmEx, DC, MC, V.

This posh modern venue has three halls (*see p180*) and often hosts foreign classical ballet companies.

Olympia Theatre

Akadimias 59, Historic Centre (210 361 1516/210 361 2461/210 364 725/www.nationalopera.gr). Metro Panepistimio. **Box office** 9.30am-9pm daily. Closed May-Sept. **Tickets** prices vary. **Credit** MC, V. **Map** p249 F3.

The Olympia Theatre, home of the Greek National Opera (Lyriki Skini), is one of the top places to go to for classical ballet. As it hosts lavish productions by some of the world's foremost companies, it's a good idea to book well in advance.

Roes

Iakhou 16, Gazi (210 347 4312/www.xorotheatro roes.gr). Metro Keramikos. **Box office** hours vary. Closed mid June-late Oct. **Tickets** prices vary. **No credit cards. Map** p248 B4.

A modern venue that accommodates some of the city's most established companies. In spring, don't miss the annual 'Diar-roes' dance festival, a meeting of highly talented new artists.

Trips Out of Town

Attica & the Mainland   205
North-east Peloponnese   213
Island Escapes   219

Features

Drive-by beaches   206
Byron the philhellene   209
Corinth Canal   214

Maps

Trips Out of Town   204

Cape Sounion. *See p207.*

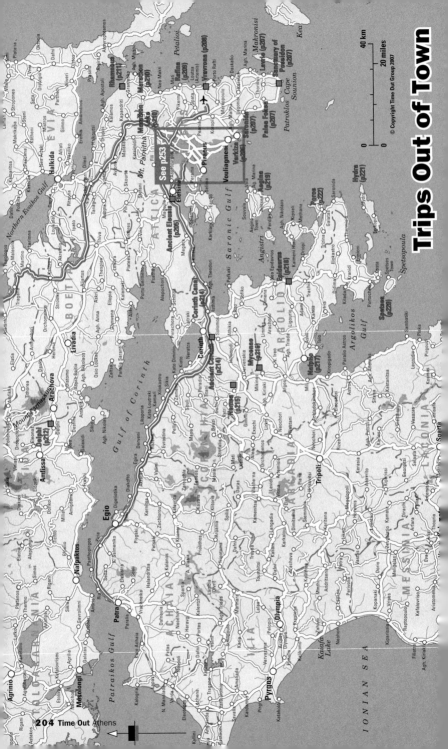

Trips Out of Town

© Copyright Time Out Group 2007

40 km
20 miles

Attica & the Mainland

Head out of the city for ancient temples, then cool off at the beach.

Sunset is a perfect time to visit the **Sanctuary of Poseidon** at Cape Sounion. *See p207.*

The fertile yet mountainous region of Attica has changed enormously in the past decade. Galloping suburbanisation, forest fires, a new airport and two new highways – the Attiki Odos and the Hymettos Ring – have all altered its topography. But it would be wrong to dismiss it. Beautiful beaches dimple its south and east coasts, and ancient sites abound, from the impressive temple of Poseidon at **Cape Sounion** to the romantic, if half-forgotten sanctuary of Artemis at **Vravrona**. You can also visit Greece's oldest theatre, at **Thorikos**, and the still mysterious **Eleusis**. You can escape the city to the wooded shores of **Lake Marathon**, or watch the shipping at the regenerating port of **Lavrio**. And further afield, a two-hour drive will bring you to the sacred stones of **Delphi**.

Athens Environs

Ancient Eleusis

Once a glorious sanctuary devoted to Demeter, goddess of harvest and fertility, Eleusis these days is not so much a lush, hallowed ground

as a marble scrapheap strewn with ancient rubble. Clinging to the edge of the dusty refinery town of Elefsina, 16 kilometres (ten miles) west of Athens, Eleusis is the rough diamond of Attica's archaeological sites.

First inhabited in 2000 BC, the site is entrenched in the worship of Demeter and became home to the Eleusinian mysteries – the name given to the cult's secret initiation process and ceremonial rites. The Romans were quick to adopt the panhellenic cult and spread it throughout the pre-Christian world.

Eventually, though, after being plundered by Alaric's Visigoths in AD 395, Eleusis was systematically destroyed by early Christian leaders, anxious to purge the shrine of memories of the goddess and a competing vision of the afterlife. Lord Elgin helped by shipping artefacts to Britain. Fortunately, a good (and air-conditioned) on-site museum filled with well-preserved relics is there to help you appreciate the sprawling remains; the site also includes a charming 19th-century farmhouse and a chapel.

Half way between Athens and Eleusis, just off the main road leading to the Athens–Corinth national road, the splendid 11th-century

Daphne Monastery has been undergoing repairs for some time – and it is still unclear when it will reopen. To find out if you'll be able to view some of the most spectacular Byzantine mosaics in Greece, phone 210 581 1588.

Ancient Eleusis (site & museum)
Gioka 1, Platia Eleusis, Elefsina (210 554 6019). **Open** 8.30am-3pm Tue-Sun. **Admission** €3; €2 concessions; free under-18s. **No credit cards.**

Where to eat & drink
Despite its grim reputation, the town of Elefsina is making efforts to clean up its act. In close proximity to the site are several old houses converted into cool cafés; the same is true for the waterfront, 10 minutes' walk away. **Kukeon** (opposite the site's entrance, 210 554 5401, snacks from €2.50) is one of the most appealing.

Getting there

By bus
Take either the A16 or B16 bus from Platia Koumoundourou near Omonia and get off at the Strofi bus stop. The site is a 5min walk away. Buses depart frequently and take 1hr. Tickets cost €0.50.

By car
Take the Athens–Corinth motorway as far as Elefsina and then follow signs to the archaeological site; or take the Attiki Odos to the Elefsina exit, turn south and follow the signs.

West Coast
The avenue that runs from south Athens to the headland of Sounion, with its quietly awe-inspiring temple, is a curvaceous corniche that hugs the coast and offers some dramatic views.

En route to Sounion

Varkiza
Varkiza, sleepy in winter but bustling in summer, has a low-key charm that contrasts with its posher, more cosmopolitan neighbour, Vouliagmeni. This little harbour town is where many Athenian families spend the summer. Preceded by a string of natural, shallow coves with calm waters, its long main beach is divided into a public and private section (*see p106*). The broad seaside promenade runs from the right of the seawall to a small but active fishing harbour. Along here are plenty of

Drive-by beaches

As well as the beaches (*paralias*) in the coastal towns, you can stop almost anywhere along the road to Sounion and find yourself a spot for a swim and a sunbathe. From organised seafronts offering umbrellas and deckchairs to secluded coves that emerge suddenly from the jagged rocks, there's a beach at every turn. (For beaches closer to Athens, *see pp103-106*).

Five kilometres (three miles) out of Varkiza lies the secluded horseshoe bay of **Lombarda Beach**. With cheery chart pop drifting from the beach bars' speakers, this sandy strip, set away from the road, has a fun, island feel. Even the sea is laid-back – shallow and calm, protected as it is by the rocky cliffs.

Further up the road is **Grand Resort Lagonissi** (229 107 6000, www.lagonissi resort.gr, closed mid Oct-Mar), a hotel with a plush pool and beach. A deckchair and umbrella are included in the €9 fee (€15 at weekends), though the fun things (watersports, massages, banana rides) are only available to hotel guests, so you might

prefer to head a kilometre (half a mile) further east to a very inviting strip of beach where you can sample the same sparkling waters for free.

Located between the towns of Saronida and Anavyssos, **Eden Beach** represents the middle ground between Lagonissi's luxury and the no-frills options. This pretty, rounded bay with crystal-clear waters in front of the Eden Hotel is served by a café-bar offering drinks and light snacks. Deckchairs and umbrellas are available for hire.

The long, flat bay of **Legrena**, on the final approach to Cape Sounion, is dotted with gorgeous secluded beaches. The Capet Cove, on the edge of Legrena Bay between Harakas and Legrena, is one of the most scenic but, like the others, can get busy at weekends. If bathing in the shadow of ancient monuments is a particular ambition, then head for the **Aegaio Hotel beach** on the western side of Cape Sounion, or, for a more rugged (and private) dip, walk down the path that cuts down the left side of the cape on the last stretch of road towards the archaeological site.

eateries, from upmarket Italian restaurants to burger joints and cafés. For an inexpensive lunch option, **Georgiadis Bakery** (on Leof Posidonos opposite DO IT, no phone, snacks from €1.60) is an institution. This bakery offers excellent-value, freshly made *tyropitas*, *spanakopitas*, sandwiches, traditional biscuits and baklava, which you can eat perched on one of the many seafront benches. Ya Banaki, the privately managed part of the beach, also has its own ouzerie, **Ya Ouzaki**.

Saronida

As the fastest-growing (and largest) of the coastal stop-offs, the town is equipped to handle the onslaught: its main strip – leading up from the beach – is filled with fashionable eateries, bars and ice-cream parlours. Among them is the swanky **Il Vento Art Café** (Leof Saronidas 4, 229 108 0080, main courses €10-€15). Further up the road is the industrial-themed **Reverso Café-Restaurant** (Leof Saronidas 20, 229 106 1331, main courses €7-€10), known for its impressive choice of ice-creams and cocktails.

Palea Fokea

Perched on the eastern end of Anavyssos Bay, Palea Fokea is more a village than a town. But with its lively café-lined main square, sandy beaches, windsurfing and splendid view over the crescent bay, it makes a great stop before the final assault on Cape Sounion.

The bustling, no-frills souvlaki joint **Ta Didyma** (Platia Eleftherias 9, 229 103 8834) serves succulent grilled chicken and lamb kebabs, as well as first-rate *gyros*. Of the fish restaurants that line the seafront at the top end of the town, **Remvi** (Leof Sounion & Galinis 14, 229 103 6236, mezedes €4-€10) and **Tessera Adelfia** (Leof Sounion 6, 229 104 0843, mezedes €4-€8) are two of the best.

Sounion

With its stunningly well-preserved columns and unrivalled position on a dramatic cliff above the blue Aegean, the **Sanctuary of Poseidon** at Cape Sounion is one of the most impressive ancient ruins this side of Delphi (hence the steady stream of tourist coaches). Dedicated to the god of the sea, the temple dates from the fifth century BC. If its proud Doric columns seem impressive from miles away, they are simply breathtaking up close – particularly in the evening, when large crowds gather to watch the sun set over this most evocative of sites. Lord Byron was so taken by this clifftop marvel that, when he visited in 1810, he etched his name into

one of the statuesque marble columns. Byron (who later referred to the temple in his *Don Juan*) wasn't the first or last to add his mark, but these days there are attendants on hand to stop you searching for his or scratching your own.

Set back behind the road that leads to the Sanctuary of Poseidon, 500 metres (1,600 feet) below, is the blink-and-you'll-miss-it **Sanctuary of Athena**. The scattered ancient rubble is pretty underwhelming, but from this smaller sanctuary you'll get a different view of the golden temple etched against the Attica sky.

Sanctuaries of Poseidon & Athena

Cape Sounion (229 203 9363). **Open** 9.30am-sunset daily. **Admission** €4; €2 concessions; free under-19s. Free to all Sun Nov-Mar. **No credit cards**. *Photos p205 and p208.*

Where to eat & drink

The site's cliffside café-restaurant (229 203 9190, main courses €9-€10, mezedes around €4) is surprisingly good value, pleasantly shaded and has excellent views.

Getting there

By bus

From Mavromateon, near Pedion Areos park, take one of the two buses (210 823 1079, €5.40) heading towards Sounion; one takes the inland route but both terminate at the Sanctuary of Poseidon. Buses leave approximately every hour, 6.30am-9pm, and take 1hr 30mins. Check the timetable for the return journey – the last bus to Athens leaves Sounion at 9pm.

By car

If you are in too much of a hurry to enjoy the calming sea views from the coast road, take the Attiki Odos motorway to Markopoulo, drive on to Lavrio and from there follow the signs for Sounion and the archaeological site.

Lavrio

Lavrio, one of the oldest industrial towns in the world, is undergoing a renaissance. In ancient times, its silver mines produced the weath that built the Parthenon and the Athenian fleet. In the 19th century, foreign entrepreneurs tried to repeat the experience, opening new mines and factories. When these fell into disuse, Lavrio acquired a grimy, gloomy atmosphere, but the past decade has brought many changes for the better. Apart from its much expanded port (229 202 5249) – serving the near Cyclades, Limnos and Lesvos – and an attractive, yacht-filled marina, Lavrio has restored (and neglected) neo-classical buildings, a lively fish market and good tavernas. Dozens of reminders of the remote and recent past are scattered around

Trips Out of Town

Cape Sounion. *See p207.*

town. The most notable is the vast **Compagnie des Mines** (229 202 7530), with 41 buildings, part of which has been transformed into a technological and cultural park, which holds occasional exhibitions.

The major ancient landmark is the sixth-century theatre at **Thorikos**. The oldest in Greece, elliptical in shape, it deserves better upkeep. It's unlocked and unattended, overrun by weeds – though this makes it all the more fascinating to explore. It shares the site with a fifth-century silver-washing basin, fragments of a temple and classical-era tombs. Remains of human habitation from the neolithic to the Classical periods litter Thorikos' acropolis on the hill above.

Lavrion Museum

Platia Iroon Polytechniou, Lavrio (229 202 2817). Not one of the greats, but it does have information on Thorikos and a map of the ancient mining installations in the area. A tiny building opposite contains extraordinary examples of Lavrio's diverse minerals, but is open limited hours (10am-noon Wed, Sat, Sun). Closed at the time of writing, the museum is scheduled to reopen June 2008.

Where to eat & drink

Try **Kafeneio** (Nea Agora Lavriou, 229 202 2092) at the corner of the fishmarket for simple, inexpensive fish mezedes. **To Petrino** (Akti G Papandreou 4, 229 202 5297), opposite the yacht harbour, offers shade, a sea breeze, excellent fish at fairly high prices and a view of the port, but the locals swear by **Kokovios** (Iroon Polytechniou 20, behind the Ethniki Trapeza on the square, 229 202 4145) for classic dishes that won't break the budget.

Getting there

By bus
Buses (210 880 8080, wait for operator) for Lavrio leave from Mavromateon, near Pedion Areos park, every 30mins and take 1hr 30mins. Tickets are €4.20. There are hourly buses from the airport (40mins, €4).

By car
Turn right out of Sounion towards Lavrio. The town is 9km (5.5 miles) to the north, Thorikos another 3km (2 miles) outside town, in the direction of the electricity plant. You can drive back to Athens, via Markopoulo and the Attiki Odos.

Sanctuary of Artemis Brauron (Vravrona)

This ancient site, 40 kilometres (25 miles) east of Athens, stands pretty much in the middle of nowhere. But its remoteness only adds to its romance. Surrounded by lush grasses and shady trees, this well-preserved temple is dedicated to Artemis, goddess of childbirth and hunting, and protectress of animals. It dates back to the fifth century BC, when the worship of the goddess was the official cult of Attica. Said to have been founded by Iphigeneia, whom Artemis saved from Agamemnon's sword, the sanctuary was known for unusual rituals involving children. In gratitude for their safe birth, parents would loan their daughters between the ages of five and ten to the goddess for a certain period. When Artemis was angered by adult behaviour, the children would intercede, performing dances and sacrifices while dressed up as her favourite animal, the bear. Apart from the Doric temple, you'll see the arcade where the girls slept, a remarkable fifth-century bridge and a 16th-century chapel. Thanks to its remote location, chances are you'll have the place to yourself. The excellent but neglected museum (closed for renovations at the time of writing) is a kilometre further along the road.

Sanctuary of Artemis Brauron & Museum

Vravrona (229 902 7020). **Open** 8.30am-2.45pm Tue-Sun. **Admission** *Sanctuary* €3; €2 concessions; free under-19s. *Museum* closed for renovations, scheduled to reopen 2009. **No credit cards**.

Getting there

By bus

Take the 304 bus from Ethniki Amyna metro station until it terminates at Loutsa. The site is a 15min taxi journey from there. Buses depart frequently throughout the day. Tickets cost €0.50.

By car

Take the Attiki Odos all the way to Markopoulo, turn left at the signs for Porto Rafti and follow them and the brown and orange signs as far as the sanctuary.

East Attica

Rafina

There's little reason to visit Athens' second port other than to catch a ferry, but there are certainly plenty of worse places to kill time in if you do happen to find yourself here. Rafina may be smaller and more out of the way than Piraeus, but ferry tickets from here to the Cyclades are generally cheaper, a taxi from the airport is around €20 and there are also plenty of buses, making the town a convenient alternative starting point for island-hopping. The ticket offices share the harbourfront with a

Byron the philhellene

The admiration and love that Lord Byron felt for Greece (a 'beautiful country, with seasons all a-smile') and especially Athens ('Athens holds my heart and soul/Can I cease to love thee? No!') are well known. The feeling was reciprocated. When Byron died in 1824, weakened by an epileptic fit and thus unable to fight off a severe cold, the Greeks insisted on keeping his heart, and buried it beneath his statue in the Garden of Heroes in Mesolongi. Their affection for the English poet carries on to this day.

Byron became fascinated by Greece at an early age. A sensitive and shy child, born with a club foot, he spent most of his time reading and became captivated by the glorious history and heroic myths of ancient Greece.

His childhood was unstable. His father, whom he scarcely knew, committed suicide, and his mother was emotionally inconsistent. His nurse was rumoured to have made sexual advances to him, and he became infatuated with three of his cousins. The emerging literary genius was a self-willed young man, who vehemently resisted attempts to control him. This is perhaps another reason why Byron admired Greece so much: despite being under Turkish rule since the 14th century, the Greeks had managed to maintain a strong cultural and national identity; the country – with its glorious classical past – was idealised by many in this period.

After leaving Cambridge, Byron set off to travel around southern Europe with his friends. He arrived in Greece in December 1809 and fell in love with not only the countryside, the sunshine, the architecture and the tolerance of the people, but also with a number of girls; he wrote *Maid of Athens, Ere We Part* about one. He left his mark, quite literally, on the Sanctuary of Poseidon (*see p207*), where he joined the vandal tradition of scrawling one's name into the columns. He even swam five kilometres (three miles) across the Hellespont (the Dardanelles).

It was 12 years before he was to return to Greece after his first visit. In 1823 the country was in upheaval and fighting for independence from the Ottoman Empire. Byron was appointed by the London Greek Committee as its agent in this cause. He threw himself into the work with gusto, personally and financially, donating thousands of pounds to set up and arm the brig *Hercules*, although he didn't see any military action himself.

Lord Byron was an enigmatic and cynical man, and perhaps there is more to his love of Greece than is known. Unfortunately, it's likely to stay that way – his memoirs, which were deemed too scandalous even by his most liberal-minded friends, were thrown into the fire after his death at the tender age of 37.

fishmarket, tavernas and cafés, while the town beach is a favourite with windsurfers. Further information can be obtained from the **Rafina Port Authority** (229 402 2300), by the port.

Getting there

By bus
Buses (210 880 8080, €2.10) for Rafina leave from Mavromateon, near Pedion Areos park, every 30-60min and take 1hr15min. There are also buses from the airport (30min, €3), roughly every two hours.

By car
Take Leof Mesogeion all the way to Rafina; or take the Attiki Odos, which cuts the time in half.

Marathon

The site of the battle of Marathon is, of course, 42 kilometres (26 miles) from Athens, near the bay of the same name, up the coast from Rafina, and about three kilometres (two miles) from Marathonas town. All that's left to remind us of it is the Tomb of the Fallen, or **Tumulus of Marathon**, a large mound that evokes a sense of the ancient past, along with the serenity of a cemetery.

It was here in 490 BC that the battle was fought. On 12 September an army of 10,000 Athenians and Plataeans defeated 25,000 Persian invaders by ambushing the foreign army from the sides. The Greeks' victory was conclusive: for 6,000 Persian dead, the Greeks lost just 192 men. The monument to the slain Athenians rises above the site where they were cremated.

Most famously, however, the Battle of Marathon gave rise to the modern race that still bears its name. After the battle, legend has it that a messenger ran to Athens to relay news of the Greeks' tremendous triumph. Once there, having informed Athens of the victory, he is said to have collapsed and died on the spot.

The **Marathon Museum** lies two and a half kilometres (one and a half miles) to the northwest. It houses relics from neolithic to Roman times and adjoins the Plataeans' burial mound as well as a prehistoric grave circle. There is no public transport between the site and the museum.

Marathon Museum
Plataion 114, Vranas, Marathonas (229 405 5155). **Open** 8.30am-3pm Tue-Sun. **Admission** (incl entry to archaeological site) €3; €2 concessions; free under-18s, EU students. **No credit cards**.

Tumulus of Marathon
Spyrou Louis, Marathonas (229 405 5462). **Open** 8.30am-3pm Tue-Sun. **Admission** (incl entry to museum) €3; €2 concessions; free under-18s, EU students. **No credit cards**.

Where to eat & drink

Cavouri (229 405 5243, main courses €27-€33), on Marathon Bay not far from the tumulus, is one of Attica's best places to eat fish. Turn off Leof Marathonas at the sign for Golden Coast Hotel and follow Fidipidou to the end. There are also plenty of decent fish tavernas on Schinias beach (*see p211*).

Getting there

By bus
From the bus terminal at Mavromateon, Pedion Areos (210 821 0872), take any bus to Marathonas, Grammatiko or Souli, and get off at the Tymvos bus stop. From there it is a short walk to the site. Buses depart every hour 5.30am-10.30pm and take 2hrs.

By car
Take Leof Mesogeion (Marathonas) towards Rafina and turn left at the junction for Marathonas. Brown and yellow signs will lead you to the Tumulus and the Museum.

Marathon Lake

Situated on the site of the ancient Marathon Lake, inland from Marathon, this massive reservoir was Athens' sole water supply up until the 1950s. The dam (built in 1925) remains an impressive sight. Made out of marble, the structure, which measures 50 metres (160 feet) in height and 300 metres (900 feet) in length, rises imposingly out of the lake, surrounded by pine forests.

Although no one is allowed too close to the water, it is possible to walk on trails in the surrounding hills for beautiful views of the lake. Fragma, a restaurant on the east side of the dam, offers a stunning view of the serene lake from its spectacular terrace. Alternatively, there are observation platforms at either end of the dam, and picnic areas on the west side.

Where to eat & drink

The fashionable café-restaurant **Fragma** (210 814 3415, main courses €10-€20) offers a selection of light snacks and traditional mezedes during the day and adventurous, well-presented modern European cuisine in the evenings (from lunchtimes at weekends). For dinner, booking is advisable.

Getting there

By car
Take Mesogeion in the direction of Marathonas. Once you reach the town, follow the well-marked signs to the lake ('*limni*').

Our advice: seek out the oracle at the **Sanctuary of Apollo** in Delphi. *See p212.*

Rhamnous

With its serene hilltop site overlooking the Euboian Gulf, the remote settlement of **Rhamnous** might look peaceful, but it's a spot steeped in military history. Dating from the sixth century BC, Rhamnous was home to the cult of Nemesis, goddess of retribution, and a grand but possibly unfinished temple dedicated to her once stood here. Appropriately, it's thought that the statue of the goddess within the temple was sculpted from the slab of marble that the Persians, confident of defeating the Greeks at Marathon, brought with them to build their triumphant memorial. Unhappily for those cocky Persians, fate had a surprise in store and Nemesis received her well-won trophy. The smaller temple belonged to Themis, goddess of justice and equity.

Further down the hill is the well-preserved fortress of Rhamnous – not officially open but accessible through a gate to the right of the temples. The fortress was permanently manned by an Athenian garrison charged with defending this vital seaway; a mighty 800-metre-long (half-mile) wall encircled it. Sadly, little remains of the sanctuary, though recent excavations inside the fortress have revealed barracks on its upper level, with a gymnasium, unique natural theatre, burial grounds and private homes below.

En route to Rhamnous, sandy **Schinias beach**, which rims Marathon Bay, is Attica's largest. Backed by tall pines, its shallow waters are very popular with Athenian families. Most of it is public, with several tavernas scattered along its length, but only one or two sections have umbrellas or lounging chairs. (Follow signs for Olympic Rowing Complex and then keep left. Several dirt roads to the right lead to the beach.)

Temple of Nemesis
Rhamnous (229 406 3477). **Open** *May-Nov* 8am-6pm daily. *Dec-Apr* 8am-4pm daily. **Admission** €2; €1 concessions; free under-18s. **No credit cards**.

Getting there

By car
Take Leof Mesogeion (Marathonas) towards Rafina and turn left at the junction for Marathonas. After about 7km (three miles) turn right for Schinias and Agia Marina. The ancient site is at the end of this road (8.5km/five miles).

Further Afield

Delphi

A majestic landscape at the foot of Mount Parnassus, the archaeological site of **Delphi** (226 508 2312) is on a plateau overlooking the silver-leaved olive groves of Amphissa and the Gulf of Galaxidi. According to ancient Greek legend, Zeus released two eagles at opposite ends of the world and Delphi is where they met.

At first a place where Mother Earth and Poseidon were worshipped, Delphi later became the Sanctuary of Pythian Apollo, before yet still more gods (including Dionysus and Athena Pronaia) became associated with the sacred location. Delphi was also the seat of the mystical oracle, the site of the first political allegiance among the city states (the Amphictyonic League) and, along with Olympia and Delos, one of the most important sanctuaries of the ancient world.

Inside the **Sanctuary of Apollo** was the sanctum of the oracle, where the Pythia (the priestess who delivered the oracle) would pronounce the dubious, and sometimes incomprehensible prophecies in a state of holy intoxication. Following the victorious Battle of Marathon against the Persians, the Athenians asked the Pythia for an oracle in view of the next expedition. The priestess pronounced that wooden walls would save the city. Interpreting this as a reference to their navy, the Athenians sailed their ships against the Persians and annihilated the Persian fleet in Salamis, ruling the seas for years to come.

Follow the Sacred Way and gaze upon the offerings of the Athenians (**Treasury of the Athenians**) and other treasuries; the **Ancient Theatre**, where theatrical and lyrical competitions were held; and the excellently preserved **Stadium**, where sports events took place as part of the Pythian Games, the second most important festival in the ancient world after the Olympic Games at Olympia.

Next to the Sanctuary of Apollo is the **museum**. On the other side are the **Sanctuary of Athena** and the **Tholos**, an impressive circular structure.

For hikers, the European path E4 offers a magical route (approximately seven hours) from the village of Agoriani (€20 taxi ride from Delphi) to the archaeological site of Delphi.

Museum

Delphi (226 508 2312). **Open** *June-Oct* noon-6.15pm Mon; 7.30am-7.15pm Tue-Sun. *Nov-May* 7.30am-3pm daily. **Admission** €6 (€9 incl Sanctuary of Apollo); concessions €3 (€5 incl Sanctuary of Apollo); free under-18s, EU students. **No credit cards**.

Sanctuary of Apollo

Delphi (226 508 2312). **Open** *June-Oct* 7.30am-7.15pm daily. *Nov-May* 7.30am-3pm daily (winter hours may be extended). **Admission** €6. **No credit cards**. *Photo p211.*

Sanctuary of Athena

Delphi (226 508 2312). **Open** *June-Sept* 7.30am-7.15pm daily. *Oct-May* 7.30am-3pm daily (winter hours may be extended). **Admission** free.

EXCURSIONS

The picturesque town of **Arachova** is 12 kilometres (eight miles) from Delphi on the main Livadia–Delphi road. There are numerous rooms and hotels as well as some excellent tavernas, and a vast market of traditional products in the main street, with wooden goods and rugs. A further 24km (16 miles) towards Athens, the 11th-century Byzantine monastery of **Osios Loukas** is beautiful both in its setting and its rich art and architecture, with notable mosaics.

Where to eat & stay

You'll find Greek specialities with a fabulous view at **Epicouros** (Vas Pavlou 33, 226 508 3250, main courses €15), while **Vakhos Taverna** (Apollonos 31, no phone) a family atmosphere, with traditional Greek cuisine, reasonable prices and a view over the valley.

Delphi's most luxurious hotel is the **Amalia** (Apollonos 1, www.amaliahotels.com, 210 607 2000, doubles from €162); facilities include a restaurant, bar, pool and a majestic view over the olive groves towards the Gulf of Galaxidi. The **Acropole** (Philellinon 13, 226 508 2675, €78 double) is ideal for those seeking peace and quiet, while the **Delphi Palace** (Apollonos 69, 226 508 2151, €120-€140 double) has nice views and serves breakfast on the veranda.

Tourist information

The Delphi tourist police (226 508 2220) can help you with hotels, eateries and sightseeing. It's located at Angelou Sikelianou 3, opposite the church of Agios Nikolaos, two streets up from the main road.

Getting there

By bus

There are six buses daily from Liosion bus station. Information is available from KTEL Fokidos (210 831 7096). Tickets cost €13. Numerous package deals are available from travel agents.

By car

Delphi is 178km (111 miles) from Athens on the Athens–Thessaloniki national road. Take the exit for Kastro-Livadia/Arachova-Delphi. You won't see any more signs for Delphi until after Livadia.

Trips Out of Town

North-east Peloponnese

From here to antiquity.

Ancient Corinth. *See p215.*

All of the Peloponnese is worth exploring, but if you have only a day or two, the north-east corner probably holds more concentrated history than any other region in Greece. Not only does it harbour the remains of ancient **Corinth**, the third most important city state after Athens and Sparta, but it is home to the Argolid, the heartland of the earliest Greek civilisation.

As you drive around Corinthia and the Argolid, it's easy to grasp its importance. The climate is mild, the land fertile, supporting vast citrus groves and vineyards. But it is also mountainous, with rocky pinnacles that were easily fortified, many of them topped by castles with Byzantine, Venetian and Ottoman additions to ancient foundations. The oldest is **Mycenae**, with its Lion Gate and beehive tombs, the newest the Venetian citadel of **Palamidi** at Nafplio.

Ruins abound, and many of them are more than just collections of old stones. The magnificent theatre at **Epidaurus**, centre of a holistic spa in antiquity, plays host to a drama festival every summer, concerts are held at a smaller theatre near **Palaia Epidavro** on the coast and the ancient games are revived at **Nemea** every four years.

For a more relaxed exploration of all these sites and more, the lazy port of **Nafplio** makes a wonderful base. The centre of town has changed little in appearance since it was designated Greece's capital for a few years after independence, but many of its historic buildings have been converted into charming hotels, restaurants, bars and boutiques.

Getting there

By car

For all destinations, take the Athens–Corinth–Patras national road. **Ancient Corinth** is signposted from the highway. For **Nemea**, turn south after Corinth on to the Corinth–Tripoli national road; follow the signs to the site of Ancient Nemea (27km/16.5 miles). For **Mycenae**, retrace your steps towards the Nemea exit, but take the overpass over the highway and follow the signs to Mycenae, via Dervenakia (9km/five miles). A new road goes past the ancient site (signed) and emerges near the coast midway between Nafplio and Argos. Turn left for **Nafplio**. For **Epidaurus** (27km/16.5 miles from Nafplio) follow the signs to Lygourio-Epidaurus. To complete the circuit (or to head for Epidaurus directly), follow the coastal Corinth–Epidaurus B-road.

By bus

From Athens: There are 15 buses daily from Kifissos station in Athens (100 Kifissou, near the junction with Athinon, 210 523 3810, 210 523 7899, 210 524 6805, www.ktel-argolis.gr) via **Corinth** (€7) and **Mycenae** (€9.30) en route to **Nafplio** (€11.30); five buses daily go to **Nemea** (210 512 4910, €10.90). From Kifissos station to **Epidaurus** and **Lygourio** (for the **Theatre of Epidaurus**), buses run at 8.45am & 4pm Mon-Sat, 8.45am & 5.15pm Sun & hols (€10.80). During the Epidaurus Festival, special buses run at 4pm Fri & Sat from Kifissos station, returning after the performance.

From Nafplio: The Nafplio bus station is on Syngrou (275 202 7323/7423). There are three buses daily to **Mycenae** (€2.50) and three to four daily to **Lygourio** (for the **Theatre of Epidaurus**; €2.20) and **Epidaurus** (€2.50). There are also hourly buses to the nearby resort of **Tolo** and every half hour to

Argos. On weekends during July and August there are extra buses at 7pm for performances at the Ancient Theatre; they return right after the show.

Organised tours: Trips to Mycenae and Epidaurus are available from **Chat Tours** (210 323 0827) and **Key Tours** (210 923 3166), which both charge €83 (incl admission and guide; lunch €10 extra).

By train

Eight trains a day run between Athens and **Corinth**. The line south of Corinth is undergoing work that is expected to last until at least 2008.

By boat

Special sailings (with candlelit dinner; €60) are timed to theatre performances at **Epidaurus**; contact the Hellenic Festival Box Office (see p200) for details.

Ancient Corinth & Acrocorinth

Commanding the narrow Isthmus of Corinth, the city of Corinth controlled the lucrative sea route between the Adriatic (via the Gulf of

Corinth Canal

But for a mere six-kilometre (four-mile) strip of land, the Peloponnese peninsula would be an island. And if it were, how much quicker and safer it would be for seafarers to get from the Aegean to the Adriatic. Such was the problem that vexed minds as long ago as 602 BC, when Periander, tyrant of Corinth, considered and then rejected (following dire warnings from the Delphic Oracle) a plan to cut a canal across the isthmus.

The journey around the dangerous southern cape of the Peloponnese added 185 nautical miles to the voyage. Such was the risk and cost of the journey that, in the early sixth century BC, the Corinthians built a limestone-paved road called the *diolkos* between the Corinthian and Saronic Gulfs. Along this road ran the *olkos*, a cart that transported ships from one sea to the other – a huge source of income and prestige for Corinth.

Yet the dreams of forging a nautical route across the isthmus persisted. In 307 BC Demetrios Poliorcetes started a canal, only to be scared off by Egyptian engineers, who persuaded him that differences in sea levels would result in the islands of the Saronic Gulf sinking under the waves.

The next serious attempt came in 67 AD, when Nero forced 6,000 Jewish slaves to start digging. They had created a trench

3,300 metres (10,830 feet) long and 40 metres (131 feet) wide before domestic troubles in Rome forced the emperor back home and the project was abandoned.

The Byzantines tried, the Venetians tried. But time and again the enormity (and cost) of the task proved overwhelming. It wasn't until the technological advances of the Industrial Revolution that the canal project finally seemed feasible. A plan was considered, then put aside, by the new Greek government in 1830. But it was the opening of the Suez Canal in 1869 that provided the spur, and the Greeks assigned the mammoth task to a French company soon afterwards. But yet again it stalled.

In 1881 Hungarian general Stefan Tyrr took over the project. The canal took 11 years to complete, and followed almost exactly the route proposed by Nero 1,800 years earlier. It measured 6,346 metres (20,820 feet) in length, was 24.6 metres (81 feet) wide at sea level and around eight metres (26 feet) deep, and opened on 25 July 1893.

The greatest irony of this feat of engineering, two and a half thousand years in the offing, is that within a century of its opening, the development of super container ships, easily able to round the Peloponnese and too large for the canal, rendered it all but obsolete.

Corinth) and the Aegean (via the Saronic Gulf), and the land route between the Peloponnese and the rest of the Greek mainland.

The city rose to prominence during the eighth century BC on the back of commerce. It founded the colonies of Corcyra on Corfu and Syracuse on Sicily, and was a major player in the various city state power struggles that characterised the succeeding centuries.

In 146 BC, following the Roman defeat of the Greek cities of the Achaian League, the vengeful Romans razed the city, which was then abandoned for a century. In 44 BC, Julius Caesar decided to rebuild Corinth on a grand scale as the provincial capital. It prospered anew, and became famous for its wealth (and moral laxity, if St Paul is to be believed), until major earthquakes in the fourth and sixth centuries AD reduced it to rubble. It is the ruins of the Roman Corinth that can be seen today.

Modern Corinth is a hot, dusty, utilitarian sort of place, re-sited on the Gulf of Corinth in the mid 19th century. Give it a miss, and concentrate on the dual attractions of the remains of Ancient Corinth, and, looming above it, the spectacularly sited fortifications of Acrocorinth, just a few kilometres inland.

The excavated area of **Ancient Corinth**, centred on a huge agora (marketplace), reveals only a fraction of what was once a vast settlement. The remains are fairly confusing, so it is wise to buy a guide with detailed information about the site. The one stand-out structure is a surprising survival from Greek Corinth: the seven remaining Doric columns of the fifth-century BC Temple of Apollo. Look out, too, for the Roman Fountain of Peirene, which stands beside a stretch of the marble-lined Lechaion Way. The site museum contains a selection of finds, all labelled in English.

While the excavations are fascinating, most visitors will get more of a thrill out of ascending the rocky outcrop that supports the ruined citadel of **Acrocorinth**. Once home to Ancient Corinth's acropolis (and, on its highest peak, to a temple to Aphrodite tended by 1,000 sacred prostitutes), Acrocorinth became a formidable fortress in the Middle Ages, and was used until the end of Turkish rule in 1830.

The approach is via three gates that provide an architectural history lesson about the castle's various keepers. The first is Turkish, the second Frankish and Venetian, the third Byzantine. Beyond them lies a range of ruins scattered over a huge expanse of the rock-strewn hilltop, still largely encircled by its walls. A Frankish keep perches on the second-highest peak. It's a tough half-hour hike from the car park to the summit, but the staggering 360° views are well worth the gruelling effort.

Mycenae. See p216.

Ancient Corinth Site & Museum
274 103 1207. **Open** *Apr-Oct* 8am-7pm daily. *Nov-Mar* 8am-5pm daily. **Admission** €6; €3 concessions; free under-19s. **No credit cards.** *Photo p213.*

Where to eat & drink

In terms of views, **Acrocorinthos** (no phone), by the entrance to Acrocorinth, has the edge over the many tavernas in the village that has grown up around the ruins of Ancient Corinth. However, for the ultimate atmospheric experience, take a picnic up to the peak of Acrocorinth.

Nemea

With its rolling chalky hills, Nemea is one of Greece's prime wine-producing regions – and it has been since mythological times, when the wine god Dionysus turned all its rivers to wine to stop Argos's seven generals in their march against Thebes, his adopted city. Parched and desperate, the generals combed the area for a spring. They finally found relief when the royal babysitter left her charge on a bed of wild celery to show them a trickle the god had overlooked. This dereliction of duty had fatal consequences: the royal babe was bitten by a viper. Faced with such an omen, the generals postponed their invasion and held funeral games instead. The Nemean Games became a panhellenic institution. Nemea was also the setting for Hercules' first labour: the slaying of the Nemean Lion.

Nemea is a vibrant, well-tended site whose excavations are carried out by the University of California and funded by private citizens. Some

Trips Out of Town

Nafplio, a lovely town with an eventful past.

of their dollars have gone to re-erect two columns at the temple of Zeus, bringing the number standing to five, and there are plans to restore more. Apart from the temple, the site contains a large baths complex, foundations of a basilica atop those of an inn, and the grave of an early Christian woman.

The site's pride and joy is the separate **stadium**, across the road and a little beyond it. You pass a mossy columned patio, where the athletes warmed up and, like them, enter through a tunnel scratched with their graffiti. The stadium, flanked by grassy slopes and surrounded by a water channel thoughtfully provided for the runners and spectators, was revived in 1996; now, every four years, athletes compete in tunics and bare feet at the Nemean Games. The exhibits in the **museum** give you a good idea of what the original games were like and how 19th-century artists depicted the site.

Archaeological Site of Nemea & Museum

274 602 2739. **Open** *Apr-Oct* 8am-7.30pm daily. *Museum* noon-7.30pm Mon; 8am-7.30pm Tue-Sun. *Nov-Mar* 8.30am-3pm Tue-Sun. **Admission** (incl stadium) €4; €2 concessions; free under-18s. **No credit cards**.

Where to eat & drink

Many of the mellow red wines produced in Nemea from the indigenous *aghiorgitiko* grape qualify for the EU's appellation of origin. Estates where you can taste them include **Palyvos**, near Ancient Nemea (signposted; 274 602 4190); **Gaia**, at Koutsi (call 210 805 5642/3

for an appointment, closed weekends); and **Domaine Helios**, at Koutsi (274 602 0360, www.semeliwines.gr). Domaine Helios has seven luxury suites and rooms (€30-€50 per person with breakfast), and can provide meals for groups if notified in advance.

Nemea is not Tuscany, despite the landscape and vineyards, and is sadly lacking in wonderful restaurants. But two places will not disappoint: **Sofos** (274 602 3070, on the main square, opposite the old Town Hall) has salads, cooked dishes and grills in newly upgraded, quite sophisticated surroundings; and **Papoutsakia** (274 602 2167, outside town) is a typical taverna with a nice garden.

Mycenae

In his epic poems *The Iliad* and *The Odyssey*, written in the eighth century BC, Homer spoke of the 'well-built Mycenae, rich in gold.' According to *The Iliad*, its king, Agamemnon – the richest and most powerful king of Greece – headed the Greek expedition to Troy after Paris, son of the king of Troy, abducted Helen, wife of Menelaus, king of Sparta and brother to Agamemnon, launching the Trojan War.

Until the 19th century these poems were regarded as little more than legends. Then, in the 1870s, amateur archaeologist Heinrich Schliemann, ignoring the jeers of his professional counterparts, proved them to be based on fact: first by excavating Troy in present-day Turkey, and then Mycenae. Here, he uncovered the graves of more than a dozen people, bedecked in gold and jewels, and was convinced he'd found the tomb of Agamemnon. Although these were later dated to at least 300 years earlier than the Trojan War, Schliemann had found evidence of Mycenae's wealth.

In the late Bronze Age, the kingdom was the most powerful in Greece, holding control over the Aegean, and building a legacy of grand palaces and fortified constructions before beginning to wane around 1200 BC.

The citadel of Mycenae is surrounded by a gigantic wall. It can be entered through the impressive Lion Gate, with the main path leading up to the ruins of Agamemnon's Palace, the Throne Room and the Great Court.

The best-preserved Mycenaean structure by far, however, lies outside the bounds of the citadel. The immense royal tholos tomb (built with blocks of stone, tapering to the top, and then covered with earth) is misleadingly known as the Treasury of Atreus or the Tomb of Agamemnon, but was actually built several hundred years earlier.

The remains of the magnificent gold treasures of the Mycenaean civilisation are housed at the National Archaeological Museum in Athens (see p90).

It's worth buying a detailed guide to the site and perusing the excellent site museum before attempting to make sense of the ruins, which, tombs aside, are relatively scant and confusing.

Archaeological Site of Mycenae & Museum

275 107 6585. **Open** *Apr-Sept* 8am-7pm daily. *Museum* noon-7pm Mon; 8am-7pm Tue-Sat. *Oct-Mar* 8am-3pm daily. *Museum* 8am-3pm Tue-Sat. **Admission** €8; €4 concessions; free under-18s. **No credit cards.** *Photo p215.*

Where to eat & drink

The village of Mycenae offers plenty of touristy eating options. One of the best places lining the main road is **Spyro's** (275 107 6115, main courses around €11). It often serves traditional regional dishes rarely found outside the home.

Nafplio

This charming little town, located 146km (98 miles) from Athens, makes an excellent base from which to explore the north-eastern Peloponnese. It wasn't until the Byzantines fortified the settlement at the end of the 12th century that it emerged as an important regional centre. The following centuries saw it pass through many hands – Franks, Venetians, Turks – until it enjoyed a brief five-year glow of national importance as the capital of the newly independent Greek state, before Athens took over the role in 1834.

Modern Nafplio is split between a workaday new town and a lovely old town that sits snugly beneath the rocky outcrop of **Akronafplia**. But its eventful history is writ in stone. From the massive fortifications of the Palamidi castle on the hill to the multicoloured marble-paved and mansion-lined pedestrianised streets that lead down to the harbour, the town is alive with reminders of its varied past.

Though you can enjoy Nafplio just by wandering among its 19th-century houses, mosques and shops, the town does have a handful of attractions worth seeking out. Its one-time military significance is obvious in the presence of not one, not two, but three castles. The first of these is the diminutive **Bourtzi**. Set on an islet, this little fortress was built by the Venetians in 1470 to guard the harbour. In the 19th century, it was the retreat of a reviled public executioner.

The second, **Akronafplia**, was the nucleus of the ancient city. Reoccupied by Byzantines, Franks and Venetians, its fragmented old walls now lend atmosphere to chic hotels. It's the mighty **Palamidi Fortress** that catches the eye, however. Its endless crenellated walls, dark passages and wide ramparts represent the Venetians' desperate, last-ditch attempt to hold on to their Greek ports in 1715. Despite its seeming impenetrability, it was quick to fall to the Turks. It can be reached either by car, or, for the fit, by an extraordinary 913-step staircase that leads out of the town and snakes up the almost-sheer slopes of a hill. Needless to say, the views are spectacular.

Back in the old town, there are a couple of museums worth a look. The award-winning **Peloponnesian Folklore Foundation** contains a beautiful selection of Greek folk costumes, though disappointingly little information about them. On the café-edged central square of Platia Syntagmatos, the **Archaeological Museum** has been undergoing renovations and should be state of the art when it reopens (some time in early 2008). The museum houses a decent selection of local finds, including the prize exhibit, a very rare set of Mycenaean armour. Also among its artefacts are some frescoes from **Tiryns**, a once-mighty Mycenaean city, the remains of which lie a couple of kilometres outside Nafplio. While some parts of Tiryns have been dated to 2600 BC, the majority of what you see today dates from a millennium later. The height and strength of its walls were famed in antiquity, and what is left still impresses, particularly when you hear that they were originally twice their current height.

For a change of pace, head for the beach at **Karathonas**, a five-minute drive east of the town. This long, greyish, likeable strand is

Trips Out of Town

popular with Greek families and is home to a scattering of beach bars and restaurants. Meanwhile the resort of **Tolo**, 15 minutes out of town, offers something a little more lively.

Palamidi Fortress

275 202 8036. **Open** *Apr-Oct* 8am-6.30pm daily. *Nov-Mar* 8.30am-3pm daily. **Admission** €4; €2 concessions; free under-18s. **No credit cards**.

Peloponnesian Folklore Foundation

Ypsilantou 1 (275 202 8379/www.pli.gr). **Open** 9am-2.30pm, 6-9pm Mon, Wed-Sat; 6-9pm Tue; 9am-2.30pm Sun. **Admission** €4; €3 concessions. **Credit** (gift shop only) DC, MC, V.

Tiryns Archaeological Site

275 202 2657. **Open** *May-Oct* 8am-7pm daily. *Nov-Apr* 8.30am-3pm daily. **Admission** €3; €2 concessions. **No credit cards**.

Where to eat & drink

Nafplio teems with tavernas. The main food thoroughfare is pedestrianised Staikopolou, which is filled with outdoor tables and waiters exhorting you to choose their joint over their neighbours'. Don't let this put you off, though. **Ta Fanaria** (no.13, 275 202 7141, main courses from €7) is excellent; try the lamb cooked with tiny pasta in tomato sauce if it's available.

If you want to eat where the locals eat, and don't mind sitting by a road opposite a car park near the cargo port, then you can enjoy some bargain-priced classic Greek cooking at **Nafplios** (corner of Bouboulinas & Syngrou, 275 209 7999, main courses €5-€10). Better for lunch than dinner, it produces superb spit-roasted pork with crackling and the most generous Greek salads you'll find anywhere.

For a romantic setting, and some seriously good fish, head round the end of the peninsula, where a couple of restaurant-bars enjoy an impossibly lovely setting right on the water. The pick is **Agnanti** (Akti Miaouli, 275 202 9332, main courses €8-€30). If you want a livelier drinking scene, the bars along Bouboulinas will deliver. For dancing, head to one of the clubs around the bay, or hop in a cab to the youthful resort of **Tolo**, 15 minutes' drive away.

Where to stay

As a well-established resort, there's no shortage of places to stay at, in all categories, in Nafplio. In summer 2003 it even got its own design hotel, the chic, sleek **Amphitryon** (Spiliadou 21, 275 207 0700, www.amphitryon.gr, doubles €190-€450); each room has a terrace with wonderful sea views. Another luxury option, the **Nafplia Palace** (Acronafplia, 275 202 8981/5, www.nafplionhotels.gr, doubles €200-€270), is

perched just above it. You don't get the views at **Ilion** (Elthimiopolou 4 & Kapodistriou 6, 275 202 5114, www.ilionhotel.gr, doubles €170-€180), back in the old town, but you do get a lot more idiosyncratic character, with individually themed rooms flamboyantly decorated and decked out with antiques.

Affordable options include the six properties that make up the **Pension Acronafplia** (central office Papanikolaou 8, 275 202 4481, www.pensionacronafplia.gr, doubles €30-€110). Other good mid-range choices are **Kapodistrias Traditional House** (Kokinou 20, 275 202 9366, www.hotelkapodistrias.gr, doubles €50-€70), and **Dafni Pension** (Fotomara 10 & Iatrou 5, 275 202 9856, mobile 697 270 8133, www.pensiondafni.gr, doubles €50-€80).

Tourist information

Martiou 25 (275 202 4444). **Open** 9am-1pm, 4pm-8pm daily.

Epidaurus

At the top of this famous archaeological site is the **Ancient Theatre**, which dates from the fourth century BC. It is the best preserved and one of the largest of its kind. The theatre seats up to 14,000 spectators and is renowned for its amazing acoustics. For a practical demonstration of this impressive venue, plan your visit in time for the annual Epidaurus Festival, when classical plays are performed just as they were more than 2,000 years ago.

At Epidaurus you'll also find the **Sanctuary of Asclepius** (dedicated to the Greek god of medicine), which includes the Katagogeion and the Temple of Asclepius, as well as the remains of a tholos, a gymnasium and a stadium.

Archaeological Site of Ancient Epidaurus

275 302 2009. **Open** *Apr-Oct* 8am-7.30pm daily. *Museum* noon-7.30pm Mon; 8am-7.30pm Tue-Sun. *Nov-Mar* 8am-5pm daily. *Museum* noon-5pm Mon; 8am-5pm Tue-Sun. **Admission** €6; €3 concessions; free under-18s. **No credit cards**.

Where to eat

Having built up a healthy appetite exploring the sites, head to the **Leonidas** taverna (Epidavrou 103, 275 302 2115, closed Oct-Mar, main courses €6-€9) in the village of Lygourio, four kilometres (two miles) away. As well as serving good Greek cuisine, Leonidas is also famous for its theatrical legacy. Displaying photographs of performances at the Ancient Theatre, the taverna was reputedly a favourite post-show hangout of Melina Mercouri and her husband Jules Dassin.

Island Escapes

Escape the frenzied pace of Athens for an Aegean adventure.

If you feel like an island break but only have one or two days to spare, the Argosaronic offers the perfect opportunity for a rejuvenating getaway. Most of its islands are just a couple of hours away by high-speed hydrofoil, with Aegina close enough to pop over to for lunch and be back by evening.

These four islands – the cosmopolitan **Spetses** (two hours by hydrofoil), picture-perfect **Hydra** (90 minutes), pine-clad **Poros** (one hour) and pleasantly bustling **Aegina** (40 minutes) – all make invigorating day trips or relaxing weekend breaks. If you do them as a quick side trip from Athens, it makes sense to take a fast boat or hydrofoil rather than the regular ferry: journey times are halved.

Getting there

All Argosaronic boats (frequent service) leave from the dockside at Piraeus (*see p100*), about 200 metres south of the metro station, beside Akti Miaouli. **Hellenic Seaways** (210 419 9200, www.hellenic seaways.gr) runs hydrofoil and conventional services to all four islands. **Euroseas** (210 413 2188, www. euroseas.com) has a service to Hydra and Spetses; **Aegean Flying Dolphins** (210 422 1766) goes to all four. Ticket booths (credit MC, V) are open from about an hour before each departure, but note that if you want to travel by hydrofoil on a weekend in high season (mid June-Sept), you must buy tickets in advance (from almost any travel agent). Tickets for conventional Argosaronic ferries are sold dockside only (for information, call 210 411 7341). A return trip by conventional ferry costs €15-€25. A hydrofoil round trip (economy) costs between €21.50 and €60.

Aegina

Aegina is a mere 40-minute jaunt from Piraeus by hydrofoil, but it's a world away from the fumes and angst of Athens, with its horse-drawn carriages and pretty neo-classical buildings harking back to its days as Greece's first capital after the War of Independence (for just a year). The biggest island of the Argosaronic, measuring 85 square kilometres (33 square miles) and with a population of 10,000, Aegina is centered around a pleasantly bustling town full of tavernas and cafés overlooking the main harbour. Rent a bike and breeze through the pocket-sized capital or join the locals buying fresh fruit and vegetables from the traditional floating greengrocers on the waterfront.

Not to be missed, 12 kilometres (about eight miles) east of Aegina Town, is the intricate and immaculately preserved fifth-century BC **Temple of Aphaia**, a local goddess, later identified with Athena. En route are the **Monastery of St Nektarios** and the island's abandoned, atmospheric medieval capital, **Paleohora**. Within walking distance of Aegina Town are the ruins of the **Temple of Apollo** at Kolona, and the **Archaeological Museum** (229 702 2248, closed Mon, admission €3), just north of the port. There are stunning views from the 532-metre summit of **Mount Oros**.

The best spots for a swim are **Marathona** or **Aeginitsa** on the west coast, and **Kleidi** and **Keri** near the southern village of **Perdika** – an ideal place for a seaside lunch.

Temple of Aphaia

229 703 2398. **Open** *Mid April-mid Oct* 8am-7pm daily. Museum 8am-2.15pm Tue-Sun. *Mid Oct-mid April* 8am-5pm daily. Museum 8am-2.15pm Tue-Sun. **Admission** €4; €2 concessions; free under-18s. **No credit cards**.

Where to eat & drink

For great seafood in Aegina Town, try **Mezedopolio Agora** (229 702 7308, main courses €7-€15) at the fish market, south of the port and a block inland. The traditional taverna of **Diogenis** (229 703 2257, main courses €6-€10) in Agia Marina is worth a visit. A short walk south from Agia Marina is the inland village of Alones, where you'll find **Costas** (229 703 2424, main courses €7-€15), sought out by discerning locals and visitors. In Perdika, **To Proreon** (229 706 1827, main courses €6-€12) is a first-rate taverna on the seafront. **On the Beach** is a pleasant café-bar in Aegina Town.

Where to stay

In Aegina town, the **Aegenitiko Archontiko** (229 702 4968, doubles €60-€70) is traditional and friendly, while **Hotel Areti** (229 702 3593, doubles €50-€60) offers sea views. In Agia Marina, the **Hotel Apollon** (229 703 2271, doubles with breakfast €82-€92) offers panoramic views of the Argosaronic from its cliff-side location. In Perdika, **Hotel Hippocampus** (229 706 1363, doubles €50-€70) is traditional and cosy.

Trips Out of Town

Hydra.

Tourist information

Aegina's tourist police, in the town centre
(Leonardo Lada 5, 229 702 7777, open 8am-3pm
daily) can assist with accommodation.

Getting around

The bus station on Platia Ethneyersias runs an
excellent service to most villages on the island.
Regular services go to the Temple of Aphaia and
from Aegina Town to beaches on the west side.

Spetses

The small, scenic, pine-clad island of Spetses
has an exclusive feel, perhaps because of its
affluent residents. Cars are banned, so hire a
scooter or wear comfortable shoes to explore
the charming courtyards and grand neo-
classical mansions of the port capital Spetses
Town. Horse-drawn carriages are a romantic,
but expensive, alternative.

The majestic Mexis Mansion in the town
centre, which once belonged to the island's first
governor, Hadziyiannis Mexis, is home to the
Museum of Spetses (229 807 2994, closed
afternoons & all Mon, admission €3). As well
as displaying relics from the 1821 Greek War
of Independence, it houses the bones of Spetsiot
heroine Laskarina Bouboulina, a leading figure
in the fight against the Turks. Other sights in
the town include the **House of Laskarina
Bouboulina** (229 807 2416, closed Nov-Mar,
admission €5) at the cannon-dotted modern port

of **Dapia**. Also check out the medieval district
of **Kastelli**, the **Old Harbour** and the **Church
of St Nicholas** (229 807 2423), with its giant
pebble mosaics. The nearby Anargyreios and
Korgialenios School was an English public school
where British writer John Fowles used to teach.

The best beaches are at **Agia Anarghiri**
and **Agia Paraskevi**, a few kilometres further
west. Water taxis are an exhilarating way for
groups to get to secluded beaches.

Where to eat & drink

For fish and lobster spaghetti, try **Exedra**
(229 807 3497, closed Nov-Feb, main courses
€8-€10), on a jetty at the Old Harbour. **Lazaros**
in Kastelli (229 807 2600, closed mid Oct-Mar,
main courses €7-€10) serves good cooked dishes
and home-made retsina. The famed **Patralis**
fish taverna (229 807 2134, closed Nov-Dec, main
courses €7-€15) in the area of Kounoupitsa, west
of the port, is also worth a visit. **Bracciera** and
Figaro, near the port, are popular clubs.

Where to stay

A short walk from Spetses town, in Kounoupitsa,
the traditional **Economou Mansion** (229 807
3400, www.spetsestravel.gr, doubles from €175)
is much loved for its huge balconies. Also in
Kounoupitsa is the luxurious **Nissia** (229 807
5000, www.nissia.gr, doubles from €245). For
more affordable comfort, try the **Yachting Club
Inn** (229 807 3400, www.spetsestravel.gr, doubles
from €90), near the beach, half a mile from town.

Trips Out of Town

Poros. *See p222.*

Zoe's Club (229 807 4447, www.zoesclub.gr, apartments for two €145-€220) is a small complex of luxurious suites in central Spetses. **Armatahotel** (229 807 2683, www.armata hotel.gr, closed Nov-Feb, doubles from €90) is a boutique venue that has been converted from a traditional island home.

Tourist information

The island's tourist police is located in the town centre (229 807 3100, open 8am-3pm daily, closed mid Oct-end May). Although it isn't active in winter, tourist assistance is available for tourists all year at the above number.

Getting around

You can reach most parts of the island by bicycle or motorbike from Spetses Town. Small boats ferry locals and visitors from Dapia to various beaches during the summer. Water taxis (229 807 2072) are an expensive alternative, but can take up to ten people for a set price (fares range from €16 to €48).

Hydra

Arriving on this picturesque gem of an island is like stepping into a painting. The distinctive neo-classical stone mansions of Hydra Town rise above the picture-pretty port, where cafés teem with customers, and donkeys await their next expedition along cobbled lanes. Hydra is twice the size of neighbouring Spetses but has an even smaller population of around 3,000.

For spectacular sea views, follow Boundouri, a pebbly path winding upwards from the port to the fishing village of **Kamini**. Alternatively, climb the mountain from town to the **Monastery of Profitis Ilias** (229 805 2540, closed noon-4pm daily), the adjacent **Convent of St Efpraxia** (229 805 2484) and the nearby uninhabited **Monastery of St Triada** – views from the top make up for the one-hour trek.

Visit the **Panaghia Mitropoleos** cathedral (229 805 2829, closed afternoons Sept-Apr); its distinctive clock tower dominates the waterfront. It houses the **Byzantine Museum** (229 805 4071, closed Mon, admission €2). Relics from the 1821 revolution are on display at the island's **Historical Archives & Museum** (229 805 2355, closed Dec-Mar, admission €4) at the port. An annual exhibition of artwork is hosted at **Hydra Workshops**, a gallery space in the harbour area.

Mandraki and **Vlichos** are the best beaches near the main harbour, but for more secluded spots, head to **Bisti** and **Agios Nikolaos** on the west of the island or **Limioniza** in the south.

Where to eat & drink

Xeri Elia (229 805 2886, closed first 3wks Nov, main courses €8-€10) offers simple but quality fare in a square near the port. **Kondylenia** (229 805 3520, closed Nov-Feb, main courses €7-€12) is situated in a charming location at Kamini. **Geitoniko** (299 805 3615, main courses €7-€12) is one of the best-known tavernas in Hydra Town, while **Paradosiako** (229 805 4155) serves exceptional *mezedakia* (small snacks). **Spilia Beach Club Café-Bar**, built into the side of a cliff just before the cannons at Hydroneta, is a great spot for a coffee or a beer during the day. At night, visit the **Pirate Bar** for rock and '80s nostalgia, and **Heaven** and **Kavos** for clubbing.

Where to stay

The stylish **Bratsera** (229 805 3971, www. bratserahotel.com, closed Oct-Mar, doubles €132-€215) is set in a restored 19th-century sponge-processing factory. At the **Orloff** (229 805 2564, www.orloff.gr, closed Nov-Apr, doubles €150-€200) guests can enjoy breakfast in a flower-filled courtyard. Both are within walking distance of the port. **Hotel Mistral** (229 805 2509, www.hotelmistral.gr, doubles €110-€140) offers rooms in a traditional stone mansion with a cool yard.

Tourist information

The tourist police (229 805 2205, 24hrs), in the town centre, can answer visitors' enquiries.

Getting around

No motor vehicles are allowed on Hydra, so rent a bicycle or prepare yourself for plenty of walking (note that the island has a lot of steps). Water taxis (229 805 3690) connect the port to all the island's beaches; prices start from €9.

Poros

Poros is a lively, pine-covered island close to some of the most striking archaeological sites in the Peloponnese, and home to around 4,000 inhabitants. Poros (meaning 'ford' or 'crossing') is actually two islands – **Sferia** (the tiny volcanic peninsula that is home to Poros town) and the larger **Kalabria** – separated by a shallow artificial canal.

Poros town's skyline is dominated by the **Clock Tower**, which looms over the café-lined waterfront. On the west of the islan is the glorious **Villa Galini**, famous for having accommodated Greek Nobel-winning poet George Seferis and US writer Henry Miller.

Also worth seeing are Constantinos Parthenis's magnificent wall paintings at the **Cathedral of St George** (229 802 3241, open Sat, Sun afternoons only), near the port, and the small **Archaeological Museum** (229 802 3276, closed Mon, admission €2), which features finds from ancient Troezen (now Trizini; *see below*), site of the ancient Temple of Aesculapius.

Elsewhere on the island, the sixth-century BC **Temple of Poseidon** (closed Mon, admission

free), near the centre of Kalabria, is an arresting sight. The 18th-century **Monastery of Zoodochou Pigis** (229 802 2926) in southern Kalabria is also worth a visit.

Good swimming spots include **Neorion Bay** and **Kanali** (north and south of Poros Town respectively), and the pretty sheltered cove of **Agapi** (or the Love Bay).

Trizini is an eight-kilometre (five-mile) bus trip from Galatas, just across from Poros on the mainland. If you make the trip, you must see the Gefira tou Diavolou, or **Devil's Bridge** – a natural rock formation spanning a gorge – and the nearby orange and lemon groves.

Where to eat & drink

For tasty home-cooked food, try **Mourtzoukos** (Neorion, 229 802 2438, closed Nov-Mar, main courses €5-€7). For great food on a jetty with an amphitheatre-style view of Poros, visit **Aspros Gatos** (229 802 5650, main courses €7-€9). For fresh fish, head to **Nikolas** taverna (Monastiri, 229 802 3426, closed Nov-Mar, main courses €7-€9), about four kilometres (two and a half miles) from the port. **Kathestos** (229 802 4770, main courses €5-€7) is a good taverna on the waterfront. The waterfront is swarming with vibrant bars; **Korali**, in town, is one of the best late-night clubs.

Where to stay

The **Sto Roloi** guesthouse (229 802 5808, www.storoloi-poros.gr, doubles €75-€150, villa with private pool €250) is housed in a restored neo-classical mansion behind the port. For minimalist luxury and great views, the **Poros Image Hotel** (229 802 2216, www.poros image.gr, doubles €130-€150, suite €265) has a prime location on the waterfront at Neorion Bay. A cheaper option is the **Hotel Saga** (229 802 5400, 229 802 5132, www.sagahotel poros.com, doubles €65-€80, suite €90), with large balconies overlooking Kanali Bay.

Tourist information

The tourist police (229 802 2256, closed end Sept-mid May) can help with where to stay or eat.

Getting around

To see the island, rent a scooter or bicycle from one of the outlets on the waterfront. Buses regularly leave Poros Town for the Monastery of Zoodochou Pigis. Frequent boats connect Poros Town with Galatas on the mainland, from where there are regular buses to Trizini and the nearby Devil's Bridge. Travel agents on Poros can also organise day trips to Nafplio and Epidaurus (*see pp217-218*).

Directory

Getting Around   224
Resources A-Z   228
Vocabulary   237
Further Reference   238
Index   239
Advertisers' Index   244

Features

Taxi tips   226
Travel advice   228
Greek etiquette   231
Average climate   236
Greek alphabet   237

National Archaeological Museum.
See p90.

Directory

Getting Around

Arriving & leaving

By air

The Greek capital is served by **Eleftherios Venizelos Airport** (210 353 0000, www. aia.gr), about 27 kilometres (17 miles) north-east of Athens, linked by the six-lane Attiki Odos highway.

Airlines
British Airways *210 890 6666/ www.british-airways.com.*
easyJet *210 353 0300/ www.easyjet.com.*
Olympic Airlines *210 966 6666/ www.olympic-airways.com.*

To & from the airport
Besides taxis, there are three ways of getting to the city centre from the airport: metro line 3, which will take you from the airport to the city centre; the suburban railway (Proastiakos), which connects with Larissa station and Piraeus; and the Airport Express buses, which run all night. All of these link up to the broader public transport network.

The **metro** runs every half hour between around 6am and midnight; journey time is 27 minutes. A single ticket costs €6, a return €10; a single for two people €10, for three €15, and for under-18s and over-65s €3.

The **Proastiakos** trains make a number of stops, including Doukissis Plakentias (where you can transfer to metro line 3), Kifisia, Nerantziotisa (transfer to line 1), and Larissa station (transfer to line 2), before terminating at Piraeus. The journey from the airport takes 30 minutes to Larissa (40 minutes to Piraeus), and fares range up to €6 (under-18s €3; two people or return ticket €10). Trains run every half hour between approximately 5am and midnight.

Several public bus routes serve the airport exclusively, linking it with central Athens, Piraeus and the suburbs. All airport buses, known as **Athens Airport Express**, depart from outside the Arrivals Hall. Routes E92, E93, E96 and E97 run 24 hours a day. E95 goes right to the city centre (Syntagma) in roughly an hour; buses leave every eight to 30

minutes depending on the time of day. Route E96 will take you from the airport to the port of Piraeus. The journey time is a little over an hour, and buses leave every 20 minutes to an hour. E92, E93 and E97 go to Kifissia, Kifisou bus station and Dafni metro station respectively. The average journey time is 45 minutes. Route E94 takes you to Ethiniki Amyna, where you'll be able to connect to the city's metro network. The E94 runs from 5am to 11.30pm and leaves every 15-30 minutes. The journey time is around 30 minutes.

Tickets cost €3.20 and can be bought from all metro stations, blue public transport ticket booths or the bus driver. Tickets are valid for one journey to or from the airport, exclusive of metro or local bus connections, which require additional tickets.

For more details on these routes, contact the **Athens Urban Transport Organisation** (OASA; www.oasa.gr) on 185. The phones are manned by bilingual staff from 7am to 9pm daily.

Taxis (*see p226*) will drop you off right outside Departures. There is a signposted queue for taxis outside Arrivals. An average taxi ride from Syntagma to the airport costs around €25 during the day and evening or €30 from midnight to 5am and takes 40 minutes (more in rush hour).

Frequent strikes and protests can bring the city centre to a standstill, so make sure that you allow plenty of time to get to the airport.

By rail

Athens' main stations are **Larissa** (for trains from northern Greece and abroad) and **Peloponnisou** (for trains from the Peloponnese). The terminals are near each other in one of Athens' less savoury neighbourhoods. Avoid accepting assistance from dodgy types outside the stations. Between 5am and 11.30pm the stations are linked to the city's transport system by buses, trams, metro and cabs, located right outside.

Greece's national railway authority is **OSE** (210 259 7777, www.ose.gr).

Larissa Station *Deliyianni 31 (210 529 7777). Metro Larissa Station.* **Open** 6.30am-midnight daily. **Map** p248 D1.
Peloponnisou Station *Sidirodromon (210 513 1601). Metro Larissa Station.* **Open** 6.30am-midnight daily. **Map** p248 C1.

By coach

The intercity coach service, **KTEL** (www.ktelattikis.gr), serves destinations all over Greece. There are two main coach stations in Athens: Terminal A (Kifisou 100), with buses to the Peloponnese and western Greece; and Terminal B (Liosion 260), with services to central and northern Greece. Coaches to Sounion, Rafina and Lavrio leave from Mavromateon (Pedion Areos); coaches to Megara and points south depart from Thissio metro station. For information on tickets and timetables, call 210 512 4910.

By boat

From central Athens you can get to the port of Piraeus by metro (line 1), the Proastiakos from Larissa station or the 24-hour 040 bus from Filellinon, next to Syntagma Square. An average taxi ride from Syntagma to the port costs €10-€15 during the day or €20 late at night (midnight-5am).

If you're planning to travel by boat in August, make sure you've reserved your tickets well in advance – it's the month when practically the whole of Athens escapes to the islands.

A number of routes for the Cyclades now leave from Rafina and Lavrion.

For information on routes and timetables, visit www.greek ferries.gr, a comprehensive database detailing many of Greece's main ferry services; www.piraeusferry.co.uk has timetables, information and booking facilities.

ANEK Lines *Akti Posidonos 32 & Leocharous (210 419 7420/ www.anek.gr). Metro Piraeus.* **Open** 7.30am-8.30pm daily. **Credit** DC, V.

Blue Star *26 Akti Posidonos, Piraeus (210 891 9800/www.bluestar ferries.com). Metro Piraeus.* **Credit** MC, V.

Hellenic Seaways *Akti Kondyli & Aitolikou 2, Piraeus (Cyclades & Sporades 210 419 9000/Saronic Gulf 210 419 9200/www.hellenic seaways.gr). Metro Piraeus.* **Open** *Summer* 8.30am-8pm Mon-Sat. *Winter* 8.30am-4pm Mon-Fri; 8.30am-2.30pm Sat. **Credit** AmEx, MC, V.

Minoan Lines (Athens branch) *Syngrou 98-100, Syngrou (210 920 0020/www.minoan.gr). Metro Syngrou-Fix.* **Open** 8.20am-8pm Mon-Fri; 8.30am-4.30pm Sat; 3.30-4.30pm Sun. **Credit** AmEx, DC, MC, V. **Map** p251 D8.

Minoan Lines (Piraeus branch) *Thermopylon 6-10, Piraeus (210 414 5700). Metro Piraeus.* **Open** 7.30am-9pm daily. **Credit** AmEx, DC, MC, V.

Public transport

For general information on public transport, phone the **Athens Urban Transport Organisation** (OASA) on 185, or visit www.oasa.gr.

Fares & tickets

Metro tickets can be bought at ticket machines or ticket offices at all stations. Ticket machines do not give change for notes or take credit cards. The regular fare is €0.70 for line 1 and €0.80 for lines 2 and 3 (€0.80 for a journey involving a combination). Children up to six years old travel free.

You need to validate your ticket at the special machines before you board the train. Tickets are valid for 90 minutes from the time of validation and

for interchanges on all three lines. However, they are not valid for return via the route already covered.

Fares for both **buses** and **trolleybuses** are €0.50. Drivers do not issue tickets, which must be bought prior to boarding, from OASA ticket booths, most metro stations and kiosks. Tickets must be validated using the special machines on the bus itself.

A ticket for the **tram** is €0.60 and can be purchased from booths or ticket machines on the platforms. Tickets must be validated in the special machines on the platform.

'**Unified**' €1 tickets are available that allow for travel on all types of public transport for a period of 90 minutes. Tickets must be validated on first and last rides.

A **day pass** (€3) is valid for an unlimited number of trips on the metro, buses and trolleybuses; a **weekly pass** (€10) allows for seven days' travel on all public transport within the city.

Metro

The underground train network is called the **Athens Metro** (www.ametro.gr) and the older line, which runs both underground and overground, is the **ISAP** (www.isap.gr). The stations are clearly marked with 'M' or 'ΗΣΑΠ' signs.

The network operates from 5.30am to midnight and has three different lines: **line 1** (ISAP) runs from the port of Piraeus to the northern suburb of Kifisia; **line 2** runs from Agios Dimitrios to Agios Antonios; and **line 3** goes from Egaleo to Doukissis Plakentias, with trains every half hour continuing to Athens International Airport. Further stations are due to open on lines 2 and 3 over the next few years. Trains run around every five minutes at peak times (ten minutes off-peak).

Suburban railway

The suburban railway, or **Proastiakos**, currently runs from Athens airport to the central Larissa station and the port of Piraeus. A new link continuing down to the Peloponnesian city of Corinth is scheduled to open by 2009. Trains run every half hour between around 5am and midnight. For more information contact 210 527 2000.

Buses & trolleybuses

Athens is well served by buses and trolleybuses, but they aren't generally useful for visitors unless they want to visit nearby beaches.

One exception is the new No.400 **Athens Sightseeing Bus**, which serves central Athens during the daytime. Frequency and hours vary according to the season; stops are marked with tall blue plaques. The €5 ticket is purchased on board and is good for 24 hours unlimited travel on all regular public transport. *See also* p60.

Blue buses and yellow trolleybuses run from around 5am until 11pm or midnight, depending on the route. For information, contact OASA (*see above*). You can pick up a bus map at metro stations.

Tram

The tram (www.tramsa.gr) links central Athens (Syntagma) with the Peace and Friendship Stadium (SEF) in Faliro – where it also links up with metro line 1 – and Glyfada (Kolymvitirio). The service from the city centre to the southern coast has been criticised for delays, but visitors will appreciate the Faliro–Glyfada route, with its sea views and easy access to the beach. Trams run between 5am and 1am, Monday to Thursday and Sunday, and

Directory

around the clock Friday to Saturday, providing a night service for coastal clubbers in the summer. Between 5am and 10pm the average waiting time is 7-8 minutes; between 10pm and 1am, 10 minutes; and from 1am to 5am, 40 minutes.

Taxis

Taxis can get snarled up in traffic, especially during rush hour, but fares are reasonable. After midnight, when most public transport stops, taxis become a necessary form of transport. The procedure is typical, but there's a definite Athenian protocol and knowing it can save you considerable grief (*see below* **Taxi tips**).

Athens taxis are yellow, with a 'TAXI' sign on the roof. They can be hailed in the street or booked by phoning a local cab company (with surcharges of €1.50 to €2.50 for a pre-arranged pickup). One useful rank is on Syntagma between Ermou and Karagiorgi Servias.

As it's pretty hard to find taxis during rush hour, most Athens cabbies have no qualms about stopping to pick up extra fares. If a taxi slows down (or flashes his headlights) as he approaches you, but has his light switched off, shout your general destination to him and he will pick you up if it suits him.

Ask your driver for an estimate of how much your journey is going to cost before you set off. If you feel you're being ripped off, suggest that you find a police officer to get a second opinion; if your cabbie really is trying to take you for a ride, this kind of threat is usually enough to bring him back to his senses.

All taxis are obliged by law to use a running meter – if the driver doesn't switch it on when you get in, ask him to. There are two basic tariffs: No.1 and No.2, which is double fare. Tariff No.1 is the day rate, used from 5am to midnight, while tariff No.2 is the night rate, valid from midnight to 5am. Also, tariff No.1 is used within the city limits and No.2 is used outside that zone. The number 1 or 2 should be clearly visible on the meter.

The meter starts at €1 and there is a minimum charge of €2.50. There is also a surcharge

Taxi tips

Not so long ago, Athens taxi drivers and their smoke-belching terromobiles had a grim reputation. Now, however – largely thanks to efforts to clean up taxi services for the 2004 Olympics – vehicles have been improved or replaced by newer, cleaner models (usually with air-conditioning), and drivers have become less loud, less rude and safer behind the wheel.

In fact, most Athens cabbies are honest, polite and helpful, but they are not saints and may succumb to temptation when encountering an obviously clueless passenger. So, even if you have to fake it, act like you know the drill. How to manage this? First of all, check the map and ascertain that the distance is really too far to walk. Rip-offs commonly occur on shorter rides, such as from Omonia to the Acropolis. Other scams involve large bills, so have a supply of small bills and coins on hand, and always count your change.

Always hail a cab travelling towards your destination. This means standing on the proper side of a two-way street or walking to the closest one-way street. A busy thoroughfare, preferably a corner – a bus stop is better – offers the best prospects and visibility. Also, unless you've got a ton of luggage, it's best to give a major street as your destination, even if this means walking a bit afterwards. There's a good chance that even the most well-meaning driver won't be familiar with smaller streets, and a search can cost you time and money.

Once on board, be prepared for a brief detour or two, a lecture in world affairs (ignorance of the language is a blessing here) or football, and don't be surprised if you find yourself sharing a ride with one or more complete strangers. Athens is the only European city we know where having one passenger on board is no bar to picking up another. In fact, this is the rule at train and bus stations, where passenger demand far exceeds taxi supply. Technically, drivers are required to ask the passenger's permission and the passenger has the right to refuse, but few do in either case. It's good for the environment, good for your waiting time and – since he gets two fares out of it – good for the driver. When entering a taxi carrying other passengers, it's proper to greet and thank your fellow passengers for picking you up.

With a fleet of some 15,000 yellow cabs, taxis greatly exacerbate the city's traffic problem. But in a city where the action starts when public transport stops – or is frequently on strike – the ubiquitous Athens taxi is nothing short of a blessing.

of €3 for journeys from and to the airport; €0.80 to and from coach and rail stations and ports. A €0.30 charge (€0.60 midnight-5am) may also be added for each item of luggage over 10kg (22lbs); drivers are required to deliver your bags from boot to pavement. During the weeks around Easter and Christmas, an obligatory 'gift' (typically €1) is added to fares.

Radio taxis

Europe 210 502 9764.
Express 210 994 3000.
Ikaros 210 515 2800/ www.athens-taxi.gr.
Kosmos 18300/www.1300.gr.

Driving

You really don't need a car in Athens, but if you do have one, map your route before setting off and be prepared to keep your temper in check. Extensive roadworks and poor signposting make driving around the city extremely hard work. Athens' traffic jams (and its collisions) are legendary. In the evening the police are on the lookout for drunk drivers, setting up checkpoints around the club districts. The summer months are especially messy, with accidents soaring around the coastal club strips.

Drivers should stick to the standard EU speed limits: 30km/h (18mph) in residential areas and around hospitals and schools, 60km/h (37mph) on central roads and 100km/h (62mph) on motorways. Seatbelts are compulsory.

Breakdown services

Check with the company you are registered with at home to find out about affiliated companies in Greece, or register with a Greek breakdown company when you arrive.

ELPA Emergency Service 10400.
Express Service 1154.

Parking

Finding a parking place in Athens is notoriously hard. Greeks tend to park in the first available space, with no regard for pavements or blocking in other cars. There are no parking meters in Athens, but spaces marked with blue lines in some areas are technically for residents only. Private car parks dot the city centre.

24Parking24 Lykavitou 3C, Kolonaki (210 361 5823). **Open** 24hrs daily. **Rates** €10 1st hr; €1/extra hr; €0.50/extra hr after 8hrs. **Map** p252 G4.

AVIN Xenofontos 4 & Amalias, Historic Centre. **Open** 24hrs daily. Rates €10 1st 2hrs; €1/extra hr. **Map** p249/p251 F5.

Ippokratous Parking Ippokratous 55 & Didotou, Exarchia (210 361 7736). **Open** 24hrs daily. **Rates** €6 1st hr; €0.70/extra hr. **Map** p252 G3.

PolisPark Platia Kaningos, Exarchia. **Open** 24hrs daily. **Rates** €5 1st hr; €6.50 1-2hrs; €8 2-3hrs. **Map** p249 F2.

Petrol stations

Avin Oil Solonos 56, Kolonaki (210 361 7767/210 362 8202). **Open** May-Sept 6am-9pm Mon-Sat. Oct-Apr 6am-8pm Mon-Sat. Year-round 24hrs every 1, 7, 17, 27 of each mth. **Credit** DC, MC, V. **Map** p252 G4.

Revoil Mesogeion 17, Ampelokipi (210 770 5876). **Open** May-Sept 6am-9pm Mon-Sat. Oct-Apr 6am-8pm Mon-Sat. **No credit cards**.

Car hire

The minimum age for car hire in Greece is 21, and you must have held a licence for at least one year. EU citizens must hold an EU licence, while non-EU citizens must possess a valid national driving licence as well as an International Driving Permit. Agencies are clustered at the beginning of Syngrou and at the airport.

Avis Amalias 48, Historic Centre (210 322 4951/www.avis.gr). Metro Akropoli. **Open** 7.30am-8.30pm daily. **Rates** from €45/day for a small car. **Credit** AmEx, DC, MC, V. **Map** p249 F3.

Europcar Syngrou 42, Makrygianni (210 924 8810/www.europcar.com.gr). Metro Syngrou-Fix. **Open** 8am-8pm daily. **Rates** from €38/day for a small car. **Credit** AmEx, DC, MC, V. **Map** p251 E8.

Hertz Syngrou 12, Makrygianni (210 922 0102/www.hertz.gr). Metro Akropoli. **Open** 8am-8.30pm daily. **Rates** from €60/day for a small car; lower rates for multiple days. **Credit** AmEx, DC, MC, V. **Map** p251 E7.

Sixt Syngrou 23, Makrygianni (210 922 0171/www.e-sixt.com). Metro Akropoli. **Open** 7.30am-9pm daily. **Rates** from €30/day for a Daewoo Matiz. **Credit** AmEx, DC, MC, V. **Map** p251 E7.

Cycling

With no cycling lanes in the city and poor standards of driving, we wouldn't recommend risking it on two wheels. If you do want to try it, you can hire bikes for €5 for four hours (€15/day) from **Acropolis Bicycle**, Aristidou 10-12, Historic Centre (210 324 5793, mobile 6944 306130). They offer city tours, as does **Pame Volta** (Agathonos 23, Ag Paraskevi, Northern suburbs, 210 675 2886, www.pamevolta.gr).

Walking

Walking conditions have improved in recent years, and there is now a ten-mile pedestrian walkway linking the city centre's archaeological sites from the Arch of Hadrian to the ancient city wall bordering the Gazi district (see also p63).

However, pedestrians must be permanently alert, as red lights, stop signs, zebra crossings and one-way street signposts are often ignored by drivers. Even a green man doesn't necessarily give the pedestrian right of way. Look both ways before crossing a street, even in pedestrian zones, which motorcyclists use as shortcuts.

And always mind your step. Hazards, structural and organic, lurk underfoot even on newly paved sidewalks.

Directory

Resources A-Z

Addresses

Most street signs in Athens are written in both Greek and Roman characters. Be warned, however, that spellings can be quite imaginative, as a standardised transliteration system was only recently introduced. For example, you could see Lykavitou, Licavittou (phonetic spelling) or even Lycabettus, all referring to the same street. In our listings we have used transliterations that sound recognisable, in case you need to ask for directions.

Age restrictions

The age limit for drinking, smoking and driving in Greece is 18. However, bars rarely ask for ID and most, especially small bars, will allow children in if they are accompanied by an adult. Driving below the age of 18 is strictly prohibited. The age of consent is 15.

Attitude & etiquette

Despite its laid-back attitude to most things, Greece is a conservative society. While you may be on a carefree holiday, bear in mind that you are visiting a country with its own set of social rules and values. Drunk and disorderly conduct, overt displays of affection in public places and rude behaviour, especially towards the elderly, are not acceptable.

While Greeks are not famed for their gushing politeness, they will be helpful and friendly towards visitors. One real point of friction between visitors and locals, however, comes when paying a bill or taxi fare. Presenting a cab driver with a €20 note for a €2.50 fare or paying for a pack of cigarettes with €50 will trigger a long, heated argument. It is advisable to carry lots of loose change and, when changing money, to break €100 and €50 notes into smaller denominations.

Greeks are notoriously fond of arguing and shouting at each other in the street. Don't dwell on this too much – they never really act on these exaggerated displays. It's just their way of letting off steam.

Many locals still take a siesta at lunchtime in summer. Between 2pm and 5.30pm it's considered unacceptable to be noisy in residential areas or to disturb people at home.

When visiting churches, men should wear long trousers, women sleeved dresses and no miniskirts or shorts. *See also p231* **Greek etiquette**.

Business

Meetings in Athens are generally held at the 'host' office or often in the lobbies of the better hotels. Lunch meetings are popular too.

Greeks may be somewhat lax in keeping time in their leisure hours, but not when it comes to business – be punctual. Also dress smartly if it is your first meeting.

Conventions & conferences

Conferences are generally held at the larger hotels. There are also a few centres for fairs and exhibitions.

Helexpo *Leof Kifisias 22, Marousi (210 616 8888/www.helexpo). Bus A7, B7 from Kanigos.*

Piraeus Port Authority Centre (OLP) *Akti Miaouli 10, Piraeus (210 428 6842/www.olp.gr). Metro Piraeus.*

Zita Congress & Travel *km1 Paianias-Markopoulou, Paiania (210 664 1190/www.zita-congress.gr). KTEL bus to Koropi from Pedion Areos.*

Couriers & shippers

All courier companies will collect from hotels and offices for a fee. Unless otherwise stated, the companies listed offer both courier and shipping services.

DHL *Alimou 44 & Roma, Alimos, Southern suburbs (210 989 0000/ www.dhl.gr).* **Open** 8am-7pm Mon-Fri; 8am-3pm Sat. **Credit** AmEx, DC, MC, V.

SpeedEx *(courier only) Spirou Patsi & Sidirokastrou 1-3, Votanikos (210 340 7190/www.speedex.gr).* **Open** 8am-7pm Mon-Fri. **No credit cards.**

TNT *Zita 7, Elliniko, Southern suburbs (210 894 0062/www.tnt.com).* **Open** 8am-7pm Mon-Fri. **No credit cards.**

Travel advice

For up-to-date information on travel to a specific country – including the latest news on safety and security, health issues, local laws and customs – contact your home country government's department of foreign affairs. Most have websites packed with useful advice for would-be travellers.

Australia
www.smartraveller.gov.au

Canada
www.voyage.gc.ca

New Zealand
www.safetravel.govt.nz

Republic of Ireland
http://foreignaffairs.gov.ie

UK
www.fco.gov.uk/travel

USA
http://travel.state.gov

UPS *Leof Kifisias 166, Marousi, Northern suburbs (210 614 6510/ www.ups.com).* **Open** 9am-7pm Mon-Fri. **Credit** AmEx, DC, MC, V.

Office services

Fast Digital Copy Centre
Kolokotroni 11, Historic Centre (210 323 9865). Metro Syntagma. **Open** 9am-5pm Mon-Fri. **No credit cards.** **Map** p249 F4.

Fototipies *Strilinga Aristidou 9, Historic Centre (210 321 2623). Metro Panepistimio.* **Open** 8am-7pm Mon-Fri; 9am-2pm Sat. **No credit cards.** **Map** p249 E4.

Secretarial services

IBS International Business Services *Michalakopoulou 29, Ilisia, East Athens (210 724 5541). Metro Evangelismos.* **Open** 9am-5pm Mon-Fri. **No credit cards.** Also offers translation services and conference organising.

Planitas *Spyridonos Trikoupi 20, Exarchia (210 330 6945-7/210 380 5663/www.planitas.gr). Metro Omonia.* **Open** 9am-7pm Mon-Fri. **No credit cards.** **Map** p249 F2.

Translation services

Executive Service Athens
Tower 2, Mesogeion 2-4, Ambelokipi (210 778 3698). Metro Ambelokipi. **Open** 9am-5pm Mon-Fri. **No credit cards.** Legal and technical translations.

Com Translation & Interpretation *Xenagora 8-10, Platia Amerikis, North Athens (210 862 3411/www.pra-zis.gr). Metro Victoria.* **Open** 9am-5pm Mon-Fri. **No credit cards.**

Useful organisations

British-Hellenic Chamber of Commerce *Leof Vas Sofias 25, Kolonaki (210 721 0361/www.bhcc.gr). Metro Evangelismos.* **Open** Phone enquiries 9am-5pm Mon-Fri.
US-Hellenic Chamber of Commerce *Mesogeion 109-111, Ambelokipi (210 699 3559/www.amcham.gr). Metro Katehaki.* **Open** 9am-4.30pm Mon-Fri.

Consumer

There is one main consumer protection service in Greece, **INKA** (Akadimias 7, Historic Centre, www.inka.gr). Though INKA can provide advice, it

doesn't have any legal power. You can also try calling the **General Secretariat for the Consumer** (1520). In disputes with shop owners, hoteliers, etc, it is better to seek advice from the tourist police (*see p230*).

Customs

Greek customs allows you to bring in, duty-free, up to 200 cigarettes (or 100 cigarillos or 50 cigars or 250g of tobacco), one litre of spirits (or two litres of wine or liqueur), 50ml of perfume and 250ml of eau de cologne. Passengers arriving from within Europe don't pass through customs. For further information about customs, contact Athens International Airport (210 353 0000).

Greece is naturally sensitive about its antiquities, which range from fragments of sculpture and architecture to a pebble picked up while touring the Acropolis, to coins and icons. Taking antiquities out of the country without a permit is a serious offence; punishments range from a hefty fine to a jail term. To apply for a permit, contact the **Central Archaeological Council** (KAS; 210 820 1293) or consult the dealer you bought from.

Disabled

Compared to many other European cities, Athens is not very accommodating towards those with impaired mobility. In theory, all public transport (buses, trams, urban railway) and many cultural and archaeological sites – including the Acropolis – are now fully accessible for wheelchair-users. Many hotels, shops and public buildings have also improved their facilities for disabled customers and (not very effective) measures have been made to improve the city's pavements for both wheelchair-users and the blind. However,

transforming Athens into a truly disabled-friendly city requires many more measures, including raising public awareness – especially that of drivers regarding their parking habits.

The **National Committee for the Disabled** (6th floor, Milerou 1, Metaxourgio, 210 523 8961, www.disability.gr/esaea) can offer advice to disabled visitors.

Drugs

Do not get involved with any kind of drug in Greece. Penalties for possession of even small amounts are harsh and getting harsher. Depending on the amount you are caught with (and whether the crime is judged as a misdemeanour or a felony), you will get a suspended sentence, which you can pay off, or face a jail sentence (between five and 20 years).

Electricity

Greece uses 220-volt electric power (AC 50Hz). Appliances from North America require a transformer and British ones an adaptor. Come equipped to save wasting valuable time searching.

Embassies & consulates

American Embassy *Leof Vas Sofias 91, Ambelokipi (210 721 2951/ www.usembassy.gr). Metro Megaro Mousikis.* **Open** 8.30am-5pm Mon-Fri.
Australian Embassy *Soutsou 37 & Tsocha 24, Ambelokipi (210 870 4000/www.ausemb.gr). Metro Ambelokipi.* **Open** 8.30am-12.30pm Mon-Fri.
British Embassy *Ploutarchou 1, Kolonaki (210 727 2600/www.british-embassy.gr). Metro Evangelismos.* **Open** 8.30am-3pm Mon-Fri. **Map** p252 H5.
Canadian Embassy *Ioannou Gennadiou 4, Kolonaki (210 727 3400/www.athens.gc.ca). Metro Evangelismos.* **Open** 8am-4pm Mon-Fri. **Map** p252 J4.

Directory

Irish Embassy *Leof Vas Konstantinou 5-7, Historic Centre (210 723 2771). Metro Syntagma.* **Open** 9am-3pm Mon-Fri. Map p252 E6.

Consulate of New Zealand *Leof Kifisias 76, Ampelokipi (210 692 4136). Metro Panormou.* **Open** (by appointment) 10am-3.30pm Mon-Fri.

South African Embassy *Leof Kifisias 60, Marousi, Northern suburbs (210 610 6645/www. southafrica.gr). Metro Marousi.* **Open** 8am-1pm Mon-Fri.

Emergencies

If you need immediate police assistance, dial **100**, free of charge, from any phone.

If you've been robbed, attacked or involved in an infringement of the law, but don't require immediate attention, you can file a formal complaint at the Athens police headquarters (Leof Alexandras 173, Ambelokipi, 210 951 5111, 210 647 6000) or at the Piraeus police headquarters (Iroon Polytechneiou 37, Piraeus, 210 411 1710).

You can also contact the **Tourist Police**, available 24 hours a day, where officers speak foreign languages (*see below*).

For hospital listings, *see below*.

Useful numbers

Ambulance 166.
Coastguard 108.
Duty pharmacies & hospitals 1434.
Fire department 199.
Poison Control Centre 210 779 3777.
Road assistance 10400.
Tourist Police 171.
Tourist Police Athens *Veikou 43, Koukaki (210 920 0724/210 920 0727). Metro Syngrou-Fix.* Map p251 D8.
Tourist Police Piraeus *New Passenger Terminal, Xaveriou (210 429 0664). Metro Piraeus.*

Gay & lesbian

See also pp175-178.
Greeks are fairly tolerant of alternative lifestyles,

although they are rather conservative, so gay/lesbian couples should use common sense about public displays of affection. The majority of the hotels in the city centre are perfectly willing to cater to gay couples. Still, you might want to check in advance.

Gay Travel Greece (210 948 4182, www.gaytravel greece.com) is a travel agency specialising in gay-friendly hotels and packages for Athens and the Greek islands.

The **Gay Greece** portal (www.gaygreece.gr) has details of events and an English-language option.

Some LGBT organisations also have websites with English pages. Try *Antivirus* magazine (www.avmag.gr), **Greek Sapphites** (www. sapphogr.net) and, out of Thessaloniki, **Cooperation Against Homophobia** (www. geocities.com/sympraxis).

Health

Visitors do not need vaccinations before travelling to Greece. The sun can be punishing and, in summer, sunscreen, a hat and light clothing are essential. Mosquitoes can be a nuisance: insect repellent helps when going out in the evening, as does a plug-in zapper (available from supermarkets) for the bedroom.

Though in the capital and on the rest of the Greek mainland tap water quality is generally of a high standard, some of the islands do not have natural water resources and rely on desalination plants for their supply; the tap water in such places is briny, and locals drink bottled water.

Accident & emergency

All visitors to Athens are entitled to free medical care in the event of an emergency. This may include

helicopter transfer if necessary. Call 166 (free from any phone) to request an ambulance. All the hospitals listed below have 24-hour accident and emergency departments.

Agia Sophia General Children's Hospital *Thivon 3 & Mikrasias, Goudi, Eastern suburbs (210 777 1811). Bus A5 or B5.*

Alexandra General Hospital *Leof Vas Sofias 80, Kolonaki (210 338 1100). Metro Megaro Mousikis.*

Errikos Dinan Hospital *Mesogeion 107, Ambelokipi (210 697 2000). Metro Katehaki or Panormou.*

Evangelismos General Hospital *Ypsilantou 45-47, Kolonaki (210 720 1000). Metro Evangelismos.* Map p252 J4.

Ippokratio General Hospital *Leof Vas Sofias 114, Ambelokipi (210 748 3770). Metro Megaro Mousikis.*

Contraception & abortion

Condoms are widely available at kiosks (some of which are open 24 hours a day in central Athens), supermarkets and pharmacies. Greek pharmacies may require a doctor's prescription for birth-control pills. The morning-after pill is available over-the-counter.

Abortion is legal in Greece. Contact one of the general hospitals or clinics, or one of the private gynaecological clinics below. Call to book an appointment or visit between 9am and noon daily.

Iaso *Leof Kifisias 37-39, Marousi, Northern suburbs (210 618 4000). Metro Marousi, then 010 bus.*

Mitera *Erithrou Stavrou 6, Marousi, Northern suburbs (210 686 9000). Metro Marousi, then 010 bus.*

Dentists

Some free dental treatments are available for EU citizens at Evangelismos General Hospital (*see above*). Non-EU travellers are advised to contact their embassy (*see p229*).

In case of emergency, check the back page of *Kathimerini*'s English edition for duty hospitals, where you will be able to find a doctor to advise you, or call the SOS-Doctors (*see below*).

Doctors

You can also gain access to medical services by calling **SOS-Doctors** on 1016 (call is free of charge). This is an international organisation of

Greek etiquette

When it comes to cultural etiquette, it's usually best to take a monkey-see-monkey-do approach. In Athens, venture out of a Saturday evening before 10pm and, bar the odd über-eager maître d', you'll find the place deserted. So, instead, heartily embrace the daily diary of an Athenian: steal a kip after lunch, reserve your dinner table for late and, while you're at it, make time to greet even acquaintances with a kiss on both cheeks.

But blindly apeing native habits is not always recommended. As in the case of the Trojan horse, there are times when there's more to Greek behaviour than first meets the eye. Like those rogue Greek letters that trick you with familiar shapes only to stump you with foreign sounds, some common gestures have altogether different meanings here.

Look out for the nod – or what to the untrained eye at least looks like a nod. Far from indicating the affirmative, the casual dropping of one's chin followed by the tossing back of the head, often accompanied by misleading smile, does in fact mean 'no'. For examples of practical usage, check out the cabbies who employ it with gusto when, as is invariably the case, they avoid being hailed.

The friendly wave is another innocent gesture lost in translation. Raise your hand – palm out, fingers splayed – and face the consequences. This is not the way to greet friends. It is an insult akin to lifting two fingers (or giving the finger).

Having unwittingly committed such a social faux pas, you can soon re-ingratiate yourself with the locals with a spot of arguing. It's no surprise that 'drama' is a Greek word – nothing tickles Athenians more than the chance to tell their side of a story. The list of suitable topics is endless: pick anything from labour strikes to the cost of meat or tales of personal misfortune. Ears prick up, opinions are voiced vociferously and before you know it you're in the midst of a lively debate. To gauge the popularity of such a forum, just tune into the evening news where everything from a mild bus crash to a high church scandal is embellished with colourful eyewitness accounts.

However, there are times where the rules of conduct aren't nearly so clear cut: for instance, what to do when someone calls you *malaka* (roughly translated as 'wanker'). The word is the most common of insults, screamed at football referees and muttered at the mention of President Bush. So what do you do if it's directed at you? Well, it's a tricky call. You could nod with defiance or wave with anger. Or you could just smile, for among friends it is also a term of endearment. Go figure.

When in doubt remember the golden rule: never ask for milk in your *cafe elliniko* and, when all else fails, grab some worry beads and fidget.

'house-call' doctors operating on a 24-hour basis. A doctor will be paged to come to wherever you are staying to assist with any medical need or emergency. For patients staying in hotels, SOS-Doctors fees are fixed at €100 (€120 between 11pm and 7am and public holidays).

If you wish to discuss your symptoms, but do not require immediate attention, the best option is to ask a pharmacist.

Opticians

See p156.

Private clinics

For those who feel uneasy about placing their health in the hands of a government-run hospital (though they really needn't – Greek medical services rank among the best in Europe, even if the hospitals might sometimes appear in need of a facelift), the following private clinics all have accident and emergency departments, and provide a range of thoroughly modern facilities. If you have private health insurance in your own country, check if this brings any affiliations to private clinics in Greece.

Athens Euroclinic *Athanasiadou 9, Ambelokipi (210 641 6600/ emergency 1011/www.euroclinic.gr). Metro Ambelokipi.*

Athens General Clinic *M Geroulannou 15, Ambelokipi (210 692 2600/www.agclinic.gr). Metro Panormou.*

Central Clinic of Athens *Asklipiou 31, Kolonaki (210 367 4000/emergency 1169/www.central clinic.gr). Metro Syntagma.* **Map** p252 E3.

Hygeia Clinic *Erythrou Stavrou 4 & Leof Kifisias, Marousi, Northern suburbs (210 686 7000/www. hygeia.gr). Metro Marousi.*

Metropolitan Hospital *Ethnarchou Makariou 9 & Leof Eleftheriou Venizelou 1, Neo Faliro Southern suburbs (210 480 9000/ www.metropolitan-hospital.gr). Metro Faliro.*

Pharmacies & prescriptions

You will find a pharmacy on just about every block in Athens, and they are clearly marked with illuminated green crosses. Generally speaking, the opening hours for pharmacies in Athens are 8am-2.30pm on Mondays and Wednesdays and 8am-2pm and 5.30-8.30pm on Tuesdays, Thursdays and Fridays. Emergency pharmacies operate after hours and on weekends – to find the nearest one, consult a newspaper, check the white chart in any pharmacy window, or call 1434.

EU citizens with an EHIC card (*see below*) may be entitled to subsidised prescriptions; otherwise you pay the full whack (as do non-EU citizens). However, prices are so low in Greece that, especially for a one-off case, the procedure may not be worth it.

STDs, HIV & AIDS

Visit the outpatient department of any of the main state hospitals (*see p230*) to arrange for free tests (a prescription issued by a state hospital doctor will speed the process up considerably).

AIDS hotline *210 722 2222.*
Kentro Zois *Diochorous 9, Ilisia, Eastern suburbs (210 729 9747).*

Helplines & support groups

For information on where to get help for various problems call a State Citizens' Information (KEP) centre. Call 1564 (24 hours) to make an appointment at your nearest centre; all the centres listed can deal with English-speakers.

Foundation for the Child & the Family *12A Herodou Attikou, Marousi, Northern suburbs (210 809 4419/www.childfamily.gr). Metro Marousi.* **Open** 10am-6pm Mon-Fri.

HAPSA (Hellenic Association for the Prevention of Sexual Abuse) *Erifilis 12, Pangrati, East Athens (210 729 0496/www.hapsa. netfirms.com). Metro Evangelismos.* **Open** hours vary; call ahead. **Map** p252 J6.

Hellenic Red Cross *Likavittou 1, Kolonaki (210 361 3563/www.red cross.gr). Metro Panepistimio.* **Open** 7.30am-2.30pm Mon-Fri. **Map** p252 E4.

OKANA *(drug helpline) Averoff 21, Omonia (210 889 8200-85/hotline 1031/www.okana.gr). Metro Omonia.* **Open** 9am-8pm Mon, Wed; 9am-4pm Tue, Thur, Fri. **Map** p249 E2.

Parthenon Group of Alcoholics Anonymous *8th floor, Zinonos 4A, Omonia (210 522 0416). Metro Omonia.* **Open** hours vary; call ahead. **Map** p252 G3.

State Counselling Centre for Violence Against Women *Nikis 11, Plaka (210 331 7305/6). Metro Syntagma.* **Open** 8am-6pm Mon-Fri. **Map** p249 F5.

ID

By law, Greeks must carry their identity cards at all times. Visitors are advised to carry a photocopy of their passports and visa (if travelling with one), especially in the capital, where it is not uncommon for police to carry out random spot checks as part of their efforts to clamp down on illegal immigrants. An EU driving licence with photo should also be an acceptable form of ID. *See also p228* **Age restrictions**.

Insurance

EU nationals should obtain a European Health Insurance Card (available at post offices or www.ehic.org.uk), which facilitates free medical care under the Greek national health service (IKA). Visitors of other nationalities should arrange insurance prior to their trips.

Internet

Internet cafés are widespread in Athens. Most hotels also offer internet access, though at high rates. If your laptop is equipped with a wireless adaptor, you can connect for free, around Syntagma, to the Athens Wireless Metropolitan Network (AWMN). For a list of hotspots throughout the city (some of which are free) visit www.jiwire.com.

For useful websites, *see p238*.

Arcade *Stadiou 5, Historic Centre (210 321 0701). Metro Syntagma.* **Open** 9am-10pm Mon-Sat; noon-8pm Sun. **Rates** €3/hr. **No credit cards**. **Map** p249 F5.

Bits & Bytes *Akadimias 78, Omonia (210 330 6590/www.bnb.gr). Metro Omonia.* **Open** 24hrs daily. **Rates** €3/hr; €1.50 minimum charge. **No credit cards**. **Map** p249 F3.

Quick Net Café *Gladstonos 4, Omonia (210 380 3771). Metro Omonia.* **Open** 24hrs daily. **Rates** €3/hr. **No credit cards**. **Map** p249 E3.

Language

Most Athenians have a basic grounding in English and many speak it well, so you are unlikely to have problems communicating. However, you will be treated with more respect, especially in the business world, if you make an effort to learn at least the basics (*see p237*). Most locals will be flattered that you are trying and keen to help.

Left luggage

The left luggage facilities at Athens International Airport are situated on the ground floor of the International Arrivals terminal.

Bags may also be left at the city's railway stations, Larissa and Peloponnisou (*see p224*). Both of central Athens' bus stations have facilities for left luggage, as do the Omonia and Monastiraki metro stations.

Legal help

Should you require any legal help during your stay in Greece, you should contact your embassy or consulate (*see p229*) and/or (where appropriate) your own insurance company.

Libraries

Visit the following libraries to browse through English-language books (but note that the books can only be borrowed by members).

British Council Library *Platia Kolonaki 17, Kolonaki (210 369 2333). Metro Syntagma.* **Open** 8.30am-3pm Mon-Fri. **Map** p252 G5.

Hellenic-American Union *Massalias 22, Kolonaki (210 368 0044). Metro Panepistimio.* **Open** 10am-8pm Mon-Fri. **Map** p252 G4.

Lost property

The Greek transport police has a lost property office on the seventh floor at Leof

Alexandras 173 (210 647 6000, 210 642 1616). For losses on the metro, there is an office in Syntagma station (210 327 960, lostprop@ametro.gr, open 7am-7pm Mon-Fri, 8am-4pm Sat). Bring your passport when making a claim.

There is also a lost property office at Athens International Airport in Arrivals in the main terminal (210 353 0000).

Media

Newspapers & magazines

International magazines and newspapers are widely available at kiosks around the central Syntagma and Omonia squares, and on the main thoroughfares in Kolonaki. *Athens News* (www.athensnews.gr) is a local weekly English-language newspaper that comes out on Fridays, while *Kathimerini* (www.ekathimerini.gr) is an English-language daily supplement to the *International Herald Tribune*. Both newspapers feature news items as well as listings of things going on around the city, TV pages, emergency numbers, duty pharmacies and other useful information.

Radio

Though there are no English-language radio stations in Greece, many play a wide range of British and American music, not to mention just about every other type, Greek and other; just zap through the stations until you find one you like.

For news bulletins in English, tune in to the following: Antenna 97.2FM at 8.25am daily; Flash 96FM at 8.55am, 3pm and 8pm daily; ERA 91.6FM at 5am, 9am and 9.30pm daily. No radio station broadcasts English-language traffic news.

Television

There are three state-run TV channels in Greece (ET1, NET and ET3) and a number of private channels, in addition to CNN International. While the state channels offer high-quality news and sports coverage and documentaries, the private stations tend to go for a tabloid style of news reporting. Their programming also includes soaps and the usual quiz, talent and reality shows. Both state-run and private TV channels feature

many familiar foreign programmes and films, mostly late at night and weekends, and they're usually subtitled rather than dubbed. You'll find listings in the newspapers mentioned above.

Money

The currency of Greece is the euro. Notes in circulation are €5, €10, €20, €50, €100, €200 and €500, while coins come in denominations of €1, €2, and in 1, 2, 5, 10, 20 and 50 cents.

ATMs

ATMs are widely available in Athens. Most accept Visa and MasterCard (you'll pay interest on cash withdrawals) as well as debit cards of international networks such as Cirrus and Maestro.

Banks

Most banks are open 8am-2.30pm Mon-Thur and 8am-2pm Fri. Selected branches of some, like Alpha, are open until 8pm.

Alpha Bank *Panepistimiou 3, Historic Centre (210 324 1023/www.alpha.gr). Metro Syntagma.* **Open** 8am-2.30pm Mon-Thur; 8am-2pm Fri. **Map** p252 E5. For general enquiries, call 210 326 0000 (lost credit cards 210 339 7250). **Other locations:** Filellinon 6, Plaka (210 323 8542).

Eurobank's 'Open 24' *Leof Kifisias 44, Ambelokipi (210 955 5794). Metro Ambelokipi.* **Open** 10am-6pm Mon, Wed; 9am-8pm Tue, Thur, Fri; 9am-5pm Sat. Not actually open 24 hours, but still good for an evening visit. **Other locations:** Sofokleous 7-9, Omonia (210 321 4811).

National Bank of Greece (NBG) *Karagiorgi Servias 6, Historic Centre (210 334 0500/lost credit cards 210 483 4100). Metro Syntagma.* 8am-2.30pm Mon-Thur; 8am-2pm Fri. **Map** p249 F1. As well as the usual banking services, this location offers a foreign exchange service (9am-1pm Sat, Sun). **Other locations:** Eolou 86 (210 334 1000).

Bureaux de change

Eurocambio *Apollon 5, Plaka (210 322 1527). Metro Syntagma.* **Open** 8.30am-4.30pm Mon-Fri; 9am-2pm Sat. **Map** p249 F5/p251 F5.

Eurochange *Karagiorgi Servias, Syntagma (210 322 6236). Metro Syntagma.* **Open** 9am-8.45pm daily. **Map** p249 F5.

Credit cards

Most major cards (American Express, Diners Club, MasterCard, Visa) are accepted at hotels, department and speciality stores, and some restaurants. Ask first if you're unsure. If you lose your credit card or it is stolen, call:
American Express 210 324 4975-9 (8.30am-4pm Mon-Fri).
Diners Club 210 924 5890/210 929 0200 (24hrs daily).
MasterCard (Citibank) 210 929 0100 (24hrs daily).
Visa 210 326 3000 (24hrs daily).

Tax

Non-EU citizens travelling in Greece are entitled to a refund of the 19 per cent VAT paid on certain goods bought during their stay here. Though this doesn't apply to hotel and food bills, it does cover items such as electronic goods and jewellery, and could save you a fair amount of money. The store will provide you with a form to fill in, which you should hand to a customs officer at the airport, port or border prior to your departure.

Normally, you receive your refund by mail after you return home. This can take four to six weeks, but should you feel that you've been forgotten about, call the store where you made the purchase. If you want to collect your refund before you leave, allow plenty of time at the airport (or port, or border).

If your purchase is cumbersome or fragile, we recommend you have the store ship it home for you, in which case you only need to pay the shipping and import duties upon collection or receipt back home, if applicable.

Natural hazards

Greece lies in a seismic zone, so there are occasional earthquakes, but most are mild and result in no damage or injuries. If an earthquake occurs and you are indoors, get under a table or doorway away from windows. Do not use lifts. If you are outside, try to move to an open area to avoid any falling objects.

In extremely hot weather, avoid overexposure to the sun and drink plenty of water.

Over-the-counter remedies are available to treat jellyfish stings and mosquito bites.

Opening hours

Opening hours vary according to the business and to the season. Generally speaking, business hours are 9am-5pm Mon-Fri (8am-2pm for public offices). Most banks are open 8am-2.30pm Mon-Thur and 8am-2pm Fri,, while post offices open 8am-3pm Mon-Fri.

Shops generally open 9am-3pm Mon, Wed and Sat, and 8am-8pm Tue, Thur and Fri. Supermarkets are open 8am-9pm Mon-Fri (8am-8pm Sat). Large department and chain stores tend to keep longer hours. Bars, clubs and restaurants tend to be flexible – usually closing only when most customers have left.

Postal services

See also p228 **Couriers & shippers**.

You can buy stamps from all post offices and many kiosks. Post boxes around town are yellow, and post offices are easily spotted by their blue and yellow ELTA signs.

Post office opening hours are generally 7.30am-2pm Mon-Fri. Several central post office branches keep longer hours. The most convenient are Syntagma (7.30am-8pm Mon-Fri, 7.30am-2pm Sat, 7.30am-1.30pm Sun); Tritis Septemvriou 28 (7.30am-8pm Mon-Fri); Mitropoleos 60 (7.30am-8pm Mon-Fri); Eolou 100 (24hr automated services).

Local postage charges are approximately €0.50 for a regular letter. Within the EU, prices start at €0.65 for a simple letter. Prices are almost double for letters going outside the EU. The price for parcels going abroad ranges from €22

(in the EU) to €25 (outside EU) for small parcels, and from €95 (in the EU) to €120 (outside EU) for parcels of 20kg (45lbs).

Tip: Parcels sent abroad are inspected, so don't wrap and seal them beforehand. You can buy brown paper, soft padded envelopes and cardboard boxes at most post offices.

Poste restante/ general delivery

If you want to receive mail while in Greece but have no fixed address, you can have it sent 'poste restante' to the main post office just off Omonia (Name, Poste Restante, Eolou 100, 102 00 Athens). It may be picked up downstairs (7.30am-8pm Mon-Fri, 7.30am-2pm Sat); you must present your passport or ID card.

Religion

Greece is a Greek Orthodox society with only a smattering of other religious groups; a sizeable Catholic community is mostly centred in Athens and on the island of Syros, and there are several small but active Greek Evangelical congregations. Jewish communities were destroyed during the Holocaust in the 1940s; most Greek Jews now live in Athens. Indigenous Muslims make up about one per cent of the population and their communities are located in the north. However, in recent years immigrants have brought Islam to Athens (migrants account for around a fifth of the city's population).

Beth Shalom Synagogue
Melidoni 5, Keramikos (210 325 2823). Metro Thissio. **Map** p248 C4.

Christuskirche & The Sanctuary of St Andrew International Church
(German evangelical) *Sina 66, Kolonaki (210 361 2713). Metro Panepistimio.* **Services** (in English) 11.30am Sun. **Map** p252 G3.

St Andrew's Protestant Church
Paraschou 117, Pedion Areos (210 645 2583). Metro Victoria.

St Denis (Roman Catholic) *Omirou 9 & Panepistimiou 24, Historic Centre (210 362 3603). Metro Panepistimio.* **Map** p249 F4.

St Paul's Anglican Church,
Filellinon 29, Plaka (210 721 4906). Metro Syntagma. **Map** p249/p251 F5.

Safety & security

Though the crime rate has risen in recent years, Athens is still one of the safest cities in Europe. What crime there is tends to be of the organised variety between rival gangs. Just to be on the safe side, however, here are a few security tips:

Keep your money and other valuable items hidden away in a safe place while walking around the city, and especially on public transport. Mind your bags too.

Avoid poorly lit or dark deserted places at night.

Beware of bar hustlers. These shady characters target men out alone at night, inviting them for a drink. The unsuspecting male is then taken to a bar where he is introduced to one or more girls for whom he will be encouraged to buy drinks, before being presented with an enormous bill. If you try to dispute the price, the bar owner will probably bring in the heavies to help you recalculate. For suspect drinks, *see p187*.

Smoking

Despite the fact that Greeks are among the biggest tobacco consumers in the world, the recent European wave of campaigns against smoking seems to be making its presence felt in the country. Smoking is now banned on all public transport and in public buildings (shops, banks, post offices, public offices, schools, hospitals, etc). Some indoor restaurants have theoretical no-smoking sections.

Cigarettes are cheap in Greece and you'll find a wide range in stock in the airport duty-free shops.

Study

Language classes

There are several institutions that hold Greek language classes for foreigners in Athens. The **Athens Centre** (Archimidous 48, Pangrati, East Athens, 210 701 2268) is one of the most popular. Many teachers of Greek also offer their services in the classified ads of the *Athens News*.

Useful organisations

For information on studying in Greece, from summer courses to language lessons, visit the **Study Abroad** website (www.studyabroad.com/content/portals/Greece_port.html).

If you are interested in longer courses, the Greek Embassy in your own country will also be able to provide information on institutions, courses, prices and procedures.

Telephones

Dialling & codes

The country code for Greece is **30**. The area code must be included even if you are calling from the same area: for example, the area code for Athens is **210** (infrequently 211 or 212) and must be dialled whether you are calling from Athens or from Thessaloniki. If you are unsure, check with directory enquiries (*see below*).

Making a call

To make an international call while in Greece, first dial 00, then the country code, before dialling the rest of the number, dropping any initial zeros as necessary (as it is for all British numbers). The country code for the UK is 44; for Australia it's 61; Canada 1; the Republic of Ireland 352; New Zealand 64; South Africa 27; and the USA 1.

Public phones

The easiest way to make local or international calls is from public cardphone booths. Public payphones only take prepaid phonecards (*tilecartes*), which start at €4 and are available from post offices, OTEShops (run by the Hellenic Telephone Organisation) and kiosks. You can also make calls from some kiosk shops where the cost of your call is tallied on a meter and you pay at the end.

A cheaper way to make calls, though, is to buy pre-paid cards that work like mobile phone top-up cards. They cost the same as payphone cards, but give you more call time for your money (approximately ten minutes for a €3 card). Smile and Talk Talk are two that give good value for money. Look out for them at kiosks, but make sure you've been given the proper card.

As elsewhere in the world, hotels charge ridiculously high rates for telephone calls.

Operator services

Directory enquiries *11880.*
International operator *139.*
International enquiries *11844.*
General information – goods & services *11811.*

Mobile phones

Mobile phone connections in Greece operate on the GSM network, so if you are visitng from the USA or Canada you should check that your phone is a tri-band or you won't be able to use it. If that is the case, your best option is to buy a 'pay-as-you-go' SIM card package to use while you're in Greece. There are many competitive packages priced at around €15. Visitors from the UK will be able to use their phones here if they have agreed roaming facilities with their service provider, or the terms of their pay-as-you-go deal allow it.

Germanos, Wind, Vodafone and OTEShop mobile-phone service shops are ubiquitous and keep regular shop hours (*see p234*). The following are centrally located branches.

Germanos *Stadiou 10, Historic Centre (210 323 6000). Metro Syntagma.* **Map** p249 F5.

OTEShop *Filhellinon 4, Historic Centre (210 322 0199). Metro Syntagma.* **Map** p249 F5.

Vodafone *Stadiou 3, Historic Centre (210 322 0615-0623). Metro Syntagma.* **Map** p249 F5.

Wind *Stadiou 7, Historic Centre (210 331 8307). Metro Syntagma.* **Map** p249 F5.

Time

Athens is on East European Time. This is two hours ahead of Greenwich Mean Time, one hour ahead of Central European Time and seven hours ahead of Eastern Standard Time. Daylight Saving Time starts at the end of March and ends in late October.

Tipping

There are no hard and fast rules about tipping in Greece. Tipping is neither obligatory nor expected in taxis, but you may want to reward a particularly helpful driver. Prices in bars and cafés are so jacked up that tipping almost seems absurd. Restaurants and tavernas are another story. Here you should leave something; around 10 per cent is normal. However, some restaurants will add a service charge of up to 15 per cent to your bill. Always check to see if service has been included.

Toilets

Public toilets in Athens are few and far between and generally little-used. Your best bet is to pop into a fast-food outlet or department store. In bars and restaurants, it is best to ask.

Directory

Tourist information

The **Greek National Tourist Organisation** (GNTO) can provide details on sights, hotels and events, but not for many hours of the day or in a very convenient location (although there is a desk at the airport's Arrivals hall). GNTO offices abroad can also help.

GNTO *Syngrou 98-100, Syngrou (210 928 7050/www.gnto.gr). Metro Syngrou-Fix.* **Open** 8am-1.30pm Mon-Fri.

Visas & immigration

EU nationals, plus those of Norway and Iceland, can travel without a visa and may remain indefinitely. Non-EU visitors can stay for up to three months without a visa. For longer periods, they should consult the Greek embassy or consulate before travelling.

Non-EU visitors are allowed only one six-month extension on their visas, which can be obtained in person from the **Aliens Bureau** (Ypirisia Allodapon, Petrou Ralli 24, Tavros, 210 340 5969/5828/ 5829); it's a ten-minute walk from metro Petralona, or take bus A13, A17, B13, B17 from Zinonos (below Omonia) and get off at stop Papadopoulou.

You must apply at least four weeks prior to the expiry date stamped in your passport. Be ready to deal with considerable red tape and then pay a hefty fee. If you overstay your time, you will be hit with a huge spot fine upon departure. Greek customs officials are uncompromising – so don't even think of taking this risk.

Weights & measures

Greece uses the metric system (kilometres, kilograms, litres, etc) rather than the imperial system (miles, pounds, pints).

1 metre (m) = 3.28 feet (ft)
1 sq metre (sq m) = 1.196 sq yards
1 kilometre (km) = 0.62 miles
1 kilogram (kg) = 2.2 pounds (lb)
1 litre = 1.76 UK pints or 2.11 US pints

When to go

Climate

Summers in Athens are dry, with next to no rainfall and lots of sunshine. Between July and September temperatures hover at around 35°C (95°F), and visitors should take precautions against the sun and heat (drink lots of water, wear a hat, and so on).

Winters tend to be wet and chilly, with temperatures around the low teens (40s-50s°F) but can feel a lot colder – and occasionally drop to near zero. However, mini-heatwaves with daytime temperatures rising up into the mid 20s (70s) are not unheard of in winter.

Public holidays

Fixed
New Year's Day 1 Jan.
Epiphany 6 Jan.
Independence Day & Feast of the Annunciation 25 Mar.
Labour Day 1 May.
Dormition of the Virgin 15 Aug.
'Ochi' (No) Day 28 Oct.
Christmas 25-26 Dec.

Movable
Clean Monday 41 days before Easter.
Easter weekend Good Friday to Easter Monday.
Agiou Pnevmatos Mon 50 days after Easter.

The Greek Orthodox calendar and its Western counterpart often diverge where Easter celebrations are concerned. It's best to check ahead.

Women

Athens is quite safe, but it's best to avoid walking alone late at night in some of its dingier central districts (Omonia, Platia Vathis, Pedion Areos).

Working in Athens

In theory, EU nationals have equal rights to work and stay in Greece as long as they have a full passport. But it's best to get a resident visa and, if necessary, a work permit from the Aliens Bureau (*see above*). You must obtain a tax number (AFM) issued by your local tax office (DOY), and at the end of the financial year you will have to submit a tax form (available at a local tax office). You will also need to sign up with IKA, the Greek social security foundation, to which your employer has to make monthly contributions.

Non-EU citizens should check requirements with their local embassy/consulate.

Average climate

Month	Temp (°C/°F)		Hours of sun	Humidity (%)
Jan	10.3	50.5	4.12	68.9
Feb	10.7	51.2	4.48	68.3
Mar	12.4	54.3	5.54	66.3
Apr	16.0	60.0	7.42	62.8
May	20.7	69.2	9.24	59.5
June	25.1	77.1	11.12	53.4
July	27.9	82.2	11.42	47.6
Aug	27.7	81.8	11.00	47.3
Sept	24.2	75.5	9.12	53.7
Oct	19.4	66.9	6.42	61.9
Nov	15.5	59.9	5.06	68.9
Dec	12.2	53.9	3.54	70.1

Directory

Vocabulary

Pronunciation
a – 'a' as in cat
e – 'e' as in net
ee – 'ee' as in Greek
i – 'ee' as in feet
o – 'o' as in hot
oo – 'oo' as in fool
th – 'th' as in thin
dh – 'th' as in that

Useful words & phrases
hello – yassoo; (plural/formal)
herete or yassas
goodbye – yassoo, ya;
(plural/formal) adeeo or yassas
good morning – kalee mera
good evening – kalee spera
good night – kalee nihta
How are you? – Tee kanees?;
(plural/formal) Tee kanete?
yes – ne; no – ohi
please – parakalo
thank you – efharisto
excuse me/sorry – seegnomi
open – anihto; closed – klisto
Do you speak English? – Milate
anglika?
I don't speak Greek (very well)
– Then milao ellinika (poli kala)
I don't understand – Dhen
katalaveno
Speak more slowly, please –
Milate pio seega, parakalo

Emergencies
Help! – Voeethia!
I'm sick – Eeme arosti

I want a doctor/policeman –
Thelo ena yiatro/astinomeeko
Hospital – nosokomeeo

Accommodation
hotel – xenodhoheeo
I have a reservation – Eho kratisi
double room – dhiklino
single room – mono
double bed – dhiplo krevatee
twin beds – dheeo mona krevateea
with a bath – me banyo
with a shower – me doosh
breakfast included – me proino
air-conditioned – kleematismos

Getting around
car – aftokeeneeto; bus – leoforeeo
bus stop – stasi leoforeeou;
coach – poolman; taxi – taxi;
train – treno; trolley bus – trollei;
aeroplane – aeeroplano; airport –
aeerodhromeeo; station – stathmos

entrance – eesodhos
exit – exodhos
tickets – isiteeria
return ticket – isiteerio met
epeestrofis
(I'd like) a ticket to –
(Thaleethela) ena isiteerio ya
Where can I buy tickets? –
Pou boro n'agoraso isiteereea?
(Turn) left/right – (Strivete)
aristera/dhexeea
It's on the left/right – Eene
ekee aristera/thexeea
straight on – eftheea

Eating & drinking
I'd like to book a table for
four at nine – Thaleethela na
klino trapezi ya tessera stis enya
A table for two, please – Ena
trapezi ya dheeo, parakalo
Can I see the menu? – Boro
na dho to katalogho?
Some water – leegho nero
Waiter/waitress – servitoros/tora
The non-smoking section,
please – Stous mi kapnizontes,
parakalo
I am vegetarian – Eeme
hortofaghos
Where's the toilet? – Poo eene
ee twaleta?
That was (very) tasty – Eetane
(polee) nosteemo.
bill – logariasmo
I think you've made a mistake
on the bill – Nomizo ehete kani
lathos sto logariasmo.

Shopping
How much does this cost? –
Posso kanee afto?

Communications
phone – tilefono
stamp – gramatoseemo
letter – gramma
postcard – kartpostal
A stamp for England/the US –
Ena gramatoseemo ya tin
Angleea/Ameriki
Can I make a phone call? –
Boro na kano ena tilefonima?

Days & nights
Monday – Dheftera; Tuesday –
Treetee; Wednesday – Tetartee;
Thursday – Pemptee; Friday –
Paraskevee; Saturday – Savato;
Sunday – Kireeakee

today – seemera; tomorrow –
avreeo; morning – prooee;
afternoon – apoyevma; evening –
vradhi; night – nihta

Numbers
1 – ena; 2 – dheeo; 3 – treea; 4 –
tessera; 5 – pende; 6 – exi; 7 – efta;
8 – ohto; 9 – eneia; 10 – dhecca;
11 – endhecca; 12 – dhodhecca; 13
– dheccatreea; 14 – dheccatessera;
15 – dheccapende; 16 – dheccaexi;
17 – dheccaefta; 18 – dheccaohto;
19 – dheccaeneia; 20 – eekosi;
100 – ekato; 500 – penda-kosia;
1,000 – hilia

Times
Could you tell me the time? –
Ehete tin ora?
It's... o'clock – Eene... ee ora.
quarter past... – ...ke tetarto
quarter to... – ...para tetarto
half past... – ...ke meessee

Greek alphabet

Αα alpha	'a' as in cat	Χχ hee	'h' as in heat
Ββ vita	'v' as in vice	Ψψ psi	'ps' as in lapse
Γγ gama	'g' as in game	Ωω omega	'o' as in hot
	'y' as in yes		
Δδ thelta	'th' as in this	**Double-letter sounds**	
Εε epsilon	'e' as in net	ει epsilon-yiota-	'ee' as in
Ζζ zeta	'z' as in zebra		Greek
Ηη ita	'ee' as in Greek	οι omikron-yiota-	'ee' as in
Θθ thita	'th' as in thing		Greek
Ιι yiota	'ee' as in Greek	αι alpha-yiota	'e' as in net
Κκ kappa	'k' as in key	ου omikron-ipsilon-	'oo' as in
Λλ lamtha	'l' as in late		food
Μμ mi	'm' as in my	μπ mi-pi	'b' as in bee
Νν ni	'n' as in night	ντ ni-taf	'd' as in date
Ξξ ksi	'ks' as in rocks	γκ gama-kappa	'g' as in get
Οο omikron	'o' as in open	γγ gama-gama	'ng' as in
Ππ pi	'p' as in pet		England
Ρρ ro	'r' as in rope	γχ gama-hee	'a' as in inherent
Σσ (ς at the end		το taf-sigma	'ts' as in sets
of word) sigma	's' as in so	τζ taf-zeta	'ds' as in friends
Ττ taf	't' as in tin	αυ alpha-ipsilon	'av' as in
Υυ ipsilon	'ee' as in Greek		avenue or 'af' as in after
Φφ fi	'f' as in food	ευ epsilon-ipsilon	'ef' as in left

Further Reference

Books

Classics

Aeschylus *Agamemnon, Persians, Prometheus Bound, The Suppliants*
Aesop *Aesop's Fables*
Aristophanes *The Acharnians, The Birds, The Clouds, The Frogs, Lysistrata*
Euripides *Andromache, The Bacchae, The Cyclops, Electra, Hecuba*
Homer *The Iliad, The Odyssey*
Pausanias *Description of Greece*
Plutarch *The Rise and Fall of Athens*
Sophocles *Antigone, Electra, Oedipus the King*
Thucydides *History of the Peloponnesian War*

Fiction

Maro Douka *Fool's Gold*
The story of a young woman who becomes involved with the resistance movement, and her reaction to the events of 17 November 1973.
Eugenia Fakinou
The Seventh Garment
The lives of three generations of Greek women reflect the history of the country, from the Asia Minor catastrophe, to modern Athens.
Panos Karnezis *Little Infamies*
A collection of colourful stories set in an unnamed Greek village.
Nikos Kazantzakis
At the Palaces of Knossos
The author of *Zorba the Greek* mixes fact and fiction in this tale about the fall of Minoan Crete at the hands of the emerging city of Athens.
Alexandros Kotzias *Jaguar*
In 1964 the wife and sister of a hero killed in the resistance meet in Athens and share recollections of the main events in their lives, from the German occupation to the civil war.
Olivia Manning
The Balkan Trilogy
(Volume 3: Friends and Heroes)
A young married couple flees war-torn Romania for Athens, where they have to contend with more historical turmoil. Made into a TV series *(Fortunes of War)*.
Kostas Mourselas *Red Dyed Hair*
This bestselling novel focuses on the lives of a group of marginalised Piraeus dwellers.
José Carlos Somoza
The Athenian Murders
When a student of Plato's Academy is found dead, foul play is suspected and Heracles sets about investigating the case. To make things murkier, a literary mystery unfolds within the murder mystery.

Non-fiction

Mary Beard *The Parthenon*
Beard demystifies the sacred temple.
AR Burn
The Penguin History of Greece
A useful intro to ancient Greece.
Brian Church
Learn Greek in 25 Years
A tongue-in-cheek crash course for the linguistically challenged.
James Davidson *Courtesans and Fishcakes: The Consuming Passions of Classical Athens*
Sex, gluttony and booze.
Diana Farr Louis *Athens and beyond: 30 Day Trips & Weekends*
Knowledgeable guide that reveals the stories behind the landscapes.
Michael Grant & John Hazel
Who's Who in Classical Mythology
A thorough compendium of mythological personalities.
John Henderson & Mary Beard
Classics: A Very Short Introduction
How the classics have influenced our lives.
Gail Holst *Road to Rembetika: Songs of Love, Sorrow and Hashish*
Excellent backgrounder on the blues of the Balkans and its singers.
Diane Kochilas
The Glorious Foods of Greece
A journey through Greece's rich regional cuisine, with recipes.
Konstantinos Lazarakis
The Wines of Greece
From agiorgitiko to xinomavro.
Michael Llewellyn-Smith *Athens: A Cultural and Literary History*
Former UK ambassador's engaging introduction to the capital's history and culture, ancient and modern.
Molly Mackenzie *Turkish Athens*
The history of Athens during its four centuries of Ottoman occupation.
David Sacks, et al *A Dictionary of the Ancient Greek World*
One-stop volume detailing the people, places and events that shaped the ancient Greek civilisation.
William St Clair
Lord Elgin and the Marbles
The ultimate volume about the marbles that were taken in 1801.
Mikis Theodorakis
Journals of Resistance
The Greek composer and activist's journal during the years of the Junta.

Films

For more films, *see pp168-171*.

Brides (Nyfes)
(Pantelis Voulgaris, 2004)
Set in the early 20th century, when many Greek women were sent by boat to arranged marriages, a Greek woman who falls in love with an American photographer during her voyage to the United States.
The Dawn (To Harama)
(Alexis Bistiskas, 1994)
A Star is Born set in Athens, complete with Greek ballads.
Edge of Night (Afti i Nighita Meni)
(Nikos Panagiotopoulos, 2000)
This film follows the ambitions of Stella, a young Athenian girl who dreams of becoming a famous singer.
End of an Era (Telos Epochis)
(Antonis Kokkinos, 1994)
An old man reminisces on his coming of age in Athens in the late 1960s.
From the Edge of the City
(Apo tin Akri tis Polis)
(Konstantinos Giannaris, 1998)
A tale of sex and drugs set in the immigrant ghettos bordering Athens.
Hard Goodbyes: My Father
(Dhiskoli Apoheretismi: O Babas Mou)
(Penny Panayotopoulou, 2002)
In the late 1960s a young Athenian boy struggles to come to terms with the death of his father.
Never on Sunday (Pote tin Kyriaki)
(Jules Dassin, 1960)
A US intellectual tries to reform a prostitute from Piraeus, believing her to be emblematic of the fall of the great Greek civilisation.
Rembetiko
(Costas Ferris, 1984)
Traces the fortunes of a female rembetika singer in Athens, from her childhood in the days of the Asia Minor population exchange (1922) to her rise to fame and eventual decline.
A Touch of Spice (Politiki Kouzina)
(Tassos Boulmetis, 2003)
The story of a Greek boy who, with his parents, is forced to leave Istanbul during the deportations of 1964, with a focus on cooking and family.

Websites

www.athensnews.gr
The site for Athens' weekly English-language magazine. Good for features and news.
www.ekathimerini.com
The internet version of Athens' daily English-language paper. A good resource for general information.
www.culture.gr
From archaeological sites, museums and monuments to cultural events, the Culture Ministry portal highlights the artistic riches of Greece.
www.gnto.gr
The site of the Greek National Tourist Organisation offers information on where to stay and what to visit.
www.gogreece.com
Loads of well-catalogued links on myriad subjects, from arts to travel.

Directory

Index

Note: Page numbers in
bold indicate section(s)
giving key information
on a topic; *italics* indicate
photographs.

a

abortion 230
accommodation 40-58
best, the 43
by price:
budget 43-45, 47-49, 50,
52, 54
deluxe 45-46, 49, 52, 55,
56-57
expensive: 40-41, 46, 49-
50, 50-51, 55-56, 57
moderate: 41-43, 46, 50,
51-52, 54, 56
see also p243
Accommodation
index
Academy of Athens 31,
77, **81**
Acciaioli, Nerio 18
accident & emergency 230
Achilles 36
Acrocorinth 214
Acropolis Museum 66
Acropolis 14, 25, 36, 60,
64-68, *65*, 167
Acropolis & around
(area) 60, **62-76**
cafés 133-134
gay & lesbian bars
& clubs 176
nightlife 188
restaurants 111-113
where to stay 40-45
Acropolis Rally 162, *163*
active sports 196-198
addresses 228
Adrianou *68*, 69
Adventure Park 167
Aegina 219
AEK Athens 195
Aeschylus **14**, 202
Agamemnon, King
216, 217
age restrictions 228
Agia Ekaterini *see* Church
of St Catherine
Agia Sophia 164
Agia Triada *see* Church
of the Holy Trinity
Agias Irini 181
Agio Georgios 164
Agios Dionysos 181
Agios Kosmas 103,
104, 166
Agnanti 106
Agora *see* Ancient Agora
Agora Walkway 34

**air, arriving & leaving
by** 224
airlines 224
airport 224
Alcibiades 16
Alexander 171
Alexander the Great *12*,
17, 25
Alimos 166
Allou! Fun Park 167
alphabet, Greek 237
Ambelokipi 61, **88**
Anafiotika 69, **70**, 73
Anaxagoras 15
Ancient Agora 60,
62, **75**
**ancient buildings
in Athens**
monuments: Hadrian's
Arch 18, **83**, 85;
Lysicrates Monument
31, 62, **71**, 72
temples: Parthenon **30**,
36, 62, **65**, *65*; Temple
of Athena Nike 31,
65; Temple of
Olympian Zeus 18, 32,
63, **83**, 85
theatres: Odeon of
Herodes Atticus 18,
32, 60, 62, **66**, 181,
199, 200; Theatre
of Dionysus 31, 60,
62, **66**
other: Ancient Agora 60,
62, **75**; Areopagus 66;
Erechtheum 31, *60*,
66; Hadrian's Library
30, 32, 73, 75, **76**;
Hephaestum 76; Pnyx
69; Propylaeum 31,
64; Roman Forum 32,
62, 73, **74**; Tower of
the Winds 17, 32, 62,
73, **74**
Ancient Corinth 13, 213,
213, **215**
Ancient Eleusis
205, 206
Ancient Epidaurus
213, **218**
Ancient Mycenae 213,
215, **216**
Antigonos 17
antiques shops 158
Anti-Racism Festival 163
Aphrodite 37, **38**
Apokries 165
Apollo **38**, 212
Apostolou Pavlou 64
Arachova 212
Archaeological Museum
of Piraeus 101

Archaic Age **13**, 25
Archimedes 25
Ardittou Hill 84
Areopagus 13, 18, **66**
Ares 36, **38**
Argonauts 37
Aristophanes **14**, 202
Aristotle **15**, 16, 25
Artemis 38
Asclepius 36
Asteria 103, **105**
Astir Beach 103, *104*, **106**
Athena 12, **36**, 207, 212
'Athenian Riviera' 99
Athens Book Fair 165
**Athens Cathedral
(Mitropolis) 69**, 164
Athens Concert Hall 181
Athens Conservatory 33
Athens Dance Festival 201
Athens Festival 162,
166, 181, **199**, *199*
Athens First Cemetery
84, **96**
Athens International Film
Festival 163
Athens Marathon 165
Athens Olympic Sports
Complex *97*, 98
Athens Polytechnic 31,
87, **88**
Athens Pride 175
Athens State Orchestra
182
Athinais 94
Athinas, shopping in 141
ATMs 233
**Attica & the Mainland
205-212**
where to stay 57
Attica (department store)
140
Attica Vouliagmeni Beach
103, **106**
Attica Zoological Park 167
attitude 228
Augustus, Emperor **17**,
25, 32

b

baklava 138
Bakoyianni, Dora 24
Balkan Wars (1912-13) 25
ballet 201
banks 233
bars 187-193
gay & lesbian 176
basketball 195
**Bathhouse of the
Winds** 62, **71**, 74
Battleship Averoff 99
beaches 103-106
'Athenian Riviera' 99

in Attica 206
best, the 103
for children 167
clubs 190
gay & lesbian 178
Benaki Museum 34, 86, **87**
Benaki Museum of Islamic
Art 92
Benaki Museum, Pireos
Street Annexe 91, *93*,
94, 95, 172, 181
Bios **94**, 95, **192**
boat, arriving & leaving
by 224
books 238
festival 165
gay & lesbian 178
shops 142
bouzoukia 185, 186
breakdown services 227
Bronze Age 25
bungee jumping 196
bureaux de change 233
buses 225
business services 228
Byron, Lord 72, 81,
207, **209**
Byzantine architecture
in Athens 19, 32
Byzantine chant 179
Byzantine Museum
19, **82**
Byzantium 18, **19**

c

cafés 133-139
best, the 134
gay & lesbian 175
see also p244 Cafés
index
Calatrava, Santiago 34
Camerata Friends of
Music 181, **182**
Cape Sounion 205, *205*,
207, *208*
car hire 227
car, getting around by 227
Carnival season 165
Catalans 18
cats, stray 67
Central Market 78
Centre for Folk Art &
Tradition 71
Chaironeia (338BC), Battle
of **17**, 25
Chalcis 13
chapel of St George 66
children 166-167
shops 142
Christianity 18
Christmas 165
Church of St Catherine 19,
71, 72, 164

Church of St Dimitrios
  Loumbardiaris 68, **69**
Church of St George of
  the Rock 73
Church of St John of the
  Column 79
Church of St Marina 76
Church of St Theodore
  19, **78**
Church of the Holy Trinity
  19, **71**, 72, 164
Church of the
  Transfiguration of the
  Saviour 72
Churchill, Winston **22**, 25
cinemas 169-170
  for children 167
  summer 169
City of Athens Museum
  78, **79**
CityLink *33*, 34
Civil War (1944-49) **22**, 25
Classical Age 14
classical music 180-182
Cleisthenes 13
climate 236
clinics, private health 231
Clock of Andronikos of
  Kyrrhos *see* Tower of
  the Winds
clubs 187-193
  gay & lesbian 176
coach, arriving & leaving
  by 224
coffee 135
  shops 153
Communists 22
computer shops and
  repairs 142
Constantine, Emperor
  18, 25
Constantine, King 22
consulates 229
consumer information 229
contraception 230
conventions & conferences
  228
Corinth Canal 21, 25,
  214
Corinth, Ancient 13,
  213, *213*, **215**
cosmetics, natural 158
couriers 228
credit cards 233
Cronus 36
Cultural Centre of Athens
  78, **79**
customs 229
cycling 227
Cyclops 36

d

dance 201
  festivals 162, 201, 202
Daphne Monastery 19, **206**
Darius 14, 25
Delian League **14**, 16, 25
Delphi 205, *211*, **212**
  Oracle of 35, 212

Demeter 36, **38**
Demetrios 'the Besieger'
  17
demonstrations, public 80
Demosthenes 16, 17, 25
dentists 230
department stores 140
designer fashion shops
  143
Despotopoulos, Ionnis 33
Deste Foundation Centre
  for Contemporary Art
  172
Dexameni 86, **170**
Diogenes 17
Dionysiou Areopagitou 74
Dionysus 38
directory 223-244
disabled visitors 229
discount fashion shops
  144
dogs, stray 67
Dora Stratou Garden
  Theatre 69
Draco 13
drama, ancient Greek 202
drugs 229
dry cleaning 147

e

**east Athens & eastern
  suburbs** 96-97
  cafés 139
  nightlife 193
  restaurants 127
Easter Week 162, **164**
Edem Beach 103
Eden Beach 206
Educational and Cultural
  Park 34
EEC **23**, 25
electricity 229
electronics shops 142
Elefsina 205
Eleusian mysteries 36
**Eleusis, Ancient
  205**, 206
Elgin, Thomas Bruce,
  Earl of 21, 25, 28, 65
Elgin Marbles 23, **28**
embassies 229
emergencies 230
Emfietzoglou Collection
  172
entechno 185, 186
**Epidaurus, Ancient
  Theatre of** 199,
  213, **218**
Epigraphical Museum 88
Epiphany 165
Erechtheum 31, *60*, **66**
Eretria 13
Erichthonius 36
Ermou 78, *78*, **141**
Eros 36
Ethniki Lyriki Skini
  (Greek National Opera)
  180, 182
etiquette 228, **231**

Euclid 25
Euripides 14, 202
Eurobaby 166
Evgenidio Planetarium
  99, 167
Exarchia 61, **87-90**

f

Faliro **99**, 166
fashion shops 144-147,
  150-151
  accessories & services
  147-152
  children's 142
  designers 150
Fates, the 36
**festivals & events
  162-165**
  carnival 165
  drama 162
  dance 162
  film 162
  literature 165
  music: classical & opera
  162
  music: jazz, rock & roots
  162, 163
  photography 165
  sport 162, 163, 165
  traditional 162, 164, 165
Fethiye Tzami 32
film 168-171, 238
  festivals 163, 175
flea markets 146
folk music 184
food & drink shops 153
football 195, **196**, 197
Forum *see* Roman Forum
Foundation of the Hellenic
  World **94**, 167
Frederick II of Sicily 18
Frissiras Museum **71**, 172
funicular 86
Furies, the 36

g

Gaia Centre 99
galleries 172-174 *see
  also* museums &
  galleries
Gärtner, Friedrich von
  31, 77
Gate of Athena Archegetis
  32
gay & lesbian 175-178
  best, the 175
  Film Festival 175
  resources 230
Gazi 61, 91, **93-95**
  nightlife 188
Gennadius Library 86
George I **21-22**, 25
George II 22
gift & souvenir shops 154
Glyfada *98*, **99**, 161, 166
  shopping in 141
GNTO 236
Gods, Greek 35-37, **38**

Golden Age of Athens 14
Goulandris Museum of
  Natural History 99
'Great Idea', the 21
Greater Athens 96-99
Greek Children's Museum
  166, 167
Greek Costume Museum
  86, **87**
Greek Dark Age 12
**Greek Myth & Legend
  35-38**
Greek National Opera
  180, 182
Greek Orthodox Church 25
**Greek popular music
  185-186**
Greek speciality food
  shops 153
Gropius, Walter 33
Guy I 18
gyms 196

h

Hades 36, **38**
Hadrian, Emperor **18**, 25,
  32, 83
Hadrian's Arch 18, **83**, 85
Hadrian's Library *30*,
  32, 73, 75, **76**
hairdressers & barbers
  156
Hansen, Hans Christian
  & Theophilus **31**, 77,
  81, 83
hat shops 148
hazards, natural 233
health 230
health & beauty shops
  & services 156
Helen of Troy 37
Helios 36
Hellenic American Union
  172
Hellenic Festival 199
Hellenic Group of
  Contemporary Music
  182
Hellenic Maritime
  Museum 102
Hellenistic Age 17
helplines 232
Hephaestum 76
Hephaestus 36, **38**
Hera 35, 36, **38**
Hercules 36
Hermes 38
Herodeion *see* Odeon
  of Herodes Atticus
Herodes Atticus 66
Herodotus 14
Hesiod 35, 36, 37, **38**
Hippias 13, 14
Historic Centre 60,
  77-85
  cafés 134-136
  nightlife 189
  restaurants 114-116
  where to stay 45-49

Historic Triangle 60, **77-82**
history 12-25
holidays, public 236
Homer 12, 25, 35, 36, 216
hotels *see* accommodation
house & home shops 158
Hydra 219, *220*, **221**
Hypnos 36

ID 232
Iktinos 30
Iliad, The 12, 25, 35, 216
Ilias Lalaounis Jewellery
Museum 74
immigration **29**, 236
Independence Day Parade
165
insurance 232
International Aegean
Sailing Rally 163
International Month of
Photography 165
internet 232
ISAP 225
island escapes
219-222

Jason 37
jazz music 184
jewellery shops 148
Jewish Museum 71
Junta, the **22-23**, 25
Justinian I, Emperor 18,
19, 25, 32

Kaftandzoglou, Lysandros
31
Kaisariani Monastery 97
Kalamata International
Dance Festival 201, **202**
Kallidromiou 87, *88*
Kallikrates 30
Kapnikarea 19, 78,
79, *81*
Kapodistrias, Ioannis
21, 25
Karamanlis, Costas 24
Karamanlis, Konstantine
23
Karathonas 217
Kavouri-Vouliagmeni 105
Keramikos 61, 63, 91,
92-93, *92*
Kifissia 61, **98**, 166
shopping in 141
Kleanthis, Stamatios 77
Klenze, Leo von **33**, 77
Kolokotronis, Theodoros
96
Kolonaki & around
61, **86-90**
cafés 136-139
nightlife 189-192
shopping in 141

restaurants 117-122
where to stay 49-50
Koukaki 74

Labour Day 162
Lake Marathon 205, **210**
Lake Vouliagmeni 99
Lalaounis, Ilias 74
Lambros 106
language 232, 237
classes 235
Larissa Station 224
laundry 147
Lausanne (1923), Treaty
of **20**, 22, 25
Lavrio 205, **207**
Lavrion Museum 208
legal help 232
legends, Greek 35-38
Legrena 206
lesbian *see* gay & lesbian
libraries 232
Limanakia 178
Limanakia A & B 106
lingerie shops 148
Lombarda Beach 206
Long Walls 15
lost property 232
luggage, left 232
luggage shops 149
Lycabettus Hill 61, **86**
Lycabettus Theatre 86,
181, **183**, *184*
Lysicrates Monument 31,
62, **71**, 72

Macedonians 25
magazines 233
shops 142
mageirion 111
Makrygianni 60, 62, **74**
Makrygiannis, Yiannis 74
Mall, The 98, **140**
malls 140
Marathon 14, **210**
Marathon (490BC), Battle
of **14**, 25, **210**
Maria Callas Museum 94
markets 78, **140**, **146**
Marousi 61, **98**
Maximos Mansion **82**, 84
Medea 37
media 233
Medusa 37
Megali Evdomada 162,
164
Megalo Kavouri 106
Megaron Mousikis *179*,
180
Melina Mercouri Cultural
Centre 76
Mercouri, Melina 23, 28,
69, 76, 96
Metamorphosi Sotiros 164
Metaxas, General Ioannis
22, 25

Metaxourgio 91
Metro, Athens *27*, 225
Mets **84**, 96
mezodopolia 108, **109**
mini-soccer 197
Minotaur 37
**Mitropolis (Athens
Cathedral)** 69, 164
mobile phones 235
Monastiraki 60, 62, **75**
Flea Market 62, *75*, **76**,
140, **146**
shopping in 141
Monastiraki Square 75
money 233
Mosque of Tzidarakis
32, 76
Mount Hymettos 96, **97**
Mount Olympus 36
Muses, the 36
Museum of 20th Century
Design 98
Museum of Ancient
Cypriot Art 94
Museum of Cycladic Art
77, **87**
Museum of Greek Folk
Art **71**, 72
Museum of Greek Musical
Instruments **71**, 73, 167
Museum of Traditional
Greek Ceramics 32, 73,
75, **76**
museums & galleries
archaeology: Acropolis
Museum 66;
Archaeological
Museum of Piraeus
101; Bios **94**, 95, **192**;
Byzantine Museum
19, **82**; Epigraphical
Museum 88; National
Archaeological
Museum *35*, 87, *87*,
90; New Acropolis
Museum 26, 28, 34, **74**
applied art: Benaki
Museum 34, 86, **87**;
Benaki Museum of
Islamic Art 92;
Museum of Ancient
Cypriot Art 94;
Museum of Cycladic
Art 77, **87**
art: Athinais 94; Benaki
Museum, Pireos Street
Annexe 91, *93*, **94**, 95,
172, 181; Deste
Foundation Centre
for Contemporary Art
172; Emfietzoglou
Collection 172;
Frissiras Museum
71, 172; National
Gallery 96
ceramics: Museum of
Traditional Greek
Ceramics 32, 73,
75, **76**

children: Greek
Children's Museum
166, 167; Spathario
Museum of Shadow
Puppets 167
coins: Numismatic
Museum 78, **81**
costume: Greek Costume
Museum 86, **87**
design: Museum of 20th
Century Design 98
folk art/tradition: Centre
for Folk Art &
Tradition 71; Museum
of Greek Folk Art
71, 72
history: City of Athens
Museum 78, **79**;
National Historical
Museum 78, **79**;
National War
Museum **83**, 167
jewellery: Ilias Lalaounis
Jewellery Museum 74
Judaism: Jewish
Museum 71
Maria Callas: Maria
Callas Museum 94
maritime: Hellenic
Maritime Museum 102
music: Museum of Greek
Musical Instruments
71, 73, 167
natural history:
Goulandris Museum
of Natural History 99
see also galleries
music
Greek popular music
181, **185-186**
jazz, rock & roots
182-186
festivals 162, 163
sacred music, classical
& opera 179-182
festivals 162
shops 159
Mycenae, Ancient 213,
215, **216**
Myceneans **12**, 25
myth, Greek 35-38

Nafplio 21, 213, *216*,
217
Nansen, Fridtjof 20
**National
Archaeological
Museum** *35*, 87, *87*, **90**
National Gallery 96
National Gardens 60,
83, 84, *84*, 166
National Historical
Museum 78, **79**
National Library 31, 34,
77, **81**
National Lyric Theatre 34
National Museum of
Contemporary Art 34

National Observatory 68
National Theatre 77, **200**
National University 31, 77, **81**
National War Museum **83**, 167
Neapoli 88
Nemea 213, **215**
Nemean Games 215
Nemesis **36**, 211
Neo-Classical University Complex 31, 78, **81**, *82*
Nero, Emperor **17**, 25, 214
New Acropolis Museum 26, 28, 34, **74**
New Year 165
newspapers 233
Nicias (421BC), Peace of 16
nightlife 187-193
see also p244 Bars & clubs index
north of the Acropolis (area) 61, **91-95**
cafés 139
gay & lesbian bars & clubs 177
nightlife 192
restaurants 123-126
where to stay 50-52
north Athens
where to stay 54
northern suburbs 97
cafés 139
nightlife 193
restaurants 129-132
where to stay 56-57
Notos Galleries 140
Numismatic Museum 78, **81**

O

OASA (Athens Urban Transport Organisation) 225
Odeon of Herodes Atticus 18, 32, 60, 62, **66**, 181, *199*, 200
Odyssey, The 12, 25, 35, 216
Oedipus 36
office services 229
Ohi Day 165
Old Palace 31
Olympiacos Piraeus 195
Olympic Complex 34, **98**
Olympic Games 22, **24**, *24*, 25, 26
Olympic Stadium 34
Omonia Square 61
open-air theatres 199
opening hours 234
opera 182
opticians 156
oracles 35
Orchestra of Colours 182
Oropos Water Park 167
Orpheus 36
Osios Loukas 212
Othon de la Roche 18

Otto I **21**, 25, 77
Ottoman Turks 18-21
ouzerie 109

P

Palaia Epidavro 213
Palamidi Fortress 213, **217**, 218
Palea Fokea 207
Paleo Psychiko 97
Pan 36, *37*
Panaghia Gorgoepikoos 32
Panathenaic Stadium 77, 84, **96**, *197*
Panathenea festival 36
Panathinaikos 195
Pandora 37
Pangrati 96
Papagou 97
Papandreou, Andreas 22-24
Papandreou, George 24
parking 227
Parliament Building 77, **81**, *83*, 166
Parnassos Literary Society 182
Parthenon 28, **30**, 36, 62, **65**, *65*
PASOK 23, 24
pastries, Greek 138
Pax Romana **17**, 25
Pedion Areos 88
Peloponnesian Folklore Foundation **217**, 218
Peloponnesisan War **15**, 25
Peloponnisou Station 224
Peloponnese, North-east 213-218
Pericles 14-15, 25, 30, 31, 62, 64, 65
Perseus 37
Persian Wars 14, 25
Peter IV of Aragón 18
Petralona 62
petrol stations 227
pharmacies 156, 231
Phidias 15, 30, 65
Philip II of Macedonia **17**, 25
Philopappus Hill 60, 62, **68**
phones 235
photography shops 143
Pindar 14
Piraeus 61, **100-102**, *100*, *102*
cafés 139
nightlife 193
restaurants 132
where to stay 57
Pireos Street Annexe 91, **94**
Pisistratos 13
Plaka 60, 62, **69**, *72*, 166
nightlife 188
shopping 141
walk 72

Platia Dexamenis 86
Platia Exarchia 89
Platia Filomousou 72
Platia Klafthmonos 78, **82**
Platia Kolonaki 86, **89**
Plato 14, **15**, 16, 25, 68
Pnyx 69
polykatoikia 33
Poros 219, *221*, **222**
Poseidon 12, 36, **38**, 207
postal services 234
poste restante 234
prescriptions 231
Presidential Palace 77, **82**, 84
Prometheus 37
Propylaeum 31, **64**
Psyrri 61, **91**

R

radio 233
Rafina 209
rail, arriving & leaving by 224
religion 234
rembetika **181**, 185
resources A-Z 228-236
restaurants 108-132
bar-restaurants 117-118, 123
best, the 111
creative 111, 114, 118-119, 123-124, 129-130
fast food 124
French 115, 119, 127
gay & lesbian 176
Greek contemporary 112, 119, 124, 128, 130-132
Greek traditional 112-113, 115-116, 120-121, 124, 128-129
Italian 121, 129
Japanese 113, 122
Mediterranean 116, 122, 129
menu, the 126
Middle Eastern 122
Seafood 122, 125, 127, 132
Thai 126
Turkish 132
with views 116
see also p243 Restaurants index
Rhamnous 211
Rhea 36
Riviera cinema 88, **170**
Rockwave Festival **163**, 182
Roman Forum 32, 62, 73, **74**
Romans **17-18**, 25
Rouf 91
Royal Palace **81**, 86
running 197

S

safety & security 234
St Paul *16*, **18**, 25
Salamis, Battle of 14
Sanctuary of Apollo, Delphi 205, *211*, **212**
Sanctuary of Artemis Brauron, Vravrona 205, **208**, 209
Sanctuary of Athena, Cape Sounion 207
Sanctuary of Athena, Delphi 212
Sanctuary of Poseidon, Cape Sounion 14, *205*, **207**
Saronida 207
saunas, gay & lesbian 178
Schaubert, Edouard 77
Schinias Beach 211
Schliemann, Heinrich 21, 66, 78, 81, **216**
School of Fine Arts 172
scuba diving 197
Second Athenian Confederacy 17
secretarial services 229
Selene 36
17 November 165
Shelley, Percy Bysshe 72
shippers 228
shipping 159
shoe repairs 152
shoe shops 149
shops & services 140-160
sightseeing 59-106
for children 166
Simitis, Costas 24
Skoufa 89
smoking 234
Socrates 14, **15**, 16, 25, 68
Solon **13**, 25
Sophocles **14**, 15, 25, 202
Sounion 207, *208*
south Athens
where to stay 52
southern suburbs 99
cafés 139
nightlife 193
restaurants 128-129
where to stay 55-56
souvenir shops 154
Sparta in film 171
Spartans 14-17, 25
spas & salons 156
Spatario Museum of Shadow Puppets 167
spectator sports 195
Spetses 219, **220**
sport & fitness 194-198
events 162, 163, 165
shops 159
Stoa of Attalos 17, **76**
Strefi Hill 87
study 235
suburban railway 225

suburbs 96-99
Sulla 17, 25
summer clubs 190
supermarkets 153
support groups 232
swimming 198
swimwear shops 148
Syngrou & southern suburbs 26, 34, **99**
Syntagma Square 60, **141**

t

tavernas **108**, **114**
tax 233
taxis 226
Technopolis 34, 63, 91, 93, **94**, 95, 172
telephones 235
television 233
temperature 236
Temple of Athena Nike 31, **65**
Temple of Nemesis, Rhamnous 211
Temple of Olympian Zeus 18, 32, 63, **83**, 85
tennis 198
ten-pin bowling 198
theatre & dance 199-202
festivals 162, 199, 202
Theatre of Dionysus 31, 60, 62, **66**
Thebes 17
theme parks 167
Themistoclean Wall 78
Themistocles 14
Theodosius, Emperor 25, 32
Theogony 35
Theseion 76
Theseus 37
Thirty Tyrants, the 16
Thissio 60, 64, **76**
Thorikos 205, **208**
300 (film) 171, *171*
Thucydides 14, 15
time 235
tipping 235
Tiryns **217**, 218
Titans, the 36
toilets 235
Tomb of Philopappus 68
Tomb of the Unknown Soldier 81
tourist information 236
tours, guided 61
Tower of the Winds 17, 32, 62, 73, **74**
toy shops 142
trams 225
translation services 229
transport, public 225
travel advice 228
travel agencies 159
trekking 198
Trojan War 25, 36, 216, 217

trolleybuses 225
Troy 12, 25
Troy Mansion 31, **81**
Tschumi, Bernard 28, 34
Turkish-Greek exchange of populations **20**, 29
Turks 18-21, 25

u

Unification of Archaeological Sites walkway 62, **63**, 92
Uranus 36
US Embassy 33

v

Valerian, Emperor 18
Varkiza 206
Varkiza Beach 103, **106**
Velodrome 34
Venetians **18-19**, 25
Venizelos, Eleftherios **22**, 25
vintage & used fashion shops 144
visas 236
vocabulary 237
Voula **99**, 166
Voula A & Voula B 105
Vouliagmeni 61, **99**
Vravrona 205
Vyronas Festival 162

w

walking 227
Unification of Archaeological Sites walkway 62, **63**
Walk 1: Exploring the old Plaka 72
Walk 2: Gardens & Monuments 84
Walk 3: Following the (flea) market 146
Wall of Nations 34
War of Independence **21**, 25
weather 236
weights & measures 236
western suburbs nightlife 193
wine & spirits shops 154
wines, Greek 130
women 236
working in Athens 236
World War I **22**, 25
World War II **22**, 25

x

Xerxes I 14

z

Zappeion **83**, *84*, 85
Zenetos, Takis 34
Zeus 35, **36**, 37, **38**
Ziller, Ernst **31**, 77, 78, 82
zoos 167

Accommodation

Acropolis House 43
Acropolis Select Hotel 41
Adrian Hotel **41**, 47
Alassia 43, **51**, 53
Anita Argo Hotel 57
Art Gallery Hotel 42
Astir Palace Resort 43, **55**
Astir Palace Vouliagmeni 53, **55**, *55*
Athenaeum InterContinental 43, **52**
Athenian Callirhoe 40, *40*
Athens Art Hotel 43, **51**, 53, *54*
Athens Backpackers 43
Athens Hilton 34, 43, 47, **49**, *51*, *194*, 198
Athens Imperial 52
Baby Grand Hotel 43, **46**, *49*, 53
Cecil Hotel 46
Divani Apollon Palace & Spa 43, **55**
Divani Palace Acropolis **41**, 47
Electra Palace **41**, 47
Emmantina Hotel 56
Eridanus 43, 47, **52**, 95
Fivos 43, **49**
Fresh Hotel 43, **46**, 53
Glaros Hotel 57
Grand O' Hotel 46
Grande Bretagne 22, 43, **45**, *45*, 47, 77
Hera Hotel **42**, 47
Hermes Hotel 42
Herodian **41**, *42*
Holiday Inn 198
Hostel Aphrodite 54
Hotel Adonis 43
Hotel Arion 43, **51**
Hotel Carolina 47
Hotel Dioskouos 45
Hotel Omega 52
Hotel Orion & Dyrades 50
Jason Inn 43, **52**
King George Palace 43, **46**, 47
King Jason Hotel 52
Life Gallery 43, 53, **56**
Magna Grecia 42
Margi 55
Metropolitan Hotel 56
Mistral Hotel 57
Ochre & Brown 43, **50**, 53, *53*
Oscar Hotel 54
Park Hotel 57
Park Hotel Athens 43, **49**
Pentelikon 43, **56**
Periscope 43, **50**, 53
Philippos Hotel 41
Plaka 43
Poseidon Hotel 43, **56**
Residence Georgio 51
Savoy 57
Semiramis 43, 53, *56*, **57**
Sofitel Athens Airport 57

St George Lycabettus 47, **50**, 86
Student & Traveller's Inn 45
Theoxenia Hotel 57
Twentyone 43, **57**
Xenos Lycabettus 43, **50**

Restaurants

Aioli 129
Alatsi 120, *128*
Alexandria 122
Aneton 111, **130**
Apia 111, **131**
Athinaikon 115
Bakaliko de Toute Façon 122
Bakaliko Ola Ta Kala 128
Balthazar **117**, 189
Bar Guru Bar 126
Brachera 117
Café Abyssinia 112, *112-113*
Cellier Le Bistrot 115, *118*
Chryssa 125
Cibus *116*, 120
Coukou Food 176
Dexameni 120
Diasimos 111, **132**
Diporto 115
Doris 115
Filistron 117
48 The Restaurant 111, **118**, 121
Freud Oriental 122
Furin Kazan 113
GB Roof Garden 116
Gefseis me Onomasia Proelefsis 132
Giouvetsakia 72, **112**
Le Grand Balcon 116, **119**
Greek House Attikos 117
Hytra 111, 121, **125**
Ikonomou 112
Ineas 125
Kafeneio 120
Kiku 122
Kitrino Podilato – Koukoumavlos 123
Kollias 132
Kuzina *109*, 112
Louizidis 128
Malabar 129
Mamacas 125
Milos 111, 116, **122**
Mommy 117
Myrovolos 175, **176**, *177*
Nikitas 111, **125**
Orizondes Kykavitou 116
Ouzadiko 111, **119**
Pandelis 128
Papadakis 119, *123*
Pasaji 111, **114**, *115*
Pecora Nera 122
Petalo 176
Philippou 111, **121**
Pil Poul Jérôme Serres 108, **111**, *117*
Il Postino 121
Pouls Podilatou 132

Prosopa 176
Prunier 119
Ratka 118
Rififi 111, **119**
Sappho 175, **176**
Semiramis 129
Soul 123
Spondi 108, 111, **127**
St' Astra 119
Taki 13 123
Tellis 125
Thalatta 111, **125**
Therepeftirio 113
Tike 132
To Kouti 111, **112**
To Paradosiako 113
To Steki tou Ilia 113
Trata 111, **127**
Tria Asteria 128
Tudor Hall 114
Tzitzikas kai Mermigas 116
Vardis 108, 111, **130**
Varoulko 95, 108, 111, 116, 121, **124**, *129*
Vincenzo 129
Vlassis 119
Zevkin 129

Cafés
A Lier Man 139
Aigli Bistro Café 85, **134**, 135
Aiolis 135
Amaltheia **133**, 134

aPLAKAfe 134
Athinaion Politeia *133*, **134**, 135
Blue Train 175, *176*
Café Brasil 139
Cafeina 136
Cake 137
Chocolat 139
Clemente VIII 134, **135**, *136*
Da Capo 134, 135, **137**, *137*
Da Luz 139
Dioskuri 134
Dodoni 134, **139**
En Athinais 134
Enidrio Internet Café 176
Ethnikon 134, **135**
Filion 137
Filistron 134
Flocafé 136
Hara 139
Ionos 134
Krinos **136**, 138
Lallabai Café 85, **134**, 135
Love Café 139
Nikis Café 136
Notos Café 166
Ostria 166
Pagotomania 134, **139**
Petite Fleur 134, **137**
Queen's Tea & Coffee 134, 135, **137**
Rosebud 137
S-cape Summer 175, **176**

Sofia's Valaoritou Café 138
Ta Serbetia tou Psyrri 139
Tribeca 134, **138**
Tristrato 134
Varsos 139
Voutadon 48 139
Wunderbar 139

Bars & clubs
Akrotiri Club Restaurant 190
Aleco's Island 175, **177**
Babae 190
Baila 189
Balthazar 117, **189**
Banana Moon 192
Bar Guru Bar 188, **189**
Big Bar 177
Bios 192
Bo 190
Booze Cooperative 188, **189**, *189*
Brettos 188
Briki 189
Caffeina 189
Dirty Ginger 188
En Delphis 189
Envy Mediterraneo 190
Fou Club 175, **177**
Frame Bohemian Bar 191
Galaxy 116, 188, **191**, *193*
Galea 190

Gallery Café 188
Gazaki 188, **192**
GazArte 95
Glam Bar 95
Granazi 176
Group Therapy Bar 177
Hoxton 188
Inoteka *187*, 188
Island 191
Kazarma Summer 175, **178**
Koukles 177
Lamda 177
Liosporos 188, **192**
Mad 95
Mamacas 188, **192**
Mao 191
Mayo 175, **178**
Micraasia Lounge 178
Mike's Irish Bar 191
Moe 178
Mommy 191
Nipiagogio 192
Noiz 175, **178**
Palenque Club 191
S-cape Army Academy 175, **178**
Sodade 175, **178**, 188
Soul 192
Soul Garden 188, **192**
Stavlos 188
Tapas 188, **192**
Thirio (Beast) 188, **192**
Tribeca 192
Vinilio 191

Advertisers' Index

Please refer to the relevant pages for contact details

Hard Rock Café   **IFC**

In Context

BBC Active   10

Arts and Entertainment

Carbon Neutral Flights   160

Trees for Cities   **IBC**

Major sight or landmark	▮
Railway & bus stations	▮
Parks	▯
Hospitals/universities	▯
Ancient sites	▯
Neighbourhood	PLAKA
Metro station	Ⓜ

Maps

Athens Overview	**246**
Street Maps	**248**
Greater Athens	**253**
Street Index	**254**
Athens Metro	**256**

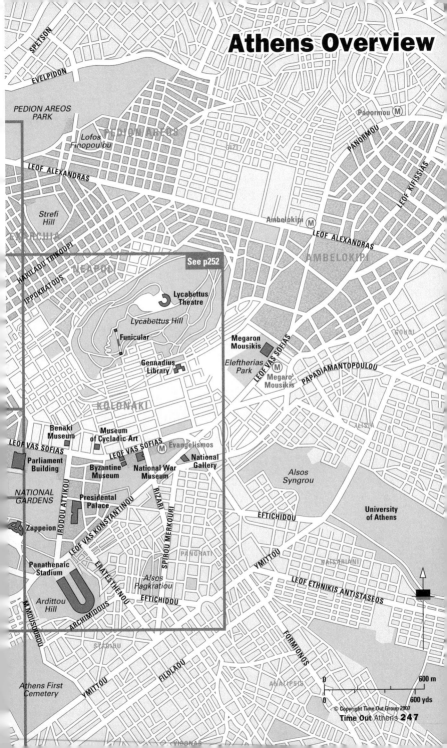

Athens Overview

SPETSON

EVELPIDON

PEDION AREOS PARK

PEDION AREOS

Lofos Finopoulou

Panormou Ⓜ

PANORMOU

LEOF ALEXANDRAS

LEOF KIFISSIAS

Strefi Hill

Ambelokipi Ⓜ

EXORCHIA

LEOF ALEXANDRAS

HARILAOU TRIKOUPI

AMBELOKIPI

IPPOKRATOUS

NEAPOLI

See p252

GOUDI

Lycabettus Theatre

Lycabettus Hill

Funicular

Megaron Mousikis

Eleftherias Park

LEOF VAS SOFIAS

PAPADIAMANTOPOULOU

Gennadius Library

Megaro Mousikis

KOLONAKI

ILISIA

Benaki Museum

Museum of Cycladic Art

LEOF VAS SOFIAS Ⓜ Evangelismos

National Gallery

LEOF VAS SOFIAS

Parliament Building

Byzantine Museum

National War Museum

Alsos Syngrou

NATIONAL GARDENS

IRODOU ATTIKOU

Presidental Palace

RIZARI

University of Athens

EFTICHIDOU

Zappeion

LEOF VAS KONSTANTINOU

SPIROU MERKOURI

PANGRATI

YMITTOU

Panathenaic Stadium

ERATOSTHENOU

Alsos Pagkratiou

KATSABUNI

LEOF ETHNIKIS ANTISTASEOS

Ardittou Hill

EFTICHIDOU

ARCHIMIDOUS

FORMIONOS

M. MOUSOUROU

STADIOU

0   600 m

0   600 yds

Athens First Cemetery

YMITTOU

FILOLAOU

AMALIPSIS

© Copyright Time Out Group 2007

VNIRONAS

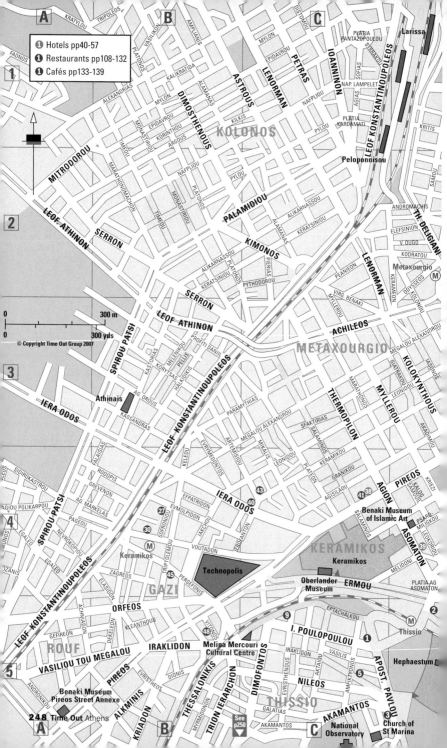

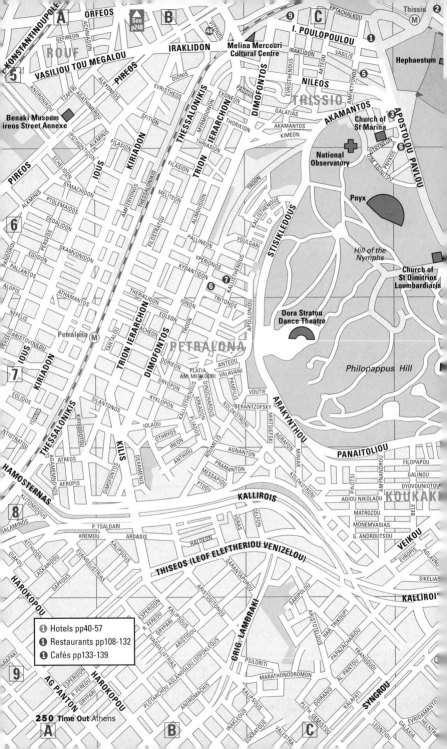

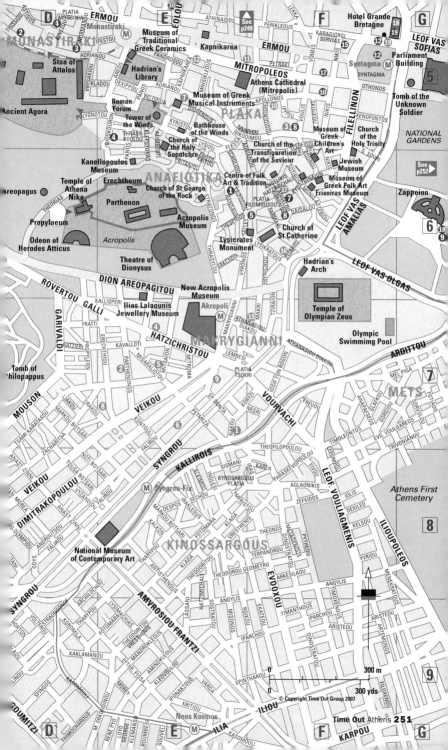

D
ERMOU
E
EOLOU
F
G

MONASTIRAKI
PLATIA
AVYSSINIA
PLATIA
MONASTIRAKI
Monastiraki

Museum of
Traditional
Greek Ceramics

Kapnikarea

Hotel Grande
Bretagne

LEOF VAS
SOFIAS

Stoa of
Attalos

Hadrian's
Library

ERMOU

MITROPOLEOS

Parliament
Building

Ancient Agora

Roman
Forum

Tower of
the Winds

Bathhouse
of the Winds

Museum of Greek
Musical Instruments

Athens Cathedral
(Mitropolis)

PLAKA

Church of
the Holy
Sepulchre

Museum of Greek
Children's Art

Syntagma

Tomb of the
Unknown
Soldier

NATIONAL
GARDENS

Kanellopoulos
Museum

Temple of
Athena
Nike

Erechtheum

ANAFIOTIKA

Church of St George
of the Rock

Church of the
Transfiguration
of the Saviour

Church of
the Holy
Trinity

See
p252

Areopagus

Parthenon

Centre of Folk
Art & Tradition

Jewish
Museum

Museum of
Greek Folk Art
Frissiras Museum

Zappeion

Propylaeum

Acropolis
Museum

Acropolis

Church of
St Catherine

LEOF VAS
AMALIAS

Odeon of
Herodes Atticus

Theatre of
Dionysus

Lysicrates
Monument

Hadrian's
Arch

LEOF VAS OLGAS

Tomb of
Philopappus

DION AREOPAGITOU

New Acropolis
Museum

Ilias Lalaounis
Jewellery Museum

Akropoli

Temple of
Olympian Zeus

Olympic
Swimmimg Pool

ARDITTOU

ROVERTOU
GALLI

HATZICHRISTOU

MAKRYGIANNI

METS

GARIVALDI

MOUSON

VEIKOU

VOURVACHI

Athens First
Cemetery

VEIKOU

SYNGROU

KALLIROIS

Syngrou-Fix

DIMITRAKOPOULOU

National Museum
of Contemporary Art

KINOSSARGOUS

LEOF. VOULIAGMENIS

ILIOUPOLEOS

SYNGROU

AMVROSIOU FRANTZI

EVDOXOU

300 m

300 yds

© Copyright Time Out Group 2007

Neos Kosmos

ILIOU

Time Out Athens **251**

KARPOU

D
E
ILIA
F
G

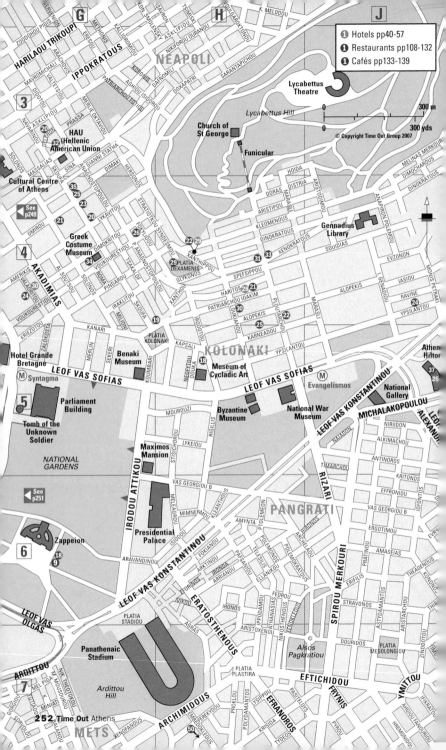

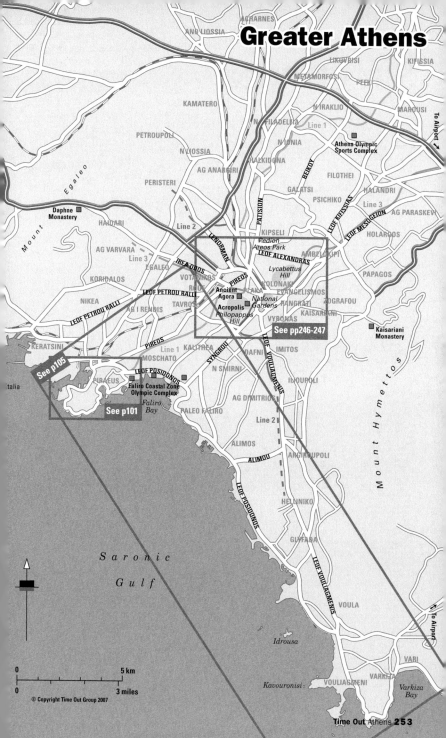

Greater Athens

ANO LIOSSIA
ACHARNES
LIKOVRISI
KIFISSIA
To Airport

METAMORFOSI
PEFK

KAMATERO
IRAKLIO
Line 1
MAROUSI

PETROUPOLI
N. FILADELFIA
Athens Olympic
Sports Complex

N. IONIA
BEIROУ
FILOTHEI
HALANDRI

AG ANARGIRI
CHALKIDONA
GALATSI
PSICHIKO
Line 3
AG PARASKEVI

PERISTERI
Mount Egaleo
Pedion Areos Park
AMBELOKIPI
HOLARGOS
PAPAGOS

Daphne Monastery
HAIDARI
Line 2
KIPSELI
LEOF ALEXANDRAS
Lycabettus Hill
LEOF KIFISSIAS
LEOF MESOGEION

AG VARVARA
Line 3
VOTANIKOS
KOLONAKI
ZOGRAFOU

EGALEO
IREA ODOS
PLAKA
EVANGELISMOS
KAISARIANI

KORIDALOS
LEOF PETROU RALLI
Ancient Agora
National Gardens
PANGRATI

NIKEA
TAVROS
Acropolis
Philopappos Hill
VYRONAS
Kaisariani Monastery

AG I RENDIS
REN
See pp246-247

KERATSINI
PIREOS
Line 1
KALITHEA
IMITOS

MOSCHATO
DAFNI
ILIOUPOLI

See p105
PIRAEUS
LEOF POSIDONOS
N SMIRNI
LEOF VOULIAGMENIS

talia
Faliro Coastal Zone
Olympic Complex
Faliro Bay
AG DIMITRIOS

See p101
PALEO FALIRO
Line 2

ALIMOS

ALIMOU
ARGIROUPOLI

Mount Hymettos

Saronic Gulf

HELLINIKO

GLYFADA

LEOF POSIDONOS
LEOF VOULIAGMENIS

Idrousa

VOULA

To Airport

0   5 km
0   3 miles

Kavouronisi
VOULIAGMENI
VARI
VARKIZA
Varkiza Bay

© Copyright Time Out Group 2007

Street Index

3 Septemvriou – p250 E1/E2
A. Metaxa – p249 F2/F3
Acharnon – p249 E1/E2
Acheon – p250 B7
Achileos – p248 C3
Achniadon – p248/p250 A5
Adrianou – p249/p251 D5/E5, p251 F6
Aeropis – p250 A8
Agamemnonos – p250 A8
Agatharchoui – p249 D4
Agathimerou – p250 A5/B5
Agathodemonos – p250 A7
Agia Dimitriou – p249 E4
Agia Irinis – p249/p251 E5
Agia Theklasi – p249 D4/E5
Agias Markelas – p248 A4/B4
Agias Sofias – p248 C1
Agion Asomaton – p249 D4
Agion Panton – p250 A9
Agiou Fanouriou – p252 H7
Agiou Isidorou – p252 G3/H3
Agiou Konstantinou – p249 D3/E3
Agiou Markou – p249 E4
Agiou Nikolaou – p250 C8
Agiou Orous – p248 B3
Agiou Pavlou – p249 D1/2
Agiou Polikarpou – p248 A4
Agisilaou – p248 C4, p249 D3
Aglaonikis – p251 F8
Aglavrou – p251 D8
Agnanton – p250 B8/C8
Agrafon – p250 C7/C8
Agras – p250 H6/H7
Aisopoui – p249 D4
Akadimias – p249 F3, p252 G4
Akadimou – p249 D3/D4
Akamantos – p248/p250 C5
Akominatou – p249 D2/D3
Aktaiou – p248 C5
Akteou – p250 C5
Al. Pantou – p250 C9
Al. Soutsou – p252 G4
Alamanas – p248 B1/C2
Alexandrias – p248 B1
Alkamassou – p248 B2/C2
Alimberti – p251 E5
Alimousion – p250 B6
Alkamenous – p249 D1
Alkifronos – p250 A7
Alkimachou – p252 H5
Alkimou – p251 E8
Alkiviadou – p249 E1
Alkminis – p248/p250 B5, p250 A5/A6
Alkyoneos – p250 B5
Alopekis – p252 H4/H5
Alopis – p250 A6/A7
Am. Merkouri, Platia – p250 B7
Amaseias – p252 H4
Amerikis – p249 F4, p252 G4
Amfiktyonos – p248 C5
Amfipoleos – p248 A4
Amfitryonos – p250 B6/C5
Aminokleou – p251 E9
Amplianis – p248 B1
Amvrosiou Frantzi – p251 E8/E9
Amynandrou – p250 C8
Amynta – p252 H6
Anagnostopoulou – p252 G3/G4
Anapafseos – p251 F7
Anapiron Polemou – p252 H4
Anargyroni – p249 D4
Anast. Zinni – p251 D8
Andromachis – p249 D2, p250 B9
Andronikou – p248 A5, p250 A5
Angelikis Hatzimichali – p251 F6
Angelou Geronta – p251 F6
Angylis – p251 E8/E9/F8
Anteou – p250 B7
Anth. Gazi – p249 F4
Anthiou – p250 B7/8
Antiatrou – p250 A7
Antinoros – p252 H5
Antisthenous – p251 E8
Antistriou – p250 A7
Apolloniou – p250 C6/C7
Apollonos – p249/p250 E5/F5
Apostolou Pavlou – p248 C5, p249/p251 D5, p250 D6
Arachovis – P252 G2/G3
Arakynthou – p250 C7
Arapaki – p250 A9
Aravandinou – p252 G6
Archelaou – p252 H6/J6
Archilochou – p250 D8/D9/E8
Archimidous – p252 G7/H7
Ardasis – p250 B8
Arditou – p252 G7, p251 F7
Areos – p249/p251 E5
Argous – p248 B1/B2
Arist – p249 E4
Aristarchou – p252 H6/H7

Aristeou – p251 F9
Aristidou – p249 E4, p250 B8/B9
Aristipou – p252 H4/H5
Aristoditnou – p252 H4
Aristofanoui – p249 D4
Aristogitonos – p250 B8/B9
Aristotelous – p249 E1/E2, p250 C9
Aristovoulou – p250 A7
Aristoxenou – p252 H7
Arkadon – p250 B7
Arkesilaou – p251 F8
Arktinou – p252 H6
Armodiou – p249 E4
Arrianou – p252 H6
Artemisiou – p248 B3/B4/C4
Artemonos – p251 F9
Asklipiou – p252 G3/H2/H3
Astigos – p249/p251 D5
Astrous – p248 B1/C1
Astydamantos – p252 H5/H6/H7
Athamantos – p250 A6/A7
Athanasias – p252 H6/H7
Athanasiou Diakou – p251 E7/F7
Athinaidos – p249/p251 E5
Athinas – p249 E3/E4
Athinodorou – p250 A7
Atreos – p250 A8
Atthidon – p250 A8/B9
Averoff – p249 E2
Avlitoni – p249 D4
Avyssinias, Platia – p249/p251 D5
Bele – p251 D8
Berantzofsky – p250 B7/C7
Boumboulinas – p249 F1/F2
Chrystokopidou, Platia – p249 D4
Dafnomili – p252 G3/H3
Daidalou – p251 F6
Dedalidon – p250 A6
Dekeleon – p248 B5
Delfon – p250 C8
Deligianni – p249 F1
Deligiorgi – p249 D3
Delphou – p252 G3
Dervenion – p252 G2/G3
Despos Sechou – p251 E8
Dexamenis – p250 B8
Dexameris, Platia – p252 H4
Dexileo – p251 F8
Dexippou – p249/p251 E5
Diakou – p250 A8
Didotou – p252 G3
Dim. Eginitou – p250 C6
Dimaki – p252 G3
Dimitrakopoulou – p250 A9, p251 D8/E7/E8
Dimocharous – p252 G4
Dimondon – p248 B1/B2
Dinocharous – p250 B7
Dinokratous – p252 H3/H4/H5
Dinostratou – p251 F8/F9
Diogenous – p249/p251 E5
Dion Areopagitou – p251 D6/E6
Dionis – p248/p250 B5
Dioskouron – p249/p251 E5
Dipyloui – p249 D4
Distonou – p248 C1
Doiranis – p250 C9
Doras Distria – p252 H4
Dorieon – p250 B7
Dorou – p249 E3
Douridos – p252 H7
Doxapatri – p252 H3
Dragatsaniou – p249 F4
Drakontos – p252 H6
Drakou – p251 D7
Dryopon – p250 B7
Dyovouniotou – p251 D8
Echelidon – p250 A6
Edesis – p248 A4
Edouardou Lo – p249 F4
Effroniou – p252 H6
Eforinos – p252 H6
Efpatridon – p248 B4
Efpompou – p251 F8
Efranoros – p252 H7
Eftichidou – p252 H7/J7
Eftsr. Pissa – p251 E9
Egaleo – p248 A4
Egidon – p250 A6
Ekateou – p251 F8/F9
Elasidon – p248 B4/B5
Elefsinion – p249 D2
Eleftherias, Platia – p249 D4
Eleousis – p249 E4
Elianikou – p252 H6/J6
Embedokleous – p252 H7
Emm. Benaki – p249 E3/F2/F3
Eoleon – p250 B7
Eolidos – p250 A7

Eolou – p249 E3/4, p251 E5
Epidavrou – p248 B1/C1
Epikourou – p249 D4
Eptachakkou – p248/p250 C5
Eratosthenous – p252 H6/H7
Erechthiou – p251 E7
Eresou – p252 G2/G3
Ergotimou – p252 H6
Erifilis – p252 H6
Ermou – p248 C4, p249/p251 D5/E5/F5
Erotokritou – p251 E6
Eschylou – p249 E4
Esperidon – p250 A9/B9
Evangelistria – p250 B9
Evangelistrias – p249 E5
Evangelistrias – p250 A8/B8
Evdoxou – p251 F8/F9
Evg Voulgareos – p251 F7
Evmolpidon – p248 B4
Evridamanto – p251 D9
Evripidoui – p249 D4/E4
Evristhenous – p248/p250 C5
Evristheos – p248/p250 B5
Evropis – p251 D8
Evrydikis – p252 H6
Evrymedontos – p248 B3/B4
Evzonon – p252 H4
Exarchia, Platia – p249 F2
Exikiou – p249 D1
Exoneon – p250 B5
Falaisias – p248 B4
Falirou – p251 D8/E7/E8
Faonos – p248 A1
Farmaki – p251 F6
Favierou – p249 D2/E2
Fedrou – p252 H6
Ferekydou – p252 H7
Feron – p249 E1/F1
Fidiou – p249 F3
Filadelfias – p249 D1
Filasion – p250 B5/B6
Filellinon – p249 F5, p251 F5/F6
Filinou – p251 D9
Filis – p249 E1
Filomousou, Platia – p251 F6
Filopapou – p251 D8
Filostratou – p250 B6
Floxenou – p251 F9
Flessa – p249/p251 E5
Fokylidou – p252 G4/H4
Formionos – p252 H6
Fotiadou – p252 G7
Fotomara – p251 D9/E8/E9
Frangoudi – p250 C9
Fratti – p251 D7/E7
Frynichou – p251 F6
Frynis – p251 F7
G. Androutsou – p250 C8
G. Sauri – p251 F5/6
Galatias – p248 C5, p250 C5
Galaxia – p251 D9
Galinou – p251 D8
Garivaldi – p251 D7
Gefireon – p248/p250 A5, p250 B5
Georg.Olympiou – p251 D8
Geraniou – p249 E3
Gianni Statha – p252 G3
Giatrakou – p249 D4
Gladstonos – p249 E3/F3
Glafkou – p251 F7
Glykonos – p252 H4
Gorgiou – p252 G7 & p251 F7
Gouveli – p251 E9
Granikou – p248 C4
Grevenon – p248 A4/B4
Grig. Lambraki – p250 A8/B9/C8/C9
Grypari – p250 B8/B9
Haldeon – p250 B8
Halkidikis – p248 B3
Halkokondyli – p249 E2
Hamosternas – p250 A7/A8
Har. Trikoupi – p250 C9
Harilaou Trikoupi – p249 F3, p252 G2/G3
Haritos – p252 H4
Harokopou – p250 A8/A9/B9
Hatzichristou – p251 E7
Hatzimichali – p251 E8/E9
Helntraich – p251 D9
Hersonos – p252 G3/G4
Hiou – p250 D2
Hironos – p252 H6/J6
Hoida – p252 H3
Homatianou – p249 D1
Horton – p251 D8
Hremonidou – p252 H7
I. Fokianou – p252 H6
I. Genadiou – p252 H4
I. Misthiou – p252 H5/6

I. Poulopoulou – p248/p250 C5
I. Tsimiski – p252 H2/H3
Iakchou – p248 B4
Iasiou – p252 H4
Iasonos – p249 D3
Idomeneos – p250 A6
Iera Odos – p248 A3/B3/B4/C4
Ierofanton – p248 B4/C3
Ierou Lochou, Platia – p249 E4
Ifestou – p249/p251 D5/E5
Ifikratous – p252 H7
Ilia Iliou – p251 E9/F9
Iliou – p249 D2
Ilioupoleos – p251 F8
Inglesi – p251 E8
Ioanninon – p248 C1/C2
Iofontos – p252 H5/H6
Iolaou – p250 B7
Iolis – p251 F8
Ioron – p250 B6/B7
Iosif Ton Rogon – p251 F7
Ioulianou – p249 D1/E1/F1
Ious – p250 A6/A7/B5
Iparchou – p251 E9/F9
Ipirou – p249 E1/F1
Ipitou – p251 F5
Iponaktous – p251 E9
Ipothontidon – p250 A5/A6
Ippodamou – p252 H6/H7
Ippokratous – p249 F3, p252 G3
Iraklexous – p250 B9/C9 & p251 E8
Iraklidon – p248/p250 B5/C5
Iraklitou – p252 G4
Iras – p251 F8
Ireon – p250 B7/B8
Irodotou – p252 H4/H5
Irodou Attikou – p252 G5/G6
Ironda – p252 H6
Ironos – p252 H6
Isavron – p252 H2/H3
Isiodou – p252 H6
Isionis – p250 A7
Ivikou – p252 H6
Ivis – p251 F7
K. Balanou – p252 G7
K. Melodou – p252 H2
K. Paleologou – p249 D2/E2
Kaklamanou – p251 D9/E9
Kalafati – p250 C9
Kalamiotou – p249 E4/E5
Kalikratida – p248 B1
Kalipsous – p250 B8/B9/C9
Kalkon – p251 E8
Kallerg – p249 D3
Kalldromiou – p252 G2/G3
Kallirois – p250 B8/C8, p251 D8/D9/E7/E8/F7
Kallisperi – p251 E7
Kallisthenous – p250 B6/B7/B8/C6
Kalog Samouili – p249 D4
Kanari – p252 G4/G5
Kaningos – p249 F2
Kaningos, Platia – p249 F2
Kapnikarea – p249/p251 E5
Kapodistriou – p249 F2
Kapsali – p252 H5
Karagiorgi Servias – p249/p251 F5
Karaiskaki – p249 D4
Karaiskaki, Platia – p249 D2
Kardamati, Platia – p248 C1
Karea – p251 F8
Kareadou – p252 H5
Karolou – p249 D2/E2
Karori – p249 E4/E5
Karpou – p251 F9
Karytsi – p249 F4
Kasomouli – p251 D9/E9/F9
Kassandras – p248 B3
Kastorias – p248 B3
Kavalioti – p251 E7
Keleou – p248 B3/B4
Kelsou – p251 F8
Kerameon – p248 C2, p249 D2
Keramikou – p248 C3/C4, p249 D3
Keratsiniou – p248 B2/C2
Kiafas – p249 F3
Kifisodotou – p252 A7/A8
Kilis – p250 B7/B8
Kilkis – p248 B1/C1
Kimeon – p250 C5
Kimonos – p248 B2/C2
Kinetou – p249/p251 D5
Kiriadon – p250 A6/A7/B5/B6
Klada – p251 E8
Klafthmonos, Platia – p249 D5/E5
Kleanthous – p248 B5, p252 H6
Klemanso – p251 E9
Kleomenous – p252 H4/H5
Kleovoulou – p251 E9
Kliious – p250 A8
Klitomachou – p252 G7

Klitomidous – p250 A8
Kodratou – p249 D2
Kodrou – p251 F6
Koletti – p249 F2/F3
Kolokotroni – p249 E4, p250 B7/C7/C8
Kolokynthous – p249 D3
Kolonaki, Platia – p252 G5/H5
Kolonou – p249 D2/D3
Kon. Smolensky – p252 G2/H3
Kononos – p252 H6
Kontouli – p251 E7
Korai – p249 F4
Korinnisi – p249 D4
Korinthou – p248 B1
Koromila – p251 D9
Koronis – p252 G3
Korytsas – p248 B3
Koryzi – p251 E7/F7
Kotopouli – p249 E2/E3
Kotzia, Platia – p249 E3
Koumbari – p252 G5
Koumoundourou – p249 D3
Kountouriotou – p249 F2
Kozanis – p248 A4
Kranaou – p249 D4
Kratinou – p249 E3
Kratylou – p248 A1/B1
Kremou – p250 A8/A9/B8
Kriadon – p248 B5
Kriezi – p249 D4
Kriezotou – p252 G4/G5
Krisida – p252 H7
Kritiou – p251 E7
Kritis – p249 D1
Kritonos – p252 H6
Kydantidon – p250 B6
Kydathinaion – p251 F6
Kyklopon – p250 B7
Kynosargous, Platia – p251 E8
Kyristou – p249/p251 E5
Lada Christou – p249 F4
Lagoumitzi – p251 D9
Laskaridou – p250 A8/A9
Lassani – p251 E8/E9
Lekka – p249 F4/F5, p251 F5
Lembesi – p251 E7
Lenorman – p248 C1/C2
Leocharous – p249 E4
Leof Alexandras – p249 F1
Leof Athinon – p248 A1/A2/B2/B3
Leof Eleftheriou Venizelou – *see*
  Panepistimiou *and* Thiseos
Leof Konstantinoupoleos – p248 A4/A5/B3/B4/C1/C2/C3, p250 A5
Leof Vas Amalias – p251 F6
Leof Vas Konstantinou – p252 G6/H5/H6
Leof Vas Olgas – p252 G6, p251 F6
Leof Vas Sofias – p252 G5/H5/J5
Leof Vouliagmenis – p251 F8/F9
Leokoriou – p249 D4
Leonidou – p248 C3/C4, p249 D3
Leontiou – p250 C9
Lepeniotoui – p249 D4
Liosion – p251 D7
Liosion – p249 D1/E2
Loukianou – p252 H4/H5
Loyd George – p251 E9
Lykavitou – p252 G4
Lykeiou – p252 H5
Lykourgou – p249 E3
Lykourgou – p250 A8
Lysikratous – p251 F6
Lysimachias – p251 E9
Lysiou – p251 E5
Lysippou – p252 H7
M. Mousourou – p252 G7
M. Srkoudinou – p251 D9/E9
Mager – p249 D2/E2
Makedonias – p249 E1
Makri – p251 F6/F7
Makrygianni – p251 E7
Mamouri – p249 D1
Mandrokleous – p251 E9
Marasli – p252 H4/J4/J5
Marathonodromon – p250 C9
Marathonomachon – p248 B1/B2
Marathonos – p248 C3
Marathonos – p250 A8
Markou Botsari – p251 D7/E8
Marni – p249 E2
Massalias – p252 G3/G4
Matrozou – p250 C8
Mavromateon – p249 F4
Mavromichali – p249 F3, p252 G2/G3
Megalou Alexandrou – p248 B4/C3, p249 D3
Meintani – p251 D8
Mei Piga – p252 G7
Meleagrou – p252 H6
Melenikou – p248 B3
Melidoni – p249 D4
Melinas Merkouri – p252 J3/J4
Mcliteon – p250 B6
Menandrou – p249 E2/E3/D4
Menekratous – p251 F8
Menelaou – p250 A9
Merlie Oktaviou – p252 G3
Merlin – p252 G5
Mesolongiou, Platia – p252 H7

Messapiou – p250 B8
Metagenous – p251 F8
Methonis – p252 G2/G3
Metsovou – p249 F1
Mezonos – p249 D2/E2
Miaouli – p249 E4
Mical Voda – p249 E1
Michalakopoulou – p252 H5
Mikalis – p248 C3/C4
Milioni – p252 G4/G5
Mimnermou – p252 H6
Miniak – p250 C7/C8
Miniati – p252 G7
Mirtsiefski – p250 C7
Misaraliotou – p251 E7
Misonos – p251 E9
Mitrodorou – p248 A2/B1
Mitroma – p251 E7
Mitropoleos – p249/p251 E5/F5
Mitsaion – p251 E7
Mnisikleous – p249/p251 E5
Monastiriou – p248 B1/B2
Monemvasias – p250 C8
Monis Asteriou – p251 F6
Monis Petraki – p252 H4
Morey – p251 E9
Mourouzi – p252 H5
Mousaion – p249 E5
Mouson – p251 D7
Myllerou – p248 C2/C3 – p249 D3/D4
Mykoni – p248 B1/C1
Myrmidonon – p248/p250 B5
N. Metaxa – p249 D1
Nafpliou – p248 B1/B2/C1
Naiadon – p252 H5
Nakou – p251 E7
Nap. Lampelet – p248 C1
Navarhou Apostoli – p249 D4
Navarhou Nikodimou – p249/p251 F5
Navarinou – p249 F3
Navarhou Skoufa – p252 G3/G4
Nefelis – p250 A6/A7
Negri – p251 F7
Neofytou Douka – p252 H5
Nevrokopiou – p248 A4
Nik. Theotokou – p252 G7
Nikiforou – p249 D3
Nikiforou Ouranou – p252 G3/H2/H3
Nikis – p249 F5, p251 F5/F6
Nikolaou – p251 D9
Nikomideias – p249 D1
Nikosthenous – p252 H6/H7
Nileos – p248/p250 C5
Niriidon – p252 H5
Nkiou – p249 E4
Normanou – p249/p251 D5
Notara – p249 F1/F2
Noti Botsari – p251 D8/E8
Odys. Androutsou – p251 D8
Odysseos – p249 D2
Ominou – p249 F4, p252 G4
Omonia – p249 E3
Orfeos – p248/p250 A5/B5
Orlof – p251 D8
Othonos – p251 F5
Othryos – p250 B7
Otyneon – p250 C5/C6
P. Anagnostopoulou – p252 G4/H4
P. Tsaldari – p250 A8/B8
Padova – p250 B5
Pafsaniou – p252 H6
Pageou – p248 A4/B4
Palamidiou – p248 B2/C2
Pallados – p249 E4
Pallineon – p250 B8
Pamfilis – p250 B7
Panaitoliou – p250 C7/C8
Pandorou – p250 A6/A7
Pandrosou – p249/p251 E5
Panepistimiou (Leof Eleftheriou
  Venizelou) – p249 F3/F4
Panos – p249/p251 E5
Pantazopoulou, Platia – p248 C1
Papargopoulou – p249 F4
Papazachariou – p250 C9
Paramythias – p248 B3/C3
Paraskevopoulou – p251 F8
Parthenonos – p251 E7
Pasiteloys – p252 H7/J7
Patsion (26 Oktovriou) – p249 E2/E3, p249 F1/F2
Patriarchou Fotiou – p252 G3/H3
Patriarchou Ioakim – p252 H4
Peanieon – p248 C2
Pellis – p248 B3
Pelopida – p251 E5
Perevou – p251 F7
Perikleous – p249/p251 F5
Persefonis – p248 B4
Perseos – p250 A6/A7
Pesmazoglou – p249 F3/F4
Petmeza – p251 E7
Petraki – p249/p251 F5
Petras – p248 C1
Petrou Ralli – p250 A5
Pierias – p248 C2
Piladou – p250 A6/A7
Pindarou – p252 G4
Pinotsi – p250 C8
Pireos – p248 A5/B5/C4; p249 D3/D4/E3, p250 A5/A6/B5

Pitakou – p251 F6
Plastira, Platia – p252 H7
Plateon – p248 C3/C4
Platonos – p248 B1/B2
Pliados – p250 B7
Plith. Gemistou – p250 C9
Plotarchou Aslanoglou (Sofokleous) – p250 B9
Ploutarchou – p252 H4/H5
Plynos – p250 C6
Polemokratou – p252 H6
Polemonos – p252 H6
Polydamantos – p252 H7
Polygnotou – p249/p251 D5/E5
Polyklitou – p249 E4
Pramanton – p250 B8
Prassa – p252 G3
Pratinou – p252 H5/H6
Praxitelous – p249 E4/F4
Pritaniou – p251 E6
Profiti Daniil – p248 B3
Proklou – p252 H7
Propyleon – p251 D7
Psaromiligkoui – p249 D4
Psaron – p249 D2
Psiloriti – p250 B9/C9
Ptolemaidos – p250 A6/B6
Ptolemeon – p252 H6
Ptoou – p250 B8
Pylou – p248 B2/C1/C2
Pyrou – p252 H7
Pytheou – p251 F8
Pythodorou – p248 C2
R. Fereou – p250 A9/B9
Rangava – p251 E6
Ratzieri – p251 D7
Ravine – p252 H4
Rene Pyo – p251 E9
Rethymnou – p249 F1
Riga Fereou – p251 D9
Rigillis – p252 H5
Rizari – p252 H5/H6
Rodopis – p248 A4/B4
Roikou – p251 E9
Roma – p252 G4
Romvis – p249 F4/5
Roumbesi – p251 E9
Roumelis – p250 B7/B8
Rovertou Galli – p251 D6/D7/E7
Sachtouri – p249 D4
Salaminos – p248 C3/C4
Salaminos – p250 A5
Samou – p249 D1/D2
Sapfous – p249 D3/D4
Sapfous – p250 A8/A9
Sarantapichou – p252 H3
Sarantaporou – p250 B8
Saripolou – p250 D8/E9
Sarrii – p249 D4
Satovriandou – p249 E2/E3
Scholiou – p251 E6
Sekeri – p252 G5
Selley – p251 E6
Serron – p248 A2/B2/B3
Sfaktirias – p248 C3
Sfinges – p251 D9
Sfition – p248/p250 B5
Sidirokastrou – p248 A4
Sikelias – p251 D8
Silantonos – p250 A7/B7
Sina – p249 F4 & p252 G3/4
Sismani – p251 E8
Skamvonidon – p250 A6/B6
Skoufou – p251 F5
Skouze – p249 E4/E5
Sofokleous – p249 D3/E3/E4
Sokratous – p249 E2/E3/E4
Solomou – p250 C9
Solonos – p249 E2/F2
Solonos – p249 F3, p252 G3/G4
Sonierou – p249 D2/E2
Sorvolou – p252 G7
Sostratou – p251 E8/E9
Sotiros – p251 F6
Souidias – p252 H4
Sourmeli – p249 E1/E2
Sp. Donta – p251 E7
Spefsippou – p252 H4
Spintharou – p251 E9/F9
Spirou Merkouri – p252 H5/H6/H7
Spirou Patsi – p248 A3/A4/B3
Spyridnos Trikoupi – p249 F1/F2
Stadiou – p249 F4
Stadiou, Platia – p252 G6
Stisichorou – p252 H5
Stisikleous – p250 C6
Stournari – p249 E2/F2
Straongonof – p251 D9
Stratiotkou Syndesmou – p252 G4/H4
Stratonos – p251 E6
Stravonos – p250 H6
Strimonos – p248 A4
Symachidon – p250 A6/B6
Syngrou – p251 C9/D8/D9/E7/E8
Syntagma – p249/p251 F5
Syrrakou – p248 C1
Tantalou – p250 B7
Telesilis – p252 H6
Terpandrou – p251 F8
Th. Deligiani – p249 D2
Tharypou – p251 D9/E8

Theagenous – p252 H6
Theatrou – p249 E4
Theatrou , Platia– p249 D4/E4
Themidos – p249 E4/E5
Themistokleous – p249 F2/F3
Theodoritou Vresthenis – p251 E8/E9/F8
Theodorou Geometrou – p251 E8/F8
Theofilopoulou – p251 F7/F8
Theonos – p251 F8
Theorias – p251 D6/E6
Theriklidon – p250 B6/B7
Thermopilon – p248 C3/C4
Thespidos – p251 E6
Thessalonikis – p248 B5 & p250 A7/A8/B5/B6/B7, p250 B5/B7
Thimocharous – p251 D9
Thironos – p252 H6
Thiseos – p249 E4
Thiseos (Leof Eleftheriou Venizelou) – p250 A9/B8/B9/C8
Thissiou – p249/p251 D5
Thorikion – p250 B5/C5
Thoukididou – p251 F5/F6
Thrasylou – p251 E6
Thrasyvoulou – p249/p251 E5
Thriasion – p250 B5/B6
Timanthous – p251 F9
Timarchou – p252 H5
Timeou – p248 B1/B2
Timoleontos – p251 F7
Timotheou – p252 H7
Timoxenous – p251 F9
Tompazii – p249 F2
Tositsa – p249 F2
Tournavitoui – p249 D4
Tousa Botsari – p251 D8/E8
Trikoupi Harilaou – p252 G2/G3
Trion Ierarchon – p248 B5, p250 B5/B6/B7
Tripodon – p251 E6
Tripoleos – p248 B1
Triptolemou – p248 B4
Tritonos – p250 B6/B7
Trivonianou – p251 F7/F8
Troon – p250 B6/B7/C6
Tsakalof – p252 G4
Tsami Karatasou – p251 D7/D8
Tsokri, Platia – p251 E7/F7
Tydeos – p252 H7
Tymfristou – p251 E8/F8
Tzaferi – p250 A5
Tziraion – p251 E6/E7
Tzortz – p249 F2
V. Ougo – p249 D2
Vakchou – p251 E6
Valaoritou – p252 G4
Valavani – p250 B7
Valestra – p250 C9
Valtetsiou – p252 G3
Varda – p251 E9
Vas Georgiou B – p252 H6
Vas Irakliou – p249 F1
Vasilikon – p248 B1
Vasiliou Tou Megalou – p248/p250 A5/B5
Vasilis – p248/p250 C5
Vathis, Platia – p249 E2
Veikou – p250 C8, p251 D8/E7
Veranzerou – p249 E2
Virg. Benaki – p248 C2/C3
Vitonos – p248/p250 B5
Volterou – p251 D9
Voreou – p249 E4
Voukourestiou – p249/p251 F5, p252 G4
Voulgari – p249 D3
Voulgari – p250 B6/C6
Vougiaroktonou – p252 H2/H3
Voulis – p249/p251 F5
Vourvachi – p251 F7
Voutadon – p248 B4/C4
Voutie – p250 C7
Voutsara – p248 A4
Vrysakiou – p249/p251 D5
Vyronos – p251 E6
Vyssis – p249 E4
Vyzandiou – p251 D8
Xanthippou – p252 H4
Xanthou – p252 H4
Xenofanous – p252 G7
Xenofontos – p249/p251 F5
Xenokleous – p252 H6/H7/J6
Xenokratous – p252 H4/H5
Xouthou – p249 E2
Ydras – p250 B8
Ymittou – p252 H7
Ypereidou – p251 F5
Yperionos – p250 B6
Ypsilantou – p252 H4/H5/J5
Yvriou – p251 F9
Zacharitsa – p251 D7/D8
Zagreos – p248 B4
Zaimi – p249 F1/F2
Zalokosta – p252 G4/G5
Zan. Moreas – p251 F8
Zefxidos – p251 F8
Zinonos – p249 D1/E6/H6/H7
Zinonos – p249 D3
Zoodohou Pigis – p252 G2/G3, p249 F3

Athens Metro

Note: Construction work is underway to extend the metro. Line 2 will be extended to the north-west to Anthoupoli (via Peristeri) and to the south to Helliniko (via Alimos). Line 3 will be extended to the west to Haidari, and three new stations are due to open between Ethniki Amyni and Halandri. Work is expected to be completed by 2009; for updates, visit www.ametro.gr.